D0974949

DATE DUE

JUN 3 0 2017			
			PRINTED IN U.S.A.

798.40
McG

HERE

COMES

EXTERMINATOR!

The Long-Shot Horse,

the Great War, and the Making

of an American Hero

Eliza McGraw

THOMAS DUNNE BOOKS

St. Martin's Press

New York

THOMAS DUNNE BOOKS.
An imprint of St. Martin's Press.

HERE COMES EXTERMINATOR! Copyright © 2016 by Eliza McGraw.
All rights reserved. Printed in the United States of America.
For information, address St. Martin's Press,
175 Fifth Avenue, New York, N.Y. 10010.

www.thomasdunnebooks.com
www.stmartins.com

Designed by Kathryn Parise

Photograph on page 75: From Press & Sun Bulletin, May 18 © 1918 Gannett-CN.
All rights reserved. Used by permission and protected by the Copyright Laws of the
United States. The printing, copying, redistribution, or retransmission of this
Content without express written permission is prohibited.

The two photographs on page 219: From Press & Sun Bulletin, May 28 © 1945 Gannett-CN.
All rights reserved. Used by permission and protected by the Copyright Laws of the
United States. The printing, copying, redistribution, or retransmission of this
Content without express written permission is prohibited.

The Library of Congress Cataloging-in-Publication Data is available upon request.

ISBN 978-1-250-06569-8 (hardcover)
ISBN 978-1-4668-7272-1 (e-book)

Our books may be purchased in bulk for promotional, educational, or business use.
Please contact your local bookseller or the Macmillan Corporate and Premium Sales
Department at 1-800-221-7945, extension 5442, or by e-mail at
MacmillanSpecialMarkets@macmillan.com

First Edition: April 2016

10 9 8 7 6 5 4 3 2 1

Because of the Bear

Contents

Preface

My horse Romeo was a red bay gelding with huge dark eyes, a sculpted head, and unclear breeding, and the two of us were very close. I'd been a horse-crazy child, so when I was twenty-three and bought Romeo, I realized a lifelong dream. Horse owning was one of those rare fantasies that turn out every bit as well as you imagine they will. Romeo was my pride and joy in the truest sense of that cliché, and when he died—at only fifteen, from a rare, undignified illness—I was undone, unmoored. There have been plenty of other wonderful horses along the way, but Romeo was different: all mine, and wholly beloved.

A few years later, I was doing research for an article about a remount depot during the World War I era. I started seeing Exterminator's name, in headlines that also mentioned records and winning and crowds. I remembered the illustrations from the children's biography of Exterminator, *Old Bones: The Wonder Horse,* and pictured him as Wesley Dennis had drawn him, which was pretty much with Romeo's doe-wide eyes and dark forelock. I read every article about Exterminator I could find—the stories of fans lining up to see him, cheering themselves hoarse, the crates of apples and ginger ale they sent him. Exterminator was a laudable athlete, but there was also something about him that drew people to visit him, write poems about him, and mail him fruit.

I knew what it was like to love *my* horse, and I was a fan of certain racehorses, but I couldn't understand how a racehorse most people would never actually know could encourage such devotion. As I read about Exterminator, I learned that besides the individuals involved, an extraordinary time in America pushed Exterminator to his extraordinary place and molded his image once he was there. I came to understand how many moments combined to make Exterminator so important, and I felt as if I needed to know all about them. I studied up on furlongs and pari-mutuels, the Hollywood star machine and turf writing. I wished I could see him the way crowds in the 1920s did: that unracehorselike demeanor, the blurred white heart on his forehead, the way he seemed to bow to the stands, his uniquely long body that could run and run.

I find shadows of Exterminator everywhere. At Laurel Park, in Maryland, which is the racetrack I go to the most, I think of the days people flocked to the track for a glimpse of Exterminator, and other days when they came masked against the Spanish flu. One summer day at Churchill Downs, I saw a retired thoroughbred standing with a pony. People lined up to pat them, and the scene reminded me of Exterminator and Peanuts, his favorite companion. But no one on the tour—including the guide—had heard of them.

As I've collated pdfs and rolled microfilm, I have realized that my work has quite a bit to do with Romeo, and what he meant to me. This is a book about the great racehorse Exterminator and the time he lived in. That means it's also about the cavalry, horse training, turf writers, Binghamton, the movies, two world wars, hope, ambition, and desire. This book is also about something I hadn't realized that I already understood, even while I was trying to absorb all I could about starters and Shetland ponies and patent medicine. It is about the enormous love—and need—we can have for one singular horse.

HERE
COMES
EXTERMINATOR!

Prologue

In 1924, Tijuana, Mexico, was a place to break rules, which made it the right place for what trainer Henry McDaniel was trying to do with the racehorse Exterminator. He should not be racing such an old horse. He should not have agreed to work with the horse's temperamental owner again after so many years apart. And most of all, he should not believe the horse could beat Man o' War's earnings record, which was the plan. In a long lifetime, McDaniel had not attempted anything this risky since the 1918 Kentucky Derby, when he had sent this same horse off at odds of 30–1. Today, at the Tijuana racecourse, there was much more at stake.

In his prime, Exterminator had performed miracles of speed, distance, and stamina. People adored him for his athleticism, for his resilience, and for himself. Exterminator was an oversized, ungainly horse with enormous eyes and a habit of nosing coat pockets for sugar. Hollywood invented a new kind of American celebrity for movie and sports stars, and fans followed Exterminator as they did Charlie Chaplin, Jack Dempsey, and Babe Ruth. Grantland Rice, the "Dean of American Sportswriters," called him the greatest racehorse. Fans packed his races, met his trains, shouted his name, and wrote poems in his honor. Reporters compared him to Cassius, Paul Bunyan, and Abraham Lincoln. Ernest Hemingway compared himself to Exterminator.

So Henry McDaniel, in the Tijuana sunshine, trained a legend. In the past year, the old horse had faltered, brought low by age and lameness. To triumph, Exterminator needed to exceed Man o' War's earnings record by winning races, and McDaniel had risked his reputation for this reunion. With a win today, McDaniel would take his place as the trainer of the iron horse of the golden age. A legend would become real. But if the horse failed, the whole trip to Mexico would be pathetic, the story of a has-been pushed too far.

"McDaniel, who is not given to sanguine prophecy, thought before Exterminator embarked on his far Western adventure, that the old fellow had a better than an average chance to train again," wrote a *Washington Post* reporter. "This theory was based on his knowledge of the horse. McDaniel knows Exterminator to be temperamentally and physically right. He does not let anything disturb his calm. He is always a quiet gentleman." It was difficult to know if the reporter was talking about the horse or the man. They had been confused with each other before.

People packed the stands, wide-brimmed hats shading them from the hot sun. McDaniel could see that the horses on either side of Exterminator were flinging their heads and shuffling, their hooves churning up white dust, but Exterminator stood, patient. He rubbed his nose against the heavy webbing of the starting "rope."

As always, Exterminator was ready.

1

Uncle Henry

How did Exterminator and Henry McDaniel find their futures bound together on that hot day in 1924, with so much in the balance? How could so many people—in the stands, gathered around radios, scattered across America—love this one horse and care so desperately if he won or lost?

Exterminator's story—and Henry McDaniel's as well—begins just after the Civil War. Looking at McDaniel's life, you could say he was made to discover Exterminator.

McDaniel used to tell reporters that he had been born on the Secaucus racetrack. His father, David McDaniel, was a brilliant racehorse breeder and trainer. By the time Henry arrived in 1867, the elder McDaniel was one of the most famous horse trainers in America; he won the Belmont Stakes three times in a row. "From the time I could first toddle I heard race horses discussed," McDaniel wrote, "their doings applauded or condemned and their shortcomings or virtues commented on. I grew up in an atmosphere of horses."

David McDaniel competed his horses throughout the South before the Civil War. Afterward, when racing was revived up north, he moved to Hoboken, New Jersey, with his wife and children. Henry was the youngest.

McDaniel did not earn as much money there, and by 1869 some horses had been seized as payments for debt. Undaunted, he pooled his talents with others' resources and formed a group of owners that became known as the McDaniel Confederacy. The group was "destined to shake the turf to its centre, and . . . dominated the race-course for a longer period than any one stable of which racing chronicles have any mention," wrote a reporter for the sportsmen's weekly the *Spirit of the Times*. Jockeys wore blue and red silks, and called McDaniel "the Colonel."

The Confederacy's pride, a temperamental, fast stallion named Harry Bassett, was only a yearling during the debt seizure, and McDaniel bought him back by 1870. Harry Bassett, named for a Confederacy member, was one of the most successful racehorses of his generation, and his jockey, James Rowe, would grow up to be a legendary trainer. One of Henry McDaniel's earliest memories was going to Saratoga in 1872 to watch Harry Bassett win the Saratoga Cup against Longfellow; the race was one of the biggest sporting events after the Civil War. "My father thought there was no horse in the world like Harry Bassett," McDaniel said years later. "The high regard that my father had for Harry Bassett I have always entertained for Exterminator."

In those days, buoyed by Harry Bassett's accomplishments and the Colonel's skill, the Confederacy reigned over American racing. McDaniel had a special gift for getting horses to succeed. "It really seemed as if Col. McDaniel had only to buy the commonest plater in order to transpose him into a winner," wrote one reporter. "He won with horses which other trainers had given up." He did celebrity endorsements for products like Dr. Tobias' Venetian Horse Liniment and Derby Condition Powders, and the advertisements said he was the owner of the fastest-running horses in the world.

But in 1876, Harry Bassett declined, winning only three of his final twelve starts. Some said the former champion deteriorated because he had been raced too hard. If that was true, it may have taught Henry a formative lesson: the ability to prolong a racehorse's health and career would become one of his trademarks. Also, the Confederacy had overextended itself, with too many horses in training who could not earn their keep. Then, Henry's mother died. The Colonel, training horses at Saratoga, learned about her death from a telegram.

By 1878, the Confederacy was over. The *New York Times* sent a reporter to cover McDaniel's dispersal sale. He saw four Hoboken policemen trying in vain to force back the crowd arriving by trains from the North and South. "These visitors were clearly of the kind that travel about with great fat wallets choking in the throats with legal tenders and checks signed in good bold hands," he wrote. Although the stallion wasn't for sale, many of his sons and daughters were, and Harry Bassett was on display to remind people that every horse was related to the famous champion. The liquidation could not rescue the Colonel, who endured a series of setbacks and then died in 1885, at seventy-three.

Henry's father had been a complex figure. "Col. McDaniel may have had enemies," read a *Spirit of the Times* article, "as men of strong individuality are bound to have, but none will deny that as a trainer he had few equals. He was a stern disciplinarian, and as such produced a disagreeable impression, but among his friends no man could be more cordial nor instructive in his discourse. His life was devoted to the turf: he had tasted the bitter and the sweet of the turfman's career."

More than a million horses and mules died in the Civil War, and in its aftermath many new horses were bred to work in an increasingly industrial and urbanized country—pulling taxicabs and delivery wagons, carrying freight—and to race. There were about seven million horses in America in 1860, and twenty-five million by 1900. Training for either work or racing was a rough business, because many people believed that breaking a horse's spirit made him ready to ride. Professional horsebreakers would simply ride a bucking colt until, shaking with exhaustion, the horse gave up. Westerners called this "bronco busting," but the general idea was that forcing a horse to obey was the same as training him. "If the animal sulks," wrote one horsebreaker, "or exhibits deliberate impatience of control, he should be conquered, then and there."

An Ohioan named John Rarey had wanted to change that. Before the war, he performed horse tamings in front of crowds in America and Europe, seeking out vicious horses—and in one case, a zebra—as subjects. Rarey allowed horses to become used to him before jumping on, and he designed special harnesses to encourage obedience. Stilling the horse to gain trust, he wrote, worked beyond whippings and bronco busting. "Any horse may be taught to do anything that a horse can do," he wrote, "if taught in a systematic and proper manner." Rarey published versions of his book *The Complete Horse-Tamer* through the 1860s and '70s. "Old theories have been exploded," wrote one veterinarian. "To those cheering indications of a better day for the horse." Some claimed Rarey overstated his own abilities, but he had inspired a new conversation and focus on the idea of humane training.

This turning away from harsh treatment and toward what we might now call natural horsemanship was a big leap, and it relied on the idea that people and animals were not very different. The ASPCA was founded in 1866, the year before McDaniel was born. As Susan Pearson writes in *The Rights of the Defenseless,* her study of children's and animal rights in Gilded Age America, "Positing both as essentially innocent and good, reformers argued that the character of beasts and babes was alike ruined through cruelty and redeemed through kindness. If animals or children behaved badly, owners and handlers, or parents and teachers, need look no further than themselves for the cause." There was a moralist tinge to all of this; the seal of the ASPCA showed a wagon driver about to beat a horse, while an angel intervened.

Horsemen of an earlier generation may not have seen things that way. But for Henry McDaniel, gentleness with horses was a way of life and of work.

Henry had galloped Confederacy horses at the Broad Rock track near Richmond, Virginia, and ridden in at least one race at Latonia, finishing second on a horse named Wellington. He saddled his first winner, Forest, on September 8, 1885, less than a year after his father died. He was seventeen.

Several other trainers had failed with four-year-old Forest, so his owners paid McDaniel $12.50 a month (about $290 today) to figure out why the horse couldn't win. Forest was odd-looking; a previous trainer had believed he suffered from rheumatism of the shoulder muscles, and had him blistered—a process involving repeated application of a caustic ointment—until the hair was entirely gone. McDaniel watched the horse move and realized the trouble was not in Forest's shoulders at all. The problem was blind splints, an inflammation of the ligament between two lower leg bones. He treated the gelding with rest, care, and gentle workouts. Afterward, Forest won five straight races.

McDaniel kept a scrapbook of his early clippings, a composition book in which he cut and pasted each article, aligned with the paper's lines. His handwriting was the horseman's careful half script, efficient for writing long lists of names, times, and pedigrees. These early articles about him invariably mentioned his father. "Henry McDaniel, youngest son of the once famous trainer, is now training for R. J. Lucas, and deserves a good deal of credit," wrote one reporter. McDaniel did not seem poised to challenge his father's outsized reputation, but he was already a gifted, insightful horseman in his own right. He trained with gentle consistency, forging a reputation very different from the Colonel's, although one reporter noted that McDaniel "had his sterling character molded by the uncompromising requirements of the old Colonel's characteristics." McDaniel's contemporary, the trainer Sam Hildreth, was also a trainer's son. He noted that "the craving I've always had for race-horses, I reckon my father passed along to me in his blood. It was horse, horse, horse, with him all day long, year in and year out." The same seemed true of the McDaniels, father and son. It was horse, horse, horse, for both, all day long.

Henry McDaniel was preternaturally talented, with an uncanny gift for communication. Over the years, various animals—a white German shepherd, a goat—trailed him around the barn. He trained a hen to jump onto his lap and carried a terrier in his overcoat pocket. McDaniel was patient, calm, and a scholar of thoroughbred bloodlines, a representative of a contemporary breed of evolved American horseman, and part of a shift in horsemanship in which working with horses became less a show of dominance and more a mixture of wisdom, care, and knowledge.

Horsemen responded to McDaniel as well as their horses did. "You are the most competent, capable, and honest man that I have come in contact with, in the thoroughbred business," wrote one of his owners to him. Reporters called him "unassuming," "modest," "reticent," "painstaking and capable," and a "thorough gentleman."

Horse tamer John Rarey's work had inspired that of other horsemen, including Oscar Gleason, who called himself the "King of Horse-Tamers" and wrote a practical treatise on breaking wild horses. In 1894, Gleason filled Madison Square Garden for an exhibition as Rarey had, claiming, "The better the horse, the better the master." Another trainer wrote about the importance of patting, praising, and blanketing the family horse: "If he is tired and worn out, it is astonishing how these little attentions will encourage and cheer him up." Understanding horses as friends and helpmeets, these trainers railed against common cruel practices, like whipping tied-up horses, lighting fires under balky ones, and "bishoping"—overfiling—teeth to make horses appear younger.

Even horses' food became less mundane. Grooms stirred a little molasses and salt into oats cooked with linseed oil. They brewed "hay tea" by pouring boiling water over a bucket of clean hay, and pampered tired horses with gruel made from cornmeal, flour, and some sound ale. There were all kinds of horse items for sale: not just saddles and halters but also straw hats for horses who pulled wagons in the sun and heavy blankets for cab horses. Horse-training ideas melded with industry, which meant that streetcar operators were asked to brush and curry the horses they drove. If they understood, and even liked, each other, the horses and drivers would be safer and more effective, using that crucial postbellum idea of kinship with animals. "Intelligence is so clear as to almost startle us by the feeling behind the full, liquid eye of the horse . . . there is a mind kindred to our own," wrote Gleason. "That [training] may require patience and self-control on the part of the instructor cannot be denied; but so does the instruction of a child."

"If any year could be said to make the apogee of the horse world, the year 1890 would be an appropriate choice," writes Anne Norton Greene in her study of urban horses. That year, the president of the Humane Association likened the British book *Black Beauty* to Harriet Beecher Stowe's 1852 *Uncle Tom's Cabin*.

Around that same time, McDaniel married a young St. Louis woman, a dark-haired beauty named Leonora Mollencott and nicknamed Lonie. Their wedding announcement went in his scrapbook. Underneath, McDaniel pasted a sentimental verse: "Sweetheart of mine, remember this / Thro' all the years to be: / True love that never, never dies / Lives in my heart for thee!" A portrait shows Leonora peering out from underneath an enormous hat, a drooping feather echoing the slope of her cheek. She evidently shared McDaniel's affection for animals; Leonora poses with her own dog, a mournful-faced black spaniel whose downcast expression echoes the feather and whose wide, dark eyes look like his mistress's.

Early in their marriage, the McDaniels lost a baby, and as the years went on, Leonora struggled with mental illness. She grew obsessed with the idea that she was going blind, although she wasn't. At times, she stayed in the private, small sanitariums, or with friends while McDaniel worked. They never had other children.

McDaniel worked relentlessly, moving around the country in rattling train cars, from Saratoga to Hot Springs to Chicago. By 1894, he was training horses for Elias Jackson "Lucky" Baldwin, who founded the Santa Anita racetrack in Los Angeles. Locals gave Baldwin his nickname when he earned millions through mining investments. Baldwin was "the kind you never forget once you laid eyes on him," Sam Hildreth wrote, "with his Prince Albert coat and large fedora hat and a look about him that only comes to the fellow who has been a pioneer on the other side of the Rockies."

The partnership between the flamboyant investor and the young trainer profited both when Baldwin's Rey el Santa Anita, a head-tossing, mistrustful stallion, won the 1894 American Derby at Chicago's Arlington Park. McDaniel discussed the race with emerging confidence. He called the famously up-and-down Baldwin "possibly the richest and the poorest man on the turf. He has never got a cent in cash but is possibly worth millions." When Rey el Santa Anita won the American Derby, Baldwin wired McDaniel from California to send his part of the prize right away. Asked if Rey el Santa Anita showed any signs of lameness, McDaniel said with pride that "he came out of the race perfectly sound." Later, McDaniel wrote that the American Derby "was the first really big race in which I had trained the winner. Things looked very good to me that day. I felt that I was riding on top of the world."

He praised the jockey, too. "I had watched his work and made up my mind that he was a good, intelligent rider . . . He is a quiet, trustworthy little fellow, and you might be around the stable here with him for a week without hearing him say a word."

McDaniel seemed to approve of hard work, calm, and reliability—qualities others praised in him. Already, he showed the reticence and concern for horses that was becoming his trademark. He told a reporter that even though Rey el Santa Anita was eligible for a long race called the Realization, he was not sure he would send him, because it might not be the right thing to do. "From the way he won yesterday it would seem that he could go on and on and do still better in a longer race," McDaniel said, "but this business is a mighty uncertain one."

McDaniel was a handsome young man, light eyed and even featured, with a full mustache that was current but not foppish. In a photograph taken at the time, he wears a white shirt and striped tie. He looks like the consummate horseman: less sober than a banker but more conservative than a gambler.

Lucky Baldwin's up-and-down ways seemed to wear on McDaniel, so he left to train for the more staid Memphis-based stable of George C. Bennett in 1899. He was continuing to climb, but with aching slowness. McDaniel needed a horse he could train for the prestigious eastern courses in New York and Maryland if he was going to ascend, but Bennett's string bound him to smaller-time venues like Memphis and Little Rock. He seemed self-assured during interviews, though: "I have often been asked why with my success in picking winners I have never been more of a plunger [habitual bettor], for I seldom bet more than a ten-dollar note," McDaniel told a reporter around 1900. "It's a great secret, but I will tell you the reason. It's because the life of a trainer is longer than that of a plunger. That's why I'm a trainer."

At first, the Bennett horses won for McDaniel. By 1902, McDaniel trained his two hundredth winner for Bennett in a little over two years. His willingness to travel the country, finding meets in which his horses could succeed, probably kept his numbers up. But a later season went less well. (A horse named Henry McDaniel had better luck; Sam Hildreth had apparently named the colt for his friend, and he won at New Orleans in the winter of 1902. Naming horses after people was a common custom at the time. There were horses named Sewell Combs, James T. Clark, Jim Heffering, and Alice Forman.) McDaniel acted unruffled about his losses: "Well, we cannot win all the time," he told a reporter.

By January 1903, however, McDaniel was still struggling. He could not win with Bennett's horses in New Orleans. The going was wet and sloppy in the Louisiana winter, and it seemed like every horse in his string preferred a fast track. McDaniel refused to train them in the mud—they might slip or pull a muscle—which kept them out of shape. Without having won a single race, he decided to send the horses back to Memphis.

But there was trouble there, too. McDaniel did not like Bennett's jockey.

William Coburn was very popular in Memphis, both as a rider and a man about town, but his eating and drinking made him overweight, which the disciplined McDaniel could not tolerate. "That boy," he said, in an uncharacteristically heated interview, "has not told me the truth in eight months. He is disreputable and cannot be relied upon, and if I can prevent it he will never ride Bennett's horses again."

Then McDaniel advised Bennett to retire his leading racer, Abe Frank, to the stud. Bennett took this so far as to decide not to buy any new horses, but race only homebreds from his western Tennessee farm. McDaniel had not meant that Bennett should never buy more horses, just that Abe Frank was ready to retire. Bennett's sentimental attachment to his own bloodlines would never yield the winners they needed. Abe Frank was a nice horse, but he was no Harry Bassett.

"That was the reason why Henry McDaniel, as nice a fellow as anyone would want to know, a good judge of a racehorse and a first-class man in charge of a stable, left my employ," Bennett said. "He was not pleased with my youngsters as yearlings, and actually disliked them as two-year-olds." Other horsemen weighed in: a bookie and former partner of Bennett named Thomas Shannon said that Bennett was spoiled by "a series of lucky strikes on the turf and cheap investments in horses turning into bonanzas . . . Shannon says Bennett can't get the notion out of his head that cheap stuff is as good as the more expensive article in thoroughbred yearlings, and as a result he has loaded up on McDaniel a lot of material that the noted trainer could not condition to get inside the money, much less win a race."

McDaniel's departure represented another lost chance, another stable of well-trained, underperforming horses left behind. A photo pasted in the composition book shows McDaniel heavier about the jaw, still with a stylishly full mustache, and some dark strands of hair showing underneath the brim of his spring fedora. He is wearing a vest, a white shirt, and a loose coat. The lightness of his eyes is still apparent, and striking, but now they look a little cooler.

———

McDaniel accepted a standing offer from a Chicago millionaire named M. H. Tichenor in 1904. One of the places he raced Tichenor's horses was Los Angeles's Ascot Park, which stood just outside the city limits. McDaniel usually stayed out of contentious situations, but even he was swept up when he got to Ascot, a new, raw racetrack overwhelmed by constant rumors of doping and fixed races. Things got so bad that a race official visiting from Montana, not exactly known as a leading horse-racing state, forbade Ascot trainers from coming to his state in 1905. "There is something rotten in Denmark," he said. "I have made up my mind that certain horsemen now operating at Ascot shall not enter Montana if I can help it." The Jockey Club hired Pinkerton detectives to patrol the track undercover. A cranky debate wore on, because some city supervisors wanted to close the track, but others insisted on keeping it open.

McDaniel added legitimacy to the troubled, upstart track. "From the time he could toddle the ways and moods of the horse were the pet study of the present manager of the Tichenor stable," one reporter wrote. (His father and lineage were still the most consistently mentioned things about him.) He took up a position in the infield before every race, glasses glued to his face, stopwatch ticking. He stood alone. He timed his horses' opponents but did not ask about them. "His own judgment is all he relies on," wrote a reporter.

The accompanying photograph shows McDaniel with his leather binoculars case looped over his arm, a flat-brimmed hat with a light band, a white shirt, dark bow tie, and light vest. A dapper horseman whose hat brim shades his eyes, and whose mouth beneath his mustache is not smiling but not grim, either. He stands with one foot a step forward, as if he hopes the photographer will hurry, because he has more important places to go.

At Los Angeles's Ascot and other tracks, in a weird mirror image of the new wave of understanding horses, outlaws imagined often cruel innovations to force racehorses to lose. Like other sports connected with betting, racing has a shadow history of rigged outcomes. Spongers placed small pieces of sponge inside horses' nostrils, so that they couldn't get enough wind to run at their usual speed. Dopers used stimulants called hop, which could contain anything from cocaine to nitroglycerin cut with rosewater, injected or mixed with molasses and ladled over horses' oats in the hopes of making the horses run faster. Other ingredients included strychnine, capsicum, and ginger. Enforcement was mostly through the night watchmen stable owners hired. Police and jockey clubs were at a loss; saliva testing for drugs did not start until 1934, and officials did not have time to probe every single horse's nostrils before a race.

In February 1906, things at Ascot came to a head when veterinarians were able to verify that a horse named The Huguenot had run under some kind of stimulant. A drugged horse sometimes behaves very oddly; one horse was so hopped up that he bucked his rider off, and then, while onlookers watched gape mouthed, ran around the track three and a half times by himself before collapsing. The case "aroused the indignation of the better class of horsemen here, and they hope some decisive action will be taken to completely eradicate this nefarious practice which has lately thrown the sport into disrepute in California," reported the *Los Angeles Times*.

At the same time, McDaniel, along with two other trainers, lodged charges against Ascot's manager. The two cases melted into one scandal. McDaniel and his friends—to add to the confusion, one of these was a defendant in the doping case—charged that one owner bribed officials to arrange races for him. (Names of the involved parties included "Overcoat Jack" Atkins and "Boots" Durnell.) After each race, the official would be given a box of cigars with a $100 bill hidden under its paper flap. Another owner, they claimed, would race horses in heavy shoes to slow them. Then, when their odds were long enough, he reshod them with lightweight racing plates so the horses could beat their old competitors. Eventually, the dopers, including McDaniel's friend, were suspended, but the board of directors merely reprimanded the crooked manager for some lapses in judgment. The *San Francisco Chronicle* sided with McDaniel: "The turf scandal at Ascot is apparently closed," an editorial ran. "That such a state of affairs was permitted to exist is a grave reflection upon the management." "The verdict in the Brooks case is considered by many as a 'whitewash,'" agreed the *Los Angeles Times.*

McDaniel left Ascot and the turmoil behind. He sold many of Tichenor's horses, except California Derby winner Good Luck, whom he took back to Memphis, another sign of restlessness. Tichenor's stable had not yielded any particular champions. Good Luck was not as promising a runner as Bennett's stalwart Abe Frank, and neither was as fast as Lucky Baldwin's American Derby winner, Rey el Santa Anita, now a distant memory.

McDaniel quit training for Tichenor. He still had not found his Harry Bassett. "While I feel very much disappointed, I want to congratulate you upon your new undertaking," wrote Tichenor in October 1906, "and sincerely hope that it will be for the good, as I know it will be, as I think that you are the most competent, capable, and honest man that I have come in contact with, in the thoroughbred business."

Time sped along. McDaniel was a veteran. He lived the horses' life: the sweet smell of hay, the muffled clatter of shod hooves on hay-strewn brick aisleways, sparrows picking at spilled grain in dawn's shaky light. Horses, he said, knew themselves best. You had to watch them carefully to understand what they were trying to tell you. "Horsemen get up early," he told a reporter in his drawl, "but horses get up earlier." He studied American bloodlines so much that he knew what each horse was bred to do, but also understood—for himself as well as his horses—that there was more to racing than blood. "Good horses have a lot of poor relations," was another of his sayings.

By 1913, McDaniel sounded pragmatic, telling one reporter that he would not take the horses he was training to Kentucky. "I feel that I must go where I can win, even if the purses are smaller," he said. "I know that my horses are not good enough to race with success at Louisville and Latonia this season." It seemed that he was recalibrating his expectations

Henry McDaniel. *(Courtesy of Muriel and Garrett McDaniel)*

and tabling the idea of rivaling his father in terms of accomplishment. No one was more respected, but plenty of trainers had earned more glory.

McDaniel and Leonora grew from a young married couple into middle-aged people. The McDaniels now lived in the Sheepshead Bay area of Coney Island. When the Sheepshead Bay track was built in what had been an oak and maple grove, horse-owning millionaires built huge homes and docks on the north shore of the bay, and the surrounding area was popular with turfmen; the Long Island Rail Road even had a special train that shuttled horses between Belmont and Sheepshead Bay.

The gambler Diamond Jim Brady—who liked to yell and jump when his horses were running—ate with the burlesque actress and singer Lillian Russell at Sheepshead Bay's Gold Room restaurant. Celebrity jockeys like Snapper Garrison and Jimmy McLaughlin lived in brownstones on the Eighth Avenue area now known as Park Slope, then called Sportsman's Row. Famous trainers Sam Hildreth, Max Hirsch, and James Rowe all lived nearby.

But many peers passed McDaniel by. He spent so much time in barns and saddling areas that horsemen called him Uncle Henry, after the member of the family who's always around, the one you turn to for counsel and support. He was a respected and painstaking hardboot. But McDaniel did not have Harry Bassett, the McDaniel Confederacy, or three-Belmonts-in-a-row fame.

During this period, McDaniel began to find himself in the local news more than in the sports pages. In October 1907, he lost his wallet—which contained $9,500 in cash—riding home from Belmont. A racetracker named Stanley French picked it up, and when he overheard conversations about the lost money, he returned it. McDaniel gave French $1,000 without counting his own money, a gesture that became a story told as an example of Uncle Henry's decency.

Next, in 1909, a talented, scofflaw jockey named Cal Shilling fought over a contract with R. L. Thomas, an owner for whom McDaniel was training. Shilling stabbed Thomas several times. As the police took Shilling off to jail, he handed over his diamond pin, ring, and gold watch for safekeeping. McDaniel had to nurse Thomas, who lay bleeding on a couch in his barn office.

Then crises began to move even closer to home. One January night in 1914, McDaniel was at home asleep next to Leonora. Suffering from one of her breakdowns, she had been living in the nearby Sunshine Sanitarium while McDaniel traveled. He awoke to find a man standing over him with a gun. "Be quiet, not a move," said the robber. He fired two shots. Leonora screamed and hid under the sheets. McDaniel removed his own revolver from under a pillow and shot once toward the fleeing robber, and then again through his bedroom door. Passing pedestrians said they saw the bullet hit the burglar in the shoulder, but the man kept running. The next morning, McDaniel found both of the bullets that had been intended for him—one in the sheets and the other in one of his boots. There was no explanation for why the robber had picked the McDaniels' house; the disturbing episode only highlighted a life that included instability and randomness.

McDaniel needed to get back to Toronto, where he was training horses for a Canadian owner. "You can't settle down and be a racing man too; it's one or the other," Hildreth's father had told him. McDaniel's life proved that. Before he left, he closed up his house in Sheepshead Bay. He took Leonora to live with some friends, and hired a nurse named Jennie Larsen to take care of her. On Valentine's Day, about a month after McDaniel shot at the robber, Larsen took a lunch tray up to Leonora's room. She found Leonora standing in a closet, fingering a revolver. Larsen ran out, shouting for help. The couple Leonora lived with rushed up the stairs, and all three—husband, wife, nurse—heard a gunshot. Pushing open the door, they found Leonora dead in a spreading pool of blood, the gun beside her on the floor. She had shot herself in the heart.

Just as his father had, McDaniel learned of his wife's death by telegram.

Only half of McDaniel's scrapbook is filled in. The last page in it contains lyrics titled "The Angel in Our House." "We did not know, when she was present here / How great a void her absence would have left / But since forever stilled her voice of cheer / Our home of all its brightness is bereft."

He would never marry again.

McDaniel kept training. In November 1914, he was working for owner Robert Davies, in Canada. Things went along in an everyday way. He missed a yearling sale because Davies's horses had distemper, and he told a reporter he had modest hopes for one colt. But by May 1915, Davies's string proved unexceptional.

More than ever, McDaniel needed a champion.

2

"One of Those Larger-Than-Life Figures"

Exterminator's owner, Willis Sharpe Kilmer, was about McDaniel's age.

That—and horses—were about the only things the two men had in common. Yet together they produced a confluence of power, talent, and desire that turned Exterminator into an icon.

Kilmer was born in 1869 in Brooklyn, where horses pulled wagons, drays, hansoms, and streetcars. Boys in knee pants knew the differences among Clydesdales, Morgans, and Percherons. People pedaling high wheels and boneshakers shared streets with horse-drawn cabs and broughams, as the use and manufacturing of bicycles shifted urban infrastructure. Industry and the accessibility of ready-made goods were changing the country, and Kilmer, a city boy who turned his family's patent medicine company into a lucrative empire, profited from that change. He lived furiously, starting and running businesses with reckless determination. With the same ferocity, he also alienated, at different times, employees, wives, and family.

Kilmer came across to horsemen as the opposite of Henry McDaniel. He had thrown himself into horse racing, it seemed, overnight, and then shouted at reporters that he was no newcomer. He bellowed for what he wanted. He fired people all the time, and lived with such flashiness that even other nouveau riche millionaires thought he was showy. At the same time, he craved the approval of upper-class racing men; thoroughbreds looked like a way in to the high society he longed for.

Kilmer was flamboyantly rich but was still snubbed by elites whose fortunes were only a little older than his. He sponsored charity projects in his hometown of Binghamton, New York. He loved many of his horses and was a good boss to some employees. "He was a millionaire, and he lived the life of a millionaire," said Bill Leighton, who was Kilmer's valet. "He may have been a tough taskmaster with his stable crew, his trainers and business associates, and what have you. But with his personal staff, he was proper and generous. He was one of those larger-than-life figures."

Kilmer built and shattered many things in his life: marriages, companies, partnerships. Throughout, there were horses.

In 1880, the U.S. Census report included an evaluation of American horses. There was no exact count, but, the report said, "the number of horses employed in trade and transportation, or owned by men of leisure, professional men, or livery-stable keepers, who are also not farmers, is large." There were no electric railways in Manhattan or Brooklyn, which had 1,764,168 people and 150,000 to 175,000 horses. The historian Joel Tarr counts 427 blacksmith shops, 249 carriage-focused establishments, and 290 stores selling harness in 1880 Brooklyn and New York.

City children like Kilmer, who was eleven in 1880, were around horses all the time: buying milk in the morning, loading a moving truck, riding a trolley to school. There were so many horses that the first international urban planning conference, held in 1898, focused on what to do about manure. People evaluated horses constantly, the way people who don't consider themselves interested in cars still have opinions about what the neighbors drive. They smelled fresh hay on busy streets and heard the clink of harness buckles when they walked by livery stables.

By the turn of the century, three and a half million urban American horses worked alongside cars and electric streetcars. There were 5,000 in Columbus, 12,000 in Detroit, and 83,330 in Chicago. Seventeen million lived in rural places. (There are about nine million in America today.) Increasing industrialization brought a higher living standard, which in turn meant more trade. Horses transported almost all of the ready-to-wear clothes, lightweight cutlery, tin toys, and other manufactured products that Americans bought.

Kilmer's Brooklyn was a separate city from New York. It was filled with everyday taxi, livery, and cart horses, but it was also a thoroughbred racing center. As Ryan Goldberg writes, the success of upstate Saratoga in the 1860s made New Yorkers want closer tracks, so they could race their horses nearer to home.

There were three tracks in Brooklyn: Brighton Beach, Gravesend, and splendid Sheepshead Bay, which was called America's Ascot because it was as lofty and formal a park as the one in England. Thomas Edison tested a camera he'd invented on racehorses there. The Brighton Beach racecourse, on Coney Island, was only a mile from Sheepshead Bay, and people got there by train or horsecar line. The Prospect Park and Coney Island Railroad took people to Gravesend; the trains that became the "most extensive railway system in the country" were started to carry racegoers to the Brooklyn tracks.

Men who worked in Manhattan could take a boat to Sheepshead Bay in the afternoon and catch the races before spending the evening at vaudeville shows on Coney Island. On Monday, Wednesday, and Friday there were races at Gravesend, and on the other days, except Sunday, horses ran at Sheepshead Bay. There was almost always a race to watch.

Kilmer's family left Brooklyn for Binghamton, in southwestern New York, in 1878. Binghamton housed the Endicott-Johnson shoe company, which aimed for progressive ideals and gave workers what they called "the square deal." Spread out over the three Southern Tier cities of Johnson

City, Binghamton, and Endicott, the company owned and donated parks, carousels, bowling alleys, and swimming pools. Binghamton was called the "parlor city," because of its gracious houses, and is still known as the city of carousels.

When the Kilmers moved to town, Kilmer's uncle S. Andral Kilmer was making patent medicine in his—and Kilmer's father Jonas's—sister's kitchen. Jonas became S. Andral's business manager, and the company, now named Dr. Kilmer and Co., moved to a big building downtown. Swamp-Root, its biggest seller, was a cure-all diuretic potion advertised as "purely vegetable," because it was made of ingredients including cinnamon, valerian root, and sassafras, but contained no cocaine. It did, though, contain 9 percent alcohol.

Medicine was not standardized yet; there was no FDA until 1906. After the Civil War, medicine trended away from dramatic treatments like bleeding and emetics. Doctors used—in doses now considered enormous—morphine, calomel (a compound of mercury chloride, which makes patients vomit), and quinine. As an alternative, many people chose patent medicines. They appealed to patients who were tired of being purged and bled. In 1859, patent medicines generated $3,500,000; by 1904, $74,500,000, just in wholesale dollars.

In later years, when people asked Kilmer what Swamp-Root was good for, he reportedly said, "a couple million a year."

In Binghamton, Kilmer did not fit in. "He was always startling the people of Binghamton in those days by all sorts of apparent innovations," wrote Jerome Hadsell, who worked for generations of Kilmers and remembered the cape Kilmer liked to wear as a young man. "I think that fact explains a great deal of the public misunderstanding of Mr. Kilmer in his earlier years." Even on the quiet streets of town, he wore a full riding habit. When he was hitting golf balls, he wore a complete golf ensemble, including St Andrews–style red cap and coat. He drove his tandem behind a fast team, hitched to a leader named Duke, and a groom in full livery rode with him. "I think I am safe in saying that some folks resented it," wrote Hadsell. One day, Kilmer lashed a cyclist with a driving whip because the man rode his bicycle in front of his carriage; he had to pay $500 to the victim.

"When we were doing a small business and making slow headway, Willis said to me one day after a session of hard work, 'Dad, I need more education than I have,'" was how Jonas Kilmer told the story of his son's headstrong personality. "Please send me to a good college and I will get the education I need to make us both wealthy. We shook hands on it . . . It was my son who made the Kilmer business big and successful." Willis became head of Swamp-Root's advertising in 1892.

Kilmer went to Cornell and then in 1893 married a young Manhattan woman named Beatrice Richardson, whose father owned a newspaper advertising agency. Kilmer and Beatrice were married in the parlors of her parents' home on East 72nd Street adorned with white flowers and palms. "Miss Richardson, the bride, is a daughter of the well-known advertising agent, A. F. Richardson," wrote one reporter. "She is a beautiful and accomplished young woman and holds an exalted position in New York society." Kilmer built a large home, and Beatrice had the finest clothes in Binghamton, as well as costly equipages and saddle horses.

The marriage bought Kilmer some social status, and his new father-in-law taught him about advertising. At the time, Kilmer's uncle and father were only haltingly marketing Swamp-Root. They used painted wooden signs, posters, and advertising circulars. Sales were steady but slow. Kilmer persuaded them to buy space in country weeklies to sell their potions with flashy copy and images. On one advertisement, a little girl playfully held her hands over her mother's eyes, with the words, "Some People Guess, the Well-Informed Know the Virtues of Swamp-Root." "X-Rays Are Not More Searching Than Swamp-Root," said another, which featured a picture of a young man staring at an X-ray machine. Kilmer's Swamp-Root ads—orange, like the labels—were everywhere. S. Andral's solemn, kindly-physician face, walruslike behind big muttonchops, appeared on the packaging. The Swamp-Root jingle went, in part: "Perchance your kidneys are deranged or liver is affected, / Don't say that life has lost its charm and be at once dejected."

It could be difficult to build a patent-medicine company. Customers shied away from medicines they had never heard of, so business owners needed to spend about $200,000 just to familiarize people with a product. They used gimmicks, like joke books, coloring books, and songbooks. Kilmer preferred almanacs, "an 1880s version of the infomercial." Between advertisements, these paperbacks had testimonials: a druggist said that he saved a client's life with Swamp-Root and kept his kidney stones on display in his store ever since. They also included information such as membership numbers of fraternal organizations, including Ladies of the Modern Maccabees (49,943) and Nobles of the Mystic Shrine (200,500), and the penalties for murder in different states (electrocution in New Jersey, hanging or shooting at the discretion of the prisoner in Nevada).

A story went that Joseph Pulitzer, the owner of the *New York World,* sent for Kilmer. Pulitzer offered the young man a salary of $25,000 a year if he would manage his advertising. "If I am worth $25,000 to you," Kilmer told Pulitzer, "I am worth more than that to myself."

Swamp-Root sales climbed, and then soared.

In 1905, a bill was up for ratification in Massachusetts that demanded better labeling on patent medicines. Kilmer sent a telegram to all the papers that carried his advertising: "Quick work necessary," it said. "Use your influence."

In 1899, Beatrice Kilmer filed for divorce. The residents of Binghamton seemed unsurprised, because the town couldn't imagine anyone getting along with Kilmer, and there had been many rumors about Kilmer and other women. The complaint she filed listed thirteen offenses—some "statutory"—and fourteen other people. Eventually, the statutory grounds were withdrawn, but the divorce stood. Kilmer left for Mexico to start a compounding laboratory. Beatrice remarried in 1903.

Around the same time, Kilmer and his father got into a fight with the local newspaper, the *Binghamton Herald*. The *Herald* had written more than Kilmer liked about the time he was convicted for horsewhipping the bicyclist, it made fun of Swamp-Root by calling it "Rump Swat," and had also published the names of all fourteen co-respondents in Kilmer's divorce suit. At first, Kilmer simply withheld Swamp-Root advertising, but when that didn't work, he threatened the owner. "I'll get even with you," he said. "You aren't through with me. I'll get even with you." A mutual friend tried to broker peace, but the *Herald*'s owner refused. "That settles it," said Kilmer.

He started his own newspaper, the *Binghamton Press*. He hired the *Herald*'s employees away and housed the *Press* in the same building as the Swamp-Root manufacturing plant. It began publication in 1904. The *Herald*'s owners sued, but the judge said that even though the Kilmers' intentions were malicious, their actions were legal. In time, the *Herald*'s business trickled away, and it went out of business.

Kilmer gave an enormous dinner at Christmas for all newsboys, regardless of which paper they delivered. One year, there were 239. He also had policemen stationed in the dining room, although that turned out to be overkill. The boys were boisterous, but they behaved fine and ate plenty. When Kilmer came in, they gave him a standing ovation.

"Goodness, boy, you can't stand much more," he said to one.

"G'wan," the boy told him. "I got room for th' ice cream yet."

Upton Sinclair's 1906 novel, *The Jungle,* exposed gruesome practices at meatpacking plants. A muckraker named Samuel Hopkins Adams wrote a similarly styled exposé of patent medicines for *Collier's* and included his thesis statement in his title: "The Great American Fraud." Adams spent plenty of his time vilifying Swamp-Root. "The way to end Swamp-Root's career of fraud is to spread understanding of what it really is," he wrote, "a compound of false promises and harmful drugs . . . backed up by a conscienceless newspaper; in all the realms of medical knavery . . . Make no mistake about that, you unfortunates who are lured by its seductive advertising. Its curative power is nil." (When Adams wrote a *Jungle*-style book directed at patent medicine, Kilmer ensured it was not advertised or sold in Binghamton.)

The Kilmers, Adams learned, told customers to mail them urine samples, so they could be analyzed in their Binghamton lab. The idea was that medical staffers would examine the specimens and figure out if the patient needed medicine. Then they could prescribe the appropriate nostrum. But when a suspicious post office inspector mailed in bottles of tea and horse urine, both came back with prescriptions for Swamp-Root.

In the end, though, the case against the Kilmers was not strong enough to prosecute. By then, S. Andral Kilmer, too, was trying to sue his brother and nephew. (Adams had not ignored S. Andral, whom he called a member of "an old, picturesque and fast-disappearing tribe of bunco-artists.") Willis Sharpe and Jonas Kilmer had bought the business from S. Andral while he concentrated on running a "cancertorium" he had founded farther upstate. But he, too, was thwarted in attempts to charge Willis and his father. An appellate court found that "Dr. Kilmer & Co. have in all respects observed the contracts made at the time the business was purchased by Jonas M. Kilmer and . . . that the defendant is advertising its business as authorized."

Meanwhile, orange-swathed bottles of Swamp-Root kept selling well. It was not until the Pure Food and Drug Act was passed in 1906 that Swamp-Root's hold faltered, and by then the Kilmer fortune was well established and flourishing.

Kilmer married again, in 1909, this time to another Binghamtonian, named Esther Wadsworth. He took up various upper-class hobbies. His speedboat, the *Vingt-et-un II,* raced at the society hub Frontenac, New York, and he went to Narragansett, Rhode Island, with his yacht, pacing the piazza wearing a wide straw hat and carrying a cane. Next it was foxhunting at Pinehurst, North Carolina, with his own pack of fifty hounds and string of hunters, and by 1911 the group was making the society pages as the Remlik—Kilmer spelled backward—Hounds. He bred show terriers and saddle horses.

Once, when he was on an ocean liner, other passengers snubbed Kilmer. Perhaps moments like these propelled him toward racing. As the historian Katherine C. Mooney writes, "Membership in the American Jockey Club was a social necessity for New York's stock market kings, steel and tobacco magnates, and railroad barons—Vanderbilts, Roosevelts, Carnegies, Lorillards, and Harrimans." Kilmer, a titan of his own industry, was inspired.

There was an excitement about racing. Dashing Alice Roosevelt, Teddy's eldest daughter, stirred up Washington in 1905 when she went to the Benning track, climbed the barrier, and clung to the track railing. Soon, a crowd collected. The starter, Mars Cassidy, whose vocabulary the sportswriter Red Smith said "would bring blushes to the foredeck of a Portuguese freighter," held his tongue that day, even though the horses for one race were plunging and hard to control. The jockeys showed off for Alice, too. Once Cassidy had launched the rambunctious field, Alice applauded him, and he doffed his hat at her as the crowd gaped.

Owning thoroughbred racehorses was thrilling, upper class, and glamorous. In 1914, Kilmer started buying thoroughbreds to race. For his racing colors, he chose green, brown, and Swamp-Root orange.

Horsemen chafed under the 1908 Hart-Agnew Act, an antigambling reform effort that prohibited certain kinds of betting in New York. Hart-Agnew affected racetrack attendance and purse sizes. Some tracks shut down; the Brooklyn tracks would never reopen. Those who could afford the costs of travel took their horses abroad to run. Between 1908 and 1913, star racers including Colin, Peter Pan, and Ballot sailed for Europe. Paris became "the new Eldorado of American racing men," and more raced in England. Many British horsemen, who considered horse racing a hallmark of culture, thought American thoroughbreds inferior to their own. They found Hart-Agnew barbaric. "It hardly seems credible that in this twentieth century a civilized community can be found that will suffer itself to be trampled on in this fashion," one wrote in the *London Sporting Life*.

In 1910, New York's Legislative Graft Committee alleged that there had been a secret dinner held at Delmonico's at which horsemen were plotting to overthrow the law. The financier and thoroughbred breeder August Belmont Jr. testified that there was no such gathering and defended his fellow Jockey Club member, Harry Payne Whitney, who was in Europe with his stable and could not appear before the committee. "Perhaps you may not think so, but the International Polo Match is a matter of great concern," Belmont said. "I don't think that he could be expected to take a steamer and come out here to testify to you about some mythical dinner that took place."

In 1911, Belmont *did* host a dinner, although he gave it at the Waldorf-Astoria, not Delmonico's. He gave a speech to the gathered horsemen, arguing for racing to be equated with patriotism, not with gambling. They should start a remount movement, donating their own horses to breed cavalry horses. Congress approved the creation of the Remount Service in 1908 to make sure the U.S. Army had a steady supply of mounts. Now it was time for thoroughbred owners to become involved. "It is upon you polo players, huntsmen, and amateur riders, as well as racing men, that the future of the thoroughbred horse in this country depends," he said. Anyone who believed racing was just a vehicle for gambling, Belmont continued, was "an enemy to the interest of our farmers, our ranchmen, military establishment, and all citizens who use and breed the horse for pleasure." Most presciently, he talked about the army.

"What would happen if in case of war, notwithstanding a growing international desire for peace, the cavalry had to be quadrupled?" he asked. "Where would they come from?"

His answer: from thoroughbred breeders.

Despite many American racehorses being impure in terms of British thoroughbred breeding, they won races. That made the Jockey Club, England's regulatory board, take a closer look at bloodlines. The lineage of thorough-bred horses has always been curated. Even today, Jockey Club–registered thoroughbreds can be bred only by two horses mating (the industry calls this "live cover"). Breeders of other registered horses—quarter horses, Stan-dardbreds, Morgans—may use artificial insemination, which means a desirable stallion often fathers thousands of foals.

English breeders had kept scrupulous records about their own horses' pedigrees and did not consider many Canadian, American, or Australian horses pure thoroughbred in terms of their stud book, which was first pub-lished in 1791 and went back much further. The *American Stud Book* (also called Bruce's, after its author, Sanders Bruce) went back only to 1868 (vol-ume 1, A–K), because so many breeding records were destroyed in the Civil War. "I have not attempted to fix any definite standard of what con-stitutes a thoroughbred," Bruce wrote.

In addition, no one in England liked their horses to lose to American ones. In 1908, an American horse won the Grand National, and England started limiting how many American trainers could work in Newmarket. By 1913, the British Jockey Club had passed the Jersey Act, which said that "no horse or mare can, after this date, be considered as eligible for admis-sion unless it can be traced without flaw on both sire's and dam's side of its pedigree to horses and mares themselves already accepted in the earlier volumes of the book."

This effectively meant no American-bred horses could be entered unless they or their parents had already been registered in the British stud book. An American-owned French horse named Durbar II won the Epsom Derby, England's biggest race. But under the Jersey Act, he was ineligible for the registry, because his dam had been bred in America. (In 1914, Dur-bar II was nearly captured by the French near Chantilly, but his groom wrapped an American flag around him and pinned a banner to him that said, "This is Durbar II, the English Derby winner. He is neutral." The French army spared him.)

During the Boer War, when Great Britain set out to annex South Africa, the British had bought thousands of horses from America. These horses lost their lives in dismal ways; 150,000 died because of poor transport conditions, like bad feed and insufficient air, alone. Horses were also forced into battle before they were trained. During one siege, soldiers even ate their horses. The whole scene was so grim that one remount director, stationed near Cape Town, shot himself. The only benefit to the wretchedness, as the historian Robert Koenig writes, was that Great Britain was far better prepared for a future cavalry war. British army officers developed methods to control disease at horse depots with pesticides and improved transport ventilation, and allowed newly shipped horses some time at pasture before sending them into battle. America would use these advances, too.

As World War I began in 1914, Britain needed American horses again. America had fewer appropriate horses because of the Boer buy-ups. Also, American horsemen, watching the war gain momentum, realized that their own army might need horses. There were not enough, particularly of the right "type." "I can . . . vividly recall the short necked, beefy withered, straight pasterned, poor moving horses obtained," said one U.S. Army official, years later. The horses the army wanted should "stand 15-2 to 16-2 hands, weigh 1,100 to 1,300 pounds, be of serviceable condition with sufficient bone and be a dark, solid color." (The color preference wasn't capricious; gray horses are more easily seen on the battlefield. Some troops actually ended up painting their horses darker colors.) From November 1, 1914, to July 29, 1915, foreign governments bought around 200,000 horses in America. The U.S. Army bought 500,000 horses between 1914 and 1918.

Front Royal, the second permanent remount depot, was activated on August 30, 1911, in the Shenandoah valley of Virginia. Soldiers there were trained in animal management, shoeing, and tack repair. Horses were examined and issued, and horsemen conditioned stallions for the breeding program. Sportsmen elected Major General Leonard Wood, who had been Roosevelt's colonel in the volunteer cavalry of Rough Riders, as the first president of the Remount Association. Roosevelt was campaigning for a third term as president but said he would serve as a vice president. Taking a step beyond merely supplying horses became a cause célèbre. Horsemen wanted to save racing, prove the superiority of the American thoroughbred, and win a war.

The Boer War had shown how important horses continued to be, and World War I, still being fought without the United States, continued to prove it. At one point in 1914, England wanted 153,000 horses; Canada, 33,000; France, 40,000. "In a nutshell," reported the *New York Times,* "the United States has over 23,000,000 horses; Germany has about 3,000,000, and France about 3,200,000. Germany and France have been breeding a re-mount type and with less than one-seventh of the total number of horses owned in the United States."

By then, Belmont and his friends had won. Bookies could no longer shout their odds, but people could place bets "among friends," which were loosely defined. That previously hypothetical war Belmont had talked about was edging closer every day. He and other horsemen donated stallions to the re-mount cause—he alone gave six. The army encouraged its officers to compete in steeple-chases and polo matches to demonstrate the athleticism of the army mounts.

Once he started buying race-horses, Kilmer was referred to as a new recruit, which drove him crazy. "New recruit" was the opposite of the impression he wanted to make. His father

Willis Sharpe Kilmer. (*Courtesy of the Broome County Historical Society*)

owned trotting horses, after all. He had show horses and driving horses and hunters. Anyway, he had arrived on the scene in style, going to the races, lunching in clubhouses. "Billy Sunday didn't know a whole lot about the scriptures when he abandoned baseball for evangelism," was his newspaper's response.

Kilmer went to the thoroughbred capital of Lexington in 1915 in a private Pullman car named *Glen Eyre,* with his wife, secretary, and guests. He had hired a man named Frank Taylor as trainer. Soon, though, Taylor resigned; Kilmer expected too much of the modestly talented horses he had, and Taylor could not deliver the winners for which his boss thundered.

Through a British agent, Kilmer bought three English-bred two-year-olds. They boarded the Atlantic Transport liner *Mongolian.* Buying those horses signified that he was not only entering racing on a "grand scale" but also would join other, longer-term members of the racing world in shipping them with Atlantic Transport, which listed some of its most famous clients, who included August Belmont, the British Tattersalls sales barn, and James Keene, a millionaire stockbroker with a large, successful stable. Now they shipped for Willis Kilmer, too.

Owners aboard Atlantic Transport Lines hired special foremen for the voyages between New York and England. Horses ate well; a sample menu was ten pounds of oats, three pounds of bran, two pounds of apples, two pounds of carrots, and piles of clover hay, fed at 5:30 A.M., 4:00 P.M., and 9:00 P.M. Some horses had double stalls, able to convert quickly into single stalls if the weather was rough, so that the horses would not slide around or fall. Stalls were padded all around with straw-stuffed burlap mattresses. Six inches of peat moss covered the floor.

When Alfred Vanderbilt sent his famous driving team of grays to England so that he could compete in coaching competitions there, they got even more bedding, and Atlantic Transport replaced the usual 2½-by-8-foot with stalls three times that size, so that the horses could lie down. (Most horses had to stand the whole way across the Atlantic.) Vanderbilt's were on the main cattle deck, which gave them more light and better breezes. Their stalls were bedded almost knee-deep with the peat moss, and the sides were padded six inches deep with wooden excelsior. Vanderbilt specifically said that he wanted the best hay and oats for the team. Grooms stayed nearby at all times; so they wouldn't wander too far when they were eating, their meals were served in a next-door mess hall. Even more peat moss padded the route of the horses to their stalls.

Horses often struggled with the long journeys. Some got sick, some died, and some were fine until the very end, which is what happened when August Belmont's prize stallion Rock Sand traveled across the Atlantic. He refused to get off the ship once he reached New York. He fought his handlers, pulling back on the lead rope, front legs extended, and then lay down, his big body blocking the path. Finally, he was pulled to his feet, but no one—not the foreman who had been with him the whole trip, not Belmont himself—could persuade the horse to step onto the gangplank. Finally, a New York City mounted police officer rode *his* horse onto the boat, and Rock Sand stepped off behind him. On another crossing, of the Atlantic Transport liner *Minnewaska,* there were so many horses that owners held a show. They cleared a space near the stalls, and grooms led each horse out. A judge from Ohio stood on a box, evaluating each one while passengers watched.

Once the war started, there were fewer horse shows and more danger on the Atlantic Transport steamers. In 1915, the German sympathizer Eric Muenter planned to sabotage the war by infecting American cavalry horses with glanders, a contagious, fatal disease. That plan failed, so he set a bomb stoppered with a cork—a crude time-release that meant when acid ate through, it would explode—to go off in the U.S. Capitol. Next, he went to J. P. Morgan's house and shot him; it turned out that he believed Morgan was financing the war. In between the Capitol bombing and the Morgan shooting, Muenter placed *another* bomb aboard the Atlantic Transport ship *Minnehaha,* which was carrying cordite and other explosives. The ship caught fire. (Muenter, a Harvard professor who had poisoned his wife before he became a saboteur, explained all this in a letter to the *Washington Star*.) The *Minnehaha* put in to Halifax to get the flames under control and was not badly damaged, because Muenter had put the bomb too far away from most of the munitions. Muenter killed himself in jail.

Kilmer kept striving. He had money and thoroughbred horses, stables and a beautiful wife. He was a "good-looking man of impressive proportions with a voice in keeping with his size," as one Saratoga regular saw him. But he still seemed unsatisfied, as if he wanted something else that Belmont had, and Vanderbilt, and Whitney, and Keene.

Horses that won.

3

All-American
Thoroughbred

In 1915, surrounded by tall oaks and the soft smells of late May—molasses, paint, grass, soap—a dark chestnut foal unfolded his legs for the first time. He did not have any markings on his legs, which was auspicious. Horsemen were just shedding the superstition that white socks and stockings were bad luck. Between the foal's dark eyes was a lopsided white mark, a "star" in equestrian terms. It looked more like a triangle, with one of its points facing down and the edges sanded round, or even, if you looked from a distance, like a heart.

The farm was quiet, out of the way, three hundred acres ringed by trees and blanketed by thick bluegrass. The foal's dam, Fair Empress, had had eleven foals already, and she knew what she was doing. The Knight farm had been in their family since before Kentucky was a state. The men who worked there knew what they were doing, too. A waiting foaling manager likely tapped the foal's hooves, rubbed his ears, and stroked his body with a soft woolen cloth or some dry straw. If his first interactions were with someone gentle, a thoroughbred foal would accept a lifetime of farriers, riders, and trainers. This foal, like countless other babies born on countless other farms in 1915, could become one of the all-American thoroughbreds every breeder and owner had been waiting for. But outside the circle of mother, baby, and man, and outside the reliable ritual of birthing horses in the spring, his world was in a tumult.

Racing's future seemed unsteady. Well before they knew that World War I would contain the last grand American cavalry effort, horsemen were fighting battles because of a welter of concerns, including the American preoccupation with blood, a denuded army remount, and the ever-nearing war. This tangle would affect everyone in racing, including Willis Sharpe Kilmer, Henry McDaniel, and the dark, wet foal taking his first gulps of spring Kentucky air.

As the fiftieth anniversary of the Civil War approached, Americans considered the concept of blood, using terms of race, identity, and thoroughbreds. The figure of Theodore Roosevelt merged conversations about the "race suicide" he mentioned in a 1905 speech if the white birth rate dropped with his image as a horseman whose Lightfoot, Little Texas, and Bleistein had carried him throughout his life: as a young man in Oyster Bay, up Kettle Hill with the Rough Riders, and through Rock Creek Park when he was president. Roosevelt and others invoked what Michael Kreyling calls "the rhetoric of 'blood,'" their preoccupation with hereditary traits and predispositions. Most crucially, they "stacked them in a pyramid from inferior people of color at the base to superior whites at the pinnacle. Not all 'blood' was the same."

Roosevelt went to ad hoc horse races when he lived out west and thrilled to the wild riding. "Cowboys," he wrote, "are certainly extremely good riders . . . Of course, they would at first be at a disadvantage in steeple-chasing or fox-hunting, but their average of horsemanship is without doubt higher than that of the men who take part in these latter amusements." In Washington, he rode often, and any companions followed rules: they had to stay at least ten feet behind him and ride with the right stirrup in back of the president's left stirrup. If they couldn't control their horses, they were to retreat to the back of the group. Roosevelt considered thoroughbred racing families like the Whitneys "kindly" but "self-absorbed." (His son Quentin had been engaged to marry one of the Whitneys when he was killed in World War I.) But he loved horses, riding, and any athletic contest, and these feelings carried over to his view of racing in general as an out-doorsy and wholesome activity. "You all know what we mean when we speak of a thoroughbred," said a boys' magazine article. "A thoroughbred has strength and heart and fire and courage. A thoroughbred goes till he drops. A thoroughbred never gives up. Every boy then should determine to be a thoroughbred, such a thoroughbred as was Theodore Roosevelt."

America, of course, complicated this picture, because there was a bit more latitude in creating thoroughbreds—men or horses. As a 1914 *New York Times* article said, "The thoroughbred horse and the thoroughbred man together can conquer the world. They have done it since the dawn of history." A problem with American thoroughbreds, as British breeders had believed when they passed the Jersey Act, was that their ancestors were "bred in the wilderness of obscurity." But August Belmont, the patrician-appearing horse breeder who seemed to be at the top of the white-man pyr-amid, was a son of a German who was born Jewish and changed his name when he came to America. Another thoroughbred breeder, James Ben Ali Haggin, was an aristocratic, landed Kentuckian and was descended from one of the state's earliest Turkish settlers, Ibrahim Ben Ali.

It was hard to know exactly what an "American thoroughbred" was; it was almost oxymoronic. The ideal "American thoroughbred" person, in the prevailing view, might have been Teddy Roosevelt. But the ideal Amer-ican thoroughbred *horse* had not yet been identified.

McGee, the sire of the newborn Kentucky colt, was a stallion imported from England. A "fiery maverick" named "Big Ed" Corrigan brought the unfashionably bred McGee to America in 1903 as a yearling and named him after his insurance agent. In 1909, Corrigan sold McGee to Charles W. Moore, a man-about-the-tracks Kentuckian who wore a wide-brimmed white hat all year round, and swung a hickory stick when he walked. McGee won twenty-four races in his time, but none were stakes races.

Also, most were short. (McGee tended to get tired after he had run a mile.) *His* sire, White Knight, never raced at all and fathered only McGee. Until Exterminator became famous, McGee was not known for siring stars. Instead, with the notable exception of 1913 Kentucky Derby winner Donerail, his get were mud runners, game horses who soldiered through wet, heavy footing. Moore called them his "daily winners."

The colt's dam, Fair Empress, was dark brown, almost black. She was born in 1899 at William S. Barnes's Melbourne Stud in Lexington. Turf writers called her a "washerwoman" and her ancestor Maria West an "American hussy," because she traced back to an unnamed daughter of a stallion with no dam on record at all. Although inelegant, the bloodline was considered hardy and useful. Fair Empress did not win any races as a filly, and went back to Melbourne to become a broodmare in 1902.

A man named W. P. Knight bought Fair Empress at a Melbourne stud sale, and when he died in 1909, Fair Empress's ownership passed to his mother, Mrs. M. J. Mizner. Accounts of who owned how much of Fair Empress and her future foal differ, but it seems that in 1914, another of the Knights—banker G. L. Knight; or F. D. Knight, the brother who registered foals for his mother, so his name appears on records—arranged for three of Mrs. Mizner's mares to be bred to McGee on a shares basis, which gave McGee's owner, the white-hatted Moore, some investment in the breeding process as well as future sales.

The Knight farm was outside Lexington in Nicholasville, Kentucky, in the kind of hills that seem to stretch to the horizon in low waves. Dry limestone walls, made from stone nestled together and stacked in layers, traversed the landscape, as did fences coated with "Kentucky paint," whitewash reapplied every spring. On May 7, 1915, news shook even the quietest roads in Kentucky: a German submarine sank the British ocean liner *Lusitania*, with 128 Americans on board. The war now seemed closer to home.

Foaling season went on, though, and about three weeks later, Fair Empress gave birth to the chestnut colt with the white mark on his forehead.

Kentucky offered a good example of the American desire to couch identity in blood, whether equine or human. By the 1910s, it was in full swing in its role as a place that inherited its love for the thoroughbred from its Old South roots. Martha McCulloch-Williams, the author of a cookbook with recipes she attributed to a "Mammy," wrote about a Confederate troop mounted on thoroughbreds: "When the coldbloods were staggering, falling by the wayside, the blood stock kept everlastingly at it—without food, almost without water." Their commander kept those horses afterward, because he "wanted them as examples to his grandchildren of how blood will tell." The state's whole identity and livelihood was wrapped up in the idea of thoroughbreds, breeding, and blood that "will tell."

As Maryjean Wall writes in her book *How Kentucky Became Southern,* the years following Reconstruction to the turn of the century gave new meaning to the tradition of Kentucky as a horse-breeding state. Kentuckians used a mythology of their home state as a genteel southern society to lure northern money. Thoroughbred breeding became the passion of northeastern industrialists and robber barons, men who had enough capital to keep up the farms, unlike many of the farmers who had bred horses before the war. Locals appealed to these investors with their heritage brand of horse nurseries, trailing images of foals chasing each other in rippling grass, fences painted white, cool springs running through the fields, bourbon served neat in a short glass.

Northerners who had farms in Kentucky included Belmont and Haggin. James Keene was born in England and lived in New York, but he established Castleton Farm in Lexington. The most blue-blooded breeding family may have been the Whitneys; they were pure northerners. At the same time, Kentucky also went from a place where celebrity African American jockeys like Isaac Murphy, who rode three Kentucky Derby winners, and Jimmy Winkfield earned fortunes during the late nineteenth and very early twentieth centuries to a state fostering a more racist structure. They were relegated to menial stable jobs, while white jockeys ascended.

During the Saratoga season of 1916, Kilmer must have realized his money alone could not bring him the winning stable he wanted. He would need to purchase some legitimacy along with fast horses.

If you were looking for a born trainer, for someone who knew all there was to know about horses, Henry McDaniel was the right man. McDaniel and Kilmer met that summer, at dressed-up Saratoga. One was the symbol of the backstretch, all savvy and history and horsemanship; the other was straw-hatted, fresh from watching the races from brand-new box seats. Each, in his own way, craved victory. McDaniel needed possibility and Kilmer needed respectability.

The two men negotiated, and by August, McDaniel had resigned from Canadian owner Robert Davies's stable, leaving his brother William in charge. For McDaniel, Kilmer represented a crucial, exciting opportunity. He had plenty of money and not very many horses. McDaniel could buy what he wanted. He might be able to train a Harry Bassett, after all, because now he could afford the best. He could leave some pragmatism behind and take a leap with this unknown, very rich owner. Kilmer's resources could offer McDaniel a chance that, in many ways, he had been preparing for nearly all of his life.

McDaniel went over to Binghamton to look things over. He found that the in-town farm on Riverside Drive—so different from the countryside Kentucky farms—had many new improvements, including a half-mile racing track. It was an unusual setup for New York's Southern Tier, but it worked. Crowds joined him, coming every day to watch the horses in the fields and see the latest, ever-changing projects.

"Mr. Kilmer has organized his stud with the idea of making valuable contributions to future breeding," a *Binghamton Press* reporter wrote, "thus increasing by rapid strides the number and quality of good horses throughout the United States."

War pushed to the front of conversation. Kilmer's idea was that McDaniel would go abroad, looking for the best horses to breed. He would buy them and bring them home so they, in turn, would better the American equine population, making not only racehorses but also good cavalry mounts available for American soldiers. "Mr. Kilmer is securing horses which are capable of going the distance, those with stamina and endurance, the best that can be secured," said McDaniel. "They are the type that will have the greatest ultimate value in improving breeding in this country." This was rich praise. He and Kilmer may have made an unusual pair, but now, his words showed, they were a team.

McDaniel's 1916 passport application shows that he swore an Oath of Allegiance to support and defend the Constitution of the United States against all enemies, foreign and domestic. He intended to leave the United States from the port of New York on November 18 on the *Saint Paul*. He would travel to England and Ireland. He would take this obligation "freely, without any mental reservation of purpose of evasion: So help me God."

Crawling up the side of the form in McDaniel's horseman's script is an asterisk, followed by: "for W. S. Kilmer, Binghampton [*sic*], NY." On the next line he entered only two words to declare his purpose for travel. But in some ways, these two words encapsulated not just his immediate mission but what he had done his whole life: inspect horses.

McDaniel traveled across U-boat-infested waters to England. Earlier in the year, thirty American horse traders had not been allowed to disembark from a steamer that had come into Manchester, because the war had changed the rules of lading and travel, and the consulate could not issue them any kind of certificate of citizenship. Those horsemen were stuck for three weeks, idling in port, imprisoned on the boat and waiting for their ship to go back to New Orleans.

McDaniel must have hoped that wouldn't happen to him. This was his first time abroad, England was at war, and the situation was very disorienting. At night, London's streets were dark, except for tiny lights at street corners, but they had large hoods over them so that German bombers would have a hard time finding the city. Locals hurried to get off the streets, and even they got lost. For McDaniel, navigation was hopeless.

Still, he kept going. He needed to get to the Tattersalls sales barn in the thoroughbred capital of Newmarket, about sixty-five miles north of London. But the British army had requisitioned the railways, so he had to hire a car and driver. As they drove past Buckingham Palace, McDaniel saw people running by, their necks craned as they looked up at the sky. His driver slowed down, but McDaniel, anxious, asked him to step on the gas. "I heard a shout," McDaniel later told a reporter, "and the next moment a loud report rent the air. We stopped. Looking back, I saw confusion and dust, rising from a hole in the pavement."

A German bomb, aiming for the palace, had instead hit the exact spot McDaniel and the driver had been. The bomb could have killed them both. Looking more closely at the palace, McDaniel saw that a false roof made of metal rose over it, protecting it from bombs. Later, he learned that the bomb was dropped from a Taube airplane that was shot down by French sharpshooters when it crossed the channel for home.

McDaniel bought eleven broodmares and left England from Liverpool on December 21. "People have to be very careful about traveling in England, and on leaving it," McDaniel told a reporter. "One cannot find out when a vessel is to leave. The sailing dates are kept secret. If you are shipping horses or anything else you are told to have your shipment aboard by a certain time, and the ship will leave 'some time later on.' And when a vessel leaves it hurries out of the harbor as fast as it can." Only forty-one first-cabin passengers were making the trip with him, and the ship carried no freight. The crew used water for ballast. The horses would travel on another ship. Christmas fell while they were still at sea, but no one celebrated, and somewhere in the middle of the ocean, the ship had a mechanical problem, which terrified the passengers. "I was glad to land," said McDaniel.

The *Minnehaha*—the ship that had almost been bombed by Muenter in 1915—was late with a shipment in January 1917. Horsemen worried. "Somewhere out in the Atlantic the *Minnehaha* must be dodging the

Kaiser's submarines," one said. As it turned out, the ship had collided with an Italian ship and needed five extra days to return to seaworthiness. To the relief of many horse owners, it finally arrived on January 15, with one of the biggest shipments of thoroughbreds ever on a ship. Four of the mares McDaniel bought for Kilmer were aboard.

The *Minnehaha* headed back to England, and the second shipment of horses McDaniel had bought there headed for America on board, just like the first. But that specter of submarines proved prophetic. When the boat left Queenstown on the clear morning of September 7, 1917, U-boats were lying in wait. Around noon, they launched torpedoes. Water poured in holes near the engine room, stokehole, and deck. The boat sank within four minutes. The bow pointed "like a column in the air," reported the *New York Times*: "The two torpedoes sounded like one great explosion, which was so terrific that the Marconi operator could only send out half a message before the wireless room went under water, and he had to swim for his life." Even though men ran right to the lifeboats, they could not get any into the water in those four minutes. The suction of the sinking boat pulled them under, and when they resurfaced, they found that two rafts had floated clear. Survivors clung to them, and a nearby, luckier ship radioed the naval station ashore. A patrol boat rescued the survivors.

The captain was cited for heroism, but he downplayed his actions. Instead, he claimed the only glory belonged to the wireless operator, a twenty-three-year-old man named Blight. As everyone on board realized the ship was sinking, Blight calmly asked, "Have you anything for me, Sir?" The captain handed him a piece of paper with the SOS call, ship's position, name, and distance from land. "He saluted and went aft on the boat deck to the wireless room and I never saw him again," said the captain, crying.

Forty-three people died and 110 survived. No horses lived. One U-boat captain, who torpedoed a different ship, told his officers, "Oh heavens, horses! What a pity, those lovely animals!" He watched men scrabbling for purchase on the deck and saw "all amongst them, rearing, slipping horses are wedged." During the war, sixty-six hundred cavalry horses went down with torpedoed transport ships, a number that doesn't include shipped racehorses, like the ones that were aboard the *Minnehaha,* which still lies underwater off of the Irish coast.

Kilmer's manager called from London with the news about the torpedoed boat right away. But Kilmer waited for the U.S. government to acknowledge the disaster before talking about it. Afterward, he decided to leave the other horses he had bought in Europe. Atlantic Transport said it would not send any more ships until after the war.

After the unnamed chestnut McGee–Fair Empress colt was weaned, perhaps through the contemporary gradual method of being tied by his mother's side at night rather than freely allowed to nurse, he was turned out with the other 1915 foals. In August 1916, he was loaded into a train car with them, bound for the yearling sales at Saratoga racecourse.

At the time, people came to Saratoga to "take the waters," bathing or just sitting by the natural warm springs. They stayed in summer homes or dressy hotels, and strolled along Saratoga streets eating potato chips, invented there in 1853. The first race season took place in the summer of 1863. With its tall elms, tended grounds, and white-fenced paddocks, Saratoga was a resort racecourse, very different from less romantic New York tracks like Gravesend and Belmont. It was different from the courses in Kentucky, too, more luxurious, dreamlike and cool under the trees. "Racing and Saratoga are synonymous," said Henry McDaniel once. "Psychology makes me believe that the worst race here is better than the best elsewhere."

"At Saratoga they don't have paddocks under an open shed as at Lexington and Churchill Downs and other tracks down in our country," wrote Sherwood Anderson in a short story, "but saddle the horses right out in an open place under trees on a lawn as smooth and nice as Banker Bohon's front yard here in Beckersville. It's lovely. The horses are sweaty and nervous and shine and the men come out and smoke cigars and look at them and the trainers are there and the owners, and your heart thumps so you can hardly breathe."

At the yearling sales held before the races, owners and trainers scrutinized pedigree charts, held endless meetings over clubhouse lunches, and examined hundreds of toddler thoroughbreds for the deep chests, strong, clean legs, and bright eyes that could win races and add to a breeding program. There were seven sales scheduled for August 1916, which was a high number; things were good for the thoroughbred industry. The war had forced European breeders to liquidate their herds, which meant that formerly untouchable horses were for sale in America.

Choosing yearlings is difficult. You can't watch them race, and they are too young to be ridden. In the Saratoga yearling sales of 1916, people watched colts—ducking, shying, striking out with their chopstick front legs—led around the shaded paddock by grooms. "It takes a lot to make up a good horse," said McDaniel years later, "and some of the most important requisites do not appear on the surface . . . Many a real good looking colt is a counterfeit because of faulty waste action, and there never was a man smart enough to tell what sort of action a colt will have by looking at him standing still or walking round a sales ring."

Kilmer and McDaniel were ready to buy. One of the first sales they attended featured twenty-four French thoroughbreds. There was one "star in the yearling division," a mahogany-colored colt named Sunday, who never would have been for sale were it not for the war. He had been bred by the immortal French horseman Marcel Boussac, whose horses all bore the same unique stamps: chiseled heads, wide eyes, and sculpted ears. There was only one off thing about the colt: he had a condition called ringbone, which meant he had a "ring" of excess bony growth on his legs, just above the hoof. Ringbone can cause lameness. Because of this, trainers passed the colt by, but McDaniel wasn't worried. Those ringbones were set up high. He was a very nice horse, beautiful and strong, the kind of expensive, well-bred colt McDaniel had not previously had the resources to buy.

Kilmer bid and won him for $6,000 (approximately $114,000 today). He also bought a filly for $9,500. Nothing seemed too expensive. "I was prepared to go much higher," he said. Horsemen know it's bad luck to change a horse's name, but Kilmer didn't care. Sunday's sire and dam were Sundridge and Sweet Briar, and Kilmer decided he liked the sound of "Sun Briar" better.

Also shopping for yearlings was an Alabamian transplant to Lexington named Cal Milam, known for his skill as a pinhooker, which meant he bought young horses, raced them as two-year-olds, and then sold them. Milam also owned an old gelding named Merrick, whom he had raced 208 times from 1905 to 1915. Usually, he turned his horses over quickly, selling and buying and reselling, but he had entered Merrick in only one claiming race. Merrick got claimed, and Milam missed him so much that he claimed him right back. When Merrick was eleven, he bowed his head in front of Milam before his 205th race. Milam promised Merrick right then that if he didn't win, he would never have to race again. He lost, and Milam retired him, naming his farm Merrick Place.

Milam liked the sturdy, Merricky, dependable horses that McGee sired, and he'd bought one of his daughters earlier in the summer. By August 19, Milam was at a sale far humbler than the one that had all the French yearlings, at which Kilmer had bought Sun Briar. Instead, this sale included all the yearlings who had come on the train from Kentucky, many from farms only a few miles from Merrick Place. Bidding was lively, and Milam bought quite a few. He bought Fair Empress's chestnut colt for $1,500 (the average price of thoroughbred yearlings sold at auction that year was $932). Kilmer bought nothing from this Kentucky sale; he didn't need to look at such homespun merchandise.

The Fair Empress–McGee colt that Milam bought was overtall and gangling, with enormous eyes. His neck was long and slender, and your eye caught on that white rounded triangle in the middle of his forehead. Resting, he looked elderly, with mule-long ears and eyes deep set beneath small hollows. He was long and tall and skinny. He looked like he should have been hitched to a family buggy for Sunday drives.

Along with the other yearlings Milam bought, the colt clambered back on a train, rattled back to Lexington, and wintered at Merrick Place. Milam worked with them all, training and gauging their athleticism and heart. A rider named Sam Johnson galloped him; like Milam, he liked the McGee colt. One day, Milam told his wife he thought that, given the right opportunities, the as-yet-unnamed chestnut colt could kill off all the competition. Belle Milam laughed, because Cal always dreamed big. "Why not Exterminator?" she said.

In the meantime, although not yet called to war, the American cavalry was using some military horses closer to home. When the Mexican revolutionary general Pancho Villa attacked the border town of Columbus, New Mexico, General "Black Jack" Pershing, famous for his horsemanship, moved his troops into Mexico to rebuff Villa's forces. This was difficult—troops rode sixty-eight miles in thirteen hours, pounding over baked deserts and scrabbling up and down mountains, and they repeated similar jobs for the ten months they were in Mexico. Afterward, more troops stayed along the Mexican border, guarding against smugglers and illegal immigrants.

Sam Harris was a private in C Troop of the 10th Cavalry, which was made up of African American soldiers. At the 1916 Battle of Carrizal, Pershing sent the troop to the town, evidently thinking they could trap Villa. But two minutes after Harris approached Carrizal, they were surrounded. All around him, horses were "rearing and plunging. Every little bit a horse or a man would get a bullet and go down. I couldn't fight, for I had to keep after those mounts." Soon, his own horse, "a great big fellow," faltered next to him, and he realized the horse had been shot in the neck. He put his hand over the wound as blood poured out. Then he himself was shot in the shoulder. Harris, a horse wrangler, realized how hopeless the situation had become. He cut the other horses loose before mounting his own. "I went right through the Mexicans. My horse brushed two of them out of the way as we charged. I owe my life to that horse, sure as you live. Don't you know, that animal was so brave and big hearted that he carried me along for ten miles before he settled down to a walk. Five miles further on his legs just gave out and he went down. Man, I hope you don't ever have to say good-by to a horse like that at a time and place like that," he said. "It seemed to me I couldn't leave him."

Harris looked behind him; no one had followed. He kneeled, poured some water onto the dying horse's tongue, and told him how sorry he was. "I thanked him for the mighty big favor he done me," he said. "I thanked him, like he was human. And I guess he understood, for he got that look in his eyes animals have when they are grateful."

Harris wanted to stay longer, but his horse was coughing blood, nearly gone, and he was bleeding, too. So he said thank you one more time, said good-bye, and walked on until he saw another army horse. He rode that one back to his camp and was interviewed from his hospital bed.

In the end, the Carrizal mission failed; the Americans never found Pancho Villa, either. But Harris's testimony brought newspaper readers closer to understanding not only the border battles but also the intensity of the bond a soldier could share with a brave, big-hearted horse.

All thoroughbreds celebrate their birthdays on January 1, and in February 1917, Milam's two-year-olds went to the Kentucky Association track. They were broken to saddle and began training to be racehorses. A little while later, Milam had Exterminator gelded, for reasons that are still unclear. Some reports have Milam claiming that the horse was just too wild—maybe part of the reason Exterminator fit as a name—and another theory holds that he was so scrawny and run-down and had never filled out like the other colts, so the idea may have been that castration could help him bulk up. This is easy to imagine, although it didn't really work, given that Exterminator stayed bony well into maturity. Yet another idea, which may make more sense in the context of the time, is that Exterminator was gelded because he just wasn't well-bred enough to bother keeping as a stallion. "Exterminator, from the beginning, was doomed," wrote one expert, "as, from the propagandized 'pur sang' point of view, he was not even 'thoroughbred.'"

Geldings often race much longer than stallions, who often quit racing once they go to the stud. Fans grow attached, watching geldings run season after season, and they have more of a chance to improve, too. Recent examples include Kelso, John Henry, and Funny Cide, but when Exterminator was born, people remembered Roseben, "the Big Train," and Raceland, "Old Bones," who had belonged to August Belmont Sr., the remount Belmont's father.

Roamer, the best-loved gelding when Exterminator was a two-year-old, was named because his unlettered sire fathered him with a blooded mare. He, in turn, had been gelded right away to avoid any more mishaps. Roamer was a tremendous athlete and had such a smooth gait that one reporter wrote, he could "carry a glass of water on his back without spilling it."

While Milam prepped his new two-year-olds, Kilmer made plans to dominate racing. McDaniel was working the Kilmer horses over the sandy roads of Virginia's Middlesex County, where Kilmer's Remlik Hall stood. The moderate climate allowed almost year-round training. "Not one has missed a work-out," wrote one reporter. Kilmer kept spending money on horses, buying fourteen yearlings from John F. Madden, who had trained five Derby and Belmont winners and was called the "Wizard of the Turf," at a high average of $2,321 each.

The 1916 racing season had seen more foreign-born horses than it had since Colonial days. "Willis Sharpe Kilmer, George D. Widener, and Joseph D. Widener have bought with a free hand and seemingly bottomless purses from the pick of the European studs," wrote one reporter. He then reminded readers: "But it is not always the high-priced, gently bred youngsters [sic] that wins all the prizes. Gift horses, or yearlings picked up for the proverbial song, have trained on to beat the best."

With money and energy coming in from rich remount patrons, and horses coming in from Europe, thoroughbred racing grew. The global

situation was bad, but thoroughbred racing in America was in a renais-
sance. "Racing Forecast," wrote one reporter, for 1917. "Increased interest, continuous sunshine, large purses and stakes everywhere."

Kilmer had a good trainer and a shining new colt. He was ready.

In April 1917, America entered the war. Despite his promise to stay out of
it when he was campaigning, President Woodrow Wilson sent the American Expeditionary Forces in to fight with the Allies. "It is a fearful thing,"
he said, "to lead this great peaceful people into war, into the most terrible
and disastrous of all wars, civilization itself seeming to be in the balance."
America responded with heightened patriotism; for horsemen, that meant
more donations to the remount. Belmont volunteered for the army at age
sixty-five and was commissioned a major. (A colt he bred and sold during
the war would grow up to be Man o' War.) He seemed a man ahead of his
time, who had seen what was coming and given the army the horses it
needed.

During the first two weeks of June, army troops headed toward the East
Coast in trains. On June 5, more than ten million men registered for the
draft. More than ever, racing linked its existence to the military. Jockeys
signed their conscription papers right away, and racing men said that they
"had come to the front for war service in a manner not exceeded by the
participants in any other sport."

Kilmer pitched in, too. He was on Binghamton's War Board and paid
the rent on four homes for Binghamton's National Guardsmen. Because
there were not enough naval destroyers, the navy needed privately owned
yachts to patrol for submarines, so Kilmer donated his steam-powered two-
hundred-foot *Remlik*. The *Remlik* sailors won the Navy Yacht League
baseball pennant in Brest, France.

In this time before starting gates were invented, racehorses simply lined up,
and the starter—a man positioned at the track's head to begin the race—

did his best to send the horses off at the exact second when they all were holding still and facing the same direction, a tricky task. Races were lost in that moment when one horse was not looking entirely forward, or got bumped as the starter let them go. A tape stretched across the track as a guide for the horses, but it did not keep them particularly straight. The starters were responsible for lining the horses up in post positions, pulling on reins and shoving horses into place, hollering the whole time. Racers could be at the post for as long as thirty minutes while starters and assistants—usually about four men—tried to line them up in the same direction. The starts could be savage, horses kicking each other, blood running. Some jockeys tried to cheat the tape, getting a jump on their rivals. Even the famous jockey Earl "Handy" Sande was punished for it. Others tried to shift post positions around, often trying to sneak their horses onto the rail. Mars (Marshall) Cassidy, the salty starter who had captured Alice Roosevelt's attention in 1905, sent one jockey at Empire City down—suspended him—for ten days for that. "Cassidy's patience with an unruly company of highly nervous two-year-olds, wheeling and turning beneath the tape, was a marvel to see, and he was a genius at his work," remembered one onlooker. "His raucous cry of 'Come on!' as he let his charges go was one of the most stirring sounds I have ever heard."

"It was tough," said George Cassidy, Mars's son and a starter himself. "The horses were hard to control, that is, if you could. They were all over the place. We used to have six or seven races a day, and you'd probably get four good starts, maybe three." Some horses, like one named Display, hated the starters handling them. "He was a demon," recalled Cassidy years later. "He'd lunge and pitch as soon as he saw the tape. I handled him, and I'm not kidding, when I was finished, I was dripping, absolutely dripping. It was like a rodeo. Every day!"

Mars Cassidy called Exterminator "the finest assistant starter I ever had." If Exterminator was one out from the rail, and the horse on the inside was fussing, delaying the start, Exterminator would pin the horse to the rail by leaning against him. Then the race could start. Others claimed that Exterminator watched the starters' hands, which was how he remained so calm at the post but was not left behind.

At home, perhaps because of being gelded, Exterminator was sluggish in his two-year-old spring. He stayed on the ailing list for a while. Once Milam got him to the Latonia track, though, he trained well. Clockers saw his fractions and took note. When finally he went out for his first race, on June 30, he was the bettors' second choice. The track was muddy, and horses sank up to their fetlocks. It was a short, cheap race—three-quarters of a mile for $700. Exterminator broke fast, swept into the lead, and stayed in front to win by three lengths. The turf writer Clinton Alwes was cashing in at the mutual window and stopped to watch the race. Years later, he remembered the victory and the mud. "Cal Milam's slab-sided gelding was at home in that sort of going, and won by himself," he wrote. Still, it was an everyday win, a slow pace, and weak competition. "None who saw him that day had any inkling of the horse he was destined to be."

Milam took Exterminator to Ontario, to the Canadian circuit, across the border from Detroit. He came in fourth at the Windsor track in a five-furlong race. Three days later, he won a race there. It was another cheap race, but his performance was strong; he came from seventh place to win by a half-length. Next, Milam took him to nearby Kenilworth Park, where he raced one more time, and lost. Then Exterminator hurt himself. Veterinarians could not figure out exactly what the problem was—perhaps a muscle strain—but Milam, cautious, retired him for the season. Exterminator was to rest—again—and stay "on the shelf" until January 1918, at least.

Exterminator had not shown himself to be anything special; in fact, he gave his owner a journeyman performance that was similar to many other horses'. But Milam nominated him for the Kentucky Derby anyway. He had worked with John Madden, who taught him always to do that. Aspirational owners appreciated horses that were nominated, Madden said, and except for Merrick, Milam bought colts to sell, not to keep.

He watched Exterminator, and waited.

On June 30, the same day Exterminator made his small-time debut at Latonia, Kilmer's Saratoga purchase Sun Briar won the Great American Handicap at Belmont Park, beating August Belmont's prize colt Lucullite. It was a big victory and meant that Kilmer no longer had to worry whether his stable would measure up. In Binghamton, his stablehands hung out giant placards saying HOME OF IMP. [IMPORTED] SUN BRIAR, CHAMPION TWO-YEAR-OLD OF 1917. With his new French colt, Kilmer was enjoying the kind of success that many far more seasoned owners could only imagine. McDaniel could take Sun Briar to the August Saratoga meeting with confidence.

At Saratoga, women knitted socks for the soldiers abroad, wet in the trenches. Some carried their work in a brightly colored bag that dangled from the arm. Julia Loft, whose husband owned Papp (named for the Pound-a-Penny Profit earned from a candy empire), could pick winners all day and never drop a stitch. Events progressed there as if the war was not quite real. The Belmonts were there. One day, Mrs. Belmont wore a light blue gown and a hat trimmed with red roses, and the Whitneys, who sailed as far as Albany on their yacht, arrived. The weather was cool; women wore summer furs and shawls. The clubhouse restaurant was full from before the races began until after they closed. Army captain Ral Parr, who was a remount buyer, passed around a box of chocolates to friends in between races.

Sun Briar's jockey for the meet was Willie Knapp, whom racetrackers called "Big Bill" because he was so small. He was thirty, on the older side for a jockey, but was a quiet rider with the "master hands" young horses listened to. Knapp was a veteran and unexcitable, but he still had the reflexes to make physical decisions in fractions of a second. Even at the end of a long day of riding, trainers relied upon him to keep his head while the bettors screamed his name. Like McDaniel, Knapp had spent his life at the racetrack.

With Knapp aboard, Sun Briar won the Albany Handicap, and then the August 11 Saratoga Special, at which Belmont disappointed fans by scratching his fast Lucullite but came to the race anyway, to watch. As expected, Sun Briar won, and turfites praised McDaniel for his eye in picking out the colt and for his training ability. People also admired Sun Briar for being a "hand horse," meaning that he hardly ever needed a whip. He seemed to run for joy, his coat shining, his muscles working, his portrait-ready head surging forward with every step. Next, on August 25, he won the Grand Union Hotel Stakes, even though another horse brushed by Sun Briar so closely that he sank to his knees. Knapp tapped him with his whip. Sun Briar had never been hit before, and, shocked, he shot forward to win by a nose. Kilmer kept the whip as a souvenir.

In the closing day's Hopeful Stakes, Sun Briar was last of eighteen to start—Knapp had been jostled and rode most of the race with just one stirrup. Kilmer watched the race from the top floor of the clubhouse, and when he saw Sun Briar win, he ran down, kissed Esther in their box, and kept going.

The only flaws anyone could find in Sun Briar were in his legs, which were still showing signs of ringbone. In the early twentieth century, ringbone was sometimes treated with cold-water-soaked cloths tied around the legs, or a salve made of mercury and lard; neither worked. "What a colt he would be if he hadn't those ringbones," one Saratoga steward said. "They don't seem to hurt him much," retorted starter Mars Cassidy.

An educated eye can see ringbone. Turf writers knew just what they were looking for when they scanned Sun Briar's body before each workout. McDaniel made light of the ringbones. In fact, he joked, he just removed them before each race.

For the 1917 season, McDaniel was right. Sun Briar was the champion two-year-old. He had won $59,905, the most money of any horse that season.

Others had labored for years to get where Kilmer was and never made it. The combination of his energy and McDaniel's expertise had worked. He celebrated with a parade.

Ten thousand people crowded the Binghamton train station by 11 A.M. on September 3, the day Sun Briar was due home on the noon train. They lined the viaduct that overlooked the train track three deep. Knapp was already there, wearing his silks, and locals gathered around him. Enormous banners were strung up: SUN BRIAR HAS MADE BINGHAMTON FAMOUS. ALL HONOR TO TRAINER H. MCDANIELS [SIC], WE WELCOME YOU, WILLIE KNAPP.

A little after twelve, the train pulled in. The band struck up a tune— maybe "The National Emblem March" or the "American Republic March," both popular gramophone tunes. Horns blared, and well-wishers hurried into Kilmer's Pullman car to greet him. He stepped out, shaking all the hands pushed toward him. Next, the door of Sun Briar's Arms Palace Horse Car opened, and the colt looked, high-headed, out into the crowd. Men brought a gangway over. McDaniel stood with Sun Briar, and Binghamtonians recognized him as soon as he appeared in the horse car's doorway. They shouted and clapped. Knapp met horses and trainer at the bottom of the walkway, and Kilmer came to greet them. The air was loud with cheering and band music as Sun Briar stepped out behind a stableboy, who led him to the street.

Once Sun Briar was out, the crowd grew even noisier. They stretched up on their toes to see him and crowded so much that it was difficult for the stableboy and horse to pick a way through. The curb was lined with even more people; one estimate said that ten thousand Binghamtonians came out to welcome Sun Briar home. Binghamton was a fairly small town, but urban, so Sun Briar walked past houses, cars, parks, and office buildings along Chenango Street from the train station to Kilmer's edge-of-town farm, which stretched for a mile along the Susquehanna River. Finally, Sun Briar arrived at his own paddock. One woman patted him, talking to him.

"This reception is not for me," Kilmer told the crowd. "It is for Sun Briar."

The week before New Year's, Kilmer gave everyone in his stable crew Christmas trees, and he held two dances. Then it was time for Binghamton to celebrate Sun Briar's turning three on New Year's Day. Kilmer opened the doors to his farm and allowed his visitors the run of the place.

They looked at Sun Briar and the other horses Kilmer owned, and walked on an indoor exercise track. They filed into the clubhouse to shake hands with Kilmer and see some of Sun Briar's relics. One was the $5,000 cup that Sun Briar had won in the Saratoga Special. Kilmer also displayed the shoes Sun Briar had on when he won the Hopeful, and Willie Knapp's whip, which touched Sun Briar only that one time, in the Grand Union, when he had been pushed to his knees. Photographs of Sun Briar winning races hung on the walls, along with pictures of the welcome-home parade and his portrait, already done by the famous horse painter Franklin Voss, who would also paint Exterminator, Man o' War, Seabiscuit, and Sir Barton. Kilmer also showed his portrait of the great Lexington, an all-American stallion who bore no relation to Sun Briar but was in Exterminator's pedigree. (He bought the picture because he owned some other descendants of Lexington.) Hundreds of people came and gaped at all of it.

Darkness fell. McDaniel looked over Sun Briar. The line of solid winners he had already trained paled in comparison to this golden horse. After all this time, it seemed like Sun Briar was his reward for the years of patience and care, for the guarding of his reputation so he would be brought to this admittedly eccentric, hot-tempered man who was not afraid to spend money for quality.

The stableboys sang as they finished feeding the horses and then went to their own party. Kilmer gave them some punch to toast the new year. It was a good night.

In Kentucky, Exterminator quietly turned three, too.

Anyone owning a two-year-old thoroughbred dreamed of the Kentucky Derby during the long winter between racing seasons, but Sun Briar's Derby readiness was an obsession. In some ways, he already represented the 1918

Derby because of his titanic two-year-old season. The management at Churchill Downs, the Louisville track where the Derby is run, wanted the colt to come train there as soon as possible. Reporters, fans, and tourists would begin focusing on the Derby as soon as the glamorous favorite arrived. So the track managers and McDaniel entered negotiations, arranging specific stable assignments, deciding how many Kilmer horses would come down, so that McDaniel would bring Sun Briar to Churchill Downs for his winter and spring training. In a letter to the track, McDaniel said that Sun Briar had grown a lot since the 1917 season ended and was in fine shape as the winter wore on. Sun Briar would be a huge draw.

Things were looking auspicious for Kilmer. He bought some Kentucky yearlings—one, he thought, looked just like Sun Briar—from John Madden.

It still incensed Kilmer to be called a beginner. "Incidentally Mr. Kilmer took occasion to correct the general impression that he is a comparatively new recruit to the sport of racing," one reporter dutifully recorded. Most of the rest kept calling him "the lucky recruit." In any case, Kilmer seemed unstoppable; no one had done what he had in such a short time. And most owners could not even be bitter, because everyone liked Henry McDaniel and agreed that he deserved the opportunities he was getting. McDaniel secured Knapp for the coming year. He was laying everything out for Sun Briar to win the Kentucky Derby.

In quieter Lexington, Milam worked with all his young charges. He had them exercised, watched them run, paired them with horses to see which was faster. Exterminator recovered from whatever had happened to him in Canada. He was healthy again, running fine. It was cold and bare-branched in Kentucky, but the ground wasn't so frozen that the horses couldn't train. Milam watched Exterminator and his other new-minted three-year-olds, and wondered if any of them had a shot at the Derby.

4

The 1918 Kentucky Derby

In February 1918, the Kentucky Derby was only three months off. But some railed against the idea of racing as an inappropriate luxury for a country at war. Other sports had paused or considered cancellations. "If I had my way I would close every theatre, ball park, and other place of recreation in the country and make people realize that they are in the most terrible war in the history of the world," said the president of baseball's American League. Why should horse racing be the exception?

Churchill Downs's manager, Matt Winn, a fifty-six-year-old Irish American who looked like Winston Churchill—down to the cigar—set out to prove the Derby was too patriotic to skip. Thoroughbred racing had created the very cavalry horses helping to win the war, he argued. He planted the infield with a victory garden of potatoes and auctioned off barrels full to benefit the war effort. He pledged 10 percent of all money handled at the 1918 meet, including Derby winnings, to the Red Cross. He pointed out that President Wilson, a racing man, wanted the Derby run. He invited army soldiers from nearby Camp Zachary Taylor to the track, planned flag raisings with color guards, and donated fans' field glasses to soldiers.

Every day, newspapers were full of soldiers, fighting in places with exotic names like Zeebrugge and Marne. Banner ads reminded readers of the upcoming wheatless Monday. Omnipresent posters adorned walls and fences. On one, a bunting-draped woman held up a mason jar, asking, "Are YOU a Victory Canner?" and on another, Uncle Sam pointed a powerful finger, declaring that he wanted you for the U.S. Army. The war effort was fueled by these images, hyperpatriotism, a uniquely American brand of exceptionalism, and horses.

To succeed, the 1918 Derby had to uphold all of its obligations, both to the beleaguered world of thoroughbred racing and to the combat-weary country. Americans could rally around the Derby as something uniquely national and horse-powered, just like the cavalry. Winn planned to prove racing's loyalty with the most American Derby ever run.

In New York, the winter was so cold that stable employees ice-skated from barn to barn on frozen puddles. Kilmer was anxious to ship Sun Briar south to Kentucky, but the war caused a shortage of train cars, and not even Kilmer could get what he wanted. It was February 1 by the time McDaniel, Sun Briar, and his eight-horse entourage arrived at Churchill Downs.

Locals lined up to see the famous colt. They were impressed. Sun Briar's shoulders were stout and well developed, and his finely drawn head was so pretty and symmetrical that it seemed incongruous to see something so elegant on such a frankly powerful body. Many, though, looked down at his legs. Rumors had flown around back east—in racing terms, Kentucky was still the west when compared with thoroughbred centers like New York and Maryland—that Sun Briar's ringbones were slowing him down. Kilmer had hired a vet for the train ride from New York to Kentucky, which seemed like a signal of a lame horse. Kilmer, who had also hired a special night watchman to call him every hour, said he had hired the doctor just because he wanted Sun Briar to have the best of everything. For his part, McDaniel never denied that the colt had ringbone or tried to hide the condition with low bandages, a tactic many other trainers used. Sun Briar remained the Derby favorite.

Sun Briar did have a quirk, McDaniel had learned: he didn't work as well by himself as he did when another horse ran alongside. So McDaniel paired him with a four-year-old named Tom McTaggart, or with Nelsweep, Kilmer's other Derby-eligible horse. Sun Briar never ran alone.

Pressure mounted for McDaniel. "The one crown of his career has been denied him so far," wrote a *Daily Racing Form* reporter. "He has never sent a winner of the Kentucky Derby to the post."

On April 4, as Derby Day drew closer, Sun Briar's photograph was on the cover of the *Thoroughbred Record*. Well inside the same edition, buried behind columns of training reports and turf gossip, was a name in a list of horses at the Latonia racetrack: Exterminator.

Each day, McDaniel tested training techniques, because what had worked with Sun Briar as a two-year-old was not working now. The colt was less dynamic, more easily distracted. He was not running in a straight line, either. One day, Sun Briar veered toward the outside rail at the head of the stretch, and the spectators who scrutinized his every workout noticed he was "going wide," or running laterally. Some thought that meant the ringbones were bothering him, which, in turn, bothered McDaniel. "The ringbones seem to be bothering these well-meaning critics more than they are bothering the colt," he said.

McDaniel put a pair of blinkers on him to block out distractions on the side. Sometimes, he would change things up by starting one horse with Sun Briar and then switching in another to run with him at the end of the workout. McDaniel sent this telegram to the *Daily Racing Form*:

LOUISVILLE, KY, APRIL 15
SUN BRIAR IS GOING ABSOLUTELY SOUND TO DATE. WENT MILE IN 1:46 TODAY WITH TOM MCTAGGART, FIRST HALF IN 48 ¾, KNAPP UP.

Later in April, with just one month left until the race, McDaniel announced that he was taking Willie Knapp and Sun Briar to Lexington to run in some smaller races before the Derby Trial, an important prep race. McDaniel believed that a real race—the jockeys in silks, the furor of the track—would help ready a horse more than six workouts. Maybe a real race would jolt Sun Briar back to his old form in a way Tom McTaggart and Nelsweep couldn't. Also, taking Sun Briar to Lexington would show reporters that everything was fine.

It didn't work, though. Sun Briar lost. "One swallow don't make a summer," Kilmer roared, "and just because Sun Briar was defeated in his first start as a three-year-old does not to my mind mean he has gone back. I still believe he will win the Derby." McDaniel, however, acted less certain. Unused to backward momentum, he rededicated himself to solving the colt's problems. He had one of the best jockeys in the business, and had tried just about every trick he knew. What was he missing? What would make Sun Briar run?

"Something had to be done," McDaniel wrote years later.

McDaniel decided that maybe Sun Briar did not need a new technique. Instead, he needed a new horse, a fast one who could offer more competition than Kilmer's others. There was only one man in Lexington with horses like that, especially this close to the big race, when the most promising had long gone to owners with Derby plans. On April 24, McDaniel went to see Cal Milam, who was well known for his eye in selecting talented young prospects. If anyone had a good horse, Milam would.

What Milam had was Exterminator. He was a dark, muddy chestnut by then: gawky, awkward, and practically lop-eared. All young horses are gangling, but he was an ugly duckling, almost bizarre with his extralong face, bony knees, and slender neck. He was now seventeen hands high and walked with such a deliberate, unfolding gait he appeared splay-footed. His withers were so prominent, and his facial bones so defined, that he looked far older than his three years. He provided a stark contrast to gleaming, burly Sun Briar stabled under heavy guard across town.

But his eyes were huge and set off by the lopsided white mark on his forehead. They also had a lot of hazel in them, a traditional promising sign. More important, he could run. "He wouldn't have captured a prize at any horse show for good looks," admitted McDaniel, "but the even way he reeled off the furlongs and the manner in which he finished his work made me take more than one look at him. Big boned, with prominent hips, this colt was a lengthy fellow, with great shoulders and lots of heart room. With no superfluous lumber, he carried nothing on his somewhat gaunt frame except what he used in galloping. Not a picture horse, but he looked all business to me, and I determined to get him if Milam would part with him." McDaniel asked one of Milam's exercise riders, Sam Johnson, a question: "Can he go in the mud?"

"Why, he was born in a muddy stall," Johnson told him.

Years later, Bill Knapp remembered thinking that he and McDaniel would go in together on the colt. But two weeks before Sun Briar's Derby was the wrong time for that kind of decision. The goal was Sun Briar's victory. "I thought it over, and decided it wasn't fair to the man I was working for without giving him first chance of purchase," McDaniel told Knapp. "Kilmer got him and that was that," said Knapp to a reporter, years later.

If Exterminator encouraged Sun Briar, he could get them all—Kilmer, McDaniel, Knapp, and Sun Briar—to the winner's circle. McDaniel had found his truck horse.

On Saturday, April 27, Milam and Kilmer met at Lexington's Phoenix Hotel and signed the sales papers. Kilmer bought the colt for $9,000 and two fillies. Milam had had Exterminator insured for $5,000, which Kilmer doubled immediately.

Kilmer's buying a new horse just after Sun Briar's reverberating defeat got people muttering, but he swore up and down that he hadn't bought Exterminator to displace Sun Briar as a starter in the Derby. Even though at least one Lexington turf writer believed Exterminator had shown "remarkable aptitude," the new colt's official job was just to serve as an exercise partner, Kilmer kept saying. Anyway, he said, anyone could see Exterminator was nowhere near as good as Sun Briar.

Exterminator climbed aboard the train for Churchill Downs alongside

Sun Briar, both swaddled in bleached-white leg bandages and saddle blankets in Kilmer's Swamp-Root orange, green, and brown colors. McDaniel rode with the horses, and Kilmer followed in a plush train car.

When they returned to Louisville, McDaniel sent both horses out for a mile workout. Kilmer was there to watch as Exterminator did his job; Sun Briar ran faster than he had recently. Kilmer was thrilled, but McDaniel would not comment, although he looked "pleased" according to a *Daily Racing Form* reporter.

Knapp told the same reporter that Sun Briar seemed like a different horse from the loser in Lexington. "I believe Mr. Kilmer made a wise move when he brought Sun Briar back to Churchill Downs," he said, "for he seems to train better there than any other track. In his work just now he fairly flew over the ground and in the last quarter it was all I could do to keep him under restraint." There was another reason Sun Briar looked sharp, according to Knapp. "The fact that he had a fast pacemaker may have had something to do with making him recover his speed," he said. "It's all over but the shouting," said a nearby railbird.

But McDaniel could not feel so relieved. "In spite of the fact that Sun Briar was training well," he wrote later, "and doing well in his stable, I still had an indefinable feeling of mistrust in the great colt. It is a little hard to explain to the average person how, under these circumstances, the feeling arose. The trainer who has been among thoroughbreds all his life will more readily understand it. It wasn't what may be termed a 'hunch.' With men who have been among horses practically since they were born, there is developed a sixth sense that we may call just 'horse sense.' That sense made me afraid that Sun Briar had become temperamental. My lack of confidence must have infected Mr. Kilmer, who was very keen on winning the Derby. He became temperamental also, and so I had two on my hands—horse and owner. I could readily understand Mr. Kilmer's feeling. He was tremendously proud of Sun Briar and shuddered at the idea of him being beaten. The race that Sun Briar had run at Lexington had shaken his confidence, and though I thought Sun Briar would win handily if he ran to his work and came back to his 2-year-old form, I couldn't give any positive assurance that he would. That's what Kilmer seemed to want."

McDaniel knew he would be one of the first people not to give Kilmer what he wanted. He couldn't bring himself to pacify him—he didn't even want to say he thought Sun Briar would win if he ran like used to. And he knew what had happened when Frank Taylor did not deliver what Kilmer wanted. So far, Exterminator had done his job; Sun Briar ran faster.

Still, Kilmer kept after McDaniel, wanting reassurance. According to Derby legend, McDaniel finally grew snappish. "If I could guarantee the horse would win," he told Kilmer, "I would take $1,000 and make a five-horse parlay. And then I would have more money than you have."

On April 20, Al Jolson made an appearance at the Palace Theatre in New York. At the time, theaters would stage briefer shows to give celebrity war bond "salesmen" time to encourage donations. Kilmer was in the crowd.

Jolson got one person to promise $3,000. "I'll take $7,500 worth my-self," Jolson joked, "though I have to borrow the money to pay." A man in the audience announced that he would take $5,000 worth, if someone else would, too. From his box, Kilmer shouted that he would take $10,000 and challenged the man who offered $5,000 to do the same thing. He said he would.

That night, Jolson sold $100,000 worth of war bonds.

Some officers from Louisville's Camp Zachary Taylor had brought home a new fashion—the trench coat—which they wore to the races. Camp Taylor, opened in 1917, was one of the country's largest camps, on 3,376 acres housing, at its peak, 64,000 troops. More than 150,000 soldiers—most from Kentucky, Indiana, and Illinois—drilled there over the course of the war. F. Scott Fitzgerald would become the most famous soldier to spend time in the camp. He was transferred to Camp Gordon, in Georgia, but he never forgot his time at Camp Zachary Taylor. In *The Great Gatsby,* Gatsby meets his beloved Daisy, a Louisville belle, at a party for camp officers.

Camp Taylor had a hospital, an artillery training school, and a theater. Its library was staffed by women from the American Library Association's War Service, who wore uniforms of middy blouses with long white skirts.

In the fall of 1918, Camp Taylor would become the center of the Spanish flu epidemic in Louisville, one of the nation's hardest-hit cities as a result of housing the camp. A primary wave, in March and April, killed soldiers in Fort Riley, Kansas. In May, the flu was on its way toward Kentucky. But on Derby Day, an army surgeon had just inspected the camp. He praised its sanitary conditions and mosquito control. Louisvillians felt lucky.

Esther Kilmer was a horsewoman; some said she had helped choose Sun Briar. When Kilmer showed horses at the New York state fair, she would watch all day from her private box, wearing luxurious gowns.

The noted portraitist Irving Wiles painted Esther. Her long neck and the underside of one arm gleam white as she stares out of the frame. She is in a darkish room, wearing a huge hat, with her eyes cast down and her mouth in a downturning pout, as if she is thinking of something sad or, at least, annoying. In her left hand she holds a white rose; a vase full of them stands to her right.

Workouts held before the Derby were an occasion in themselves. As soon as McDaniel walked to the infield so that he could see each furlong pole, clockers hurried to arrange themselves around the track, evenly spaced, assigning themselves short lengths of track for greater accuracy. All the guests Kilmer had invited from Binghamton were making their way to Louisville on private train cars. Big hotel rooms were booked, dresses bought, hats trimmed, menus planned, parties scheduled. In fact, despite the war, all the private boxes at Churchill Downs were sold. The New York delegation included many Binghamtonians there to cheer on Sun Briar.

On May 9, McDaniel sent Sun Briar and Exterminator out to work the full distance, carrying Derby weight. It was like a dress rehearsal for the race. Matt Winn had come out of his office to watch. He knew that Sun Briar's Derby depended on this workout, even if Kilmer did not understand that yet. McDaniel sent out Exterminator as the pacemaker for Sun Briar's first mile, and Exterminator galloped right alongside him. The workout was off, somehow. Sun Briar gave McDaniel an "uncomfortable feeling that he might not do so well in the race," as he wrote later. Even Kilmer could see that there was a problem. He finally admitted that Sun Briar was no longer a Derby contender.

Owner and trainer conferred. Kilmer sent a telegram to Binghamton: "The report of my trainer shows that Sun Briar has not been training satisfactorily. I feel it is due my friends to make this public announcement of his probably [sic] withdrawal from the Kentucky Derby. He will be shipped East to try and be ready for his Eastern engagements." The telegram was written as a courtesy to Sun Briar's local fans, but you could feel Kilmer's devastation.

For McDaniel, though, a life of experience biding his time was paying off. The work and effort he had spent on Sun Briar could not be recovered, but it wasn't wasted, either. Like so many horses McDaniel had trained over the years, Sun Briar just needed some time.

Exterminator, though—he had been right about the truck horse. Later, he pointed out that "there are many who run fast past the furlong posts in the morning, but don't run so fast in the real test, with the colors up in the afternoon. I'd made up my mind that Exterminator was no 'morning glory.' 'Honest' should have been his first name." Equine honesty is a highly valued quality; calling a horse honest is a compliment. An honest horse is willing and responsive, and will not sulk—refuse to speed up even when asked—and will always run as fast and hard as he can. McDaniel knew that Exterminator would give all he had.

But McDaniel could not simply swap Exterminator for Sun Briar, because Kilmer thought he was crazy. He seemed to hate Exterminator. "You've bought me nothing more than a cussed billy goat!" he yelled at

McDaniel, and said it was against his better judgment that he did not send Exterminator to a livery stable.

Matt Winn did not know McDaniel's plans, but he noticed that Kilmer was "the most disappointed man in Kentucky." In his memoir, Winn remembered that day. He asked Kilmer who Sun Briar's work partner had been in that last workout.

"A truck horse that Henry McDaniel bought, and got me hooked for $12,000," Kilmer spat.

"I was watching rather closely," Winn said. "He ran very well. If the boy hadn't been checking him down when he tried to run past Sun Briar—"

"That horse isn't fast enough to run past me," Kilmer snapped and brushed by Winn.

Later, Winn was still thinking about Exterminator. He had seen so many racehorses over the years and knew he had seen something extraordinary. He could not leave it alone. He tried to praise Exterminator one more time. "He's no race horse—regardless of what you think," Kilmer told him. But an hour later, he called back.

"You still think Exterminator is a Derby horse?" he asked.

"Yes."

"If he were your horse, would you start him in the Derby?"

"I certainly would."

"All right; he starts."

Kilmer capitulated, but McDaniel, Winn, and Knapp seemed to be the only three people in America who thought Exterminator had a chance. With Sun Briar out of the race, the crowd turned its attention to the second favorites. Many chose Escoba, "the pride of the Bluegrass," since he belonged to Kenneth D. Alexander, a Kentuckian who was also a U.S. Army officer. Alexander, fighting abroad, had vowed to give his Derby winnings to the Red Cross. The overall favorite was War Cloud, who was fast and had a patriotic name.

Besides these two, most racegoers thought there was little else to see. In fact, hardly anyone noticed a thing about the pinch-hitting Kilmer entry. Exterminator's odds were listed at 30–1.

War Cloud was not the only patriotically named horse in the race. Exterminator's half sister, also entered, was named Viva America. Others registered with the Jockey Club included War Loan, War Smoke, War Strength, Camouflage, Rifle, Captain Rees, and Whizz Bang.

Wearing an ornate Derby hat had been a tradition since 1875, but this year, many women did not have extra time or money, and it would have been in poor taste anyway. Instead, with dye and fabric shortages on, they wore mended skirts, shortened to save material. Many cropped their hair short, more practical for work in factories, at Camp Taylor, or for the Red Cross. (Flappers would morph this pragmatism into style in a few years.) At home, they altered housekeeping. "Without Wheat" was a popular pamphlet, along with "Sweets without Sugar" (molasses, dates, maple) and "Potato Possibilities" (potato fish balls, potato spice cake, potato-oatmeal soup).

In 1914, Wilson had signed a proclamation making Mother's Day the second Sunday in May. Now Pershing commanded each of his soldiers, "general to private," to write to their mothers and wear white flowers to honor them. Censors would work all night to get the letters back to the United States in time.

On Derby Day, weak dawn light spilled over the twin spires of the grandstand at the Churchill Downs racetrack, where grooms carried sloshing buckets to waiting horses, rustling in straw-strewn stalls. Sunlight lingered over the infield, where a ragged outline was imprinted in the grass, the souvenir of an early-harvest victory garden. It caught on the wet-paint white rails surrounding the racecourse and leaked in through small windows onto drowsing lead ponies. The drizzly air carried a scent of hay and molasses. In his stall, Exterminator ate his light competition-day ration and lowered his neck to have his mane twisted into short plaits.

Winn had pulled off a pageant as well as a sporting event. Soldiers ceremonially hoisted the flag, and women sold war bond stamps. The Red Cross reaped benefits from auctioning off a dog. The enormous American flag snapped and whipped over the racetrack. Soldiers and civilians shook warm May rain from their hat brims and scrutinized dampened racing forms. Mud clotted the grounds and forced people to pick their way along, oxfords and low boots sinking.

The band played the national anthem as the horses paraded in for the first race on the card. Soldiers stood at attention, and men in civvies uncovered their heads. The heightened patriotism of a country at war gave the day of racing meaning beyond its usual significance. Even a very brief moment of sunshine during the flag raising seemed like a sign that the day would hold better things for the race and for the country. "Earnest that our fighting forces and their allies will make the world safe for democracy . . . the sun shone out from behind the vanishing clouds," wrote one reporter.

The thoroughbreds running were the same stalwart animals carrying soldiers in the American Expeditionary Forces. The year before, a foreign-born colt had won. This year, maybe the roses would go to an American horse.

At a party the night before, Knapp's friends had teased him about his bad luck, because he had traded a mount on the Derby favorite for a ride on the longest long shot in the race. But thinking about Uncle Henry's faith in his last-minute horse, Knapp did not smile. Instead, he told them that Exterminator would win. The other jockeys—Johnny Loftus with the ride on War Cloud, Joe Notter who would be aboard Escoba—laughed even harder.

The next morning, the jockeys started their day of competition as they always did, sweating off any excess weight their stripling frames still held in a long Turkish bath. Holding still as the steam swirled around them, the riders fretted about the footing, which was already deep from the days of rain, and getting worse. They knew every step of the Churchill Downs track, every spot that worsened in wet conditions, every hole that could trip a horse. As the rain continued to fall, Joe Notter sighed. He knew Escoba had plenty of speed, but he also knew that the officer's horse was no mud runner.

The morning papers revealed to the world outside Kentucky the surprising end to the long-simmering questions about Sun Briar. Writers widely viewed the last-minute changeover as a hopeless measure. Along with that of American Eagle, a horse who was starting at similarly terrible odds, Exterminator's picture was featured in one paper as a joke. The caption said that if one of those absurdly ill-favored two colts were to win, their backers would earn a "hatful" of money.

One bookie gave a reporter some odds. War Cloud at 6–5, Lucky B at 8–1. The writer asked what odds he would lay on Exterminator. "For you, 3,000 to 1," he said. A gambler from nearby Paris, Kentucky, wanted to put $200 on Exterminator, but his friends teased him so much that he bet on War Cloud instead.

Puddles formed, and trees, overladen with moisture, dripped steadily. No one could remember a muddier Derby Day since 1912. Matt Winn looked out the window and gave up his hope that the crowd would be anywhere near as large as it had been for previous Derbys. But he had misjudged how badly people wanted to see the race.

By a little after 1 P.M., the sky was still dismal, but the rain held off. Despite the wet ground and heavy clouds, people kept coming. Their shoes soaked through, they lugged mackinaws and umbrellas. Women hitched up their skirts to keep them from dragging in the muck. Admission cost $2.50, with a 20¢ war tax. Winn's team had encouraged patrons to keep exact change ready to avoid delays, but attendants still took extra time to collect all those dimes, and the line crawled. Forty mounted officers and the entire motorcycle police squad ushered people toward the gates and quieted disputes. "Give me three conductors, and I'll get the whole crowd inside!" shouted a streetcar driver.

Spectators packed every inch of space in clubhouse and grandstand, and a solid mass of people lined the lawns over a quarter of a mile. The splashy oranges, blues, and yellows of the women's dresses dotted the capacity crowd of about forty thousand. Army officers and society people filled the private boxes, while poor people who wanted to watch for free carved out space along the fence by the stable yards.

In the betting ring on Derby Day, turfites chose horses, scratched those out, and started all over. War Cloud emerged as the favorite, and some said that it would take a very dark horse to beat him. "I had the winner picked before it rained," one muttered. One man noticed the symmetry of the entry of the fifth horse in the fifth race and hollered out some eccentric advice, "Two fives is lucky, it's Exterminator!" More than $500,000 went through the pari-mutuel machines.

In the stands, umbrella-wielding women placed their own bets, a change from previous years when they had to send down messengers to the betting windows. Now too many young men were at war to work as runners. Even though the back of the Derby program forbade woman from betting, women elbowed their own way through the crowds to do just that. In two more years, these women would vote for the first time, their final push for suffrage inspired by the independence they gained during the war.

Down beneath the crowds, in the smaller bustle of the saddling area, McDaniel looked at Exterminator. The colt's eyes were large and unflustered. He seemed poised but not frantic. On this rainy day, Exterminator could prove that McDaniel, too, was special. Much hung in the balance.

"It was with very mixed feelings that I watched our foreman get Exterminator ready for the big race," McDaniel wrote later. "The thoughts that ran through my mind as he adjusted the saddle to the colt's high withers, picked the mud out of his feet and stretched his forelegs to straighten out the wrinkled skin under his girths may be imagined. I was responsible for recommending his purchase. It was through my lack of faith that Sun Briar was withdrawn—and by the way Exterminator acquitted himself I would be judged! If he failed, I would be the goat. That happening is too often part of a trainer's job, but in this case I felt that, to a greater extent than is ordinary, the responsibility lay on my shoulders. Just as the foreman was putting up the finishing touch by tying up the colt's tongue to prevent him from getting it over the bit, the paddock judge's sharp inquiry, 'Are you ready, McDaniel?' came as a welcome relief. Quickly followed by the command, 'Mount your jockeys,' it meant action that would soon put an end to the cruel suspense."

"Hurry home," McDaniel told Knapp, boosting him into the saddle. "You are on the best horse, even if a whole lot of people don't believe the same way I do." McDaniel instructed Knapp not to hurry Exterminator along at the beginning of the race, but to let him settle, and push him once they were rounding the turn for home. He felt certain of one thing: if the race came down to a stretch battle, Exterminator would win.

Once the day's other races were finished, Winn had the track "floated" with a six-mule drag, to improve the footing. Next, an outrider on a gray horse, wearing the traditional Churchill Downs fire-scarlet coat, led the eight contestants out. Each horse paraded past the grandstand and club-

The start of the 1918 Kentucky Derby. (*Courtesy of Churchill Downs, Inc./Kinetic Corporation*)

house. The crowd started to cheer when they saw Escoba and grew louder when favorite War Cloud came along. Exterminator picked his way through the mud without special cheers.

It was a good start, only two minutes, and at 5:19 they were all facing the same way. There was a moment of charged hush. "Come on!" shouted the starter. And they were off, hooves throwing up wet mud with every flying step.

The lone filly, Exterminator's half sister Viva America, took the lead, and maintained it around the first turn until the three-quarter-mile mark. Loud cheers erupted from the spectators in the free section. They hung over the rail and waved their hats, shouting. War Cloud's fans yelled for him to move up, move up, for God's sake, and Johnny Loftus tried to oblige them, but his horse could not handle the miserably wet footing. Defeated, War Cloud fell back.

The others pressed on, their hooves slipping in the mud as they pounded along, the jockeys' silks now spattered with dark wet clods. War Cloud forgotten, Escoba passed Viva America. Exterminator was right at his heels, his legs relentlessly unfolding open to gobble more track. Who was that tall drink of water racing to catch up with Escoba? wondered the crowd, squinting as the horses turned down the stretch. Viva America clung to third place.

Escoba and Exterminator drew farther and farther away from her. Down the stretch they dueled, neither giving an inch. Onlookers grabbed each other's sleeves and stared in disbelief as the impossibly long legs continued their machinelike cycle. The horses could have been yoked together, Escoba's head reaching forward with effort. About two hundred yards out, Knapp looked ahead at the nearing finish line. He crouched down and tapped Exterminator with his whip to ask for speed. His hands came forward to give Exterminator some rein, his legs tightened around the horse. Here was the stretch battle McDaniel had hoped for. Knapp pulled Exterminator alongside Escoba, and he ran in front. Exterminator won the Derby by a full length.

The crowd was speechless, shocked. People checked their programs to see who the hell Horse Number 5 was. "A pall of gloom seemed to

Exterminator after the Derby, Willie Knapp up.
*(Courtesy of Churchill Downs, Inc./Kinetic
Corporation)*

spread all over the inclosure as its occupants watched the plain-looking chestnut stepping back to weigh in, with his cocky, confident gait and a look in his eye that seemed to say, 'This is nothing to what I'll do to these guys later on.'" wrote McDaniel.

The Kilmers had watched the race with the Binghamton party from a lofty box. Smiling, they hurried down and through the muck. Governor Augustus Stanley congratulated them with handshakes and a grin as the roses were placed around Exterminator's neck.

After the initial shock of the upset, spectators found their voices to give Exterminator his due, cheering him and Knapp with the pure joy of witnessing the impossible. Knapp wiped the mud from his face. "I always have something up my sleeve," he said, grinning. More seriously, he said, "I have always thought that I would ride a Derby winner since Mr. Kilmer shipped his stable to Louisville, but I never dreamed that Exterminator would be my mount."

McDaniel was more measured in his comments, but he could not hide his pride. "After Exterminator beat Sun Briar so handily in his trials I realized that the son of McGee was a good colt," he said. Then he spoke more diplomatically, adding, "making due allowance for the fact that Sun Briar was not near his best form." He was finally where he belonged: the winner's circle at the Kentucky Derby. McDaniel had found his star, his Harry Bassett.

Even Kilmer seemed pleased. "Gee, but it is great to win a Derby," he said. "I am delighted that I purchased Exterminator. He is sure a great horse and he can have anything in Binghamton. The same goes for Jockey Knapp

The Derby crowd, and Knapp, Kilmer, and McDaniel moments after the Derby.

and Trainer McDaniel." He announced that he would give them each $1,000, and double even his stable workers' salaries for the month of May. Some of his friends, though, were surprised that he was not happier and suggested that maybe he just didn't "realize what an honor it was to own the winner of this great race."

A reporter asked Cal Milam his reaction to seeing Exterminator, so recently his own horse, in the winner's circle with racing's greatest prize. Milam's response exemplified sportsmanship: "It was the old story of a bird in the hand is worth two in the bush."

Moviegoers around the country saw the race as part of Screen Telegram No. 23, a Mutual newsreel, as soon as forty-eight hours after the race.

Binghamtonians who could never afford to go to Churchill Downs especially loved watching the hometown success. Crowds went to three show-
ings of Exterminator's victory film at the Stone Opera House. They were
shocked by the mud; it looked far worse than the newspapers described it.
When the celluloid Exterminator crossed the finish line and trotted to the
winner's circle, tossing his head as the roses were wrapped about his neck,
they responded with exuberant applause.

Exterminator's victory was one also for the country, for homebred horses
in unspoken contrast with royally bred Sun Briar or the previous year's winner, English-bred Omar Khayyam. "The splendid victory gained by Exterminator in Kentucky's greatest race is a veritable triumph for the stout
strains of American blood. All honor to the blood of the American thoroughbred," was how Milam's mentor, John Madden, put it.

There were a few people who believed Exterminator's story was too
good to be true. Where had this horse come from? In a time when racing
was filled with spongers and dopers, skeptics were suspicious of a horse
coming out of nowhere to replace a star and win the Kentucky Derby. The
Cincinnati Enquirer even published a series of op-eds claiming foul play
and called for the Churchill Downs commission to launch an inquiry. The
racing community said no, using Exterminator as a symbol of patriotism.
The idea was like running down cavalry horses. "This is the glorious uncertainty of racing," wrote one reporter. "The war has demonstrated the
absolute necessity of thoroughbred blood in the Army horse, and there is
only one way in which the standard of the breed may be maintained, the
race course test." To disparage Exterminator was to put down the country; no one would take away Exterminator's glory.

"That was the Derby of all Derbys," Knapp said years later. "That was
the story book Derby."

On Derby Day, though, Exterminator startled when the blanket of roses
fell over his neck. He pulled from the groom, feet hustling backward. Then

he seemed to consider chewing a rose. In the saddle, Knapp wiped his face and tried to steady the horse underneath him. And then, while Exterminator's owner and trainer met the governor, shaking hands and bowing before a cheering crowd, the horse was walked, through the still-wet mud, back to his stall for some hay.

5

"One of the Greatest
Three-Year-Olds of the Season"

"Exterminator, the horse I bought to work with Sun Briar, won the Derby," Kilmer wrote in a telegram to his *Press* the day after the race. "If Sun Briar had started, he would have won by five lengths, making Sun Briar first and Exterminator second in the Derby." Whatever transient delight Kilmer may have taken in Exterminator's victory seemed dampened by the time he was dictating to the telegraph operator in Louisville. Now, people understood that Sun Briar was still first in his heart. A dream of winning the Derby had come true—a dream that most horsemen hold but never realize—but Kilmer was still unsatisfied. Exterminator's win, it seemed, just wasn't the one he wanted.

Many disagreed with Kilmer there. "If such a contingency ever occurs where both horses start in the same race," wrote a *Daily Racing Form* reporter, "Exterminator, in the event that they are both ridden out, will lead Sun Briar at the finish." That contingency would arise during the rest of the 1918 season, but often only Sun Briar would be "ridden out," or pushed to the utmost. Kilmer's campaign to keep Sun Briar on top could be helped by a racing rule of the day called the "declaration to win." The rule was complex, but basically said that if you entered two horses in the same race, you could declare one to win. That is, a jockey would not be penalized for holding back the other horse, the one you had not declared. Normally, of course, jockeys were forbidden to hold horses back. This was the one way they could. The rule also helped bettors, who could then understand which horse they should put money on.

It was a controversial rule, but it was used in some important races. August Belmont Sr. had Fenian declared to win for the 1869 Belmont Stakes. In the 1875 Belmont, Calvin beat Aristedes, who had won the Derby, only because the owner declared Calvin to win.

Declaring Sun Briar to win gave Kilmer a way to favor him while keeping Exterminator racing. By winning the Derby, Exterminator had shown he could be far more than a truck horse. But Kilmer still saw Exterminator as a pacemaker for Sun Briar, and the rule gave him a method to treat him that way.

The question of whether geldings like Exterminator should compete plagued racing's leaders, and it became critical during the war. Geldings did not contribute to the national effort of producing more thoroughbreds. European tracks had been forbidding geldings for years, the argument ran, and owners there did not even dare to geld any thoroughbred stallions until government veterinarians said they wouldn't be useful to the cavalry. American horsemen wanted to maintain that crucial tie between racing and the army. "Racing in the United States is no longer a mere sport," said Winn. "It must henceforth be regarded as an essential factor in our great scheme of national defense." This meant that only horses who could contribute to the country's cavalry should be allowed to race.

That rule would mean no more Roamers or Exterminators. Some racing men cautiously agreed, but they wanted time to adjust. The trainer H. G. Bedwell said they should wait so that geldings currently in training—he trained the speedy gelding Billy Kelly—could have the careers they had started. He had another suggestion, too: that there be certain races in which the winner would go to the government as a remount stallion or broodmare. Forbidding geldings caught on for some races but never wholesale; still, the conversation stood as a reminder of the unwavering cavalry-racing bond.

When one army official suggested suspending racing, August Belmont gave a chilly, arch response. "In well informed quarters," he said, "racing is regarded as a military necessity."

The Kilmer pair had a weak early summer. Sun Briar was supposed to be ready for the Withers Stakes by June 2, but instead he lost with "no excuse." He was such a disappointment, in fact, that some thought he was jinxed. Horsemen were superstitious; jinxes, or hoodoos, were nothing to take lightly. There was a jinx on a certain jockey cap, riders were sure, because two riders who wore it fell and fractured their legs. Some riders thought that turf photographer C. C. "Red" Cook was a jinx; you saw him only when you fell. The trainer Sam Hildreth avoided $2 bills and cross-eyed mares; both were unlucky, he thought. He did not allow photographers to take pictures of his horses before races, and when one did, he scratched the horse. A mare named Kathleen broke badly in a race, lost, and returned limping, proving to onlookers that the jinx "was on the job." All you could do was wait for a jinx to lift.

In late May, racegoers at the Jamaica racecourse in Queens, New York, gathered around Exterminator. They were impressed by his long body, which seemed to be made only of muscle and bone. Even his head, with his enormous, cervid eyes, seemed larger than other horses'. But Exterminator lost that day, not living up to his Derby performance. People wondered if he was jinxed like Sun Briar, or just a one-time kind of winner. "Exterminator is mostly legs," said one horseman. "He has good shoulders and is deep round the heart, but he is not a high class horse, and his winning the Derby was a fluke. He belongs to the overnight handicaps and is worth about $3,500."

Maybe the next race, the Latonia Derby back in Kentucky, would suit him better. He would race against the Belmont Stakes winner, Harry Payne Whitney's Johren. Johren was "not unbeatable," said Knapp. "I expect to see Exterminator give him a stout battle." As the Kentucky Derby winner, Exterminator drew the largest crowd Latonia had ever had, so big that the managers expressed relief that they had just enlarged the viewing area.

A. B. Hancock, the owner of Claiborne Farm in Kentucky and a captain in the army, was there along with other remount men, looking for stallions. The remount's connection to racing had shoved away images of parasitic bookies and desperate gamblers. Instead, as one reporter wrote, standing among the thousands of people from Ohio and Kentucky, watching a horse race was "one of the greatest outdoor diversions of red-blooded Americans," a hardy, Rooseveltian pastime.

Even with the "red-blooded" crowd rooting for Exterminator, Knapp had been wrong. Johren won. It was an unremarkable race, but afterward, Mrs. Stanley, the Kentucky governor's wife, did something new. She took her absent husband's place in the steward's stand. An army general presented roses to the winning jockey, who then handed them over to Mrs. Stanley. As far as anyone could remember, she was the first woman ever to be in the official stand.

Kilmer did not make the trip to Kentucky to watch the Latonia Derby, and there were no flowers for his second-place winner. McDaniel decided both horses needed to rest before they made their bid for Saratoga, in August.

For the most part, American cavalrymen and their grooms treated horses well. Stables were whitewashed often, to hold down disease, and feed boxes were disinfected once a week. Sweaty horses were rubbed with dry straw and buckled into warm blankets. "Each cavalry man, as a rule, loves his horse far more than words can describe," wrote a lieutenant in the veterinary corps at Camp Greenleaf, in Chickamauga, Georgia. One soldier, stationed in France, abused a horse. He was given only half of his food for the day, and the other soldiers "shunned" him. They also nicknamed him "the Hun," which stuck.

The rules that AEF horsemen lived by seemed very much a product of the ASPCA, of John Rarey's legacy, and the focus on kindness: "Get acquainted with your horse, so that you will know when he is fit," ran an article in *Stars and Stripes*. "Treat him kindly and he will trust you. Always carry one day's feed of grain . . . If you have no water bucket, use your helmet. When mounted, if you know your horse, you should know when he needs a rest. If you dismount and lead him, you will readily see how much it refreshes him. Never lose an opportunity to put your horse under shelter at night."

The *Manual for Stable Sergeants* took a more practical view, with clear instructions on how to put a horse down humanely. "An imaginary line is drawn from the base of the right ear to the left eye and vice versa," it said. "The bullet should enter at the point where these two lines cross, the pistol being held close to the head." But even this hard-bitten guide allowed that if a horse was very sick, only one, trusted man should be allowed to nurse him.

Since the Spa was where Sun Briar had his extraordinary first season the year before, much rode on him recapturing his glory and shaking off his jinx there. McDaniel had laid both colts off for a long time and hoped that he would be ready to train winners at Saratoga the way he couldn't in Kentucky. "Trainer Henry McDaniel has given Sun Briar a long rest since his disappointing showing earlier in the year," wrote a *Daily Racing Form* reporter, "and it may be that that astute trainer will have another surprise at Saratoga."

The year before, Exterminator had been rattling around Canadian tracks, and now the question was if he could face the kind of competition Saratoga offered, the kind that Sun Briar had faced—and dominated—all the previous year. So far, it looked like the answer was no.

Kilmer seemed in a despairing, petulant mood. Some of his two-year-olds had a cough, and he wasn't sure how many of them would even be healthy enough to race. He told a reporter he "would probably have to be satisfied with a few crumbs at the Saratoga meeting."

The war seemed closer at the Spa than it had in 1917. The horsiest things stayed the same: the smell of liniment mingled with that of the woodsmoke from the fire grooms heated for hot water after morning rubdowns, the sound of horses stamping. But American soldiers had been fighting for almost a year and a half now. Men had died, lost limbs, and come home with the tin or plaster masks that covered faces ruined by gas, guns, and fire. Soldiers had become more than ghostly creatures who could use some hand-knitted socks, although a list of local contributions to the Red Cross still included two pairs of wristlets from a Miss Merchant, four pairs of socks from a Mrs. Howard H. Hall, and $5 from Miss Burrit's music class. There were fewer young men around—one estimate said that 20 percent of the men who would normally be in the clubhouse were off at war—and there were six new service stars on the flag in the jockey's room; four, for the four Roosevelt sons, on the flag at the Roosevelt farm, Sagamore Hill. Eight-year-old Julius Sighulz stood in the clubhouse dressed in a complete miniature army uniform, selling War Savings Stamps. Few refused him, and he sold $7,500 worth.

The *Daily Racing Form* listed jockeys who were at war; sixty-two from Yonkers, New York's Empire City course alone. Those who stayed home were there for specific reasons, like being too small, or bearing old racing injuries that meant they couldn't fight. Others were supporting families. Local car dealers posted signs saying that it was the "patriotic duty of every owner to make minor adjustments and repairs, to the end that every expert mechanic available for war work may be released to the government." There were auctions: George Bain, who normally voiced the yearling sales, said nothing was too small for him to auction off for the war effort. Lots included a black kitten, for $75, and a pin that was given to the seller by the kaiser. The pin sold for $5,300, and the buyer had to pledge he would destroy it.

Other sports continued to abridge or cancel their games. The War Department requested that college football be suspended, even though Big Ten practice was supposed to start in days. A. A. Stagg, who coached at the University of Chicago, thought this was ridiculous, given that West Point players were still practicing. "Football undoubtedly would make better officers," he said. In the end, schools made different decisions: some, like Cornell and Dartmouth, canceled varsity football but still played games against nearby teams.

But the horses—the cavalry horses' cousins and daughters and uncles—ran on. The Kilmers watched from their box.

Things changed for the Kilmer stable when Sun Briar set a record at Saratoga in the August 6 Delaware Handicap, a race Exterminator did not run. It was an astonishing, fiery performance. Sun Briar was playful after the race and seemed comfortable, without a sign of ringbone lameness. Racegoers crowded to congratulate Kilmer and McDaniel. "If I had waved him on, as I usually do in his trial work, when he came into the home stretch, he would have made the mile in one thirty-five or one thirty-five and a fifth," McDaniel said. But he couldn't conceal his pleasure. "He was a good horse today," he said. For McDaniel, that was effusive praise.

Kilmer had, of course, bet on Sun Briar to win the Delaware. But he told his wife to bet on a horse named Drummond across the board for the third race. "I have no money to throw away," Esther told him. "There," said Kilmer to nearby men. "You see how much a woman respects her husband's word." That was his kind of joke, seeming to pander to the other owners in the clubhouse, while Esther made an uncomfortable reference to how much money they had but she couldn't use.

When Kilmer gave dinner parties, he would sometimes announce, midmeal, that it was time to move. He would lead all of his guests to another house on the estate for the next course. "The move would be made with varying degrees of enthusiasm from his guests and I often wondered with what re-action from his chef," remembered one guest.

In Saratoga, though, Kilmer entertained with expensive restaurant din-ners, keeping up with other owners, who hosted parties at houses they had rented for the season. The Riddles were famous for the mint juleps they served in mugs "thick with frost." Some held gatherings or charity events at the grand Canfield Casino. Guests included Enrico Caruso and Chauncey Olcott, the tenor who wrote and sang "My Wild Irish Rose."

Saratoga continued to be a charmed place for the Kilmer stable, because Sun Briar kept coming in first. The next big race at Saratoga was the Trav-ers, which is for three-year-olds. Even today, it is a highlight of the season at Saratoga, and the 1918 race was particularly significant, because al-though the term "Triple Crown" was not used yet, the Travers was only the second time in history that three horses who had won a Triple Crown race the same year met later. Exterminator had won the Derby, his Derby rival War Cloud won one of the two 1918 Preaknesses (the field was so big it had to be split), and Whitney's Johren had taken the Belmont.

Sun Briar (on inside) and Exterminator (on outside) working out at Saratoga, August 1918. (*Courtesy of Keeneland-Cook*)

Ten owners donated $1,000 to the Red Cross, and the Travers's whole purse, except the entry fee paid by the winner, went to the Red Cross, too. Even the jockeys rode for free, and they collected extra money from other riders for the cause. It gave Kilmer the perfect opportunity to declare Sun Briar to win—if he beat War Cloud *and* Exterminator, it would mean he was faster than two success stories. It also meant he declared Exterminator to lose.

Knapp rode Sun Briar, and Andy Schuttinger, another accomplished jockey, rode Exterminator. To ride a horse knowing his stablemate is "declared" is very difficult; emotionally, it goes against everything you usually fight for as a jockey. Celebrity jockey Isaac "Honest Ike" Murphy, who rode during the 1880s and '90s, refused to ride stablemates of horses declared to win. He felt it was dishonest to pull up, ever, no matter what the rulebook said. It is tactically difficult, too. You have to see the race about four steps ahead, because you're thinking not only of riding your horse, you are also thinking of not winning, and how you can help some other horse to win, or, at the very least, stay out of his way. You have to do all of this on a thoroughbred bound for the finish line with the determination he has been taught from infancy. In some ways, it can be harder than winning. Schuttinger had a hard race ahead.

The Travers was held on a beautiful summer day, and the start was one of Mars Cassidy's best: clean and quick. Right away, before the first turn, Sun Briar took the lead. Schuttinger kept Exterminator just behind him and to the outside, protecting him. As the race went on, Sun Briar stayed on the rail, with Exterminator just far enough out that any challenger would find him right in the way. Schuttinger kept Exterminator focused and forced Johren into a pocket—a spot where he was so closely flanked that he couldn't get ahead. War Cloud, pushed far out on the turn, got tired. All these moves paved the way for Sun Briar's victory, giving Knapp a clear road to race down. In the end, Exterminator came in fourth behind Sun Briar, Johren, and War Cloud.

Kilmer was still "the luckiest recruit." He kissed his wife, sped off to find McDaniel and Knapp, and "all but snuggle[d] Sun Briar to his bosom."

The sportsmanlike patrician Harry Payne Whitney, whose warm laugh echoed through Saratoga, was the first to applaud Sun Briar, even though he had beaten Johren. "Sun Briar was the greatest two-year-old last year and his comeback has been a wonderful thing," he said. Then he put an arm around Johren's jockey and told him, Teddy Roosevelt style, not to worry; he had ridden a "bully race."

Kilmer was so buoyed by Sun Briar's performance that he considered starting him in the Saratoga Cup, which was run at a longer distance than Sun Briar was used to. "I am convinced that the farther he had to go today," he said, "the further off he would have won. I am also reasonably positive that when in the stud Sun Briar will sire horses that will stay a long route."

Shouting Sun Briar's praises was an advertisement for his future stud services, for any potential mare-owning customers who might be listening. Kilmer was still a patent medicine man.

Exterminator had succeeded in his Travers goal, too. By pinning in Johren, and staying well back, he had given his stablemate his path to victory.

In each issue, the *Daily Racing Form* reported on horsemen who died in the war. While leafing through your copy to find out the latest from Latonia or Hot Springs or Aqueduct, you might learn about a jockey who joined the infantry, was sent with a regiment engaged after the second advance to the Marne, and was killed in France. A gentleman rider from Tennessee was also killed in France, leaving a widow and two children. The son of a racehorse owner was killed while driving an ambulance. The registrar of the Jockey Club had two sons: one died, and one was wounded in action and confined to a hospital. A bomb blew off one of his legs, and he died the next day. The son of the president of the Empire City Track died from injuries he got while fighting in the forest at Argonne. He was twenty-three and just married. Martin Kearns, the foreman for a big stable called Greentree and the youngest of four brothers, all of whom were in the service, died in France. It wasn't just men, either. A Canadian racehorse named

Rockspring proved that "blood counts with horses, as with men, in war-fare," when he fell in France after three years of serving as a cavalry horse. His owner marked his grave with a rough wooden cross.

The racing press reported some more uplifting war-related news, too. President Wilson's saddle horse, Democrat, was a son of Octagon, one of the Belmont-donated remount sires, and the *Thoroughbred Record* put his picture on the cover. The son of one Jockey Club member, an aviator, had run away and joined the French army, since he was too young to join the AEF. He was taken prisoner but escaped from a German camp into Swit-zerland when he was being transferred on a train. Pudd'n McDaniel, a jockey cousin of Henry's, was a corporal at Camp Upton, on Long Island. Soldiers staged a race with the cavalry horses, and Pudd'n rode a sorrel gelding belonging to his quartermaster. "It was an exciting thing, that race," wrote a reporter in the camp newspaper. "One rider was dismounted in the melee." Pudd'n, who, like Henry, had inherited the family's talent, won.

And C. C. Cook, the photographer some riders thought was a jinx, was a lieutenant and a head photographer in the aviation service. He liked it a lot and hoped to get to the front. "The work is interesting," he said, "and I take photographs from a height of 10,000 feet, which reproduce so dis-tinctly that the stump of a tree is discernible. In fact, one can almost tell if we are going to have corn beef and cabbage for dinner or ham and spin-ach, by looking into the cook's boiler."

The wins at Saratoga were not quite enough for Kilmer. He wanted to prove Sun Briar could run a mile faster than any other horse, so he decided to send Sun Briar after the time made by gelding Roamer, whose record stood at a very fast 1:34 ⅘. "I will send my colt against the record of Roamer's," he said, "under the same conditions as regards weight next Saturday if I can get two pacemakers to assist Sun Briar . . . Roamer really did not need a pacemaker, while my horse will do better with aid."

Because the season had ended by the day Sun Briar ran, it was not an official run against the record. Another pacemaker started with him, and then Exterminator joined him for the last half mile. Sun Briar sped by them both. The track superintendent said that the track footing was faster than it had been the day Roamer made his record, which would mean that Sun Briar had a slight advantage, but he did run it in 1:34 flat, four-fifths of a second faster than Roamer. Because the mile wasn't during a race or any formal event, it did not technically break Roamer's record.

The whole episode seemed slightly patent-medicine shady, because declaring your own day and conditions to set a record was atypical and seemed like an example of Kilmer making his own rules. Kilmer boasted tirelessly about the time. Finally, a reporter put the question, instead, to McDaniel, who responded, "The mile was run in 1:34," he said. "I timed it and know."

After that, no one questioned the time again. It was the new record.

Kentucky passed a "work or fight" rule to keep men from shirking their duty to the army. Many African American grooms were rounded up and jailed, as if they were not working enough. One groom, named Rabbit, said a man with a badge "as big as a pie plate" approached him, announced he was a federal officer, and asked why he wasn't obeying the law. When Rabbit told him that he was at work, the officer told him that tending horses was "no work at all."

In fact, the daily life of grooms was hard. Grooms—also called rubbers or swipes because they rubbed the horses dry after they worked—were in charge of four or five horses at most well-off stables. A groom woke up at sunrise to feed and water horses. Next, he mucked out stalls, laying fresh straw or shakes down for the horse to have clean bedding all day. He would saddle and bandage the first horse of the morning.

By then, the exercise rider would be back from breakfast, and he would take charge while the groom ate. But the groom would need to be back to get the second horse ready, and then take the first horse from the exercise rider. The just-worked horse needed to be cooled off by slow walking, then cleaned—"rubbed"—with water and towels, depending on the weather. If he needed to be bandaged again, the groom did that. He would do that all morning, repeating the ritual with each horse. After lunch, it was time to do laundry—all the bandages, towels, and rubbing cloths he had used. He might have time for a short nap, but soon it was time to walk the horses so they could stretch and graze. Next, he might lay down some more fresh bedding, give each horse hay and water, and then have his own dinner. At night, grooms took turns sitting up with the horses, checking that they were not sick, or distressed, or "cast," which happened when a horse rolled over, sometimes in his sleep, and got himself pinned in the narrow shed row stall.

As one race official said, "His work is a highly specialized kind of work, and an ordinary laborer could no more perform it than he could fly."

At Saratoga, Exterminator lost whenever Sun Briar was entered with him, but he also just lost. It really did begin to seem possible that he had won the Derby by luck. McDaniel gave Exterminator a change of scenery. They went to Maryland, to race at the recently renovated Laurel Park. Besides landscaping, there was a new covered walkway, so people who drove could walk to the clubhouse under cover; the car was becoming integral to members of the racing crowd.

In the fall of 1918, the Spanish flu was taking hold in Maryland, as in many other parts of the country. During the 1918–1919 course of the pandemic, 47 percent of all the deaths in the country were from flu. It forced the American life expectancy down by ten years. The flu was not mainly killing old people and children, either. Instead, it killed people who were young and hardy, including one out of every sixty-seven soldiers. It also struck grooms, trainers, racegoers, and jockeys, including Earl "Handy" Sande.

Turfites had hoped that because the tracks like Laurel were mainly open-air facilities, they could stay open even though other public gathering places were closed to limit contagion, but most health officials did not allow them to do that. Exterminator placed third in Laurel's Washington Handicap on October 12, and the next day health authorities shut it down. Other racetracks had to alter their schedules, too, and at least one made everyone wear gauze masks. Some preferred a perforated zinc mask, dosed with creosote for antiseptic properties, with eucalyptus and pine needle oil sprayed inside.

Only sixteen of the Laurel meet's twenty-seven days were held because of the flu. Despite that, Exterminator's luck began to change at Laurel. In those sixteen quiet, worried days, he won three races and was emerging as a winner again. When he won the Artillery Liberty Bond Purse, Kilmer was there to watch. After the race, Kilmer addressed the crowd from the winner's circle and announced he was donating $10,000 worth of bonds. Next, McDaniel took Exterminator to nearby Pimlico, won one minor race, and then raced two other Kentucky Derby winners in the Bowie Cup. He came in third; the horses who beat him were the other two Derby victors.

Exterminator was showing promise as a handicap horse, which meant he performed well while carrying extra weight. In a handicap race, horses receive weights—lead bars that slide into the saddle pad—based on their previous performances. A horse who tends to win will be assigned more weight than others, with the goal of evening out competitors. Because many of these races awarded big silver cups as trophies, they became known as "cup" races and had names including Saratoga Cup, the Jockey Club Gold Cup, and the Autumn Gold Cup. Horses like Exterminator, who succeeded in these, were called cup horses.

Handicap races are no longer as popular as they were in Exterminator's time, when most horses carried weights in the 120- to 126-pound neighborhood. Exterminator, by contrast, lugged 130 pounds or more thirty-five times in his ninety-nine-race career, and twenty of those times, he won. That was how he got the nicknames "the Big Train" and "the Iron Horse."

Germany surrendered. At Empire City track in Yonkers, the mayor of Yonkers interrupted a day's racing to read an AP bulletin, while overhead, airplanes dropped patriotic brochures, and racegoers shouted until their voices rasped.

McDaniel planned for Exterminator to race at Latonia, the Covington, Kentucky, track near Cincinnati. People were excited to see him again, since he had escaped Sun Briar's shadow.

But just as in Maryland, flu hung over Kentucky and Ohio, so the Latonia meeting was pushed back, waiting for Kentucky to lift its ban on public gatherings. By November 19, horses were running. The race meeting had been shortened from twenty-one to fourteen days, which racetrack management thought would give enough time to raise the $300,000 that the Kentucky racing men had pledged to the Red Cross to convince governments to keep racing going. They had increased the values of some of the purses so that the flu could not stop the Red Cross fund-raising.

At Latonia, Exterminator was welcomed as a "distinguished arrival" and a "crack three-year-old." Kilmer was scheduled to come watch, and McDaniel appeared confident that Exterminator would win. Every win Exterminator notched testified to his work. Also, McDaniel and Exterminator were growing more attached to each other. Exterminator would bump McDaniel's shoulder with his long nose and huff into his coat pockets, hoping for sugar.

In downtown Covington, shoppers gawked at the Latonia Cup prize sitting in the window of a local store. It was pieces of solid silver: a punch bowl with a relief image of a racing horse, six mint julep cups with the Latonia Jockey Club's seal, and six ice spoons. The day of the race was cold and cloudy, but crowds still turned out. McGee's owner, Charles Moore, with his white hat and walking stick, came to watch his stallion's most successful foal. Exterminator took it all home, but Kilmer never did make it to Kentucky, so jockey Johnny Loftus wore the floral wreath, and McDaniel accepted the bowl, cups, and spoons.

With that race, Exterminator recaptured some of the excitement that had surrounded him on Derby Day. He was versatile and competitive, and his uniqueness was beginning to emerge, as a horse who "will shoulder top weight dependedly and gamely give the best there is in him to the contested end . . . Exterminator proves conclusively his distinction as one of the greatest three-year-olds of the season."

He won one more race against good competition on Thanksgiving Day, and he and McDaniel got on a train back to Binghamton, heads high.

In November 1918, World War I ended. Soldiers came home, and so, people hoped, would Kidron, Black Jack Pershing's warhorse, who had carried Pershing in French victory parades. But Kidron was stuck in quarantine. Horse disease is a serious thing; at one point, Teddy Roosevelt tried to intervene for fellow Rough Rider General Leonard Wood, who wanted his own horses to come home sooner from the Philippines, but the Department of Agriculture said it was impossible. And a saboteur named Anton Dilger had planned to harm the army by sickening its horses. Kidron had been all over France, near thousands of other horses, many of whom were ill, and probably contagious.

Still, Kidron's quarantine was crushing. "A great captain and his horse are almost inseparable in the memory of the soldier," wrote a reporter, remembering how Ulysses Grant, on Cincinnati, and Robert E. Lee, on Traveller, said good-bye to their troops at Appomattox.

The day before the big parade in New York, Pershing greeted fifty thousand children in Central Park. Each child held an American flag, and each school had its own flag, so the field was shot with color. After that, he went to a riding academy, where officers from the Jefferson Feigl Post of the American Legion gave him a six-year-old thoroughbred. They had named the horse after Pershing, but he changed his name to Jeff, after the legion. (The officers tried to make Jeff jump a four-foot jump, but he wouldn't. "They all do that some time," Pershing reassured the officers.)

As it turned out, though, refusing that jump was just the kind of thing Jeff did. He wasn't mannerly enough to be a parade horse, so Pershing ended up riding yet another horse for the parade. The crowd didn't even know about Jeff, but they were disappointed; they'd wanted Kidron. Somehow, seeing Pershing on a new horse was not quite the same.

After five months in quarantine, Kidron was released to Pershing, who stabled him in Chevy Chase, Maryland. When the horse grew older, Pershing retired him to a remount farm in Front Royal, Virginia. Visitors could visit Kidron—and Jeff—there, and buy postcards with the horses' pictures on them. Kidron died in 1942.

Kilmer and Esther divorced. Another woman had sued Kilmer for $100,000 the year before, and even though it never went to trial, Esther was apparently finished. The divorce proceedings—and what exactly that $100,000 was for—stayed secret, although Kilmer's "course of life" was listed as a primary issue. Binghamton legend holds that Kilmer found out when Esther would be at her lawyer's office and sent a process server after her, to give her papers. The server waited, but Esther never emerged. Her lawyers had used a rope to lower her down two stories. She entered a different office through the window, and walked out the front door of the building while Kilmer's process server sat waiting. More shocking than the divorce—or climbing out an office window—was that Esther turned down $25,000 in alimony. She wanted to get remarried right away, to a young aviator named John Redondo Sutton. Her wedding to Sutton was so much of a surprise that many guests had not even realized that the bride had gotten divorced in the first place.

At the wedding, in the Rose Room of the Ritz-Carlton hotel in New York City, a temporary altar stood in a grove of palms, ferns, and pink roses. Esther wore a mauve chiffon gown and a diamond-and-ruby bracelet, a gift from Sutton. Her days as Mrs. Kilmer were over.

There is another story in Binghamton that says one day, the pressure of wondering which horse was better got to Kilmer. He had to know what would happen if Sun Briar and Exterminator went head-to-head. This race would be unofficial, with no reporters invited, only Kilmer's employees. "Sometime after the Kentucky Derby there was a race between Exterminator and Sun Briar," longtime Kilmer employee Bill Leighton told Binghamton writer Jack Shay in 1977. "Sun Briar had won races, too. Both were champions. And this was a race between the two champions. Mr. Kilmer always insisted that Sun Briar could beat Exterminator. Period. Anytime, anywhere. No qualifiers needed. And when they had this race, there was to be no reporting afterward. This was not an official race. Exterminator won. By a head over Sun Briar. But Mr. Kilmer wanted this suppressed. I'll give you names and contact information on people who can verify this. But I have to caution you not to ask Mrs. Ellison [Kilmer's third wife and widow] about this. She's very loyal to Mr. Kilmer's memory and his wishes. And she will deny that Exterminator ever beat Sun Briar." Shay followed up and interviewed locals, who said that the story was true. Everyone warned him not to talk to Ellison about it, and he didn't, even when he first interviewed her for an article about Exterminator for a local magazine. But after a month of interviews, Shay had to ask if Exterminator could have "ever beaten Sun Briar, head to head?"

"Oh, surely he could," Ellison told him. "Yes. And he did. He surely did. He could race anyone anywhere." Ellison would not have even known Kilmer when the race took place—they married in 1932—and Shay didn't press her. Ellison could have been making a general point about Exterminator's dominance, but her words seemed to indicate that he had, at some point, beaten Sun Briar.

Right around the time that the "match race" was supposed to be taking place, McDaniel said that his own timing was enough as far as Sun Briar's mile was concerned, and other horsemen thought it was, too. Also, he had been the one giving exercise riders orders to use Exterminator as a pacemaker. He knew exactly what each horse could do. Could he have known that Exterminator stood a good chance of winning against Sun Briar? He never said a word about it, which seems in line with his usual reticence. The story seems possible on so many levels—the way Kilmer used a closed Saratoga for Sun Briar's mile time, McDaniel's ability to stay quiet, and Shay's investigations.

Later, Henry McDaniel was often asked which horse he thought would win such a race. "Up to a mile and a furlong I always believed Sun Briar the better horse," he said, "but after that distance Exterminator would wear him down." That sounds like he saw it happen, as if it was right at that mile-and-a-furlong mark that Exterminator began his relentless cycling, and Sun Briar ran out of power. It is easy to imagine McDaniel standing there, with his watch, wondering as much as anyone which of these two horses, both of which he knew so well, would win.

But if he actually saw the two horses race all out—if the race ever happened—McDaniel never mentioned it.

The writer Sherwood Anderson became famous for his collection of short stories, *Winesburg, Ohio*. With his direct, simple prose, Anderson's work influenced the so-called lost generation of writers like F. Scott Fitzgerald and Ernest Hemingway. Anderson had worked in a livery stable as a young man and saw Exterminator's Derby. He modeled a horse in his short story "I Want to Know Why" after Exterminator. In the story, a boy goes to Saratoga to watch two hometown horses race. One is an unhandsome gelding named Middlestride. "Middlestride . . . isn't such a much standing in a paddock that way," he wrote. "[He] is long and looks awkward and is a gelding . . . He goes away slow and is always way back at the half, then he begins to run and if the race is a mile and a quarter he'll just eat up everything and get there."

Kilmer issued decisions and then unmade them. First he said would retire Sun Briar. "This will be the last year of Sun Briar on the turf," he told reporters. He'd decided that given Sun Briar's ringbones, he would not race any longer.

A French syndicate offered to buy Exterminator and train him as a steeplechaser, jumping over high rails on cross-country courses. His long-bodiedness and way of going suited him to jumping. Kilmer didn't want to sell him to become a jumper, but he did consider sending him abroad to race in French steeplechases. Then he had a moment of wanting to send both horses abroad, to show the Europeans how good they were. That did not happen.

Odder were his decisions about trainers. Kilmer hired a second trainer, named J. Simon Healy, and it was unclear in what capacity he was to work with McDaniel. Like McDaniel, Healy was a hardworking old-timer, popular with other trainers. As a young man, the story went, he had saved Man o' War's grandsire from castration, thus ensuring Man o' War's existence. Healy had trained horses for the eastern millionaire Edward Cassatt, the nephew of the artist Mary Cassatt. Healy came across as optimistic; when Cassatt, evidently losing interest in racing, sold all but three horses, Healy seemed undaunted and said, "We have weeded the stable down to the real racehorses."

In July, Healy was running a training stable, and Kilmer said he would give him some horses to train once Healy got to Saratoga. "W. S. Kilmer is going to turn one or two of his horses over to Simon Healy to train, according to authentic report . . . This does not mean a change of trainers, nor the entire stable, but Mr. Kilmer intends to have two strings," reported the *Daily Racing Form*. The echo of Kilmer protesting that it didn't mean a change of trainers rang a little hollow.

In September, Healy was the one pleased with a Futurity candidate named Mormon's workout. And when Kilmer still thought he would send his horses to Europe, a reporter wrote that he couldn't decide which trainer he would send. The situation was confusing and added uncertainty to McDaniel's position. Who was Kilmer's trainer? McDaniel or Healy?

At times, the racing press seemed to ignore the recently ended war—the dead, the lost, the maimed—and just focus on how good things were for the sport, now that the days of Hart-Agnew and the antigambling zealots were gone. Those days without racing "were dark days, but not so dark that the spark of resumption was invisible to those who were industrious enough to step into the blackness and fan it into a flame . . . Racing today in this country is as well clothed in influential and financial raiment as it ever has been in its history."

McDaniel's reputation had grown again. With what Sun Briar and Exterminator had accomplished, he had won the Saratoga Special, the Hopeful, the American Derby, and the Kentucky Derby.

Everyone was looking ahead.

6

Remarkable Gameness

In 1919, glamour seeped back into America. The wartime-practical bobbed hair morphed into fashion. All the sports were back, too, with many athletes returned from the front. Americans followed boxing, baseball, and racing the most. Sports columnists wrote about Jess Willard and Jack Dempsey, about Shoeless Joe Jackson and Buck Weaver, Sir Barton, Sun Briar, Man o' War, Purchase, and Exterminator.

Even though the war was over, the connection between horse racing and cavalry horses stayed strong. Theodore Roosevelt died, but his legacy still pervaded the country as the glory of cavalrymen like Pershing gave color to the Allied victory. "These swift and exquisite creatures, miracles of endurance and grace and strength, in the hour of peril are as essential to the nation's security as fleet or fortress of frowning guns," said the governor of Kentucky in a speech. "Second only to the warrior's laurels is the coveted crown of the winner of a Kentucky Derby." Exterminator was cast as a real American warhorse, a stouthearted, homebred winner who was a miracle of endurance, grace, and strength.

McDaniel was winning races with Kilmer's horses, but Kilmer and McDaniel's propulsive chemistry sputtered. Both were very different men than they had been when they met, and Exterminator was a very different horse.

Sun Briar Court was a 487-acre combination farm and training center, all on the edge of town, alongside Binghamton's Riverside Drive, under the shadow of a low mountain. Southwestern New York, people thought, could never have the famous limestone-nourished bluegrass that legendarily strengthened "hickory-boned" Kentucky foals. But Kilmer proved them wrong by seeding different fields until he came up with a reasonable approximation and made the bluegrass grow with "Kentucky luxuriance." Then he said he would bet anyone $1,000, "horse for horse," that his two-year-olds would be as healthy as any brought up somewhere else in the country. His colts looked wonderful. No one collected.

At least one writer pointed out that growing bluegrass in New York was prohibitively expensive, "but that is beside the question. Mr. Kilmer is breeding to race. He is a sportsman, not a commercial producer of running horses. Economy in production is not the ruling consideration with him." It was a gentle way of bringing Kilmer's prodigious spending into the conversation. You could almost hear Kilmer's own defense in that one phrase: "I am a sportsman, not a commercial producer." The grass may have cost a fortune, but it was good for racehorses. All you had to do was look at them.

Sun Briar Court already had a well-appointed barn, as guests had seen during Sun Briar's birthday party in 1918—oil paintings, trophy cases, the framed whip—but it now became a destination. Poplars and elms shaded the facility, and Kilmer and his staff welcomed reporters, fans, and locals. He wanted everyone to see what he had, and to marvel, which they did. Reporters loved being given free rein and visited often to see the horses and be amazed by the farm. It was just like Kilmer to build such an over-the-top stable, but even the most seasoned horsemen had to admit that the "lucky recruit" had a terrific barn.

Kilmer's training stable alone took up an acre and half, and had been built over the old wooden stable. It was made of fireproof tile on a concrete foundation, instead of the less-costly wood still used in most barns. The mares' stalls were lit with electricity, ventilated, and roomy enough for them to stretch out, along with their foals. An underground steam plant warmed the floors.

There were three training tracks. One, a straightaway, ran alongside the Susquehanna River, flowing along the south side of the farm. Another, built along the lines of the one at Sandown, in England, was a racing oval. Inside, the building enclosed a quarter-mile riding ring, tan bark with straw scattered on top for dryness. Working in the enclosure, Kilmer's horses didn't lose workout time because of icy footing. Sliding glass panels stretched from five feet to the roof, so that the track could be almost open-air on nice days. In winter, the sun through the glass warmed the track. On the outer edge of the straw track were the box stalls, so roomy that a horse could roll over safely. They were electrically lit and had two doors. One led to the indoor track, and one outside. Enough hay and grain for the two hundred horses was stored above. In the same building were offices for the staff and trainer.

Today, many otherwise unimpressive riding schools have observation rooms with windows that look into an indoor arena, but Kilmer's was a novelty, and an invitation to watch training sessions. It was another sign of Kilmer's advertising-man desire to show off. VISITORS ARE WELCOME read a sign, and turf writers did gather at Sun Briar Court. One tour group included Harry Williams, who wrote under the name "Hindoo" for the *New York Telegraph*; Al Copland, from the *Evening Telegram*; and Ed Farrell, who covered East Coast racing for the *Chicago Racing Forum*. They saw Sun Briar, Mormon, and Exterminator, strolled the aisleways, admired trophies. Kilmer's staff served lunch.

Another innovation was a predecessor of the modern hot-walker, a machine with arms that radiate out. A groom hitches a horse to each "arm," and the whole apparatus revolves to exercise horses, keeping them moving. Instead of a motor, another walking horse, ridden by a groom, propelled Kilmer's. Hot-walkers are commonplace today, but to contemporary reporters, the machine was a miracle. "This machine-like arrangement looks for all the world like a carousel," one wrote. Another machine sifted fodder, pouring oats into separate buckets.

Even with all the press recording Sun Briar Court's advantages—and the easy availability of tours made it very appealing to reporters looking for a feature or color story—Kilmer also published his own pamphlet. "With the war, too," it read, "has returned a truer valuation of the robust elements of life, as distinguished from the narrow and effeminate standards that often prevailed before. America's future is to be a future of red blood—an open-air regime in which men and women will pay frank homage to the best product of field, forest, and farm. Of such an era Sun Briar Court is a type and a prophecy." Kilmer saw his farm as a paradigm of Rooseveltian hardiness and outdoorsy masculinity.

Others just took in the luxury. "The stable they keep [Exterminator] in," wrote Will Rogers, years later, after a visit. "I wanted to go right back to the hotel and give up my room."

Kilmer's two-trainer system persisted. He planned that Sun Briar would spend the first part of the year in the breeding shed, with Simon Healy overseeing his daily gallops, and then debut at Saratoga, in August. This was an uncommon idea. Most horses, once they went to the stud, stayed there.

Meanwhile, McDaniel took Exterminator to Hot Springs, Arkansas, a warm-weather meeting that would prepare him for the $10,000 Kentucky Handicap, a long race suited to his ground-covering speed. Some of the jockeys were riding again for the first time since they had come home from the war.

Exterminator won the first prep race; the next race was a little more challenging but still easy enough that his jockey held him back at the beginning. As soon as he let go, Exterminator sprinted in front and came in first. For McDaniel, this kind of competition warmed up a horse and got him ready not only to run, but to win. One turf writer wrote that McDaniel was "well satisfied" with how Exterminator was doing, which probably meant that he didn't say anything in particular to the press. But from the way he smiled in the winner's circle, they could see he was pleased.

Also in Hot Springs, the Hollywood director Harry Revier was shooting scenes for his movie *The Challenge of Chance,* a vehicle for world heavy-weight boxing champion Jess Willard. Willard—also called the Kansas Cowboy or the Pottawatomie Giant—had said no one wanted to see him defend the championship during the war. Now he was ready to expand his fame even though, as one reporter wrote, he was already "the most widely known American in the world outside of President Wilson and General Pershing."

Revier took his crew of cameramen and assistants to Hot Springs and secured permission from the track management to take pictures and film. They took close-ups of Exterminator, some footage of him before racing, and then they filmed the Hot Springs handicap, his second race of the season. One camera, mounted in a car, got a little close to the horses. In his hurtling drive to the finish line, Exterminator almost ran it down.

Willard and Exterminator were two of the first athletes to cross over into Hollywood; a few years later, the football star Red Grange was in some movies, and the swimmer Johnny Weissmuller played Tarzan. But the boxer and racehorse on-screen was a novelty that demonstrated some dawning ideas of celebrity. Both athletes had already been on-screen in newsreels, and now they were moving into the features.

"One end bites and the other end kicks," was all that Sam Riddle, Man o' War's owner, said writers knew about horses. Turf writing became more stirring, hyperbolic. Racing reporters highlighted equine personalities and rivalries for color. Many of the turf writers were very knowledgeable, often from time spent on the backstretch. Today, this is still true—Eclipse Award–winning writer Sean Clancy, for example, used to be a jockey. In the press pool covering Exterminator's races, Bert Collyer, a handicapper who also uncovered baseball's 1919 Black Sox scandal, had been an amateur jockey, and W. C. Vreeland had worked as an assistant trainer, a steward, and a track clerk.

Sports—primarily racing, boxing, and baseball—were an "American obsession." The legends surrounding athletes flourished, morphing the men into superheroes. Americans followed horse racing as closely as they did boxing and baseball, and the writers of the postwar years into the 1920s—sports' "Golden Age"—controlled much of how racing was understood. They excited readers with descriptions of unseen horses and races, and rendered thoroughbred racing as its own world, which sometimes seemed like a small town in that the same names tumbled through, day after day: Hildreth, Rowe, Keene, Kilmer, Whitney, McDaniel, Belmont.

Many papers, like the *Daily Racing Form*, didn't always use bylines, and some writers took horses' names for their pseudonyms. There were columns by writers called Exile, Omar Khayyam, Salvator, Roamer, and Exterminator. They used their own jargon, too, a slangy bettors' language that Damon Runyon would make famous with the short stories that became the musical *Guys and Dolls*.

"This bird has been in the brine preparing for this race," wrote Collyer about a horse named Secret Greetings. "From where I sit this looks softer than taking candy from the infant."

Writers like Collyer and Grantland Rice set a tone for the idea of sportswriting as its own genre, affected by contemporary diction, and putting forth sports as something crucial, magnificent, and American. Their stories made it unclear if the athletes had really become greater, or if it was simply the stories surrounding them. "What, then, made the Golden Age Golden?" writes Mark Inabinett in his book *Grantland Rice and His Heroes: The Sportswriter as Mythmaker in the 1920s*. "Is the period remembered this way because the athletes of the time possessed unapproachable skill? Or has its glow endured because of the words used to record their achievements?"

Of all the contemporary writers and mythmakers—O'Neil Sevier,

Peter Burnaugh, John I. Day, C. J. Savage, Grantland Rice, Henry V. King—Bill Vreeland may have adored Exterminator the most. "Would I were a Homer to write an Iliad about Exterminator," he wrote. "His deeds stand forth as the virile American thoroughbred—stout-hearted, space devouring, and oblivious to fair or foul track conditions." Vreeland was a traditionalist, a Brooklyn native who wrote with a pen instead of a typewriter. He beat track handicappers with his own exhaustive knowledge of thoroughbreds.

Although not Manhattan-based like the *New York Times* or even the *Evening Telegram*, Vreeland's *Brooklyn Eagle* was an important paper. Walt Whitman edited it in the 1840s, and it shaped Brooklyn's identity. At one point, the *Eagle* was the country's most widely read afternoon newspaper. The *Daily Racing Form* aggregated material at times, and so did the *Thoroughbred Record*. It just wasn't always practical to send reporters all over to cover the widespread tracks. If a race took place in New York, you could count on excellent coverage from the *Eagle, Herald,* and *Times.* Almost every paper sent correspondents to Saratoga, particularly for the Travers, Hopeful, and Saratoga Cup. The *Daily Racing Form* covered everything that happened in Kentucky, and much more.

The *Binghamton Press* gathered countrywide news items, too, pulling attributed paragraphs about racing from various newspapers. Kilmer had a clipping service, and on occasion his *Press* served a similar purpose. There were sometimes editorial decisions that favored Sun Briar, though. For example, once, when the *Press* borrowed Henry V. King's description of the trains coming into Saratoga, it left out the part he had written about Exterminator being pretty much as good as Sun Briar.

Different publications had different specialties. The *Daily Racing Form* and *Thoroughbred Record* had gossip columns, listing which trainers were leaving which owners, which two-year-olds looked strong, which gamblers had lost. The *New York Morning Telegraph*—a copy of the "Telly" and a cigarette was called a "whore's breakfast"—advertised tip sheets in the back. These had names like Clocker's Review, Frankie O'Brien, Famous Clocker, the Daily American Handicapper. They touted results in their ads. W. E. Wilson's said he was an owner, trainer, and clocker. "To-Day! To-Day!" ran one ad. "We Expect To 'Clean Up.'" "From what the 'boys' all tell me, I do not hesitate to say that THIS 'UN LOOKS LIKE 'HAY IN THE BARN.'"

Turf writers maintained enormous control over horses' reputations and images. They gave Exterminator many of his nicknames, including the Abe Lincoln of Race Horses, the Animated Hatrack, the Galloping Hatrack, Lincoln on Stilts, Old Poison, Old Reliable, the Evergreen Gelding, Slim, Stermy, and Slats. They shaped Exterminator's legend, starting with the Cinderella Derby.

McDaniel trained Mormon alongside Exterminator in Arkansas. Mormon was supposed to be Kilmer's 1919 Derby candidate, and he had been working soundly. But he kept losing races without any evident reason. Racing underperforming horses rather than keeping them on the shelf was one of McDaniel's training methods. The idea was that being in an actual race instead of just workouts would enliven a sour horse, taking him out of a stale routine and exciting him with crowds, flags, and applause. That's why McDaniel had taken Sun Briar to Lexington before the Derby the year before—but it didn't work with Mormon, either.

McDaniel brought both Exterminator and Mormon to Churchill Downs. He told a reporter that Exterminator "was never in better condition." In fact, he said he expected Exterminator to be the "stable's main reliance this year, the same as he was last." That was a daring thing to say, given that Sun Briar had had a powerful season late in the year and that Kilmer read the papers. But it was true that Exterminator, in the end, had raced more and finished stronger. He, not Sun Briar, was the "main reliance."

In the pre-Derby furor, Exterminator started in the Ben Ali Handicap in Lexington. Before the race, he stood in the paddock. "It was evident that Henry McDaniel had taken great pains with the gelding," wrote one reporter.

McDaniel patted Exterminator's head, and the horse tugged on McDaniel's coat. Exterminator walked to the post in a leisurely, but attentive, way. His eyes and ears were forward, and his body moved with deliberation. He didn't shy or pull. Horses around him plunged and dove; he stood still. One writer called him "the best mannered horse in the world." Of the five horses in the race, Exterminator carried the most weight and came to the front to win easily. His stride amazed onlookers with its deceptive power. "His action is low and frictionless," wrote one, but "while he does not waste motion, he springs like a rubber ball."

McDaniel accepted the silver trophy in front of the grandstand, apologizing for Kilmer's absence. Photographers pressed in, flashbulbs exploding.

"Open your eyes, Henry!" Cal Milam shouted.

"I had my eyes open when I bought this horse from you, Cal," drawled McDaniel.

Exterminator's next race was the Camden, another handicap. Rain came down in sheets, seemingly never ending. One owner after another scratched his horse, until only Exterminator and a horse named Midway remained. Exterminator won, a credit, the turf writer named Exile believed, to McDaniel, who sent him to the race in "splendid fettle." Kilmer, waiting for Derby week, was still not in Kentucky. This time, Governor Stanley presented the prize plate straight to McDaniel, who again said he was sorry that Kilmer couldn't be there. "It is a pleasure to see such a horse as Exterminator run and win," said Stanley, "as he is a thoroughbred of remarkable gameness."

Afterward, Exterminator's photograph was on the cover of the *Thoroughbred Record*. In it, his ears look particularly long, canted forward, and he stands still under the blanket of roses instead of trying to eat them. He looks all grown up, an unhandsome, race-ready handicap horse, the best-mannered horse in the world.

McDaniel made a quick trip up to Binghamton, checking on how Healy was coming along. He told a reporter that he was happy with how Sun

Briar looked, and that there were some "likely colts" among the young ones. Healy would ship some Kilmer horses to Aqueduct, and had some in hand at Empire City, too. Clearly, Kilmer didn't think of Healy as just an underling.

McDaniel raced back to Kentucky. He had another Derby to run and the Kentucky Handicap to win. Since Mormon was faltering, McDaniel went to see Milam again. This time, Milam sold him a colt named Frogtown. (Milam charged Kilmer quite a bit more money for his last-ditch effort this time.) Frogtown had run some fast trials, so the purchase was hopeful. Trying to re-create the upset from the 1918 Derby seemed a bit desperate, though, and Frogtown came in second to last.

Meanwhile, McDaniel was unsurprised that Frogtown lost the Derby. "[Frogtown] just didn't have class enough for that kind of race," he wrote later. He found what he thought would be a more suitable race for him in New York, but there was some confusion over which jockey would ride the horse. He and Kilmer disagreed over how to handle the situation, and Kilmer, McDaniel wrote, "flew off the handle, declared it would be better not to start the colt, and that he would go home and not wait for the race." Finally, after a lot of arguing and intervention from other owners, Kilmer hired the jockey McDaniel originally wanted, and bet $5,000 on Frogtown, a way of showing public confidence in horse, trainer, and rider. "Frogtown won handily enough and Kilmer won his bet," McDaniel wrote. "It would have been too bad to let the chance slip by, but I never remember having so much trouble in smoothing matters out. It was harder work than Frogtown had to do to win."

The Frogtown kerfuffle, which included McDaniel appealing to others for help, bickering with Kilmer, and then finally having the horse succeed, was how the owner-trainer relationship went that season. Everything seemed debatable, from the number of trainers to which horses would run which races, and as Kilmer became self-assured in the world of thoroughbred racing, he second-guessed McDaniel oftener. Kilmer even told people that he had "made" Henry McDaniel. Their original understanding was shifting, straining under the burden of both men's strengthening confidence.

Exterminator kept racing to prepare for the Kentucky Handicap. He lost one race at a mile, which appeared to be the jockey's fault: he kept him under "choking restraint" too long, which exhausts a horse, because he's fighting the jockey. It looked like he might have made the mistake because he wanted Exterminator to win, but not by too much, so he wouldn't get huge weight penalties the next time. But if that was the plan, it didn't work. Exterminator did win his next race, which was against much slower horses, carrying an enormous 134 pounds.

McDaniel's overall plan also failed. Exterminator lost the Kentucky Handicap to Midway, a horse he had beaten earlier. Their stretch duel gave the audience reason to shout, but Exterminator could not pull ahead. He came third, just off the winning pace. McDaniel blamed himself, not the weight. He felt like Exterminator would have won if he "had had the gumption to have got a good strong rider for him." Jack Morys, he said, was just not enough jockey. Typically, trainers were more likely to look at the weights, or the other horses, or the footing, or the start, when they wanted to account for a loss. McDaniel didn't even blame Morys, who had turned in the bad ride. Instead, he blamed himself for assigning Morys a job he was not able to do.

It seemed like Kilmer blamed McDaniel, too.

The largest crowd of the year was expected for the Suburban, at Belmont. Exterminator, the favorite with bettors, would carry a fairly heavy 128 pounds. McDaniel was pleased with how he was working and thought Exterminator was ready for the race. One *Daily Racing Form* reporter was a little more worried, especially seeing what had happened in the Kentucky Handicap, when Exterminator also had to carry a lot of weight. "He is a fine race horse; fast, a sturdy weight carrier and as game as they make them. But he is set a tremendous task here, and it may be doubtful if he is equal to its exactions." That turned out to be the case when Corn

Tassel, who was carrying twenty fewer pounds than Exterminator, won. After he lost yet another race, McDaniel gave him a rest.

Exterminator had been in active training since August 1918. He was winding down, struggling to carry the heavy weight handicappers assigned him. He had had some stupendous wins, but the price for those was doled out in the lead bars slid into his saddle pad before every race.

The release of *Challenge of Chance* was timed to coincide with Willard's boxing match against Jack Dempsey on July 4th. The print of the film that got to New York from Los Angeles arrived in a tangle, so the first New Yorkers to see the movie saw it in a bewildering jumble, a horse race in the middle, what seemed like random fights breaking out, a sudden wedding. In Binghamton, movie prices were 25¢ for a matinee, 35¢ for the 9 P.M. show.

The movie seems to have been lost, but reviews and other articles detail the plot. Willard plays Joe Bates, a ranch foreman who is the kind of man who steps in when he sees horses being abused. He helps Fay, the ingenue lead, played by Arline Pretty, save her string of racehorses, while getting in many fistfights along the way, often with enormous groups of men. The Pottawatomie Giant couldn't quite convince audiences as a romantic lead, so Pretty's character married a good-hearted horse trainer; Willard's character was rewarded, instead, with his own ranch.

Exterminator's role was less complex. He played Silver Moon, Fay's prize racehorse, the champion of the Juarez track. A villain named El Capitan wants to swindle Fay out of Silver Moon and her other horses, but he doesn't count on Bates coming to the rescue. After a huge chase scene with sweeping herds of horses, the good guys win.

Reviewers appreciated Exterminator's appearance. "It is the best horse race that the screen has known. Thousands of race lovers will remember 'The Challenge of Chance' for this feature alone," one read. "Big Scenes," said the poster for *Challenge of Chance*. "A real horse race, a reproduction of an actual big stake race won by the famous Exterminator." Together, he and Willard made an already big movie into a blockbuster.

Unfortunately for Willard, the Toledo fight that the movie was supposed to help promote ended with little Jack Dempsey beating him in a bloody, drawn-out battle. Dempsey became the new heavyweight champion of the world. When Sir Barton, who beat Frogtown and others for the 1919 Kentucky Derby, became famous, one racing-stable agent nicknamed him Dempsey, because he was a giant killer of a horse.

Dissent burbled between Kilmer and McDaniel. Kilmer said that he didn't think McDaniel could get Sun Briar, who had been servicing mares in the breeding shed, to the races before Saratoga in August. McDaniel, however, had instructed Healy to keep Sun Briar's weight down throughout the breeding season and work him only in slow gallops. The stallion looked strong.

But when Sun Briar did come back to racing, Roamer beat him in a short race. Roamer, considered aged at seven, carried sixteen fewer pounds, but McDaniel stood up for Sun Briar: "Sun Briar's race did not take any of the glory away from him in my opinion, though he was beaten," he said. In his next race, though, Sun Briar was beaten again. This time, no rationale was offered for his loss.

Kilmer had more at stake than records. Allowing Sun Briar to come back was a sally to better his reputation, too. "Willis Sharpe Kilmer has displayed admirable sportsmanship in racing Sun Briar after he had been to the stud," wrote John Fitzgerald in the *Morning Telegraph*. "He has the best interest of the American turf at heart."

Postwar Saratoga could let loose. No more knitting and war drives and flourless luncheons. Instead, there were big flashy improvements for the 1919 season. Hoteliers renovated, and one reporter wrote that the bright new lights installed along the city's main street could make New Yorkers forget Broadway. There was a new theater that would show movies and plays all through the August season. A new entrance for racehorses allowed them into the paddock without having to share the main gate with cars.

A high, happy mood prevailed. Knapp, flushed with victory, dismounted from a fast colt named Purchase after a race. "Anybody could have won with that fellow," he said.

"You have proved it," McDaniel teased.

As a robust stallion now, Sun Briar's beauty was awesome. There was never "a better balanced horse than Sun Briar, nigh unto a model horse," wrote Exile. His neck was crested, his carriage majestic. As another writer wrote in the *Daily Racing Form*; he was "a living model for one of J. F. Herring's exaggerated portraits of the extremely bloodlike old English turf champions. No one would ever mistake him for a gelding."

On the other hand, no one would mistake Exterminator for a stallion. He was just as "raw-boned," as ever, as a reporter for the *New York Herald* wrote. "He is 16.2 hands high, and he has the tall, ungainly, gangling form of an equine backwoodsman, with the amiable, affectionate disposition of a family buggy horse . . . He is hollow above the eyes like an old horse, and is such a homely, awkward, dejected looking figure when standing around without anything to do with those long legs of his."

McDaniel nicknamed Exterminator "Chang," after another tall horse he knew called that, who in turn was named for a gentle giant who had toured with P. T. Barnum. The stable help turned that into Shang. Because of that gracious, elderly demeanor, also, he was four in 1919, one of Exterminator's barn nicknames soon became "Old Shang."

In the Delaware Handicap, a horse named Hannibal got close to Sun Briar. Johnny Loftus pushed Exterminator up to Hannibal, making Hannibal run all out before he was ready, a move that exhausted both. Then he went on to catch Sun Briar, who was in turn trying to catch a filly named Fairy Wand. Exterminator, by the end, was galloping the fastest, "pressing" Sun Briar and Fairy Wand, "as if urging on his stable mate," language that indicated Exterminator's jockey had never urged *him* to run as fast as he could. Sun Briar just missed Fairy Wand—"his gallantry or something got the better of him," joked the *Morning's Telegraph*'s John I. Day—and he came in second.

Exterminator came in third. "If horses talked," wrote Day, "one might have heard the honest gelding [Exterminator] saying to the gallant Sun Briar: 'Go on and get Fairy Wand and beat her. Don't leave it for me to do, and I could do it at that . . . Forget your harem manners learned at Sun Briar Court and be a real racehorse once more. I had to come to the front and pull you out of trouble and win the Derby for you last year when you were such a pampered pet they didn't think you could win on that muddy track.'"

"Sun Briar will win," Kilmer boomed, while Sun Briar and Exterminator were being curried to a high shine in the paddock before the Champlain Handicap the following week, "but if he makes any mistakes Exterminator will come along and save the day for us." "Exterminator is the best horse that I ever owned in the opinion of the public," Cal Milam said, as he looked at Exterminator. "He is a great horse today and I am proud to have developed him, and am glad that Mr. Kilmer has been so successful with him." Then he thought for a minute. "Even as great a horse as Exterminator has proved to be, I believe that the best thoroughbred I ever raced was dear old Merrick."

The Saturday attendance for the Champlain was the biggest yet. Trains from all directions funneled in spectators, who climbed out of the cars carrying lunch baskets, and thousands more drove. Towns around Saratoga declared Champlain day a holiday, so middle-class clerks and shopgirls mixed with the rich vacationers in the sunshine.

The horses for the Champlain were off. The crowd shouted when Sun Briar and Exterminator swooped past the judges' stand. Toward the end of the race, both were moving fast and easily. But spectators' eyes were

Sun Briar wins the 1919 Champlain Handicap. Exterminator is second.
(Courtesy of Keeneland-Cook)

glued to Loftus, who sawed and pulled on Exterminator's reins, trying to keep him behind Sun Briar. Knapp gave Sun Briar an extra squeeze, and he rushed into the lead. A horse named Hollister briefly tried to edge Exterminator out for second place, but Exterminator shoved by him, finishing just behind Sun Briar. The race had been speedy; Sun Briar set a new mile-and-a-furlong track record.

The holiday crowd was thrilled with the performance, but careful onlookers saw something else. "A majority of the thousands who saw the race and watched Loftus tugging on Exterminator's reins during the last furlong of the contest are certain he would have won if allowed to do his best all the way," reported the *New York Sun*.

Kilmer gave McDaniel $1,000 for the new record, and Knapp and Loftus $500 each.

At the end of August, Saratoga hosted the Saratoga Cup, the distance-race highlight of the season. The race was charged with history. McDaniel's father had trained horses that won it three times in a row; Harry Bassett's Saratoga Cup was his big victory over Longfellow, the one McDaniel remembered watching as a small child. McDaniel remembered standing on

Sam Hildreth's shoulders that day; today, Hildreth saddled one of Exterminator's rivals, Purchase. James Rowe had been Harry Bassett's jockey, and now he was at Saratoga as the Whitneys' trainer.

Kilmer deliberated for a long time about which jockey would get to ride Exterminator; he finally settled on veteran Andy Schuttinger. Willie Knapp would compete against him, on Purchase. Sun Briar wouldn't run in the Saratoga Cup, because the mile-and-three-quarters distance seemed too long for him.

Rain had fallen for a couple of hours. Owners scratched their horses as they watched the ground grow slippery, and rain continued to sluice down on the three horses left at post time. Wet weather always gladdened Mc-Daniel, because he knew Exterminator liked the going. Cassidy gave the three contenders a "walkup start." Exterminator was in the lead in the beginning, pounding and splashing through a Derby-evocative river of water and mud, his low, extended stride carrying him along.

Knapp, however, knew better than anyone else how to go after Exterminator, and he had a good horse, a year younger, in Purchase. He moved him up to challenge, forcing Exterminator to run as fast as he could, cycling his legs with force, eyes ahead, ears back. "The horses had been "hooked up at hurricane speed," reported W. J. Macbeth. "It was pretty to see them sweep around the far bend for the second time." Once Purchase's head, pushing farther and farther forward with every stride, reached Exterminator's middle, Schuttinger hit Exterminator with his whip, and he surged forward. Purchase stuck with him. Knapp gave Purchase one tap with *his* whip, then as he swung it a second time, it slipped from his rain-wet hand.

The whip landed behind him, turning in the mud. Without it, Purchase faltered. "Purchase hung on gamely against the mud-running fool he had been asked to beat," Macbeth wrote, "but he couldn't do it." "The way that race was run is one of those things I like to forget," Hildreth wrote.

Even with the rain and muck, Exterminator met the track record of 2:58 for a mile and three-quarters, which had stood since 1903. Exterminator looked fine after the race, drenched but alert. Kilmer ran from the stands to congratulate Schuttinger, and trainers and owners raced to congratulate McDaniel. Given the history his father had with the race, McDaniel's win meant a lot to old-timers, and to him. Also, any Exterminator victory seemed good for America these days. "He has more sturdy native strains in his make-up than his rival Purchase, whose sire and dam are both by English horses," wrote one reporter.

Even though Kilmer and McDaniel were at odds, Kilmer worked to make public gestures to the contrary. He had given McDaniel that $1,000 when Sun Briar broke the track record, and also gave him a half share of the Saratoga Cup stake, which amounted to $2,675. "Mr. Kilmer is setting a good example in recognizing that the preparation of a horse is the foundation of success," the *Form* noted, another nod toward Kilmer's growing legitimacy as an owner and racing man.

With the ending of the Saratoga season, Sun Briar had run his last race. "He will always be remembered as a most wonderful race horse," wrote the *Morning Telegraph*'s reporter, in an elegiac article. Sun Briar was finished. It was time for him to sire foals. The unspeakable was finally aired. Sun Briar had had a good season, especially since he had returned from stud service, but at Saratoga in 1919, he was "not nearly as great as . . . his stablemate, Exterminator. This gelding is fifty pounds better than he ever was in his life and there are a host of practical horsemen who firmly believe that he is superior to the more renowned Sun Briar," another reporter wrote.

Kilmer turned his attention back toward Sun Briar Court. One project was having Sun Briar's dam, Sweet Briar, shipped over with a staff of attendants. Her shipboard stall was lined all over with mattresses, and the posts were covered with padded cotton burlap. Healy met her in New York and brought her home to Binghamton in a private car, a venerable dowager, honored at her son's court.

The year 1919 arguably belonged to another horse entirely: Man o' War dazzled Saratoga in a way that even Sun Briar had not. If Exterminator was the faithful warhorse, carrying America through wartime racing and now emerging powerful, the red colt Man o' War symbolized the new feeling in the country after the war, shiny, strong, rich, and fierce. Bred by August Belmont, Samuel Riddle bought him as a yearling in 1918. The next year was his two-year-old season, and he obliterated memories of other juvenile champions. The same day that Exterminator won the Saratoga Cup, Man o' War won the Hopeful Stakes with "ridiculous ease."

Exterminator came when McDaniel called or signaled for him, even if the trainer didn't have any sugar. And McDaniel was equally fond of Exterminator. McDaniel was happy to praise Sun Briar, wrote a reporter in the *New York Herald*, "but somehow the conversation drifts to the chestnut gelding, and then there is enthusiasm in his speech as he tells you that Exterminator is the most honest, generous, admirable horse he ever trained."

"He has never run a poor race when he was in condition," McDaniel told the *Herald* reporter one day, as they stood in the summer shade, under an apple tree in the Saratoga paddock.

Exterminator gave McDaniel a nudge, his long nose gently shoving the trainer in the shoulder.

"He didn't look it," McDaniel said years later, "but he was the healthiest, strongest and happiest horse I ever saw . . . There wasn't a blemish on him when I trained him, and he could do anything any thoroughbred could do . . . He was a truly great horse and, with the exception of Man o' War, I believe he was the best ever foaled in America."

Horse and trainer went to Maryland. Exterminator lost the Harford there, even though it was raining. He seemed to lack his usual "dash," disappointing local fans who wanted to see a repeat of the Saratoga Cup. But then he won the Republic Handicap, getting his revenge on a horse named Cudgel for beating him in the Merchants' and Citizens', back in Saratoga. Those two went back and forth; Cudgel won the Havre de Grace Handicap, beating both Exterminator and Sir Barton, who banged into Exterminator at the end. Knapp filed a complaint, but it came to nothing. Knapp and Exterminator won their next race easily and came in second in the one after that.

Maryland gamblers passed around the rumor that a fix was in on the World Series, and that it had something to do with someone the local racing world knew well, Havre de Grace and Redstone stable owner gangster Arnold Rothstein, "the Man Uptown" or "the Big Bankroll."

Yet another rumor went around the New York tracks: that McDaniel would train the horses of Robert Livingston Gerry. Unlike Kilmer, the Gerrys were genteel. Gerry, younger than McDaniel, was a patrician financier. His wife was Cornelia Averell Harriman, a daughter of railroad magnate E. H. Harriman, and the first dinner dance they gave was at the posh Sherry-Netherland hotel in New York. The guest list included Belmonts, Vanderbilts, Whitneys, and Iselins. Guests received favors: silver pincushions, leather card cases, canes, and Japanese fans. Cornelia Gerry was an expert rider and coach driver, and the couple had been the underbidders of Man o' War, whom Belmont had told Gerry about. (The story ran that the Gerrys wanted to buy him for foxhunting.)

The Gerrys' trainer had recently died. They wanted to improve their racing stable, and McDaniel was one way to do it. They had the resources to bid on costly horses and would probably be far easier to work for, not bragging that they had "made" McDaniel, or second-guessing him. At the same time, Gerry's stable was much smaller and far less accomplished. McDaniel would be starting over.

On October 7, McDaniel signed a contract that would change the pattern of current racing, his life, and Exterminator's. For the 1920 season, he would train Gerry's horses.

McDaniel and Exterminator went to Latonia next, to recapture the Latonia Cup, but Exterminator lost. After that, they headed back to Bowie in November. In Maryland, racing was just as popular as it had been in Saratoga. There were so many people at Pimlico the day of the Bowie Handicap that spectators could hardly move, even in the infield.

The 1919 Bowie was one of the worst races Exterminator had ever run. He was so far back that McDaniel "thought he had been lost or stolen during the journey," wrote Vreeland. "He was slower than the Senators in Washington signing the Peace Treaty."

Both McDaniel and Exterminator redeemed themselves, though, in the inaugural Pimlico Cup, which Exterminator won in the rain so handily that the race was more a "procession rather than a contest." Maybe he had been ill during the Bowie, or maybe the Pimlico competition suited him better. Vreeland pronounced him transformed. "He had all the pep of a Bolshevik when informed where the Czar's diamonds were hidden," he wrote. "His coat in the Bowie was as dry and crusty as a handout from a miser's door. He looked like a forlorn hope out of a job. But yesterday, some change! His coat glistened like a new $10 goldpiece just from the mint."

A shiny gold piece: It was a good end to the season.

McDaniel and Exterminator headed back to Binghamton. It would be their last trip together. McDaniel would see Exterminator home safe and turn him over to Kilmer and Healy. Then he would sever his connection with Sun Briar Court.

McDaniel told reporters that Exterminator was the most honest and admirable horse he ever trained. "I never had a horse in my charge that I was as fond of as Exterminator, and I hate to give him up," he said.

But he did.

Racing had lost horsemen—and horses—in the war, but it had also gained a foothold. Resplendent with the borrowed glory of the cavalry—Pershing parading through Paris on Kidron—racing, rousing and alluring, was the perfect sport for a newly moneyed society.

Exterminator, in some respects, was an unlikely representative of the flashy, exciting time. "Exterminator is no oil painting, but when at his best is a thorough workman," wrote Exile. Diligent, homely, methodical, Exterminator was less showy than Sun Briar or Man o' War. He reminded people more of uncomplaining old-time distance runners than of the dashing new crop of winners to which he actually belonged. But his accomplishments and personality intrigued new race fans as well as old-timers.

"The gaunt and angular gelding is galloping on," Exile continued, "his neck outstretched and his head set for home."

But how could he gallop on without Henry McDaniel?

"The Color of the 1920s"

People loved the little gelding Roamer, whose mile record Sun Briar had beaten. He was an appealing horse, homely and personable, much like Exterminator. "Ungainly in appearance," wrote a *New York Times* reporter, Roamer "developed into a great race horse by a homespun trainer, [and] has a strong hold upon the affections of the man in the street who goes to the races." Roamer was eight years old in the winter of 1919, resting after the season. Then, calamity struck.

First, his owner, Andrew Miller, died of a heart attack on New Year's Eve 1919. Early the next morning, Roamer fell on an icy patch in his paddock and broke his right front leg; he had to be destroyed. Roamer had been Miller's special pet as well as a favorite champion. Their twinned deaths lingered and seemed like they revealed some kind of unearthly connection between men and horses. Roamer's death also left a space for America's favorite stouthearted gelding.

"Now that Roamer is sleeping the long sleep," wrote Vreeland, "Exterminator looms large as his successor in the affection of the racegoing public." Exterminator was fast, long running. He was an American heritage brand of racehorse, an old-fashioned stamina horse. "What we like most about Exterminator is the fact that he is none of your six furlong stars," wrote a turf writer named Daniel. "He is a two-miler—a stayer after the old cup horse type which is becoming extinct." Exterminator was easy to love, the kind of horse who lost enough for him to need fans rooting for him, but was also an exceptional athlete. He was something people wanted to keep from the patriotic war era, like bobbed hair and trench coats, and he reminded them of something valuable about the past. He won races in such familiar style—rushing ahead at the very end—that one journalist called him "Old Reliable." As soon as they saw he was beginning one of those charges, the crowd would stand, stamp their feet, and yell, "Here comes Exterminator!"

Andrew Miller had cherished Roamer, but Kilmer saw Exterminator as a kind of also-ran. Kilmer was busy building Sun Briar's court, buying his relatives and adding to his farm.

Fans turned toward Exterminator. His owner remained less besotted.

Exterminator debuted shakily in 1920. Perhaps he missed McDaniel; Healy's training method differed. For one thing, Exterminator's first race was late, with no warm-up season in Hot Springs. He did not make his initial start until late May, and he came in second.

Racegoers hoped Exterminator would win the Suburban, a big New York race run at Belmont. His jockey, Teddy Rice, wore a green cap that the first Suburban winner's jockey had worn; the cap's owner gave it to Rice because Exterminator seemed like a sure thing, and the once-bright green matched the Kilmer orange, brown, and green silks. The cap was a good-luck charm, the opposite of a jinx. *New-York Tribune* turf writer W. J. Macbeth spent an unpleasant Suburban day at Belmont with what he called a "bedraggled, wet and peevish throng." "The rain transformed the paddock into a swamp," he wrote. "It soaked into the stand through every conceivable crevice. It was all permeating. It could not be dodged no matter where one went . . . The club house was as deserted as a wreck at sea. But the area in front of the grand stand looked like a sinister ocean on which black billows called umbrellas bounded up and down. Here and there the olive drab of a raincoat or the whitish unprotected straw on the head of a venturesome onlooker provided some slight chromatic relief from the sameness of the uninviting vista." In addition, the deteriorating roof let down showers of iron dust and old paint. The concrete floor was awash in a shoe-high "sea of dirty water and muck and slime."

The five Suburban entrants shared the beleaguered mood. They slogged to the post, pokey and joyless. And then Exterminator lost, sliding by Upset—the only horse ever to beat Man o' War—to come in third. "No excuse," chorused onlookers. Some wondered if his loss was a jockey issue—Healy had added Rice late, and he hadn't ridden Exterminator often—but for the most part, they agreed that he had simply run the Suburban too "sedate and careful."

After that outing, though, Exterminator improved. He won the Long Beach Handicap at Jamaica on June 19, and set a record of 1:51 ⅕ for the track on a day so crowded that people pushed past each other to catch glimpses of the race.

Exterminator was the favorite for the June 24 Brooklyn Handicap, but came in fourth. Cirrus, a horse he had beaten the week before, won. Only five days later, Exterminator won the Luke Blackburn Handicap, setting another record while he carried 126 pounds and ran into a "half gale" blowing toward him down the stretch. "It was one of the very best horse races of the season," wrote Macbeth. Four days later, he won the Brookdale. Next, he lost the Frontier Handicap on July 14, and then the Saratoga Handicap to Sir Barton on August 2.

To race this much, Exterminator had to travel all the time. He was what McDaniel called a "suitcase horse" because he was on the road so much. "He spent as much time on the road as a traveling salesman and he didn't miss many stops from Toronto to Tia Juana," said horse shipper John Brady. "He never gave anybody the slightest trouble. All you had to do was to let him alone. He'd walk into a car, look it over, just like a human being, pick out his spot and lie down as much to say: 'Well, I'm settled. Let's go.'"

McDaniel remembered once leaving Baltimore for Louisville with Exterminator. "Any road you take west out of Baltimore runs over the mountains, and there are sharp turns that aren't so easy on the horses. We had five other horses in the car, and when we came to the turns they were thrown up against the sides of the stalls and bumped around, but Exterminator just braced his legs . . . and rode those turns as nice as you please."

As Exterminator, journeymanlike, ran and ran, Man o' War soared. Man o' War was so fast, strong, and dominant that fans began calling for a match race with Sir Barton, Canadian owner J.K.L. Ross's four-year-old speed horse, and Exterminator, the strongest five-year-old. For sure, Man o' War was the best three-year-old out there. Sir Barton was a Triple Crown winner, but the term wasn't commonly used yet. He was a surly, fast horse with the "look of eagles," a phrase horse people use to describe a thoroughbred with a regal presence. (Friendly Exterminator was not a look-of-eagles sort of horse.)

So for each age division—three, four, and five—many people could agree on the fastest racer. But which was the best horse?

Exterminator came in second in the Champlain Handicap, run at Saratoga on August 14. Next, Healy hustled him to Ontario for the Windsor Jockey Club Handicap. Sir Barton was entered, but Bedwell scratched him when the footing was iffy. A week later, still in Canada, Exterminator won the Hendrie Memorial Cup. One turf writer joked that Exterminator wasn't even cooled off from the Hendrie when Healy hurried him back into an express car and shipped him back to Saratoga. Exterminator returned on a Sunday, and the following Tuesday, August 31, Healy saddled him for the Saratoga Cup.

Kilmer criticized Healy often. Mostly, he made the decisions that a trainer likes to make, all the way down to how each horse should be conditioned. Healy obeyed, but like McDaniel before him, he was wearying of Kilmer's interference.

Because it was not age restricted, the Saratoga Cup seemed like the perfect race for Exterminator to meet up with Man o' War and Sir Barton. With all three, the race could "easily be the greatest racing attraction of the year," wrote Vreeland. He knew that it was unlikely, though. "Which one will be the 'Artful Dodger'?" he asked. The *New York Times*'s reporter agreed that the time had come to let Man o' War race opponents other than three-year-olds. He won almost everything against horses his age. "There is nothing to be gained by keeping his record clean through picking spots for him," he wrote. Other owners made a gentleman's agreement to keep their horses out of the Saratoga Cup if it developed into a three-way match race.

It was around this time that Vreeland first used the nickname "Old Bones" for Exterminator. It had previously belonged to a gelding named Raceland, who had died in 1894. Like Exterminator, Raceland was tall and skinny. The nickname stuck. Exterminator became "Old Bones" to railbirds, turf writers, and fans until few remembered that the name originally belonged to a different horse entirely. "Sir Barton and Man o' War had better be on their best behavior or 'old bones' will grab 'em and eat 'em alive," Vreeland wrote. If the two younger horses tired themselves out in an early duel, Exterminator could pass them both with the speed he habitually reserved.

Turf writers nudged the owners. They wanted a match race, and invoked the deserving fans. "The public which has made it possible to hold a month's high-class sport at this point through their generous patronage should be considered," one wrote. The leaders of the Schenectady Lodge of Elks decided flowers might work, and offered a special $500 floral piece in the hopes that would make the race more appealing. Someone asked Healy what Exterminator needed to win the Saratoga Cup—maybe a muddy track? "It will make no difference," he said. "But I would like to see both Sir Barton and Man o' War go in the race."

In the end, though, Riddle decided Man o' War would not run in the Saratoga Cup, even though he was "being 'ridden' and 'goaded' almost to distraction" about it. Riddle wanted to win the Lawrence Realization—a race for three-year-olds—more. He was worried the two races were too close together, and even though people thought he was letting Man o' War off easy, he wanted to win all the three-year-old races rather than tire Man o' War out racing Exterminator and Sir Barton. Then Ross scratched Sir Barton.

Vreeland was having none of it. He said Sir Barton was scratched because it was wet, and Exterminator was the better mud runner. As for Man o' War, he wrote that Riddle's trainer, Louis Feustel, "dodged the issue with Exterminator. It was the one big chance that Man o' War had to prove that he was a cup horse as well as a champion at all other distances . . . in history's pages you will have to read that Man o' War did not win the Cup because his trainer was afraid that if he delayed too long for a car he would miss the glorious chance of beating Hoodwink in the Lawrence Realization. C'r'I'ps, wouldn't that give you a pain!"

And that was exactly what happened. Man o' War *did* beat every other three-year-old in the Lawrence Realization, and Exterminator, for his part, won his second Saratoga Cup. Only one other horse entered—a filly named Cleopatra—but he established a new record for a mile and three-quarters, and a new record for winning two cups in a row, which was exciting. The performance also made people really wish the other two horses had shown up. Exterminator did get those flowers, and the Schenectady Exalted Ruler named him an "equine Elk." Healy, Kilmer, and jockey Charles Fairbrother were all Bills of the Elks. (The greeting from one Elk to another was "Hello, Bill!") The horseshoe of flowers was enormous, the largest and most elaborate that many in Saratoga had ever seen. Kilmer walked underneath it as men in white hats lined the way, gawking.

Racehorses were becoming athletes first—still linked to the cavalry through remount operations, but not as much as they had been. They were less part of daily life. Horse-drawn buggies transitioned into expensive novelties. Studebaker moved from making buggies to making cars. "You can no longer hear the tink-tink of the anvil in the horseshoe shop. The horseshoer quit to run the garage," said C. D. Wilman, a Chicago Studebaker manager. Buying a used car was cheaper than buying a custom-made buggy, and as people moved into the cities, they had less need of the buggy.

McDaniel's boss, R. L. Gerry, once had to pay a fine of $500 because he was driving his brightly colored car so fast that it frightened a team of horses, who pitched their driver into a roadside bank. On just one summer day in Brooklyn in 1920, nine people were hurt on the street by cars; lacerations, a scalp wound, a bicycle messenger was hit and wounded.

Once, a reporter asked McDaniel how he could tell one horse from another. "I don't mean your own horses," said the reporter. "I think if I had some horses I could tell them apart all right. But other men's horses, I mean."

"Why, that's simple," said McDaniel. "They don't look alike."

"They do to me," another reporter said. "Do they look as different to you as people?"

"Certainly," said McDaniel.

Then the first reporter asked if McDaniel could tell one make of car from another.

"No," he said. "They all look alike to me."

So much was changing around McDaniel. Women's right to vote was ratified in August; thoroughbreds were named Suffrage, Voter, and Suffragette. Livery stables morphed into garages, taxicabs were motorized. The new generation of race fans was drawn by beauty and dressed-up excitement but didn't know horses quite as well. They idolized the champions in a new, starstruck way.

Exterminator as a grown gelding. *(Courtesy of Keeneland-Cook)*

What was it like to see Exterminator now? What did it mean to call him homely, especially now that he was in his prime, a full-grown horse? He was clean legged, without blemishes. His neck was long, and as plain as he was, there was something compelling about his head. His eyes were so wide set that he appeared wise, knowing, sure. His white mark gleamed. His shoulders were strong, with the right amount of slope; his withers, the bone at the base of the neck, ran smoothly into his back. It was his hips, more than anything else, that made the name "Old Bones" fit. They were angular and jutted upward. His long, long legs made them seem to stick out more, too.

People appreciated his idiosyncrasies. " 'Tis an axiom of the track that if Exterminator gets within a length of any hoss an eighth from the wire he wins," one reporter wrote. That quality—of seeming to push forward even when another horse surged in front—was what people crowded to see. Many horses falter toward the end of a race; it's exhausting, they're spent, and they want to stop. A horse that kept driving like Exterminator did—eyes ahead, legs eating up the ground in rhythm, ears forward, tail streaming—was something to see, whether he came in first or not. As one *Saratogian* reporter wrote, "On some of his forays Exterminator has been beaten, but his dauntless spirit has never been dismayed."

There were three horses running in the September 15 Autumn Gold Cup, at Belmont, and Exterminator carried 128 pounds; his three-year-old rivals had 98 and 105 pounds up. One of them, Damask, was a Harry Payne

Whitney horse, trained by James Rowe. Jockey Charles Fairbrother made a mistake early on by keeping Exterminator throttled too far back for too long. But then Cleopatra hugged the rail, Damask laid wide, and Fairbrother slid Exterminator between them. Damask and Exterminator ran head-to-head, fighting it out. Two-mile races are more exciting, in some ways, because there's simply more to watch; viewers gaped as the two horses seemed locked to each other. Then Exterminator leaped ahead, so fast that he broke the American speed record for two miles.

The audience thrilled to the battle, the Autumn Gold Cup victory, and Exterminator breaking a record. They whooped and cheered. Even Kilmer was flushed and happy. For ten minutes, he made "profound and sweeping bows." First, he bowed to the camera. Then he climbed up to the stewards' stand to receive his prize cup, and bowed to all the officials. August Belmont shook his hand and congratulated him on owning Exterminator, a moment that must have filled Kilmer with righteous pride. When he clambered down, people gathered around, congratulating him. "I'm all flustered," he said. He spirited the cup away, bowing as he went. Vreeland noted that before Prohibition, that gold cup could have been filled with champagne and emptied all afternoon.

Healy was in a more sober mood. The Autumn Gold Cup was his last race as Kilmer's trainer. "Exterminator is a great horse, in my opinion one of the best any man ever trained," he said. "I hate to part with him and am glad to wind up with a victory, particularly a victory of that kind. He ran a really wonderful race."

"Healy isn't sorry," wrote Vincent Treanor, in the *New York City Journal*. "[He] for some time has had no peace of mind and felt that his efforts weren't appreciated."

Besides antagonizing Healy that summer and fall, Kilmer spun through other decisions that he made and then regretted right away. For one, he put Exterminator up for sale. He said he was going to spend a year or two on his yacht. He would give up racing altogether and maintain the breeding farm at Sun Briar Court at a distance. One buyer offered $50,000 for Exterminator, but by then, Kilmer had changed his mind. He would stay in racing. And Exterminator wasn't for sale.

With Healy gone, Kilmer hired Henry McDaniel's brother Will. Henry had always said that Will was the more talented horseman; both men had trained horses who won the American Derby. And Will knew what Henry had been through, how Kilmer's volatility energized and demoralized you by turns. But Kilmer kept Will at arm's length. As Healy had told Treanor, with each trainer, Kilmer became more confident of his own judgment and less convinced he needed to listen to the horsemen he hired.

Exterminator was now one of a very few horses who had won $100,000. He was unique in that he had won that money, for the most part, bit by bit, handicap by handicap, cup by cup. Other high earners, primarily Man o' War, ran only in very rich races, which meant they racked up money much faster. Writers kept calling him things like an "old time 'cup' horse," who ran "the finest race over a two-mile course that has been run in America in many a year." Henry King took this further, positioning Exterminator as a distance prodigy. "With the possible exception of Man o' War there is no horse in America that can beat him over a long distance of ground," he wrote.

That prompted a burning question: *could* Man o' War beat Exterminator at his kind of old-time race?

The Kenilworth Jockey Club in Ontario offered $50,000 and a gold cup for a three-way-match race among Man o' War, Sir Barton, and Exterminator. Matt Winn tried to lure the race back across the border, offering $75,000 and a gold cup.

But Kenilworth Park's leader, Abe Orpen, prevailed. He opened negotiations with the race at one mile and a quarter, a distance that made sense because Man o' War and Sir Barton had the same speed record for it. But that was too short for Exterminator—Sir Barton had beaten him at that distance. Kilmer wanted a mile and a half, the distance of the English Derby. Exterminator would have the time to win in the stretch that way. Kilmer's other demand was for Walter Vosburgh, a handicapper who gave older horses less weight. In Canada, Exterminator would carry the same weight as the other two, but Kilmer hoped Vosburgh would allow Exterminator to carry less. Both Sir Barton's and Man o' War's handlers agreed that would not work. They wanted weight for age, meaning Exterminator, the oldest, would carry the most.

Riddle was not exactly known to be easygoing, but Kilmer outdid him. He had produced too many sticking points, and Orpen had a marquee event as long as he had Man o' War. The other two owners shook on it.

Kilmer felt slighted. Later, he told a *Telegraph* reporter that he'd thought from the beginning that it was to be a three-horse race. He had made those propositions, yes, but said he had no opportunity to negotiate. He said he would have suggested that the purse should go to a hospital, and that he was down in Remlik, Virginia, when the other two met at Havre de Grace. He gave his telegrams with Orpen to the *Telegraph* to publish. In them, Orpen asked for his conditions, and Kilmer outlined his desire for one and a half miles and apologized for his late reply—he had been cruising on his yacht.

Some turf writers complained. "There can be no genuine championship race between the matured horses of the current season that does not let Exterminator in," wrote O'Neil Sevier. A *Chicago Daily Tribune* reporter wrote that the match race "lacks only the presence of Exterminator . . . to make it truly an American championship." But many also believed that Kilmer, as always, simply wanted it all: he wanted Exterminator begged to run, and he wanted Exterminator set up to win. When he couldn't have that, he refused. Years later, examining Kilmer's actions, Salvator wrote that "Mr. Kilmer and not Mr. Riddle was the owner that 'took to the woods.'" Like many things concerning Kilmer, the truth seemed more complex.

In the end, the debate didn't matter. Kilmer and Exterminator were out.

Exterminator won two races in the ten days before Man o' War and Sir Barton's match race. When "the Race of the Century" finally took place, Man o' War beat Sir Barton easily, which just made Winn long to see Man o' War and Exterminator race even more. He offered Riddle and Kilmer $50,000 for another match. It could have been a good time to ask Riddle, because with one more rich purse, he could make Man o' War the highest money earner in the world before he retired.

"I am considering the offer from Kentucky," Riddle, standing next to a parrot in a golden cage, told reporters, "but as I have not heard from Mr. Kilmer direct I cannot say as yet whether anything will come of it. You know how long it took to arrange the race between Man o' War and Sir Barton, and it may not be possible for us to get together on this new proposition before winter arrives. On the other hand, everything may go smoothly and the race may come off this fall." He touched the parrot's cage. "Come on, Man o' War; Come on, Man o' War," the parrot said.

Exterminator, meanwhile, chewed hay in a big box stall at Pimlico, and Will McDaniel told reporters he had not heard anything about any match race.

The next day, Riddle showed reporters the telegram from Jockey Club cofounder James Keene, offering the $50,000 match race with Exterminator. Before his gathered audience, he dictated a telegram to his stenographer. In it, he thanked Keene but said Man o' War would not race again. "You may state positively that the horse will remain in strict seclusion," Riddle said, "this is flat and final: even my dearest friends will not be allowed to see him, so any persons who may go to the trouble and inconvenience to try to see the horse are wasting their time."

Man o' War and Exterminator would never meet.

In 1922, O'Neil Sevier wrote that "the fact that Man o' War did not meet and beat Exterminator before he retired left a not unreasonable doubt in the minds of discriminating students of racing as to whether he was really the champion distance runner of his time." Because the race was supposed to be a distance race, which was more Exterminator's specialty than

Man o' War's, it seemed to Sevier that Man o' War would not have "lost caste" if Exterminator won.

Years later, Salvator wrote that "perhaps no greater nonsense was ever written or printed than the statement that Man o' War was 'hastily retired to the stud' in order to avoid the issue with Exterminator . . . Could any man in his senses see [Exterminator] giving Man o' War 6 lbs and a beating?"

The strength of these convictions characterize the Man o' War–Exterminator fantasy race debate. Ruminating about what that race could have been has provided plenty of lively conversation. Both horses meant a tremendous amount to the era. As the turf writer David Alexander wrote, "The color of the 1920s was the chestnut shade of Man o' War and Exterminator."

Away from Kilmer, McDaniel enjoyed limited success as Gerry's trainer. Gerry's stable was unprepossessing, and his chances for competition were "limited." Maybe he had longed for peace and autonomy, but Gerry's stable may have been a bridge too far. Another owner, Kingsley Macomber, asked McDaniel to train his horses. Macomber, a millionaire who led explorations in Africa, owned Exterminator's old Derby rival, War Cloud.

At first, Gerry didn't want McDaniel to leave. Perhaps another year would turn their joint fortunes around. Eventually, though, Gerry said he would release him from his contract. McDaniel hurried to tell Macomber he would take the job, but Macomber had sailed for France; he planned to race there. McDaniel briefly considered the offer but decided he didn't want to move abroad. He was still stuck.

The Macomber option seemed to make McDaniel recognize that being Gerry's trainer wasn't working. He needed another change.

At Pimlico, as the season wound down, Exterminator was entered in the Bowie Handicap along with Man o' War's half brother, August Belmont's

Mad Hatter. "The Kilmer crack is awfully good," wrote Bert Collyer before the race. But Exterminator, trapped in a pocket near the end, never got to stretch out in his best ground-covering way, and Mad Hatter won. After the Bowie, Kilmer switched jockeys, from Fairbrother to Buddy Ensor. Ensor avenged the Bowie loss when Exterminator beat Mad Hatter and Boniface in the Pimlico Cup. Exterminator also clipped twenty seconds off the track record, which was also his, for two and a quarter miles.

In the window of the *Press* building in downtown Binghamton, Kilmer placed two trophies. People trooped by to look at them. The George Hendrie Memorial Cup, from Windsor, was a rococo item with three silver horses on it—two, mounted, on the base, and one saddled but unridden on the top. The Saratoga Cup, more genteel, was rounded and striated, with two handles, patterned sides, and a finial on top.

Racing kept expanding, and all financial and attendance records were broken at Saratoga. Kilmer's other horses had not done very well; for the 1920 season, he'd had "a one-horse stable." Exterminator had won more money than any other gelding and had stood up during the remarkably trying season. "With the mighty Man o' War setting the turf world ablaze with his marvelous achievements, there appeared remote chance of any other horse to bask in the spotlight of public favor during the racing of 1920," wrote a *Daily Racing Form* reporter. "But the gallant Exterminator was not to be denied his place in the sun, and before he was retired for the winter his praises were sung far and wide."

In the sun and in the shadow of Man o' War, Exterminator made his own way. He had progressed beyond inheriting the role of hardy, beloved Roamer, and he was also something entirely different from Man o' War. Not undefeated but, in the echoing words of racing writers, a soldier, a veteran, a gallant campaigner.

Old Reliable, Old Shang, Old Bones.

In February 1921, the owner and breeder of thoroughbreds E. R. Bradley told Walter Vosburgh how he imagined luck. "My luck has always come in cycles, good and bad. I've had my cycles of bad luck and I've had my cycles of good luck. Lately I've had a cycle of bad luck, but my next cycle may be one of good luck."

This conversation made Vosburgh start thinking about cycles in general. He remembered Henry McDaniel's father and the teetering fortunes he gathered and lost. "I began to meditate upon the word. I began to recall that there are periods when all things seem to go wrong, other times when they are quite the opposite. I remembered when the late Cal [sic] McDaniel's fortunes had fallen so low that his horses were seized by the sheriff: yet in a year or two later he had the strongest stable in the country . . . Certainly, we have had a realization of that in the events of the past five years when the whole world seems to have gone crazy." Racing, as Vosburgh saw, was a kind of metaphor for the current state of affairs. It remained old and new, a touchstone and a harbinger.

Thoroughbred racing grew glitzier. August Belmont spent $600,000 to make over Belmont Park, and Latonia was renovated, too. The physical surroundings of horses running races were festooned with flowers, repainted, shined. A fundamental love for the animals' beauty fueled the American love for racing. "When great beauty of form, perfection of coloring and magnificence of physical development is found in the same horse," wrote a *Daily Racing Form* reporter, "he commands the admiration of those who love the beautiful in nature as well as those whose taste runs to the more material affairs of racing."

The world *had* "gone crazy," as Vosburgh wrote. Racing had returned as big and splashy as in David McDaniel's heyday, and the horses were astonishing, breaking speed and time records, refashioning racing.

In the early spring of 1921, the McDaniel brothers were heading for Maryland, Will with eight Kilmer horses, Henry with fifteen of Gerry's. Trouble developed there with ex-jockey Cal Shilling, who assisted trainer H. G. Bedwell with the Ross stable. Shilling and Henry McDaniel were together, most memorably, when Shilling stabbed owner R. L. Thomas in 1909;

McDaniel nursed Thomas, bleeding in the office, while Shilling was arrested, and McDaniel appeared in court when Thomas prosecuted Shilling in 1910. Shilling claimed the whole incident was self-defense. The only reason he even *had* a knife when Thomas hit him, he said, was that he had just happened to be eating an apple right then. The case was eventually dismissed, and in 1911, Shilling earned more than $60,000 riding (about $1,500,000 today). By 1912, though, Shilling was banned for rough riding.

Bedwell tried to force the Jockey Club into reinstating Shilling. Shilling was an incredible talent, the tutor of Earl Sande. He had been Bedwell's assistant trainer, and Bedwell wanted him to ride Ross's gelding Billy Kelly. But August Belmont had warned Ross that if he ever wanted to race his horses in New York again, he had to fire Bedwell. (Belmont was acting in his capacity as president of the Westchester Racing Association, which operated Belmont Park, but his warning stood for all the big New York tracks.) Maryland officials followed: one steward swore he wouldn't serve if Shilling was allowed to ride, and the clerk of the course said he would not weigh him in with the other jockeys. Even the governor of Maryland got involved. A mob attacked Joseph P. Kennedy, one of the members of the Maryland Racing Commission, over the whole thing. Shilling was dressed to ride when the crowd learned he couldn't. "There's Commissioner Kennedy; he just set down Shilling," someone shouted when Kennedy was leaving the Pimlico stewards' stand. A woman lunged at Kennedy and hit his hat with a folded program. Someone else hit his neck, and yet another attacker pummeled his body. Kennedy ended up with a broken finger and a lot of bruises.

Ultimately, Ross could see that given the Shilling situation—lawsuits, beating racing officials with programs—the future with Bedwell was mired in dissent. He was "tired and sick of the trouble," he said. Ross let Bedwell go in April 1921.

Right away, Ross hired Henry McDaniel, paying him what was reportedly the largest retainer ever for a trainer. Securing McDaniel made all Ross's troubles evaporate. People were happy for Uncle Henry. "The news that McDaniel would take charge of the Ross stable met with hearty approval among horsemen," reported the *New York Times*. With a barn full of fine horses, and a wealthy owner, McDaniel had returned.

Bedwell had one last day with the Ross horses. Ross and Bedwell chatted in the saddling area of Havre de Grace, acting as if nothing had happened. Bedwell seemed jolly, and it was a good day for Ross's horses. "Although his heart must have been heavy, Bedwell was like a youngster every time he saw the Ross silks borne to victory by his pets. He shouted like a schoolboy as his Elemental won . . . [When Billy Kelly won he] leaped with joy," wrote Edward Sparrow in the *Sun*.

McDaniel wasn't much of a leaper, but soon the fast Ross horses—Billy Kelly, Elemental, Boniface—would be his to train and cheer for.

Bedwell's story became a cautionary tale. "Bedwell has nobody but himself to blame for the predicament he now is in," wrote Joe Vila in the *Philadelphia Inquirer*. "He had a fine position at the head of the biggest stable on the Canadian and American turf and was under contract to a wealthy and liberal sportsman. Yet Bedwell failed to see breakers ahead when he attempted to force the stewards of the Jockey Club to reinstate Carroll Shilling."

Bedwell eventually returned to training, but he never again achieved Sir Barton–level glory. Shilling never rode in another race. He started drinking, and in 1948, Maryland police picked him up on a vagrancy charge. In December 1951, he was found dead underneath a van parked outside Belmont Park.

Will McDaniel had Exterminator sharp for the spring. He was strong, his usual almost-too-lean self, and fit. Kilmer set a high goal for Exterminator: earn $200,000 in winnings by the end of the 1921 season. If he did that, he could retire. Exterminator needed to win $79,000 worth of prize money; win, place, or show.

Exterminator started off slowly in New York. He would meet his 1920 Bowie Handicap and Pimlico Cup rival, Mad Hatter, the Sam

Hildreth–trained half brother to Man o' War. Mad Hatter could be danger-
ous. He had the temper of his grandsire, Hastings. Hildreth didn't allow
Mad Hatter's riders to carry whips, because they made him shy, and he
would try to scoot, flailing, in the opposite direction. Being around everyone else's whips couldn't be helped, but the flapping and whistling made
Mad Hatter hard to control, especially in the frantic before-race minutes.

Mad Hatter beat Exterminator in the Kings County Handicap. Exterminator then lost to Blazes in the Excelsior, a race that was delayed
because Mad Hatter and a horse named On Watch kicked each other for
about six minutes.

But Exterminator was able to shake off Mad Hatter and get back to
his best form for the Long Beach Handicap at the Jamaica track on May 21,
a summer-warm day when crowds poured in from the Locust Manor station. Special trains ran to accommodate the crowd. The racing secretary
said the track clocked the most people who had ever come through the turnstiles, and the biggest crowd for the New York tracks that season. Two
hours before the first bugle call, race fans massed in the stands, and even
the steps leading up to them "were packed to choking suffocation."

Exterminator began moving up on Mad Hatter in the backstretch, and
the crowd shouted for him. They stood, stamping their feet and waving.
Right at the stretch turn, he took the lead, and did not yield, even as Earl
Sande urged Mad Hatter on. Mad Hatter pushed Exterminator to run fast
but could not catch him. Watching Exterminator call on that extra engine
he seemed to have delighted the twenty thousand onlookers. "It will be
many a day before a better contest of horses is seen on any racing ground,"
wrote the *Daily Racing Form*'s reporter. "Exterminator's time of 1:50
knocked a second and a fifth off his own Jamaica track record of 1:51 ½
made under 119 pounds last June."

Such performances elevated Exterminator above the fast, strong competitors he faced each new season. Even if they could beat him sometimes, Exterminator's general consistency was new, incredible to see and
understand as his career went on. He had rewritten history. "I believe that
most students of American racing agree that Exterminator is about the best

gelding the American game has developed," wrote O'Neil Sevier. "No longer can there be found among the Eastern trainers a man who will put up an argument for Banquet, Parole, Roamer or Boots."

Sevier was concerned, though, too. Without a big match race with an oversized prize, Exterminator couldn't win the $79,000 Kilmer wanted in a regular season's work, even with all the races he ran.

Also, each win meant the handicappers might be inspired to assign more weight the next time around. Exterminator was a wonder horse, the Big Train, but Kilmer's ambition still seemed ludicrous.

At the Suburban Handicap, on June 4, Exterminator faced Mad Hatter yet again. As starter Cassidy hollered, cursed, and tried to line all the horses up, Mad Hatter kicked out. His flying hoof slammed into Exterminator's right hind leg.

Cassidy, waving and barking commands, then moved Mad Hatter to the far outside, so he couldn't kick any more horses, but it was too late. Exterminator ran, but he was clearly hurt, without his customary ability to rally. At the stretch, the crowd tried a "Now watch Exterminator!" cheer, but it didn't work. He actually fell farther behind as they yelled. "Just what would have been the result if Mad Hatter had not kicked Exterminator while the horses were lined up at the barrier must be placed in the column of the unsolved problems of the turf," wrote Vreeland.

Two weeks later, Exterminator came in third in his next race, the Brooklyn Handicap, to Grey Lag and John P. Grier, but seemed recovered from Mad Hatter's kick. "Old whalebone and steel Exterminator," wrote one reporter. Will McDaniel shipped Exterminator to Kentucky.

Bert Collyer liked Exterminator for the Independence Handicap at Latonia. "Weight don't bother him, and all he needs is a 'cook' to hold the reins tight," he wrote. "Just slap what you can afford to lose right smack on his nose and don't worry." He was right. "Exterminator, of Course," was the

Daily Racing Form headline. Exterminator drew the largest crowd the track had yet seen, even though the day was broiling, and men sweated under their collars and hat brims.

Meanwhile, Will McDaniel couldn't stand working for Kilmer anymore and found another job. A man named Fred Curtis is listed on Exterminator's racing chart for the next two races. He placed third in both. Kilmer's next trainer—Willie Knapp—testified to the small town of racing. He and Exterminator would reunite. Kilmer had always liked Knapp as a jockey, but whether the two could get along now that Knapp was a trainer was anyone's guess. He was certainly less experienced than many others who had trained for Kilmer—he had received his training license one month before—which Kilmer may have found appealing.

At Saratoga, waiters, bellboys, and tourists paused to watch beautiful thoroughbreds parade through town, their knees and hocks wrapped in white cotton bandages. Exterminator arrived with Ross's horses; Henry McDaniel watched out for him during the trip. Then, just as he had in the moments before the 1918 Kentucky Derby, he turned Old Shang over to Knapp. It was another of Vosburgh's cycles.

People were pulling for Knapp. It was Exterminator's job, the *New York Telegraph*'s Dan Lowe wrote, to give Knapp his first win as a trainer. "Willie Knapp has all the qualifications," he wrote. "More power to him." For the Merchants' and Citizens' Handicap on August 27, in which Sun Briar had beat Exterminator two years before, people packed into Saratoga, traveling by car and train. Under jockey Bill Kelsay, Exterminator won in one of his trademark driving rushes.

The victory credited trainer Knapp. Could he and Exterminator make it three Saratoga Cups?

As it turned out, no other horses even entered the Saratoga Cup that year. The "walkover" was still staged, for tradition's sake, and Exterminator still earned money toward the $200,000 Kilmer said he needed to retire. The moment had some pageantry, but was far less exciting than it could

Exterminator winning the Merchants' and Citizens' at Saratoga on August 17, 1921.
Mad Hatter is second. *(Courtesy of Keeneland-Cook)*

have been with another horse, although the crowd clapped the entire time.
"The old fellow took the track alone," reported the *Evening Telegram,* "and
calmly galloped over the route, a beautiful specimen of the American race
horse in his faultless gait and chestnut splendor. As he returned to the stand
where he had already been crowned champion twice before, a huge wave
of applause burst out in recognition of a truly great race horse."

Without another horse to contest him, the victory seemed a little hollow as Exterminator cantered around by himself. Still, it was its own kind
of triumph that no one dared to race Exterminator, the old fellow in all of
his "chestnut splendor."

Kilmer entered Exterminator in the Autumn Gold Cup at Belmont again.
Only one other horse entered, a filly named Bellsolar, whom one reporter
saw as "more or less of a joke and a travesty on the name of thoroughbred
sport," and blamed other owners for ducking out.

The race was predictable: Bill Kelsay tried to hold Exterminator back
for a while, but it was no use.

"That fellow ain't a horse. He's a steam engine," said Bellsolar's jockey
after the race. "The only reason he [Exterminator] was near me was because

Kelsay was choking him to death. When Kelsay gave him his head he bounded away so quickly I thought my mare had broken down." Kilmer cheerily climbed the steward stand and waited for August Belmont to hand over another gold cup. The race may have been put on to encourage distance running, wrote a *New York World* reporter, "but so far it has served only as a means of increasing Mr. Kilmer's collection of trophies."

Kilmer said he would put his newest on his sideboard at his farm in Remlik, Virginia, with the others.

At Aqueduct on the Fourth of July, Arnold Rothstein had someone else enter his horse Sidereal. Rothstein had kept Sidereal's fast workouts secret, so he seemed unimpressive; he had just turned in three out-of-the-money races. He went off at 30–1—Exterminator's Derby odds—and Rothstein bet thousands on him. Sidereal won, and Rothstein earned $800,000, the largest payoff in America.

Rothstein didn't just own racehorses; he owned part of a casino in Saratoga, too. It had been converted from a farm called Bonnie Brook, and patrons called it "The Brook." Rothstein paid Saratoga's "boss" Democrat $10,000 for protection, and then he gave $60,000 to the Republicans. Rothstein was careful with his stacks of money. He invited the sports editor Donald Henderson Clarke to ride with him to and from Empire City in Yonkers, and Clarke watched as Rothstein counted rolls of bills worth tens of thousands of dollars. He observed that Rothstein never took him home until after he had gone to the bank. "He knew that the underworld knew that if I were killed," Clarke wrote, "my paper would move heaven and earth to catch and punish the murderer. I never rode with him after that."

August Belmont had warned Rothstein to stay away from the tracks, but one day, the two men ran into each other at the track, and Belmont asked Rothstein why he was there. Rothstein replied that it was a holiday. "Why yes, you ought to know, Mr. Belmont," he said. "It's Rosh Hashanah."

The rest of the season unspooled. Exterminator won the Toronto Autumn Cup, drawing Ontarioans to see him run while carrying a crushing 137 pounds. Next, Knapp took him to Laurel, and he lost a race there in which he carried 35 pounds more than some of the other horses. "No horse can do the impossible," wrote Ray Hegelsen in the *Washington Herald*. "Not even Exterminator. Conceding anywhere from 15 to 35 pounds and stepping a distance of a mile and a half on a track as sloppy as yesterday's comes as close to approximating the impossible as one can imagine offhand." For his next race at Laurel, thousands poured in from Washington and Baltimore. Collyer predicted that the "Big Train" would win, which he did when Jockey Albert Johnson moved him up, Omar Khayyam wrote, "and all was over but the shouting." Next, he went to Lexington, lost, and then came back to Pimlico to run in the Pimlico Cup.

Exterminator, now a public figure, paraded at Pimlico to raise money for the Baltimore County Children's Aid Society. A special rival waited for Exterminator at Pimlico; Henry McDaniel was there with the Ross horses, and entered the stayer Boniface in the Pimlico, too. McDaniel was credited with Exterminator's successes, but Exterminator was also the most formidable opponent to Boniface. He had to wonder what would happen.

The other horses faded away as Exterminator and Boniface headed into the stretch. Both jockeys sat down in the saddles, hunched as low as possible, and the crowd roared. At the finish wire, "the ancient warrior's head [was] in front." Exterminator had won.

A friend tried to comfort McDaniel. "Why, didn't you see?" asked McDaniel. "Exterminator pulled a knife on him."

Exterminator had had a strong 1921. Most incredibly, he seemed unweakened by age, beating much younger horses, and weathering a punishing competition schedule as well as shifts in trainers. He was a real iron horse. As a *New York Times* writer put it, "It seems that seasons may come and seasons may go but Exterminator goes on forever."

8

Iron Horse

In the frigid, dim New York January of 1922, some turf writers took advantage of the lull in the eastern racing schedule and traveled up to Sun Briar Court. Along the straight outdoor track, lined by winter-bare trees, the Susquehanna River sparkled and glittered. One reporter wandered into the warm stables and was surprised when he peered over a stall door and found a mild-mannered, large-eared animal loafing. "Exterminator, seen in his box, is not as attractive as when the bugle arouses his fighting spirit," he wrote. The skinny horse he regarded bore little resemblance to the champion in his imagination, the great race-boldened Exterminator who bucked the conventional wisdom that a seven-year-old racehorse's career should be on the wane.

Exterminator proved an unending surprise. And in that cold January, no one knew that 1922, which the poet Ezra Pound titled Year One of a New Era, would be an astonishing time for the country in general. In *Constellation of Genius: 1922*, his book about the birth of modernism, Kevin Jackson writes that "on all sides, and in every field, there was a frenzy of innovation." The first AM radio station was founded, and Louis Armstrong moved to Chicago. Albert Einstein won the Nobel Prize in Physics. James Joyce published *Ulysses,* and Alfred Hitchcock directed his first feature film.

In Exterminator's own way, he took his place in all this novelty. He was now the first American racehorse to complete a "double triple," which meant he had won two important races—the Saratoga Cup and the Pimlico Cup—an unheard-of three times each. He was considered the greatest distance runner in the country and was poised for greatness or cataclysm as he faced his fifth season on the track. Exterminator had forged his own brand of innovation, flummoxing handicappers, racegoers, and turf writers by improving with age. Even though he had much in common with the star geldings of the past, he had far outpaced those old heroes. Now, he stood alone. To borrow the classical diction of the day, when turf writers blamed "old Jupiter Pluvius" for a wet track, Exterminator had become something of a Janus figure. He looked backward, to the surprise Derby win that propelled him to fame, but astoundingly for a seven-year-old, he was still looking toward the future.

The question now was whether Exterminator would remain a specialty celebrity—best gelding, best distance horse—or could he be more? What about greatest racehorse?

He had proved he was anything but typical. "A horse as sound and kind as he is is capable of almost anything," wrote O'Neil Sevier. And in 1922, sports barriers were falling along with other cultural mores. Riding racers had been men only, but now a "real she-flapper," a bobbed-haired dancer who claimed riding would improve her figure, exercised horses at Belmont. Stories about Exterminator shared sports pages with the record breakers Babe Ruth, whose 1921 season ended in his hitting the most home runs in history, and Jack Dempsey, whose Fight of the Century with Georges Carpentier yielded the first million-dollar boxing gate ever tallied. Was Exterminator the equine Dempsey or Ruth?

Kilmer had his own plan to find out, spelled out in dollars rather than fame or record books. He wanted Exterminator's winnings, which were $173,000, to pass the $200,000 mark, and he had another new trainer in place to do it. Willie Knapp had quit.

No one had to ask anymore why a particular trainer left Kilmer. His rages and unreasoning tirades were so familiar that you had to wonder why anyone *would* work for him. The answer, of course, was stabled in his immaculately kept barn. Gene Wayland, who succeeded Knapp, was a decent trainer in his fifties, and Exterminator was the most famous horse he had ever saddled. He was humble and delighted with his charge, his earnest cheer a good foil for Kilmer's irascibility. He couldn't say enough good things about his new situation. "Exterminator is a wonderful horse," he said, "and I scarcely know how to bestow enough praise on the old fellow. He is as frolicsome and as jaunty as any youngster." Wayland particularly appreciated Exterminator's unique calm; he reminded the trainer of a child's pony, the kind who hunted for sugar in your pockets. (McDaniel had carried treats in his coat, and Exterminator nosed newcomers with hope.)

Wayland was entirely "in love" with Exterminator "as all his trainers have been," reported the *Daily Racing Form*. *Form* reporters rarely skipped an opportunity to remind their readers just how many trainers Kilmer cycled through. Another pointed out that "Exterminator is the kind of stout, sound, kind and always willing thoroughbred that would be formidable in a training tyro's hands." The idea that even a rookie could train Exterminator may have diminished Wayland, who had trained a leading filly named Careful, but the trainer was so humble that he probably would have agreed. He felt lucky to train a horse he adored.

On March 15, Exterminator led a midnight procession of seventeen Kilmer horses to board a train bound for Maryland's Havre de Grace racetrack. Guests at Binghamton's Alfred Hotel and hundreds of locals lined the streets to watch. If Exterminator's renown was growing in the racing world, Binghamtonians already knew him as their hero, and Kilmer, with an impresario's sense of production, made even the night his racehorses loaded on a train worth staying up for.

Eddie Campbell, Exterminator's exercise rider, led the parade through town to the Lackawanna freight station astride a white pony. The other horses trailed behind, their legs swathed in shipping bandages, metal-shod feet sounding a tattoo on the pavement. Campbell shuttled the horses up the plank to the platform and into their accommodations—rolled hay and a freshly bedded stall. Fourteen Kilmer employees would make the trip, including a private farrier. "Binghamton is just right. I like it," jockey Albert Johnson graciously told the gathering, as he fussed over Exterminator. Finally, the white pony was loaded. A kitten, stashed aboard to keep Exterminator company on the long ride, meowed from inside his stall. Exterminator eyed the carrots waiting for him, and the train chugged south.

The attention only ramped up when Exterminator arrived at Havre de Grace, Maryland, a sleepy town about forty miles from Baltimore, on the banks of the Susquehanna. Maryland's Pimlico and Laurel tracks primarily drew fans from D.C. and Baltimore, but "the Graw," as northerners called the track, often brought spectators from Philadelphia, too. An iron grandstand seating six thousand overlooked the homestretch.

One of the best sights at Havre de Grace was Dr. and Mrs. Tubbs exercising their horses. Dr. Tubbs was a local veterinarian, and his wife was the stable's "exercise boy." She rode sidesaddle, in a full riding habit. She "would be the jockey if women were given all the privileges they seek," reported the *Morning Telegraph,* especially since she had no trouble controlling her "bad acting mare that runs away any time they put a boy on his back."

The track at Havre de Grace provided a perfect gathering place for bootleggers, middlemen, and customers. One supplier had contraband delivered by air. Prohibition agents, learning that a plane regularly hovered over the track, believed that the "ether ship" had something to do with reports of a man entertaining what seemed like far too many friends in his two-story house near the track. Inside, they found "one hundred pint-bottles of gin, two cases of Jack Cranton's cocktails, five quart-bottles of

Benedictine cordial, one 10-gallon keg of whiskey and 200 quarts of whiskey bottled in bond."

Other agents, intrigued by the long lines at the lunch stand next door, found twelve and half jars of corn whiskey in a nearby field. One day, the same bootlegger was moving pints when police arrived, but they caught only him, because someone had already told the Havre de Grace racing crowd that "dry" officers were heading that way. "An incident on the way up, according to John M. Barton, agent, added color to the tipping-off suspicion," reported the *Baltimore Sun*. "Their machine was passed near Aberdeen by another containing three men. A little farther on the agents' car was stopped by State police, who told them they were under arrest for speeding. The three men who had passed, the police said, had informed on them."

There was a Prohibition joke about Exterminator: They said the anti-saloon leaguers bet against him, because he was always "in his cups."

Some visitors to Havre de Grace, however, were actually there to watch racing, not buy whiskey. They streamed in to catch a glimpse of Exterminator, lining up to look in his stall as Wayland stood proudly by. They saw more horse than last year. Exterminator had put on about a hundred pounds over the winter, going from a "lean and hungry-looking Cassius" to a more hefty figure.

Johnson, meanwhile, was trying to sweat off his own excess weight before the spring campaign. He likely joined other jockeys swaddling in wool before running, spending hours in saunas, and subsisting on lettuce and water. Exterminator was readier. The off-season spent in steady endurance training had left him fit, with legs "like hickory saplings and thews [muscles] as tough and supple as tire rubber."

Kilmer made an offbeat decision to enter Exterminator in the Harford Stakes, the first stakes race of the season at Havre de Grace. Typically, the race was suited for sprinters, not distance runners like Exterminator. Henry McDaniel now trained Ross's three-time winner Billy Kelly, and when he saw that Exterminator was entered, too, McDaniel confessed that he still liked Exterminator as much as he did the day he bought him. He said he worried his old Chang—he still used the stable name he had given Exterminator—could beat Billy Kelly in the Harford.

On April 15, the pocked track showed remnants of mud from recent rains, but skies stayed blue, and flocks of people turned out, clambering off special opening-day trains from Washington and Baltimore. Ross arrived in a private Pullman car laden with his Montreal friends, planning to see Billy Kelly seize his fourth Harford. Even during Prohibition, the Pullmans offered luxury: white-jacketed porters, baize seats, lamb chops. Instead of alcoholic cocktails, passengers could order from an extensive dessert menu. The "Pullman Special Sundae" included preserved figs, maraschino cherries, chopped nuts, and sweet wafers, and sold for 40¢. Of course, passengers could always add any of their own contraband beverages to orangeade (30¢), Perrier water (30¢), or imported ginger ale (45¢).

The fifteen-thousand-person crowd proved a little too big for the Graw; it was hard to move around and the betting ring was shoulder to shoulder. Bettors managed to stay jovial, but not without plenty of shoving. Kilmer was there. Wayland boosted Johnson into the saddle and said to let Exterminator run his own race. For his part, Johnson thought that in a sprint like this, if Exterminator finished even close to the winner, it would be a "good workout for the horse."

Most everyone liked Billy Kelly for this short six-furlong race, even with Exterminator in the running; the Harford belonged to the little speed horse. Also, like Exterminator, Billy Kelly was a personable gelding, ewe-necked and undersized, and people appreciated his quirks. Fans cheered for both horses as they paraded to the post for the race, pausing only for no-name Dextrous, wedged in between. The race started clumsily, with the horses, staggered, almost taking off in single file, raggedly running after each other.

Johnson conserved Exterminator's speed, while Billy Kelly pulled ahead of the rest, which brought the crowd to its feet to see what looked like Billy Kelly making history with his fourth win. Then, so deliberately that it looked like the horses were slowing down, Exterminator's nose appeared in front of Billy Kelly's. Next came his head, and then his shoulders. By the time the two horses were before the judges' stand, Exterminator had won.

Exterminator's effort so dominated the field—and his size so dwarfed Billy Kelly's—that reporters likened him to various natural phenomena. He was "a chestnut avalanche" to the *New York Times*'s reporter, and a "mountain" to Omar Khayyam in the *Baltimore Sun*. Johnson explained how the race had felt from the saddle. "Passing the eighth pole, I looked up. I quickly saw that Billy Kelly had the opposition anchored, but in less time than I can tell it I also noted that 'Bones' was closing ground on Kelly with every jump, and at a rate that would soon bring him up to even terms with the Ross gelding. No, I didn't set down to ride. It wasn't necessary. I had an electric dynamo under me that was fairly burning up a wet track. Had I hit 'Bones' again we would never have made the clubhouse turn. A sixteenth out we passed Kelly so fast I could smell the hair singing on his side. Billy Kelly, nor any other horse, could have withstood that charge of Exterminator. Going by the paddock gate I barely recognized Weland [*sic*] standing alongside the fence. His features were spread with a grin, but to me it appeared as though he was chuckling into his own ear. I reached over, took a good, strong hold, deciding to take 'Old Bones' up. The old fellow turned his head ever so slightly, but I could see the white in his eye. Any one— owner, trainer, rider or horse—who has ever looked 'Bones' in the eye when he had his dander up, knows just what to expect. I called upon him with both voice and strength. It was so much wasted effort. As we swung around the clubhouse turn I again caught his eye, and if ever a horse grinned he did right then, as much as to say, 'Well, young fellow, you've had your fun. Guess I'll have mine.' When I finally slowed him down to a canter we had circled the track and were well into the main stretch for the second time. That is one jockey fee I earned. I couldn't balance a spoon of soup for ten days."

Exterminator all but winking, Wayland grinning, Johnson shaking with excitement and sheer exhaustion, and a brilliant victory. The performance was the exact kind of stretch run Exterminator had grown famous for, and every patron, even those who had wanted Billy Kelly to win, thrilled to see him do it. For years, Exterminator had been taught to hang on to his speed until late in the race, but now he had won a sprint against horses trained to unleash their power right away. The " 'lion of the turf,' surprised the spectators at Havre de Grace when he was returned winner," reported the *Daily Racing Form*. "Few believed the champion American Cup horse and long-distance racer would show to advantage at such a short distance as that of the Harford." But he had.

"His quality, long accepted," wrote the *New York World*'s George Daley, "is now raised to the nth power."

Only a week later, McDaniel had to send yet another Ross horse—Boniface again—to face Exterminator. What happened during the Philadelphia Handicap, run on April 22, a week after the Harford, was unclear at the time, and never was entirely sorted out. Some said they saw Johnson try to shoehorn Exterminator into an overly small gap, but others insisted that Turner, Boniface's jockey, crowded Exterminator unlawfully in the last seventy yards. The track stewards lacked enough proof to level a charge of foul play, and gave Boniface the win. So Kilmer sent Exterminator right after Boniface in the Pimlico Spring Handicap two weeks later. The two met on a sloppy track in front of a near-record crowd of sixteen thousand, which was leaning forward and holding their breath to learn whether Exterminator's loss had been a fluke. This time, as Boniface and Exterminator battled in a stretch duel that uncannily resembled the previous one, Exterminator surged in front, his long head safely in front of Boniface's. The crowd, whipped up, gave him "the homage that is the right of kings" as he went to the winner's circle.

This continuing Ross-Kilmer rivalry left McDaniel in an unusual position. The Canadian magnate Ross was a more respected owner, a longer-tenured member of the thoroughbred racing world than Kilmer. His Sir Barton had won the Triple Crown only three years previously. And by now, Kilmer was notorious for his never-ending carousel of trainers. But McDaniel had been the one who brought Kilmer his success. As Kilmer picked up speed, seeming to care less about whom he hired and fired over any given season, McDaniel's early consistency seemed more and more to have helped Exterminator become the steady winner he was. McDaniel knew very well—for Exterminator proved it—that his old favorite could beat the horses he now had in training. He had probably gotten lucky with that bad ride that had served Exterminator up to Boniface. But seeing the self-effacing Wayland admit he had nothing to do with Exterminator's success demonstrated McDaniel's influence more than if Wayland had tried to take credit for Exterminator's greatness. McDaniel was in charge of two of racing's best—Billy Kelly and Boniface—but they couldn't seem to top good old Exterminator.

Exterminator's accomplishments piled up over the spring of 1922. He set a new weight-carrying record of 133 pounds during his Clark Handicap victory at Churchill Downs, defeating a field of eight other horses who carried up to 34 fewer pounds than he did. And he won the Clark, according to the *Thoroughbred Record,* in a "matter of fact manner." Next, he won the Kentucky Handicap, which only one other horse entered. That race was important; Exterminator passed the $200,000 mark in winnings. Only Man o' War, with $249,465, was ahead of him on the American earning charts.

In June, Exterminator headed back east to Aqueduct, far more of a celebrity than he had been when he had left New York only three months earlier. People had lined up to see him at Havre de Grace, but they now packed stands to see him race, sometimes traveling distances just to watch him wear down an opponent in one of his famous stretch runs. Now Kilmer had a new dilemma: few owners wanted to challenge his horse. Most of the entrants bowed out when they saw he was entered in the Bayside. But the crowd did not care. They had come to see Exterminator, and they be-

gan clapping for him the moment he appeared on the track in the parade
to the post. That day, Exterminator ran as if he understood they were cheering for him, and no matter how Johnson pulled, he would not slow down.
It took Johnson an extra half mile after the race was over to control the
horse. Shouts of excitement continued as Johnson, his arms sore from pulling, jogged him lightly back to the judges' stand. Exterminator won the
$1,070 Bayside purse as easily "as John D. Rockefeller earns that amount
from his invested interests," wrote Vreeland. "He's the best yearling I've got
in the barn," teased Wayland.

"Exterminator won the Kentucky Derby of 1918, in that year worth only
$14,700," wrote a reporter in the *New York World,* "but since that day he
has won his way to the hearts of all racegoers by his dependability, his consistency, and his real greatness." Along with the glamour surrounding athletes like Dempsey and Ruth, the allure of the film industry, churning out
silent movies, was in full swing, and the way people responded to Exterminator was not that different from how they looked at Mary Pickford
or Douglas Fairbanks.

Fairbanks played swashbuckling roles like D'Artagnan (the fourth Mus-
keteer) and Robin Hood. Fairbanks was a superhero, fighting villains and
leaping onto parapets on-screen. Off-screen, he lived a thrilling life with
his movie star wife, Mary Pickford. Charlie Chaplin spent the night at Fairbanks's house, but "somewhat regretted the strategy at 6 o'clock this
morning, when he was awakened by Fairbanks hurling pillows at his head."

Readers liked to know that Douglas Fairbanks was just like them—
pillow fights with friends—but also completely different, elevated. His pillow fights were with Charlie Chapin.

That was the idea of celebrity: same but different. Exterminator, with
his unaccountable, unprecedented success and approachable demeanor, embodied the image of a star.

Exterminator beat Mad Hatter in the June 13 Garden City Handicap, even though he was carrying seven more pounds than Mad Hatter, who came in second. It was his fifth consecutive win. The race proved to be nothing more than a glorified "workout," Johnson's reins yanked so tight that the horse won with a kink in his neck. "Exterminator! That's All" ran a *Daily Racing Form* headline.

"My operative thinks that was a fixed race," joked a writer from the *Morning Telegraph*. "His assistants stationed at the head of the stretch caught the old gelding shifting that 135 pounds from his own to Mad Hatter's back as he passed." Heavyweight and fellow Binghamtonian Jack Sharkey, watching the race, said he wished he had a punch like Exterminator's.

Gene Wayland was unsurprised by the easy win. In fact, nothing Exterminator accomplished could astonish his happy, satisfied trainer. "He's an iron horse," Wayland said. "Added weight or a heavy track, conditions that hold other horses back, make no difference to him. He just seems to call on a secret reservoir of strength and does as well as if the conditions were favorable."

Vreeland's waxing became even more fulsome. He wrote as if he were in love. "There's no telling how great Exterminator is at the present time," Vreeland crowed. "He takes them all into camp—those that are on top of the handicap division, those that are in the middle section and the little fellows with scarcely more weight than a 25 cent package of postage stamps. He plays no favorites—he treats them all alike. He makes them acknowledge that he is the champion of champions."

For Vreeland, Exterminator's performance outshone the one horse whose accomplishments hovered over Exterminator's. "Talk about your Man o' War!" he wrote. "Where is the horse that better deserves the distinction of 'wonder horse' than Exterminator? Show me one in the long galaxy of stars that strutted their hour on the turf stage that ever won so many notable races over so many notable courses and at such various distances? And please don't overlook the fact that when Man o' War was in the zenith of his glory that his owner declined to send him against Exterminator in the race for the Saratoga Cup." Vreeland became positively Shakespearean in trying to explain Exterminator's uniqueness. And even two years after Man o' War retired, the question of whether Riddle or Kilmer had blinked at matching up his champions chafed. Vreeland would not let it rest.

Neither would Kilmer. He was formulating one of his plans.

With Boniface, Mad Hatter, and Billy Kelly dispatched, the only horse that posed a threat to Exterminator's domination of the racing scene was far younger, only four years old. Grey Lag wasn't actually gray; he was a chestnut, like Exterminator, but lighter in color. He had some "painted" gray patches on his belly, but he had been named after a breed of gray goose. Harry Sinclair, the horse's owner, was an oil magnate who, by 1924, would wind up in jail as a result of his involvement in the Teapot Dome scandal that shamed the Harding administration. Grey Lag had beaten Exterminator in the Brooklyn Handicap of 1921. Of all the horses racing in 1922, Grey Lag was the only one who actually seemed like he could be better than Exterminator, as if he were just getting started on a Man o' War–like ascent. If Grey Lag defeated him again, Exterminator could fall—no more "right of kings"—and yield to Grey Lag as the rightful crown prince.

The two would meet once again in the Brooklyn Handicap, a mile-and-a-furlong race that was one of the four eastern handicap races—along with the Metropolitan, the Suburban, and the Brighton—that determined which horse was the best in the all-aged division. In 1922, the Brooklyn gained even more import than usual, because during Derby season, many young horses had to be scratched from the classic races because of a coughing epidemic. Now that they had healed, owners pointed them toward Brooklyn to prove themselves.

Track handicapper W. S. Vosburgh did not seem to think that Exterminator's age should grant him a break, and for the Brooklyn, he assigned him 135 pounds to Grey Lag's 126, an enormous gap. After he had watched

Grey Lag win a race, Wayland announced that Exterminator should carry 130 pounds, not 135. He and Kilmer wondered if Exterminator should even race under such unequal burdens. It was a lot of weight and was "a sort of left-handed compliment," Vreeland wrote. "It makes him great, but at the same time it lessens his chance of winning."

Many Brooklyn entrants scratched their horses. With Exterminator *and* Grey Lag running, finishing in the money seemed unlikely, and owners decided to pull their runners rather than enter them simply to see them fall far behind in a two-horse contest. Bettors seemed less concerned about the weights than Exterminator's trainer and owner, and made him the favorite. "Certainly the prospects are excellent for one of the greatest races of the year," wrote a *Daily Racing Form* reporter, "and all New Yorkers who can crowd into the Aqueduct course will be there to see it." People came from Philadelphia and New Orleans. Boys wearing knickers and flat caps and men stood directly inside the track to get as close to the racing as possible. About twenty-two thousand people—too many for Aqueduct—crowded in, elbowing each other, stepping on each other's feet, jockeying to get a glimpse of the horses. They were there to find out if Exterminator could possibly continue doing the impossible.

On Brooklyn day, the wooden stands and walls of Aqueduct were freshly painted, and jewel-green turf filled open spaces. As the horses went to the post, there were ovations for both Exterminator, his mane tightly braided, and Grey Lag, who wore his mane loose and a hood with blinkers over his head. The start was clean, and a small mare named Polly Ann set a fast pace. Grey Lag and Exterminator, both under restraint, let her speed ahead. They were biding their time until the head of the stretch. Then they pulled ahead and began the race all twenty-two thousand people had come to see.

Grey Lag's jockey forced his mount so close to Exterminator that Johnson could not raise his arm to use his whip. The crowd's cheering grew into frantic, out-of-control yelps. The two horses were locked together, pulling farther and farther away from the pack, but neither yielded. John-

Exterminator wins the 1922 Brooklyn Handicap; Grey Lag (in blinkers) is second. *(Courtesy of Keeneland-Cook)*

son gave Exterminator some taps with his whip, and Exterminator flung his tail in the air, often a sign of exhaustion. People gasped. Was he giving up? But Exterminator called on his last bit of strength and swept under the finish line, a scant head before an exhausted Grey Lag.

Carrying far more weight, Exterminator had defeated a horse a little more than half his age. The crowd started cheering the second Exterminator's nose poked in front of Grey Lag's, and instead of slowing down after the finish, their applause increased. People who had spent their lives going to the races could not remember any horse receiving the same kind of reception. Something new was happening. In this furious outpouring of people clapping, stomping, and cheering for his mount, Johnson walked him back to the winner's circle. He gave the horse a pat, and Exterminator flicked his ears back in response. Many saw humanlike qualities in Exterminator at that moment: "He stood like a perfect equine god as though he knew what that tumult meant and that he appreciated it," wrote Vreeland. He "seemed to know he had done something out of the ordinary," agreed Vincent Treanor. "All the while he seemed to be saying: 'Well, I beat him, didn't I?'"

He flung up his head once and then held it high in the air, ears forward, seeming to pose like Douglas Fairbanks for all the clicking, whirring cameras pointed at him. Many said they saw Exterminator bow, as if he were acknowledging his fans. Then he stood perfectly still, surveying the crowd, comfortable with the applause washing over him.

For his part, Johnson doffed his cap, all respect and smiles as he gave the joyful mass its due. Tumbling over one another, onlookers pushed to the finish line, shouting Exterminator's name and cheering, arms outflung as they tried to touch his neck and sides. Finally, Johnson dismounted and a groom flung a blanket over Exterminator. As he was being led down the stretch, back to his stall, fans continued stretching out, their bellies over the rail, fingertips extended, straining to pat him as he passed by.

In their elation, men threw their lightweight straw hats—sennits, leghorns, tuscans, split straws—into the air, where they sailed away on the light wind. "Men on the lawn gave free vent to their joy," wrote Vreeland. "Men, total strangers to each other, whirled one another about in a dance of ecstasy." The vision of 1920s racegoers joining hands and spinning each other like square dancers symbolized Exterminator's extraordinary effect on his fans. His reception after the Brooklyn made more history than the race itself, as if the applause were the most concrete proof of the horse's astonishing popularity. "Seldom if ever before in the history of the turf in this country have the followers of the thoroughbred paid such tumultuous homage to an animal," reported the *New York Times*.

There were other tributes, too. A ginger ale salesman had a case delivered to Exterminator's stall. (One parched racegoer said he wished he had something stronger to toast the victory with.) Another said he thought Exterminator's name was perfect, since "They all look alike after he gets through with 'em."

Guy McGee, a *Chicago Tribune* writer, published a poem called "Old Bones." Here is a verse: "Who is it laughs at years that flow? / Who is it always gets the dough? / Whose only creed is go and go? / Exterminator." And the idea that Exterminator somehow occupied a boundary between person and animal continued along the lines of his "bow" to his audience. As one sportswriter wrote, "In Exterminator beats a heart whose gameness might well be envied by a human."

Beyond the extreme reaction on race day, Exterminator's performance in the Brooklyn Handicap of 1922 cemented the belief that he was a symbol, an idol, emblematic of what an American thoroughbred should be. Even for Vreeland, whose store of superlatives seemed boundless where Exterminator was concerned, the horse's Americanness was special. "Talk about bulldog courage!" he wrote. "Talk about Airedale tenacity! It was all embodied in Exterminator, the greatest American racehorse that ever looked through a bridle—the horse that typifies the American thoroughbred in pedigree, in looks, in stoutness of heart and ability to travel fast and far."

The Brooklyn also revived the idea that despite his humble breeding, Exterminator should be recognized as equal to his European counterparts. Some even wanted Kilmer to make good on his on-again, off-again promise to ship Exterminator abroad, to prove that American thoroughbreds could beat British ones over their long courses. The largest injustice American thoroughbred people saw was that, according to European standards, Exterminator did not even qualify as a thoroughbred, because he was, as the *Thoroughbred Record*'s Charles Brossman wrote, "the old fashioned American . . . rugged, stout hearted and dependable. There is probably no better race horse in the world today than Exterminator, yet American breeders have been advised by the so-called English experts, to quit breeding to mares with blood lines like his dam, Fair Empress. The only thing he lacks is a number and eligibility to be registered in the English Stud Book." Brossman used the elevated response to the Brooklyn to prove his point: "The crowd at the track was enthusiastic. Hats were thrown into the air and the applause was long continued and spontaneous; demonstrating that great achievements on the track are what the people desire and recognize and care but little whether the horse has a number or not." Exterminator symbolized an American meritocracy, as opposed to a more European model in which bloodlines guaranteed inclusion. It wasn't only his athleticism, either. Exterminator's "stout heart"—with its connotations of American-valued effort, stamina, and courage—proved more meaningful than the prim charts of the British stud book.

The explosion of excitement over Exterminator at the end of the Brooklyn Handicap was a distillation of the celebrity machine along with American racing's undying hopefulness, the idea that anything can happen on the track. In 1922, Exterminator embodied that image of possibility and of upended expectations. At seven years old, he was something new. More than Exterminator's shocking 1918 Derby win, the Brooklyn victory rewarded Americans' belief that he could prevail.

"I have been a rider and a trainer for many years," Sunny Jim Fitzsimmons told Vreeland in 1929. "I have watched many races, but I don't think I ever witnessed a race that thrilled me or gave me a greater kick than when Exterminator with 135 pounds beat Grey Lag with 126 and Polly Ann with 103 for the Brooklyn Handicap of 1922."

9

Paper Record

Directly after the Brooklyn, while men retrieved their flung hats and talked about the astonishing, affirming race they'd just seen, Exterminator did something very unusual back in the barn: he refused to eat. Normally, Exterminator was what horsemen call a "good doer"—he would eat no matter what. If a groom tried to give him any kind of medicine capsule, he would find it lying in the bottom of the feed bag, carefully avoided, but every scrap of bran or oat mash would be gone.

Wayland came in. "How is he, Blink?" he asked the foreman.

"He turned his tail to the feed box and won't eat. He never done that before," was the answer. "Boss, he looks like he's all through."

"For the first and the only time since I've known him he refused to eat his supper after that race," Wayland said later. "He was all in—dead on his feet."

Outside the stall, though, celebration reigned. Wayland was beside himself. "Let the race tracks hang up the money, and Exterminator will race any horse in the world at 1¼ miles on an equal basis of weights," he said. Kilmer was back on another let's-race-in-Europe tear, but that did not even seem ridiculous anymore. Nothing did, because Exterminator seemed like a giant in a folktale: unstoppable, with new powers that only increased yearly.

Writing about Exterminator soared to new heights, taxing the descriptive powers of even the most florid turf writers. Exterminator earned a profile in *Vanity Fair,* a magazine usually dedicated to nonequine celebrity. O'Neil Sevier wrote the piece; it was his job to capture how important Exterminator had become. "The career of Exterminator is an American racing epic," he wrote. "His racing glory is the glory of a fixed star, not the ephemeral, meteoric kind of the wonder horse or the horse of the century."

"Behold Exterminator," wrote Peter Burnaugh in the *New York Times,* "quiet, powerful, marching at the head of the parade to the post, standing motionless as he awaits the rise of the barrier. Observe his frictionless stride as, for a furlong or so, he trails the field. And then, as the race progresses, see how he moves on his devastating way. One by one his adversaries quiver and expire as he goes on, indomitable, the epitome of his name." "A bet on Exterminator has come to be as reckoned as sound as an investment in Government bonds," wrote Davis Walsh in a syndicated color piece. "He always runs true to form, his heart is as big as a Burbank cabbage."

A cartoon titled "Exterminator, the Wonder Horse" appeared in many papers. The caption read, "Many folks think Exterminator . . . is an iron horse, taken apart in the evening, high-tensioned motor removed and oiled, guarded throughout the night and bolted together again in the morning. From Exterminator's super-performance on the track, he does seem more than just horse." There was a pen-and-ink picture of Exterminator running, a more sober head study, and then a figure of a smith at an anvil, hammering out some metal, to evoke Exterminator's made-of-steel quality. He was the horse of the hour, the true meaning of horsepower, a somehow industrialized horse, still steeped in the tradition of the past.

He had already gone from being an American soldier to a folk hero. Now he was Paul Bunyan, a freight train, Abraham Lincoln, a fixed star, and a Burbank cabbage.

Within the confines of the sport, handicappers responded to his victories with more weight. He was assigned 138 pounds in the Queens County Handicap, and Wayland didn't send him to the post. It was too much. In June, Exterminator went to Latonia for the Independence Handicap. He was assigned 140 pounds, which was the highest weight ever carried in a Kentucky handicap. Kilmer and Wayland wanted to try; no one could remember any horse in Kentucky carrying 140 pounds for a mile and a half. Joe Estes, the sports editor of the *Lexington Herald,* wrote a poem:

> *There was a camel*
> *Whose back was broke*
> *One sprig of straw*
> *Made the poor beast croak*
> *It's a dang good thing*
> *For them that gamble*
> *Exterminator ain't no camel.*

Exterminator's fans rallied and made him the favorite, but he couldn't win under all of that, and poor Firebrand got very few cheers for winning. "It is just probably that the horse has had a trifle too much of it and would be benefited by a rest," wrote J. L. Dempsey, voicing many people's thoughts.

Wayland gave him a rest, but by late July, Exterminator was back in training, at Saratoga.

The Independence Handicap loss marked the beginning of a turning tide for Exterminator. After the Brooklyn Handicap, there were whispers that maybe this was enough. He was seven years old. He had crossed the $200,000 winnings mark Kilmer had gone after, and he had galloped into legend. So how long did Kilmer plan to make him keep running? people wondered when they saw Exterminator was heading to Saratoga. The Spa had been renovated again, with new clusters of hydrangeas and phlox. There were flowers around a swan-filled lake, and the clubhouse and grandstand shone with new paint. The Saratoga Racing Association named a street Exterminator Avenue.

As Exterminator grew older, he remained unhandsome. Stallions deepen in the chest as they age, neck growing crestier, haunches muscled. Sun Briar, by 1923, was stouter and more regal than ever. Exterminator's legs were still clean and looked overlong, coltish. His shoulders were even slopier these days. The way he moved, unless he was in a full gallop, was still a little ungainly, and did "not impress as possessing co-ordinated excellence," as one reporter wrote. His head, though, was well set, and his too-long neck tapered down into "compact" withers. When you saw his expression, and the wide space between his big eyes, he was appealing and intelligent looking.

Kilmer entered Exterminator in the Saratoga Handicap, an opening-day prep race. Grey Lag would have to carry only 130 pounds to Exterminator's 137. "If Exterminator can carry 137 pounds to victory his performance will outrank the triumphs of every other racehorse in America," wrote Vreeland, keeping the furor alive. But that seemed unlikely.

Early-season crowds gathered to watch the Saratoga Handicap. Men dominated on the lower grounds of the clubhouse, where they wrote down their bets to be given to the bookmakers, called "oralists," signifying that the bets were just between friends, and legal. On the upper verandas, women chatted over lunch. All the tables had been reserved for the season, and the club manager said he could have filled hundreds more. The clubhouse crowd wore diamond pendants and carried silver flasks so they could siphon whiskey into their mineral water and tea. Below, in the grandstand, "enthusiasts balanced themselves on one toe to get a glimpse of another inch of the track in close finishes; here onlookers tumbled off seats or sprawled over one another in their frenzy; here, in short, was a genuine bit of bedlam."

Against the backdrop of diamonds, silver flasks, and bedlam, the handicap horses were off. Exterminator was wild, running with his head in the air, very unlike his usual determined self. He swished his tail and crumpled, finishing last. "Old Poison was a complete physical wreck to what he was early in the year," wrote Vreeland. The crowd was so concerned about Exterminator that Grey Lag got only a "ripple" of applause for coming in first. Watching Exterminator's uncharacteristic floundering and unease, even Kilmer seemed undone. "I probably will not ask him to compete again," he said. "He's done all and more than can be expected of any horse." He admitted that he'd actually felt unsure even sending him into the Saratoga Handicap. He felt obligated, he said, since the Saratoga Association had advertised that Exterminator would be there on opening day. Also, one paper reported, it was "the ambition of his life for Exterminator to win his fourth Saratoga cup, so he clung to the frail chance that the old horse would come through again."

The sight of Exterminator struggling seemed to have unnerved Kilmer. "We had better not start him, Gene, for the Cup," Kilmer told Wayland. "He has won it three times, and three times spells out. You wouldn't want to be the only trainer to start him for the Cup and bring him home beaten, would you? Better not start him.'"

"Exterminator is not as good as he was, I'll admit," Wayland said, "but he possesses so much courage that he will tear the heart out of any horse going one mile and three-quarters. Let us start him and he'll make a record that no other horse in America is ever likely to repeat. If he isn't good enough to win, in my opinion, I won't start him." Kilmer agreed. Exterminator would run in the Saratoga Cup, to be held in four weeks.

No one took Kilmer's anxiety too seriously, given the way he made and unmade decisions. They were pretty sure that the handicap wasn't Exterminator's last race, either. They saw him as exceptionally durable. "Horses like Man o' War and [1922 Derby winner] Morvich seem coddled, done up in cotton, compared with Exterminator," wrote one reporter.

This year's end-of-season Saratoga Cup wouldn't be another walkover. Since Exterminator appeared enervated, trainers saw a reason to enter their own horses; now they had a chance to win. Also, his return for a potential fourth cup would be the biggest thing to happen in the closing week of the Saratoga season. No one would take it easy on Exterminator. "If Exterminator is beaten it will just be another story of a champion that tried to stay too long," wrote Peter Burnaugh.

In the weeks before the cup, Wayland entered him in a prep race, the Merchants' and Citizens' Handicap. The other horses entered seemed slow, and Wayland thought Exterminator could go into the cup with a victory under his belt. On the day of the race, Kilmer walked under the elms and headed toward Exterminator's box. He looked up and was shocked to see Exterminator's name written on the day's entry board. Furious, Kilmer scratched Exterminator and roared for Wayland. Wayland explained: Exterminator would win, it would be a good preparation for the cup, but Kilmer was unhearing, irate. If Exterminator was going to run, he wanted the cup most of all. Adding a race—any race—jeopardized their chances.

Meanwhile, people stopped Kilmer at his hotel to tell him they didn't want to see Exterminator start in the cup. "I don't know just what was their motive," Wayland told Vreeland, "but I believe they wanted to get the horse out of the way in order to make it a sure thing for some other horse . . . I didn't like the way everybody was telling me that Exterminator was going to be beaten in the Cup." In fact, Wayland thought these suggestions were kind of menacing. "Night raiders had been placing sponges in the nostrils of horses during the summer, and I didn't like the looks of things," he told Vreeland.

"Take a chair," Wayland told the foreman, "place it with its back to the door of Exterminator's stall and sit there all night." Another Kilmer employee slept in Exterminator's stall with him, so he spent the night before the cup doubly guarded.

In the morning, all was fine. Exterminator stepped along briskly on his way to the post, well filled out and alert. Kilmer brought a big Binghamton contingent down to watch and a film crew to capture the race. In the end, Sinclair scratched Grey Lag, but Mad Hatter was still in. Wayland told

Johnson that if the race didn't start off too fast, it would be all right to take Exterminator to the front.

The race was on, and Johnson sped right to the front with Exterminator, a move that also wore Mad Hatter out. But then Exterminator, too, seemed tired all of a sudden. He wrung his tail, whirling it in a tight, uncomfortable circle, as he had in the handicap, and the crowd shouted, "That ends Exterminator; he's throwing up his tail!" Johnson closed his legs around "Slim's prominent slats" and hand-rode for all he was worth.

"Go on, Exterminator!" yelled the crowd. He held his lead. Then Mad Hatter caught up. "Mad Hatter has him!" they screamed. Kilmer, watching from the stands, cried as Exterminator, with his body arrow straight, his head out in front, wore Mad Hatter down. "The greatest cup horse of history was laughing himself to death as he breezed through the final sixteenth under triple wraps," wrote W. J. Macbeth.

"I nearly died while the race was being run," Gene Wayland's wife told Vreeland later. "I was more anxious to have Exterminator win the Cup than any other race that he or the other horses in the string might win. Mr. Kilmer had set his heart on it. During the running of the race I jumped up on my seat and kept silently praying for Exterminator's success. I closed my hands so tightly that my nails cut into my flesh. When Mad Hatter challenged in the homestretch and gained inch by inch on Exterminator I thought I'd die. My heart began to beat like a triphammer . . . Johnson did not seem to worry about Exterminator. He had great confidence in him. But when both horses were near the finish and Mad Hatter got up to Exterminator's head I couldn't contain myself any longer but yelled, 'Albert, don't let Mad Hatter beat you!' Albert answered my prayer. Exterminator won. Then I flopped in a heap. I did not fully recover for a long time . . . I was afraid to go to the track, fearful that the excitement would kill me!"

The twenty-five-thousand-person—besides Mrs. Wayland—crowd was wild, applauding and shouting. The president of the track, up high in the stewards' stand, tipped his hat and bowed to Exterminator, and the band struck up "Hail to the Chief." Wilson gave the tearstained Kilmer his fourth Saratoga Cup, and racegoers pressed around him to congratulate him.

The *Thoroughbred Record* printed a poem titled "Exterminator." It was a version of Rudyard Kipling's famous poem "If." A verse:

> *When you have won in sprints and in the dashes*
> *And then repeated on a longer ride;*
> *When you have carried on each year more able*
> *To hold esteem in spite of others' loss,*
> *And yet each night lie down within a stable,*
> *Why man, you've done no better than a hoss!*

After the Saratoga Cup, no one could imagine that Exterminator would need to keep racing. Kilmer's tears, the victory, and the money all seemed to point to a fitting finale. What more could he accomplish? Turf writers and fans alike called for his retirement. There was a real fear that Exterminator would go stale, or embarrass himself. "He has earned his retirement," wrote John Fitzgerald in the *Morning Telegraph*. "He well deserves repose," agreed a *New York Times* reporter.

Vreeland was particularly worried. He had loved watching the Saratoga Cup, but he also wanted Exterminator to be retired. "If he doesn't show a desire to train he ought to be retired for good and all because it would serve no good purpose to have this one time champion humbled in the dust," he wrote.

Vreeland didn't mention that had already happened once.

It was around this time that Wayland first mentioned a new goal Kilmer had. Now that Exterminator had won more than $200,000, he wanted him to win more than Man o' War's $249,465. "It will still be remembered that Mr. Kilmer was desirous of starting Exterminator on the notable special between Man o' War and Sir Barton, but failed to have it framed so that his gelding could be one of the starters," wrote a *Daily Racing Form* reporter. Kilmer had evidently not forgotten. He had conjured up another way to prove that Exterminator was greater than Man o' War—on paper.

In business, in Binghamton, Kilmer liked to win on the record. He had needed the other newspaper out of business, and he had needed Swamp-Root as his own. Beating Man o' War's earnings record would give him a similar victory. "Earnings Second Only to Man o' War," ran one headline.

Kilmer intended to change that.

Kilmer packed Exterminator off to Ontario to win his third successive Toronto Autumn Cup on September 20. Then he sent a telegram to the Hawthorne racetrack in Al Capone's headquarters of Cicero, Illinois. It said that Exterminator was coming.

Chicago, unlike New York, hadn't had racing since 1916, and that was only a thirteen-day meet. Before that, there had been no racing since 1905. Hawthorne, the local track, had been a quartermaster's depot during the war, and the army's lease had just expired. The track's reopening would be Chicagoland's first chance to enjoy horse racing again. Somehow, Kilmer decided that Chicagoans should get to see Exterminator at the same time. He wired the Illinois Jockey Club that he would be happy to have Exterminator shipped down from Toronto for a special race, or even a contest against time, with a pacemaker or two. A cup would be enough of a prize, he said; he did not need the money. Kilmer's message fired up the locals more than the track's opening.

The stable manager reserved the best stall for Exterminator and had the barn whitewashed. On the twenty-second, Kilmer sent a telegram saying Exterminator would leave Toronto at 3:20, and Illinois Central arranged a special car for him. There were last-minute arrangements made to remove the remnants of the army's railroad track from where the racetrack would be. When Exterminator arrived, hundreds of Chicagoans flocked to see him that first afternoon. An assistant trainer named Joe McClennan had gone with him, and he saddled Exterminator and let a rider gallop him slowly around the track. Visitors were struck by how calm Exterminator was and how he accepted "the homage in a regal way such as becomes the reigning king of the thoroughbred world."

The *Daily Racing Form*'s reporter pointed out that these moments—people hurrying from their jobs, lining up to see Exterminator, even for a moment, even when he wasn't racing—are what kept racing going. Horses like Exterminator and Man o' War, he wrote, do "so much for the turf. Such horses become national characters and those who know nothing of the sport still take a lively interest in the performances of such a horse." The Jockey Club heeded local requests and lowered admission so that more people could come see Exterminator. Carpenters worked on the racetrack until noon of the day Exterminator would run; many were so exhausted by the rush of work that they didn't even stay for the races. Kilmer took his private car down, loaded with three boxes' worth of friends.

The plan for opening day was to have three pacemakers go out, ridden by silks-clad jockeys, to parade and race with Exterminator. He would race against the track record for a mile and a quarter. The cup for Kilmer was already made. It was sterling silver and said "Exterminator, Champion of Champions" on one side, and "Presented to Willis Sharpe Kilmer by the Illinois Jockey Club" on the other.

About twenty thousand people went to Hawthorne on opening day, excited and expectant. Some came by train or el, and many in far more cars than anyone had imagined. Roads were at a standstill for a mile leading up to the track. Around two thousand cars were parked on nearby streets, and people who owned vacant lots charged 50¢. "Track builders of the future will have to make due allowance" for cars, warned the *Daily Racing Form*. At the track, flags and banners flapped in the wind, and a hundred-piece band played. A crowd gathered around Exterminator's stall in stable nineteen, craning to see him. A young girl, wearing a silk dress and a lavender jockey cap, stepped through the stands and sold pictures of Exterminator. She ran out by the time she got to the first tier.

Many—including people who had never before been to a horse race—came just to catch a glimpse of Exterminator. The other horses running that day did not impress the visitors very much. "I've been here an hour now . . . and I ain't seen none that can run yet," said one man. "Have to wait for Exterminator, I guess." Local reporters adjusted to the sights of the track; one saw horses with white leg bandages and white blankets, and thought they looked like "Ku Kluxers if there had been a red cross to the costume."

As soon as Exterminator appeared on the track, the crowd started cheering, wild at the sight of him. They stood up. Johnson wheeled Exterminator around, alone; there were no pacemakers, in the end. He was by himself. He broke from the corner pole and started his tail wringing again. Apparently that had turned into a habit, since it didn't actually seem to signify fatigue, sourness, or anything else.

Exterminator didn't appear to be running very fast. Onlookers were confused. Their cheers slowed a bit. Was this it? Then Johnson let go and Exterminator sped on, his long legs raking the track. With that burst, the crowd began to stamp, whistle, and shout again, and they stayed standing and clapping until he returned to the judges' stand. Watching Exterminator move into his high gear was what the crowd wanted to see, and be a part of.

Afterward, Exterminator bowed his neck for a wreath of flowers, and Kilmer accepted the big silver cup. He thought of Exterminator as a "national asset," he said, and the people of Chicago deserved to see him. "The name of Exterminator is a household word," wrote the *Daily Racing Form*'s reporter. "Chicagoans will not forget that [Kilmer] did not merely send a horse here. He sent the best he had, and no man owns better than that best."

The moment in Chicago did not make Exterminator faster or stronger, but the outpouring of emotion and desire that people focused on him differentiated and elevated him anew. "Now, the great running horse is almost as difficult of description as the gentleman," wrote one reporter. "But certain qualities he must have to be truly great. He must have speed to run with the best. He must be able to carry weight. He must have the endurance to go a distance. He must have the courage to hook up with a rival in the stretch, look him in the eye, and go on to win. He must have the intelligence to understand the game and the will to win. He must be sound physically and have the stamina to stand training and race often. He must be

Head shot. *(Courtesy of Keeneland-Cook)*

honest and always do his best. And he must not be temperamental. Exterminator has all these qualities."

New York had disallowed geldings in many of the cup races, which meant Exterminator could not race against some of the younger champions. The Jockey Club Gold Cup, for example, could have pitted him against some of them. This was "obviously unfair," wrote Vreeland. He still didn't believe that rule was made only to encourage owners to breed more thoroughbreds who could then fortify the cavalry. He thought the stewards were just prejudiced against Exterminator, because some owners scratched their horses when he was entered in a race. Stewards wanted more entrants. Besides, he wrote, Saratoga had made an exception to the no-geldings rule so that Exterminator could win that fourth cup; why couldn't other tracks do the same? "When one considers that Exterminator in his five seasons on the turf has beaten all the great racehorses of this country and that even the great Man o' War dodged him in a race for the Saratoga Cup, wouldn't it have been that much better for the stewards of the Jockey Club if they had discriminated in Exterminator's favor in making their ruling against geldings?" Inviting racegoers to a race without Exterminator, as he'd written when this had come up the year before, is "like asking patrons of a theater to go and see Hamlet with the Melancholy Dane missing. Who would give three whoops for Hamlet if Hamlet was on the side lines?"

People seemed to have forgotten that they had been clamoring for Exterminator's retirement only a few months before. Exterminator lost a race at Laurel on October 14 but won another one week later, delighting the biggest crowd of the meeting when he went the last eighth of a mile of the Laurel Handicap in his "usual cyclonic rush," then went back to the scales in "that unconcerned manner for which he is noted."

"There are many who would take exception if one were to say that he is not the greatest of all thoroughbreds bred in this country," wrote a *Thoroughbred Record* reporter.

Kilmer's drive wasn't the only force behind the desire to see Exterminator on top. Many in the public and press seemed to want the same thing. Why did anyone besides Kilmer care?

The answers may have been best put in an unattributed article that was syndicated in many publications, subtitled "Racing Public Roots for 'Old Bones' to Pass 'Red's' $249,465 Mark": "Exterminator, not so much of a turf aristocrat as Man o' War, has worked hard for his winnings during seven strenuous years of campaigning, during which he has dodged no man's horse and has run at all distances and under all conditions."

"If Exterminator were able to express himself at this juncture," wrote another reporter, "he might remark that some guys certainly have it soft. But being a thoroughbred gentleman, there is no danger of Exterminator saying anything of the kind."

Exterminator managed somehow to be both a gentleman *and* an American, a horse with a rugged constitution *and* class. America wanted him to win because he represented the best of them. He may have been owned by a rich man, but Exterminator was their soldier, a horse with a work ethic. "Exterminator never had a chance to win a $75,000 purse like Man o' War did against Sir Barton," reported the *Baltimore Sun*. "He has been plodding away year in and year out since a youngster in 1917."

Also, Exterminator seemed so very close to getting that record. He lacked only $6,749 to equal Man o' War's earnings, and he had enough races left on the 1922 schedule that he should have been all set.

Meanwhile, Henry McDaniel was headed to Tijuana, Mexico, with the Ross horses for the Thanksgiving opening day. Racing at Tijuana was gaining steam, and even eastern horsemen trained their horses cross-country to be a part of the scene there. Tijuana—then sometimes spelled Tia Juana—functioned as a far wilder Saratoga. WHERE EVERYTHING GOES AND WHERE EVERYONE GOES read a local banner.

The track was "in a Mexican village where peons slept beneath their sombreros on dusty streets and stray curs had the starved and humpbacked look of coyotes," wrote David Alexander. As its clubhouse, the racetrack had a casino, and directly outside the racecourse gates, Tijuana lawyers offered bargain divorces. Behind them, a sign for a bordello called the Molino Rojo flickered on and off, all day and all night. Clubs lining Tijuana's main street were called El Caballito, the Klondike, and the Black Cat.

Tijuana was a key destination for people from Los Angeles. On opening day of the races, the plan was for more than a thousand to be on one train that left the city at 8:30 and pulled into San Diego at noon. They would eat at San Diego and then hop on one of the "race track special" trains. The track drew Hollywood stars including Fatty Arbuckle, Tom Mix, Gloria Swanson, Will Rogers, and Charlie Chaplin. Once, a San Diego police officer stopped Chaplin for speeding. There was a plane above carrying a movie friend back to L.A.; Chaplin waved to the pilot, who landed nearby. Chaplin left his car, waved to the police officer, and climbed into the plane.

The border town, with its strong earning potential and warm climate, was a good place to take the solidly talented Ross string. It was a new place for McDaniel's fresh start.

Wayland felt confident that Exterminator could sweep by Man o' War's earnings record with a big enough chunk of the $25,000 purse in his next race: Laurel's Washington Handicap. Crowds swelled; Laurel management ordered extra train cars from Baltimore, D.C., and New York, and extra parking. Even after the opening bugle, lines of cars stretched along the two roads alongside Laurel. "May be the best horse win, and may that be Exterminator," wrote a reporter in the *Daily Racing Form*. "Man o' War's Mark in Danger Today," ran a hopeful *New York Times* headline.

Nothing went Exterminator's way in the Washington, though. The start was delayed, all the horses antsy and knocking into each other. Exterminator couldn't truly begin to settle down and stretch out until the last eighth, and when he did, the crowd yelled, shouting for "Slim." With even another half furlong, he would have won, but he didn't have it. "On he came with the courage of a lion and the speed of a deer, but alas, though going faster than all, it was too late," reported the *Daily Racing Form*.

Oceanic, who did win, was a stablemate of Man o' War. (Also, Oceanic's dam was McGee's daughter, making him Exterminator's "nephew.") His victory charged the situation with irony. Oceanic wasn't impressive overall, so it left a feeling that he had come out of nowhere just to spoil Exterminator's bid. "[The loss] completely changed the result of turf history," wrote Vreeland. "There is not the slightest doubt that if Exterminator had won that race that the year 1922 would have marked his last appearance on the turf . . . He would have been retired to the green pastures of Sun Briar Court to round out his days in a few scampering canters in his paddock."

Vreeland knew Kilmer would never let that happen now. Without that win money, there would be no paddock, no scampering. Kilmer may have teared up during the Saratoga Cup, but those days seemed to have evaporated. Now he was concerned only with beating Man o' War.

Kilmer and Wayland were still somewhat at odds, Kilmer never having gotten over Wayland's entering Exterminator unbidden in the Merchants' and Citizens' Cup. He had shown his lack of faith in his way, by adding another trainer, William Shields. "The Association of Ex-Trainers of Exterminator will get a new member in Eugene Wayland," guessed a reporter in the *Evening Telegram*.

"Jolly Willie" Shields was a "rotund" old-timer who was handling a string of low-rent horses. He had ridden his first race at thirteen. His size was one of his most noticeable features. "One would never think to look at the now corpulent trainer that he once tilted the scales at 85 pounds," wrote one reporter.

Wayland kept working Exterminator, and when he did two miles in fair time, entered him in the Pimlico Cup for another shot at getting the record. It would be a glorious time to do it, since only Exterminator had ever won the recently founded race, and he had done that three times already.

Something wasn't quite right, though. Exterminator seemed ill. Wayland stayed with him day and night, and wouldn't commit to starting him. It was after noon on race day when he gave in. Wayland teared up when he told the secretary of the Maryland Jockey Club that Exterminator could race. "Mr. Riggs, I am sending an ailing horse to the barrier," he said. "Just what is wrong with 'Slim' I am at a loss to know, but I do know that I am making a mistake. In a way he is public property. Being a gelding, he is unfit for anything other than racing. The public demands that he start, but it is going to be against my better judgment and wishes."

That was inauspicious enough, but the gathering scene of another attempt was starting to have a familiar pit-of-the-stomach feel. Pimlico's management had made plans for the enormous crowd that would gather—it turned out to be about thirty-one thousand people—and that huge crowd crossed their fingers. Unfortunately, Exterminator did not face a particularly easy group of competitors: Paul Jones and Captain Alcock were both fast and young. "Old Slim—the whole wide world is pulling for him to stick his snoot in front at the wire today," wrote Bert Collyer. "Here's hoping he wiggles home on the front end. It's a tuff race, however."

Albert Johnson was sick, so Kilmer borrowed a jockey named Johnny Marinelli from trainer Max Hirsch. Marinelli had had a successful meeting and was proud to be rewarded with the chance to ride Exterminator, especially on such an important day. But at the beginning of the race, Marinelli either gave Exterminator his head, or was simply not strong enough to hold him back; Exterminator's height and pull made him hard to hold. Exterminator rushed ahead, galloping fast. That was a mistake. With fast competitors, Marinelli should have tried to keep some speed in reserve for Exterminator's customary late bid.

A year earlier, Johnson had told Peter Burnaugh that Exterminator needed a jockey to "let him know the distance of the race—to keep him in check if the route is long, like the Saratoga Cup, so he won't think it's a sprint race and make him run too soon," an observation that now seemed prophetic. Marinelli had never "let him know" how long this race was. "The old fellow must have been completely bewildered when he discovered that the race wasn't over on the second swing past the grand stand," wrote Burnaugh.

As the horses swept into the backstretch, Paul Jones pulled up along-side Exterminator, who was flagging, then stumbling and running side to side. The crowd gasped. Then they almost seemed to wait, because Exterminator seemed to stop short. Marinelli, sensing something wrong, tried to take control. Captain Alcock pulled in front of both Exterminator and Paul Jones to win. "Men turned away with lumps in their throats," wrote Leonard Collins, recalling that day, "while mist gathered in women's eyes." Wayland slumped by the paddock gate. Henry McDaniel, watching, called it a "bungling ride."

Kilmer went in a different direction. He "was about the maddest man that ever watched a race from the Pimlico clubhouse porch, when Marinelli wore 'Old Bones' out in the first mile of the cup race yesterday," wrote Burnaugh. Kilmer swore Marinelli's ride was the worst he had seen on Exterminator. Then he said no, it was the worst ride he had ever seen in his life. Everyone clapped louder for Exterminator, heading back to the barn in defeat, than they did for Captain Alcock on his way to the winner's circle.

In these days, when they had to watch Exterminator lose, people fell back on remembering his earlier races. He had worked so hard, and so often. Exterminator was becoming an object of sympathy and adulation. The crowd was pulled in two directions: they wanted to see him beat that record, but it was starting to be painful, watching the campaigner "rap-idly ebb" along with his campaign, during which there were so many "try-ing struggles."

Also, while people agreed that Marinelli had done a bad job, there was also the fact that he was asked to ride in the first place. "Summing it all up, it would seem that Exterminator was not treated fairly," wrote the *Daily Racing Form*'s reporter. "In the first place he was not up to such a race . . . Then, on top of that, he was ridden in a manner that would have brought about his defeat if he had been at the top of his form. Marinelli was to blame, but more blame attaches to his being selected when there were many riders of better riding experience over a long route available." Writers skirted around the issue with extensive passive-voice usage, but they blamed Kilmer. Because, as Kilmer himself said, Exterminator had become a "na-tional treasure," he was also anthropomorphized. The notion of him being treated "unfairly" made him sound like a person rather than a horse.

"[Captain Alcock] beat Exterminator but not that Exterminator the American public had learned to love," wrote the *New York Tribune*'s re-porter. It was as if the real horse wasn't even out there, as if Kilmer was sending a shell out over and over again, chasing this record that, as close as it had originally seemed, was getting farther away all the time.

True to form, Kilmer would not back down. He had sworn that he would keep Exterminator racing until Man o' War's record fell, and even after the Pimlico Cup disaster, he never wavered. He seemed to have entirely forgot-ten his conversations before the Saratoga Handicap, the tears he shed at the Saratoga Cup. If anything, he redoubled his will to keep going. He said that both he and Exterminator would "still be found trying" and then sent Exterminator over to nearby Bowie to train for the Bowie Handicap.

Articles about Exterminator's races focused on dollars now, rather than furlongs, pounds, or seconds. Over and over, writers cited Man o' War's $249,465 worth of winnings. Exterminator was only $4,754 short. If he could win the Southern Maryland Handicap, he would get to within $792 of the record. "That could readily be picked up in shares of purses, even should the old fellow never win another race," wrote a wistful *Daily Racing Form* reporter.

Training for the Bowie Handicap, Exterminator wrenched a shoulder. He was out for the season and couldn't try to beat the record anymore. "It would have been better for his reputation if he had remained away from the post [at the Pimlico]," wrote O'Neil Sevier.

The idea that Exterminator could beat Man o' War's earnings record spurred a new round of comparison of the two horses. The juxtaposition that Kilmer insisted upon by focusing so intently on the record seemed to encourage many others to take it on. A writer named Neil Newman started off one conversation by calling Man o' War the greatest racehorse ever seen. A letter from a man named Colin Campbell followed, disagreeing: "I need only mention one, the great 'Exterminator.' I feel sure many would place him, at the end of his wonderful career, ahead of Mr. Riddle's good horse."

Newman responded: "Insofar as the personal equation is concerned I sincerely wish I could honestly believe Exterminator was Man o' War's superior. Like thousands of others I have a softer spot in my heart for Exterminator than any horse that has raced in years. Nothing will please me more than to see Exterminator supplant Man o' War as the leading money winner." Newman understood that Man o' War had earned much of his money because of the match race, and he didn't even care for Man o' War in the first place. Still, he recognized his greatness. "Despite a luke-warm feeling for Man o' War personally and irrespective of the antipathy with which I have always regarded his connections, I am nevertheless forced to admit Man o' War was a superhorse in all that the term implies." Newman *liked* Exterminator more, but he had more respect for Man o' War. That was—and is—a common sentiment; Exterminator was more beloved, Man o' War more revered.

Campbell wrote back that he didn't judge horses only on their times and earnings; he focused on their entire careers. The way he saw it, had

Man o' War raced more, he "might justly be termed the Horse of the Century, but we must take things as they are, and I still maintain EXTERMINATOR has proved himself the greater of the two."

There were rumors that Exterminator might ship out west, where McDaniel had taken Ross's horses, to try the Coffroth Handicap at Tijuana, scheduled for March 1923. The Coffroth was a long race, and suited to him. He could win some money; Exterminator was an agonizing less than $5,000 behind Man o' War's record now, and Wayland said he would pass that record in the 1923 season.

One reporter was at Sun Briar Court when Exterminator was on the road. He stood at his stall, remembered the Saratoga Cup, and cried. "I felt again the tightening of the heart and moisture about my eyes as when I rose to my feet and cheered him home in his heroic win for the fourth time of the Saratoga Cup. Everyone loves and reverences this brave and honest creature, and he will be remembered as long as generous hearts warm to brave and noble deeds." That was where people were comfortable with Exterminator now: the kind of memory of bravery and honesty that could make you cry, a horse to be recalled and honored. Their hearts could afford to be generous as they warmed to his noble deeds, but they also seemed to want something that said he was the best.

Kilmer had vacillated in the past, back at Saratoga before that fourth cup, but now, he seemed hell-bent. He didn't want to tear up and remember Exterminator's great past. He had to have that earnings record. He had to beat Man o' War somehow.

10

"I Could Stand Against the World"

Over the course of his long career, Exterminator's "clean legs" had always been a point of pride. But by 1923, he had developed osselets, a form of fetlock arthritis that is common in older racehorses. Kilmer and Wayland decided to have these pin fired. Pin firing a horse means cauterizing points along his legs with a red-hot pin; the healing process from the resultant blistering is supposed to increase blood flow to the area. Today, many veterinarians believe it is actually the enforced rest after the procedure that helps horses, not the firing itself. "The scene must have bordered on the tragic when it was found that the firing iron would be necessary to restore him," wrote Peter Burnaugh.

For Exterminator, pin firing meant withdrawal from the 1923 Coffroth. He needed to rest. So Wayland moved the finish line. In January 1923, he promised that before midsummer, Exterminator would pass Man o' War's earnings mark. Bowing out of the one-sided contest did not seem to be a choice. Wayland and Kilmer appeared to have mended their rift, to a point. William Shields, who had been hired as a second trainer while Wayland and Kilmer were at odds, never left, but neither did Wayland.

————

Vreeland took a trip from Brooklyn over to Sun Briar Court one snow-covered day in February. As he approached the farm, a shaft of light hit a sign that said THIS IS SUN BRIAR COURT. HOME OF SUN BRIAR, EXTERMINA-TOR, SALLY'S ALLEY. VISITORS WELCOME. Vreeland loved that sign. It made him feel at home. (Kilmer also took out full-page advertisements in racing publications, saying, "Race Men—Race Fans You Are Invited to Visit Sun Briar Court.")

Vreeland watched Exterminator lead the string of younger horses out to gallop around the straw-packed mile course. He was spirited and fast, but still obedient. After his workout, Exterminator's rider said, "Whoa, boy!" and he stopped right away. He knew when he'd reached his own stall, and waited, patient, for his blanket and sugar. He was a little heavier, Vreeland saw. Long, tall, but not as bony. Age-mellowed. An older geld-ing, an "angular but stout hearted chestnut racing machine." Also, there were the osselets, which had left distinctive "bracelets" around his fet-locks.

It seemed cozy and familiar at Sun Briar Court that winter. Wayland and Kilmer appeared to be getting along. Albert Johnson would ride for Kilmer again in 1923. There was something about Johnson's ability to negotiate distances that made Exterminator race with less apparent ef-fort, and in a more relaxed way, as if he understood Johnson's theory about "letting him know" how long a race was. Johnson's Airedale ter-rier, Dick, slept in Exterminator's stall. "Exterminator is the greatest horse that I ever trained, or any other man, I guess," Wayland said.

In March, Wayland started feeling sick. He told friends he wondered if his sudden illness had to do with the long New York winters. As he prepared to take the Kilmer string south to Maryland, he said that once he left Bing-hamton, he might not come back; it was just too cold there for him. But when he got to Havre de Grace, Wayland felt worse, and in early March, he died. The cause was listed as "acute dilation of the heart." He was fifty-two years old, and left behind his widow, who had so vividly described watching the Saratoga Cup.

Ten days later, Kilmer was interviewing prospective trainers at Havre de Grace. He said he would wait until April to decide whom he would hire, so for the time being, "Jolly Willie" Shields would have control of all of the horses. "What trainer would not strive for employment in charge of a racing string with a Sally's Alley and an Exterminator at its head?" asked a *Daily Racing Form* reporter. (Sally's Alley was a fast Kilmer filly; as a two-year-old, she had won the 1922 Futurity in record time.)

Kilmer finally unearthed a trainer named John I. Smith, who had had some minor successes. His goal in life was to have his own farm in Kentucky, which he could afford if things went well with Kilmer. Smith took some of the Kilmer horses to Kentucky. Their names included Sunfey, Sun Magne, Sun Silent, Sunspero, Sun Altos, and Suncar. Kilmer didn't want anyone to miss which horses Sun Briar had sired.

Meanwhile, Henry McDaniel was having a wonderful spring in Tijuana. Celebrities including Jack Dempsey and the silent film stars Harold Lloyd and Norma Talmadge poured in to watch the Coffroth Handicap, the valuable race Kilmer had considered for Exterminator. McDaniel entered two Ross horses in the Coffroth, Feylance and Rebuke. He thought Feylance would be the horse to beat, but Rebuke pulled ahead. "What a triumph it was for that veteran of trainers, Henry McDaniel, the discoverer of Exterminator," reported the *Daily Racing Form*. It was the richest all-age stake in America, winning Ross $29,475. McDaniel was thrilled. The Coffroth was a new, shining accomplishment for the elder-statesman trainer.

Ross was back on his Howard County farm after a trip around the world, and said he'd wait for McDaniel to come back from Tijuana before he made any decisions about which horses would race in Maryland. And Will McDaniel was working with his brother again. It was a comfortable situation for McDaniel, with an owner who respected his opinion and his brother by his side. He was an expert at Tijuana, too, often sought after for his opinion. "No less an authority than Henry McDaniel," one reporter called him.

Meanwhile, Shields trained Exterminator at Havre de Grace, and he looked better with each passing week. Exterminator would be entered in the Harford Handicap, the six-furlong race he had beaten Billy Kelly in the year before. Reporters were heartened when they watched Exterminator training. The extra weight looked good on him, they thought. "The old fellow was on the bit," wrote one reporter, meaning that Exterminator was willing and fast in his workouts.

To get to Man o' War's record now, Exterminator needed to win just one large handicap, or even a few smaller races. He was so close.

Larger-than-life sports figures were crucial in the new age of fame; even as an elder statesman, Exterminator held his own. "Those who have never been to the races must know of Exterminator," reported the *Daily Racing Form,* "as those who know nothing of pugilism know Jack Dempsey. One need not go to the ball park to know Babe Ruth. These big figures of all the sports bring the widest interest." As a *New York Times* reporter wrote, "[Exterminator's] magic name has appeared in the lists, and the 1923 season is on."

The Havre de Grace track was heavy again, just as it had been in 1922. In the morning, crowds began to gather, arriving in cars, in trains, and on foot. Gamblers came from New York. All seemed to anticipate that Exterminator would repeat the Billy Kelly performance. They cheered riotously when he first appeared, but Exterminator, carrying a hefty 132 pounds, couldn't rally and was "forced to bow his head in defeat." Blazes, the winner, carried only 106 pounds.

Lately, crowds clapped more for Exterminator, even when he lost, than they did for the winners. Onlookers agreed that he finished a strong third in the Harford on the pure strength of his "courage" and "class."

Kilmer reloaded and entered Exterminator in another, longer race called the Philadelphia Handicap, which seemed well suited to him. "Listen Baltimore," wrote Bert Collyer on April 21, " 'Old Slim' . . . is my selection for the Philadelphia Handicap . . . The old horse is on his toes and the distance suits him better today . . . Ye'wekkum!"

As soon as Exterminator emerged from the saddling area, the crowd began applauding for him. Hoping they would see him get closer to Man o' War's record, twenty thousand people had come to the track. The horses lined up for the race. Next to Exterminator, a horse named Comic Song plunged and bronco-kicked until his jockey flew off. He pitched down and, hooves paddling the air, wound up almost under Exterminator's belly. "But darn if that Exterminator would even twitch a muscle," the assistant starter said. "He just stood there, contemptuouslike. Then, after a time, he turned his head, looked down, and cocked an eye at Comic Song. Then he carefully stepped over Comic Song without even touching him." The jockey clambered back aboard, and the race was on.

Johnson was ill again, but jockey Linus "Pony" McAtee would not make Marinelli's mistake. He let Exterminator start out front, but McAtee kept him under control so that he wouldn't get too tired. He coursed on. McAtee brought him up around the outside, and when he moved up for one of his typical finishes, everyone stood. McAtee asked Exterminator to move up, and he responded, surging old-style to win by a neck. "The roar that greeted him on his return was by far the greatest ovation tended an equine here in these parts," reported the *Washington Post*. Men flung hats, and the stands shook from stamping. "He is still the big hearted piece of racing machinery that has endeared him to all who go a-racing," wrote the *Daily Racing Form*'s reporter. It was an enormous relief as well as a joy to see him win. He was painfully close to breaking the record, edging closer almost a dollar at a time. "No event in thoroughbred racing will be more pleasing to the great mass of followers of the turf than the breaking of the present American money-winning record by Exterminator," reported the *New York Times*.

Each race now meant far more than another victory for Exterminator. "He is now in an unfinished race that is watched all over this land. That is his race against the record of Man o' War as the greatest money winner of American turf history," wrote a *Daily Racing Form* reporter. He had won $3,850 at Havre de Grace so far. Everyone hoped he would earn the remaining $1,140 in the coming weeks. It was such a small sum. Why did it still seem so far away?

When the management of Havre de Grace realized that Exterminator's next race, the Old Dominion Handicap, would get him within $500 of Man o' War's record, they added $500 to the purse, to try to get him over the line. Because of his performance in the Philadelphia, people thought he could do it. "He came through with his old-time honesty and now there need be no fear of his going back from that form," said the *Daily Racing Form*.

Instead, it was a disaster. Exterminator came in a bare second to a horse named Chickvale, who was carrying about a hundred pounds to his 132. "To say that the defeat of Exterminator was a bitter disappointment to the crowd that cheered him in his heroic failure is stating it mildly," reported the *Daily Racing Form*. People were unimpressed with Chickvale's trainer and Harry Bassett's jockey, James Rowe. They thought it might have been time to let Exterminator win enough to earn his retirement, since Kilmer would not let up.

"Many sportsmen regretted that trainer Jimmy Rowe should have brought the fresh, speedy young Whitney horse on to halt Exterminator's going over the top. The old fellow deserved more consideration," wrote the *Morning Telegraph*'s reporter.

Just let him win, they seemed to be saying. Please.

———

Horses had vanished from everyday life. In 1923, people in Pasadena thought they were being haunted because they heard hoofbeats at night. A group armed themselves and waited for whatever it was; the sound turned out to be made by a man riding a horse. He was a cook and didn't have a car. He was just coming home from work on horseback.

There was a nostalgic renewal of the Pony Express that same year, marred when an officials' car following the riders crashed into an embankment, which seems like a symbol of the futility of trying to combine the two ways of life.

"High tide for the horse," reported Arthur Chapman in a state-of-the-horse-union article for *McClure's* magazine, "was reached in the years between 1914 and 1920. The average number of horses on farms during that six-year period was 21,047,000." By 1927, that number was 15,279,000. Horses were now needed as saddle and pleasure horses, polo ponies and the occasional milk wagon, but not for the cavalry, deliveryman, or streetcar.

One day, Exterminator came in lame from a workout. He couldn't work any longer, and racing was impossible. "Should the old son of McGee and Fair Empress never come to the post again he will still go down in turf history as one of the greatest horses that ever raced in this or any other country," wrote a *Form* reporter, which seemed like an admonition to Kilmer to consider letting Exterminator retire.

After Exterminator was pulled from training, Kilmer did take some sweeping actions, including selling thirteen horses at Belmont for $395,900, a New York record. He said Exterminator could retire at the end of the season, implying that Exterminator would have beaten Man o' War's record by then. Retiring Exterminator now seemed out of the question.

But Exterminator stayed lame. He couldn't run again that spring. Man o' War's record stood fast.

———

In August, most of Kilmer's horses went to Saratoga to race. Exterminator, left behind, moped around Sun Briar Court.

Perhaps remembering how attached Exterminator was to Dick, Albert Johnson's Airedale, and to the white pony who used to lead processions through Binghamton, farm employees bought him a Shetland pony.

Exterminator perked up as soon as the pony arrived. He started crunching carrots again, and his eyes brightened. "He's tickled to death with the pony," his handlers said. They named the new resident Peanuts.

"The pair are inseparable now," a reporter wrote.

By the fall, Exterminator was sound again and training well. Kilmer had been thinking about Tijuana for a while. Late in 1922, he had mentioned the idea of sending Exterminator there for the Coffroth in March 1923, but then Exterminator faltered, and he didn't mention it again. But the idea of sending Exterminator west appealed to him in the same way he said that sending him to Chicago did; he wanted all Americans to see his "iron horse in action." The Tijuana scene was alluring, too, with its glitziness, the over-the-top atmosphere, and the big purses.

The problem was that neither Shields nor Smith seemed up to the challenge. They didn't know Exterminator very well. The past year had had its moments of glory, when people gathered to praise and see Exterminator. But the halting, stammering progress toward beating Man o' War's record was excruciating. Shields couldn't figure out how best to prepare him. But he kept him galloping just the same, first at home, then in Maryland.

There was only one man who could get that earnings record, Kilmer realized. He had broached the subject with him in 1922, but then Exterminator had been so on-again, off-again that the question was moot. In 1923, Kilmer asked McDaniel again. Would he train Exterminator? More important, would he get the old horse to beat Man o' War's record?

There was a lot at stake for McDaniel. He was well installed with the Ross horses. The stable had never reached Sir Barton heights, but training there was an excellent job. He and "Alphabet" Ross got along, and the horses were strong. Not that Kilmer ever did things in a typical fashion, but it was not customary to take on one horse from an outside stable when you were training a perfectly successful string.

But McDaniel's discovery and training of Exterminator remained his most important accomplishment. The two of them were linked, forever. Bringing Exterminator west could fail miserably. If he continued to deteriorate, it would be McDaniel's fault. The very turf writers who had created the Exterminator-McDaniel legend worried now. "If he is brought back he must be brought back to something approaching his former greatness," wrote a *Daily Racing Form* reporter. "It would be better never to make the attempt of having him come back than to have him come back racing among the cheap horses. He has done too much for the turf to suffer the indignity of descending to the selling plater ranks. If ever a horse earned the right to honorable pension and a life of ease to the end of his days it is this same Exterminator."

A horse named Zev, who had also raced in very rich purses including a $100,000 match race with a horse named Papyrus, had passed Man o' War's record already and had won $296,673. (Zev and Exterminator never raced, but Kilmer's strong filly Sally's Alley had beaten him.) There was no way Exterminator could catch Zev's record, so his goal remained the same: beat Man o' War's earnings. It was as if McDaniel were caught in a broken time machine: Exterminator was supposed to beat Man o' War when he had been at the top of his game, even though it was years past.

If the plan failed, McDaniel would be responsible for pushing the old campaigner too far. He would be as culpable as Kilmer. But in the end, it was simple. In 1918, Exterminator had rescued him. Now it was his turn.

He said yes. He would train Exterminator with the goal of besting Man o' War's earnings. "I would be satisfied," he said, "and would consider I had the greatest stable any man ever handled, if I had only two horses, instead of 52. With Billy Kelly and Exterminator, I could stand against the world, and you could have all the other horses in America."

If anyone could do it, it would be Uncle Henry.

McDaniel thought Exterminator had stepped badly in the mud back in his last Graw race, and that the stress of that sprain had caused the osselets. They were nothing serious, he felt, much like Sun Briar's ringbones back in 1918. Kilmer happily told everyone gathered for the Maryland meet that McDaniel would take Exterminator west with the Ross string. Turf writers enjoyed the reunion story: "The man who found Exterminator in the West and saddled him for his first great victory, his triumph in the Kentucky Derby renewal of 1918, is the same who will take Old Bones West in his quest for the world's thoroughbred money-earning record," wrote a reporter in the *Morning Telegraph*. McDaniel said that Exterminator had a better than average chance to train again. "This theory was based on his knowledge of the horse. McDaniel knows Exterminator to be temperamentally and physically right," reported the *Washington Post*.

McDaniel and Exterminator in Tijuana, 1923. (© *San Diego History Center*)

A crowd of horsemen, jockeys, and race fans waved good-bye to Exterminator in Baltimore as he got onto his special car, which was attached behind the fastest cross-country passenger train. The trip took about four days.

Exterminator traveled in his usual relaxed way, but when he got to Tijuana, there was a special ceremony. Mrs. Ulysses Grant (the general's granddaughter-in-law), who was a great fan, decorated Exterminator with a floral horseshoe. A crowd applauded.

Exterminator had come west.

McDaniel took things very easy with Exterminator, and reporters watched them both. He trained slowly, carefully. McDaniel watched Exterminator's legs and felt them for heat. He inspected those osselets. "A horse must have plenty of good, hard flesh worked on his frame by slow work before he is asked for speed," McDaniel had said. "There is an old saying, 'No foot, no horse.' It is equally true to say, 'No flesh, no horse.' A thoroughbred is much like a human athlete, and he can show a careful and observant trainer in many ways when he requires a 'let-up,' when the strain of work is beginning to tell its tale. Easing him off in time has saved many a horse for the future. Perseverance with him when he is getting tired has ruined many a one."

Exterminator did so well under the old, familiar training regimen that McDaniel, with uncharacteristic bravado, said he thought Exterminator was primed for a "triumphant comeback." On Christmas Day, Exterminator paraded before the big crowd present at Tijuana, which gave him the largest ovation a racehorse had ever received. In January 1924, Exterminator felt so strong that he pulled his exercise boy's arms as he did a quick mile in 1:52. "Henry McDaniel will have him fit to run for a king's ransom ere long," reported the *Washington Post*. The crowd liked seeing Exterminator appear sound and stout, "fit and ready after careful training under the watchful eye of Henry McDaniel, who developed the horse for Mr. Kilmer as a three-year-old." By early February, McDaniel said he was "training wonderfully" and ready for his first race back.

"If McDaniel is successful in his efforts to restore the old fellow to soundness he will have done a tremendously big thing for racing," wrote a *Daily Racing Form* reporter. McDaniel had to contend with Kilmer's need to win, and also the country wanting Exterminator to be brought back. On top of that, he had turf writers and cognoscenti wanting him to do it— but only in the right way. If he was ever perceived as pushing Exterminator too far, he could undo their whole storied legacy. He had built everything on being the man who found Exterminator. That alone made him famous for being keen eyed and cautious, a reward for a lifetime of patience and hard work. It was a lot to think about and must have weighed upon him as he watched the old horse run.

McDaniel booked Johnson, who had already ridden Exterminator to victory fourteen times, to ride. "He [McDaniel] also is well pleased with the way Exterminator is going," wrote a *Washington Post* reporter.

The following joke appeared in the *Morning Telegraph*: "Two hopheads were kicking the stem around one night and a discussion of great horses came up. 'Well,' said one of them, yawning, 'Exterminator's my favorite. I'm thinking of buying him and putting him at the head of my stud.'

" 'You must be off your nut,' replied the other. 'Don't you know Exterminator's a gelding?'

" ' 'At's all right,' was the answer. 'I haven't any mares, either.' "

McDaniel wanted to enter Exterminator in a short mile-and-seventy-yard-dash race, just as a kind of warm-up, but owners of the other horses, who were supposed to be some of the strongest in Tijuana, scratched them. One owner said he would be satisfied running for second-place money, but the local jockey club wanted more of a race. They would try again later.

Finally, some owners agreed to race their horses. McDaniel entered Exterminator in another mile-and-seventy-yards race against some local talent. The heart-wrenching losses of 1922 and 1923 were fresh in everyone's mind. That churning feeling was back. Exterminator was in a new place, though, with a new audience, and his old trainer. He seemed ready.

McDaniel gave Johnson a leg up and had him warm Exterminator up on his way to the starting gate. He was sending Exterminator to the post for the first time in five years. This was it. If Exterminator won, he was as good as his word, and their Derby magic had held. If Exterminator lost—or, worse, pulled up lame—then McDaniel had been wrong, and had hurt America's horse for nothing.

Starter Mars Cassidy could see that Exterminator was "on his toes." One of the other horses kicked out, heels flying, and Exterminator edged away from him. "I had no worry with [Exterminator], for he appeared to have an understanding that was almost uncanny," said Cassidy. Exterminator rubbed his nose on the barrier webbing, his signal that it was time to go. No one watched the other horses; all eyes fixed on Exterminator. It was a short race, but there was enough time for Exterminator to win in one of his trademark stretch drives over a horse named Supercargo.

The reaction to the comeback victory was as raucous it had been at the Brooklyn. Hats went in the air. No one could remember a noisier celebration. "The crowd simply went wild," the *Daily Racing Form*'s reporter wrote. "The old fellow has probably never had a greater triumph than today's," added the *New York Times*'s reporter in an article called "Exterminator Wins in Come-Back Race." It was a little race, but an enormous win.

After stopping at the stewards' stand, Exterminator headed back toward the stables, shaking his head with each step, "as if he knew just why the spectators were so jubilant." He had won only $490, but it was an enormous step and a real comeback. The race was a trial for the bigger ones to come, and so far, Exterminator and McDaniel had passed the test. The victory testified to McDaniel's skill. He had brought the old hero back. "It is small wonder that his return to racing means so much," wrote the *Daily Racing Form*'s reporter.

"Horses may come and go," said Cassidy. "There will be runners to top the amount which Exterminator has won, but if I remain a starter for the rest of my life, I know that the greatest thrill I ever had came when I sent

Exterminator away for the first time in the West and for the first time in winter racing."

Then there was a setback. Exterminator was supposed to get a special purse at last—$1,000 to race a local horse named Osprey. But after his morning gallop that day, McDaniel paused. Something was wrong with Exterminator's front left leg. He felt the leg and examined his shoe. It seemed like it was too tight, so McDaniel had the farrier take it off and reset it. That didn't help, though. The track vet said the lameness was not serious, but it was there.

The episode served as a reminder that Exterminator, even trained by McDaniel, was not impervious. "The judges excused Exterminator from the race, which was then declared off. Questioned, McDaniel couldn't say whether the lameness meant that Exterminator would be able to run in the Coffroth handicap or the Tia Juana cup," reported the *Washington Post*. He didn't know yet, and he was not going to make any promises he could not keep.

McDaniel kept training Exterminator. He may really have thought the lameness was just from that faulty left shoe, or he saw something else that showed him that the horse was all right. In fact, he changed his usual way of working with him and let him run as fast as he liked, which shocked reporters. It was the opposite of how McDaniel usually trained, and Exterminator had never been a "workhorse"; that is, he always ran his fastest time in races, not during his workouts. Clockers weren't used to seeing him stretch out during a workout. He did a fast 1:40 ⅘ mile one day, stunning onlookers. "Of course Henry McDaniel is bringing the old horse back after rather a long retirement and it is natural that he should have some speed tests," wrote the *Daily Racing Form*'s reporter. "If Exterminator goes along as he has recently, there is good reason to expect that he will again rapidly become the idol of the turf."

Also, he seemed fine, healthy, and sound, pulling on his exercise rider to go faster. As the Coffroth neared, it seemed that McDaniel was pushing him to step out in these fast times so people did not think he was sending Exterminator out unfit, especially since he would carry the top weight of 130 pounds. If he ran fast during training, people could understand that he felt good.

More and more hung in the balance for McDaniel. "Should Exterminator vanquish this [Coffroth] field then McDaniel will have gained the sobriquet of the turf's miracle man," wrote a reporter in the *Daily Racing Form*.

On the Wednesday before the Coffroth, the sky opened. It poured again Thursday. Six crews, using rollers and harrows, worked the course from Friday to Saturday night, trying to make it raceable. Watching the harrows move back and forth, gouging then smoothing the earth, seemed just like watching Winn's preparations for the 1918 Derby.

The day before the race, a red sun edged over the hills surrounding the track. It was hot, with a soft, steady breeze from the Pacific. The course would be dry and fast.

Crowds pressed into San Diego on special trains, steamers, and cars. They filled hotels, streets, and restaurants, talking about Exterminator. They had come to watch him break that record at last. Only Kilmer had not made the trip.

"Boys, it isn't even going to be close," wrote Collyer. "Henry McDaniel has the 'big train' keyed to concert pitch and all jockey Johnson has to do is stick his toes in the saddle irons and let Exterminator do all the paddling."

"I will have no excuses to offer if Exterminator is not the winner tomorrow. In fact, I am extremely confident that he will be first to the wire," said McDaniel.

On Sunday, the sky was cloudless, clear and blue. There were fifteen acres of parking at Tijuana, but so many thousands of cars came that the sheriff of San Diego County, working on Sunday to manage the crowds, had to tell people to find a place to park on the American side of the border. There was no more room at Tijuana. All across the country, people gathered around their radios.

Most of the people at the track came from Los Angeles, but others came to San Diego from as far away as San Francisco, Denver, Omaha, Kansas City, and El Paso. Hollywood came "almost en masse." The Pacific breeze blew again, and people began funneling through the turnstiles by ten o'clock. At a hot high noon, the grandstand and clubhouse were both shoulder to shoulder. The sunlight was bright. By 1:15, the general manager had the infield opened, because hot crowds now filled the pathways, betting rings, and paddocks, too. Several thousand people poured into the infield and watched the races from there. There were about twenty-five thousand all told, the biggest crowd in the track's history, ten thousand from Los Angeles alone.

They filed into their seats or found places to stand. McDaniel stared down at the track. The Coffroth was about to start.

Exterminator broke first. And at the head of the stretch, just like always, he rushed the three leaders. Johnson urged him on. It was all falling into place, with only a furlong left to go. "Here comes Exterminator!" roared the crowd, and for a brief, shining instant it looked like he would surge past the other horses.

But he couldn't. That one burst was all he had left. "The old fellow's heart was the same as ever," wrote one reporter, "but his old legs were weary and he could not hold on." The three in front finished almost together about a length ahead; a horse named Runstar won.

But Exterminator had finished in the money. He won in the way that counted for him: he broke the earnings record. With his meager $1,250 for fourth place, his total winnings were finally, finally more than Man o' War's.

The crowd did the arithmetic fast. They had wanted him to win the race so badly, but this was good, too. It was all right. Everyone cheered and whistled for Exterminator, and no one paid Runstar particular attention.

McDaniel had promised that he wouldn't make any excuses, and he didn't.

He and Exterminator had won.

"Exterminator's goal has been achieved. The best-loved horse on the American turf has eclipsed the winning record of Man o' War. And now, as his reward, he may be sent into retirement, to end his days on the W. S. Kilmer farm petted, pampered, and idolized by farm and stable hands," one reporter wrote, joining a chorus of valedictories and well-wishes for Exterminator.

But Kilmer had other plans.

"A Finer, Truer Horse
Never Lived"

After Tijuana, the Ross string loaded onto train cars and headed back to Maryland. McDaniel seemed to have one thing left to do: show people back east that he really had brought Exterminator back. He started at Havre de Grace, and reporters gave him plenty of approval. "Henry McDaniel has old Exterminator in great condition," said one. "The son of McGee was on the track this morning bucking like a colt."

A crowd turned out for the day of his first race back. It was chilly, but people kept coming, huddled in overcoats, hands in their pockets. Exterminator was set up to succeed; competition was light, and he carried only 107 pounds, a weight that would have seemed ludicrous only a few years before. After he won, Exterminator bowed his head toward the stands as he came back to the scales, delighting people with his courtly nods. They praised him directly, and it appeared to one onlooker that "his amiable face beamed." Applause started in the clubhouse, spread through the grandstand, and waved over him all the way back to his stall.

With the victory, the *Daily Racing Form* allowed that McDaniel "brought the old fellow back to at least something like his old form." With a victorious horse who seemed to be "beaming," McDaniel showed that he hadn't hurt

Exterminator by asking him to run in Tijuana. All the easterners who had missed the Coffroth could see what he had done. He had brought Exterminator back—to at least "something like" himself—safe, whole, and smiling.

One reporter imagined what Exterminator was thinking as he ate his hay in his stall: " 'Here I have been doing everything they've asked of me for seven years,' he grumbled, 'and now they want me to commit grand larceny. And at my age, too . . . Mr. Kilmer, my boss, ought to be ashamed to take the money, but it'll give me a chance to get the kinks out of my joints from that long trip across the country. Besides, as Charlie Chaplin says, I belong to my public.' " Even though it was written as a kind of joke, Exterminator's internal monologue covered some crucial points. Now that McDaniel had gotten the earnings record *and* returned Exterminator safely east, there was not really another quest out there.

Was it time for Exterminator to retire? The question seemed to have one obvious answer—yes—but it was also complex. It was easy to vilify Kilmer—it was always easy to vilify Kilmer—but if the press was any reflection, there were still plenty of people who wanted to keep Exterminator going. Kilmer was not wrong that the public seemed to want the horse.

"The statement frequently is made that Exterminator . . . should be retired. This is a mistake," wrote a *New York Evening Post* reporter. "He is better provided for by Willis Sharpe Kilmer at Binghamton than most people in this country . . . If he were turned out among wild horses on a prairie he would run long races with them every day."

McDaniel had done all he could. And Exterminator was adored. The *Sun* piece was charged with the same tension that people felt. Should he still be out there? Should we still be cheering? If he does belong to us, what do we want?

Next, Exterminator lost the Philadelphia Handicap on April 19. He never looked at the crowd, which made him appear abashed. "His action in defeat is convincing that he knows what winning a race means and how a loser should act as well as a victor," wrote one reporter.

Now McDaniel wanted to see Exterminator retired. He had gotten him past Man o' War's earnings record and even brought him home in victory. But after the Philadelphia loss, when Exterminator himself seemed all in, he wanted to be done, too. He told Kilmer he was through with their special arrangement and devoted himself to Ross's string.

McDaniel's quitting—again—did not, however, stop Kilmer. He turned Exterminator over to John I. Smith, who took Exterminator to Blue Bonnets track, in Montreal, back to the Canadian circuit where he had begun his racing career. In June 1924, Canadians trooped to the track to see him. Exterminator stood in the first stall of one barn, and by the morning after he arrived, there was a line of cars parked around the entrance. Exterminator seemed unconcerned and accepted any sugar given him over the half door of the stall. Smith acted as a tour guide, telling onlookers about all the races Exterminator had won. He won one race at Blue Bonnets.

Exterminator's next race was his ninety-ninth. He was still in Canada, on closing day. It was raining. The crowd was small, huddled. Exterminator broke fine, and was racing along when he began to shorten his stride, clearly in pain. His jockey, Jim Wallace, tried to pull him up, but he forged on. The chart read: "Exterminator moved up at the same time as Spot Cash (winner), and saved ground at the head of the stretch, but could not menace the winner, and pulled up lame." He finished gallantly, never flagging, running through obvious pain. He came in third. But it was a little pathetic, too—the 113 pounds, the paltry crowd. It was probably exactly what McDaniel didn't want, and why he had turned away.

Exterminator had run his last race.

Kilmer gave Henry King an interview in which he summed up Exterminator's past couple of years. Reading it, you can imagine Kilmer looming over the reporter's notebook. "There is nothing that money could buy that he'd fail to provide for his aged pet," King dutifully wrote.

"Exterminator is in training because he wants to be in training," Kilmer told King. "Twice I retired him to a life of ease, and each time he nearly died on me. When he first went wrong two years ago I ordered him sent to Sun Briar Court to spend the rest of his days roaming about in the fields. I instructed my employees to take better care of him than the best youngster in my barn. I forbade any one to work him and insisted that he receive the best of feed obtainable. And he nearly died. He pined for the races. He lost nearly 200 pounds and looked worse than any junk cart horse I ever saw. One would believe, if the truth were not known, that I was starving him. I couldn't understand it. Veterinarians couldn't explain why he was falling down. Except for bad legs he was sound. At the suggestion of my trainer we put him in racing. Immediately he began to pick up. He thrived on work and filled out into a good looking horse in less than a month. He wanted to race, so we sent him to Tia Juana [*sic*]. There he improved still more and he raced and won. Then one of his bad legs went back on him, and a second time I ordered him retired. This time we decided to gallop him at the farm to keep him fit. But as when he was turned out, he began to lose weight and within a few weeks he became a skinny scrawny thing with less fire and vim than an aged goat. He didn't want exercise. He wanted the excitement of the races and I sent him to Canada. As soon as he was put in training with my other horses he again began to thrive. His legs mended gradually and we found a few races for him. The old fellow seemed to know a week ahead of time that he was going to the races and he acted as if he were the happiest thoroughbred in the world. We raced him a few times and before and after each contest he displayed all the snap he did when he was the champion of champions. Last week he went lame behind and we had to throw him out of training again. He probably will never race again."

Then Kilmer seemed to catch himself. "But we are going to keep him in training and if his old legs mend sufficiently to allow him to breeze, I am going to let him race if I have to make half mile races for him with my other horses . . . I don't want him to win another dollar, but I want him to enjoy

himself, and I am sure he
receives more pleasure
out of training for and
competing in a race than
anything else."

So Exterminator stayed
"at the races." He acted
as a sort of assistant
trainer. Sometimes, he
traveled with the other
Kilmer horses, ridden
as a lead pony, the calm

Exterminator and Franklin Delano Roosevelt at the
New York State Fair in 1925. *(Thoroughbred Racing
Associations)*

horse who helps exercise riders usher the two-year-olds—mostly sons and
daughters of Sun Briar—along to their morning workouts. He nickered
each time exercise rider Eddie Campbell approached. He also knew if one
of his usual companions was left in the barn and would balk if the whole
string was not together.

Just as Mars Cassidy had, the Kilmer stablemen found that Exterminator had a calming effect on other horses. Sometimes, he would break for-
mation and gallop right up to one of the young horses. To one reporter,
Exterminator seemed to be saying, "Come on if you think you're running
good and I'll show you some running that's running."

Exterminator also would go to the track to lead parades, like the one
at the 1925 New York State Fair, on its first day of racing. That day, Franklin Roosevelt sat in an open-topped car by the track rail. As onlookers
smiled, a groom led Exterminator over. The future president grinned as he
looked at the tall horse.

In 1925, one of Kilmer's prize colts, Sunny Man, was doing well and
pointed for a winning career when he died at Pimlico. "Sunny Man was

poisoned," said track veterinarian R. W. McCully. "He was given a dose of chloral and arsenic with intent to kill. The horse was in terrible pain and died a terrible death. No one in the stable would have known how to administer chloral if they had even wanted to do so."

"I can not understand, however, how he was poisoned, for every precaution was taken to protect him with stable guards," said John Smith. There were lurid, murder-mystery aspects to the case: somehow Sunny Man's body was removed to a rendering plant before a full investigation was made. Insurance officials ran to recover his stomach, but all of his innards had already been put into an acid bath. Kilmer offered a reward, and he vowed to quit racing, which no one believed, since he had threatened to do that plenty of times before.

The case was never solved—the most likely scenario is that a stableboy accidentally overdosed the horse with what he thought was a mildly anesthetic dose of chloral hydrate—but Sunny Man's death became a call for action. "Racing authorities have become too thick-skinned in matters such as this," wrote the sports editor of the *Washington Post*. "If a comparable incident happened in any other form of sport there would be a hue and cry which would not be stilled until at least a real and decent effort had been made to apprehend those who originated and carried through the plot."

Instead of quitting racing, Kilmer bought another breeding farm, this one near Newmarket, Virginia. He named it Court Manor.

One day Grantland Rice came to Sun Briar Court along with about twenty other writers. (They were in town covering a boxing training camp.) Rice wanted to see Exterminator, and Kilmer decided he wanted a picture of the writer and horse together. A groom brought Exterminator out of his stall but left Peanuts inside. Rice had taken hold of Exterminator's lead rope, and Exterminator "took the writer for a ride which threatened to carry the gelding and man all over Binghamton." Turf writers scattered as Exterminator flew around. Peter Curran, the stable manager, yelled for a stableboy to bring out Peanuts, and as soon as he appeared, Exterminator settled right down.

Exterminator and sportswriters at Sun Briar Court, 1925. Grantland Rice is holding his bridle. *(Courtesy of the Broome County Historical Society)*

Boxer Benny Leonard holding the bridle of both Exterminator and Peanuts, with Kilmer and Rice. *(Courtesy of the Broome County Historical Society)*

There are two photographs from that day. One shows Exterminator with the entire assemblage of writers. Two wear plus-fours; all are hat-

less for the picture. Rice is holding
Exterminator's bridle. The next
shows Kilmer, in white pants and
holding his white hat, next to a
boxer named Benny Leonard, who
holds Exterminator's bridle. Rice
stands off to the side, looking
dubious. On Leonard's other side,
looking at the camera with evident
cheer, is Peanuts.

Exterminator arrived at Aqueduct with the rest of the Kilmer
horses in May 1925, and Kilmer's
latest trainer, a man named Lew
Williams, said he was "galloping
miles, sometimes a mile and a
quarter, in surprising time."

Kilmer's trophy room; painting is of
Sun Briar. (*Courtesy of the Thoroughbred
Racing Associations*)

"Is Exterminator back for the races?" asked a reporter.

"I can hardly say," said Williams. "He is going fine. Something may happen that he will be sent to the post. You will understand, however, that the
wish is father to the thought. Really, I cannot say definitely. I can tell you he is
taking kindly to his work. Exterminator is best satisfied on the racetrack.
What finer thing than to have him in the midst of metropolitan atmosphere?
He fits into the picture."

"The old fellow was raced too long as it was," wrote a *Daily Racing Form*
reporter, appalled at even the mention of Exterminator fitting into any picture as a racehorse. "If the old gelding was a mere selling plater, the idea of
bringing him back after he is obviously through would not be quite so repul-
sive."

Exterminator poses with actress Kay Gordon. *(Courtesy of the Broome County Historical Society)*

Sun Briar Court still attracted visitors. The cowboy humorist Will Rogers strolled through the stables and grounds, examining the harness, the hot-walker, and the observation room. He looked over the horses and watched the stableboys at work, carrying buckets, currying horses. "It would be great to spend a day here just looking over the pictures and trophies. They are wonderful," he said.

In September 1929, a starlet named Kay Gordon came to town by airplane. Locals noticed that she was wearing all the latest fashions, including a cloche hat and narrow dress. She was filming a movie short, which was supposed be a tour of America, featuring various American scenes and figures, like Exterminator. She fed him sugar, patted him, and they posed for pictures together.

———

Eventually, Exterminator and Peanuts moved down to Virginia. The original Peanuts died. A groom at Remlik Hall named Wilford Bray, whom Kilmer called "Pitchfork" because he couldn't remember Bray's name, said that when that happened, "Exterminator dug a hole in the stall as deep as this chair I'm sitting in and wouldn't let anyone in. It took three men to hold him while I got the pony out. He wouldn't eat and wouldn't come out of his stall. We tried putting goats and donkeys in with him, but he just had a fit." Finally, he accepted a new pony, Peanuts II, but the II was soon dropped. He would be the longest-lived Peanuts in the dynasty.

When people visited Exterminator, Peanuts would sulk in a corner, and Exterminator would shove him over to the crowd. Sometimes, Exterminator and Peanuts took off across the field, the pony always in front at first. Then Exterminator galloped by him, looking back. They stood together, Exterminator nipping Peanuts's withers, sunbathing and grazing. Exterminator would lean on Peanuts, increasing the pressure until Peanuts turned around and gave him an aggrieved look, which one reporter likened to a comedian's "slow burn."

When Count von Luckner, who had been a World War I hero in Germany, came to visit, he let himself straight into Exterminator's paddock. Exterminator looked at him. Then, for the only time anyone could remember, Exterminator attacked. He chased Luckner, monocle clenched, lanyard streaming, across the field. Luckner scaled the fence, just ahead of Exterminator, who pounded behind him, teeth bared.

Horses, people joked, just don't forget.

Kilmer cycled through trainers, faster and faster. One day in 1931, a bunch of turf writers sat in a press bus, trying to count just how many "Whimsical Willis" had employed. Neil Newman, one of the newer generation, counted twenty-two but thought he was missing a few. "Kilmer undoubtedly wants his horses to win every time they go—and we don't blame him—but a man can't expect the impossible," wrote one reporter.

Binghamton, too, still suffered from his mercurial moods. A former mayor made a speech at a dinner for Kilmer that included the following: "Willis Kilmer, I wonder if you know all that you have missed in your life-time in not having made more friends in the Valley of Opportunity . . . Their hands are outstretched to grasp yours. Their hearts are open to take you in. But if you will not come half way to meet us we must stay apart." Next, six dancers performed dressed as jockeys—two wore the Kilmer silks. As they danced, they sang a song called "Horses," which included lyrics about Sun Briar and Exterminator. After an encore, they gave Kilmer a flo-ral horseshoe, the kind his horses had worn so many times.

In 1927, McDaniel's employer J.K.L. Ross lost his money. Ross had made some unfortunate investments, and his expansive generosity had also cost him. His stable was dissolved. Ross decamped to Jamaica, where he fished, sailed, raised German shepherds, and represented the Montego Jockey Club. McDaniel went back to Kilmer, who paid him $20,000 a year plus win bo-nuses, which was reported to be the highest ever paid a trainer in America. This time, McDaniel wrote a very specific contract. In it, "all agreed that I am not to be interfered with in any way, shape or form with the training, handling, and racing of said thoroughbreds . . . It is up to me to get the best results possible because it is to my best interests, as well as my employer's, to do so and in order to be successful, I must not be interfered with."

Kilmer owned some fast horses, including Reigh Count and Sun Beau. "Racing is an uncertain proposition," McDaniel told a reporter, "but, as far as appearance goes, this is the best lot Mr. Kilmer ever raised." Then, look-ing proud, he turned and gestured toward Exterminator. "Look at old Ex-terminator over here," he said. "He looks like a two-year-old, and is enjoying the best of everything, as he is entitled to do. A finer, truer horse never lived."

But McDaniel did not spend very much time training for Kilmer this go-round. He stayed long enough to start Sun Beau, a Sun Briar colt who would turn out to be the all-time money winner. But then he quit—again—when Kilmer sold Reigh Count against his advice. As it turned out, McDaniel was right about the sale being a mistake; Reigh Count went on to win the Kentucky Derby, the Saratoga Cup, the Lawrence Realization, and the Jockey Club Gold Cup for his new owners.

"Just as he had defended Sun Briar against Exterminator," Edward Bowen wrote in the *Blood-Horse* years later, Kilmer "was to hold later that Sun Beau was the best horse he ever bred, even in the face of Reigh Count's Kentucky Derby victory and his English triumph in the Coronation Cup."

McDaniel went on to train for Joseph Widener, an art collector who helped found both the National Gallery of Art and Hialeah Racetrack. Widener once sent McDaniel the following telegram: IF THEY WONT WIN FOR YOU THEY WOULDN'T FOR ANYONE ALWAYS REMEMBER THAT IS MY FEELING.

McDaniel gave a reporter a tour of Widener's barn in 1932. McDaniel's white German shepherd, Kleiner, stayed at their heels the whole time. Reporter and trainer passed a floppy-eared billy goat, which had irritated McDaniel by sitting in his personal chair. "The nerve of him!" McDaniel said. "He'll be giving orders to the jockeys next."

The reporter asked who was the best horse McDaniel had ever trained. "I'd say

McDaniel in the 1930s. *(Courtesy of Bettmann/Corbis)*

Sun Briar and Exterminator," he said. "Sun Briar was the faster, probably up to a mile and an eighth, but, somehow, I always favored Exterminator."

Exterminator and Sun Briar spent time at both of Kilmer's Virginia farms. Bray, the groom, recalled that Swamp-Root was sent down from New York during the winters in five-gallon clear glass jars. Grooms mixed it with brown sugar, oats, grain, and olive oil and gave it to the horses. There were two buckets in Exterminator's stall; one was for Peanuts. Exterminator wouldn't eat unless Peanuts ate first.

Writers and photographers visited Exterminator, who always greeted them with Peanuts at his side. "All visitors are anxious to see him," said Maryland starter Jim Milton, "and he welcomes all with a lordly and gracious air as much to say, 'I was truly great.' He knows he was good." When the *Morning Telegraph*'s Nelson Dunstan drove up one day in 1935, he felt like he could see Exterminator standing in the paddock before a race. "I thrilled at the thought of seeing the old rascal I had not laid eyes on since that memorable afternoon at Saratoga in 1922," he wrote. Exterminator seemed to be waiting for him, looking over the paddock fence. "Hello, Slim!" Dunstan called. When a groom opened the paddock gate, Peanuts scooted away, but Exterminator stood quietly, watching. "His head is a fascinating study today for those interested in animal intelligence," Dunstan wrote.

A *New York Press* reporter noticed that Exterminator was more interested in the camera than Peanuts was. "[He] wanted to know, with that old curious trait of his, what it was all about," he wrote. The reporter also wrote a poem. A verse:

> *When the gallant deeds of valiant steeds*
> *Are inscribed on the equine scroll of fame,*
> *You may be sure none will endure*
> *Longer than Exterminator's name.*

"How long will Henry McDaniel train for Willis Sharpe Kilmer?'" asked Vreeland in 1933, after McDaniel had returned to Kilmer for yet another stint. The first thing McDaniel did when he got to Remlik Hall this time was to ask to see Exterminator. Later, he sat and talked to the *Morning Telegraph*'s Newman. "No one had ever taught Exterminator the rudiments of arithmetic," McDaniel said. "He never knew the difference whether he carried 115 pounds or 135 pounds."

That McDaniel was still training horses wasn't surprising; McDaniel had said—and shown—so many times that the racetrack was the only place for him. It was a little more confusing that something always pulled him back to Kilmer. Part had to have been the enormous salaries Kilmer paid trainers, but it seemed that there was more to it. Kilmer represented his most frustrating moments—and his most thrilling. Kilmer had been a crucial part of McDaniel's most striking success. Whatever their alchemy was, it was worth it for McDaniel to try again, not just once but twice.

As Vreeland wrote, "I think of all his achievements [McDaniel] stands out as the man who discovered . . . Exterminator."

Kilmer remarried again. His new wife, Sarah Jane Wells, went by Jane. She had been Kilmer's manicurist on board a cruise ship and was in her thirties when they married in Paris in 1932; Kilmer was sixty-three. When they returned to Binghamton, Jane Kilmer gave teas, served on boards, and became an important figure in Binghamton society. She kept her own saddle horses at Sun Briar Court and would become a guardian of Exterminator's legacy.

As they all grew older, McDaniel, Kilmer, and Exterminator became legends in their own time—depicted in the press as simplified characters rather than as human—or animal—beings. McDaniel seemed more esteemed, "the Mark Twain of the turf, who never fails to see the humor in a situation." Turf writers used him as a sort of walking reference library. "A good listener and not much of a talker," wrote Frank Graham. "But when he says something, you listen because he knows how to use words, and he has been around and seen about everything and when he talks about the places he has been and the horses he has seen, he makes pictures in your mind so clearly that you can see the places and the horses and you can almost hear the roar of the crowd."

Kilmer seemed more established, an ever-larger figure in racing as horses like Sun Beau kept his name in the *Daily Racing Form*. He also seemed crabbier, and smashed a radio one day when he heard that a jockey had put come-from-behind Sun Beau up front; a move sure to cost him the race, which it did.

Exterminator seemed even more venerable and anthropomorphized than ever, a sort of cross between a revered athlete and the kinds of half-human animals who starred in movies, like Tom Mix's "wonder horse," Tony, or the valiant German shepherd Rin Tin Tin. "A hero who is questioned and then is able to answer is more compelling than a figure who is so powerful he is never doubted. The war had made that even more real," writes Susan Orlean in her book about Rin Tin Tin. Like "Rinty," who rescued children and climbed trees on-screen, Exterminator had been tried and tested. With his idiosyncratic appearance and history on the public stage, he—and now, Peanuts—shared this heroic space with Hollywood's heroic animals.

As Exterminator's generation of racehorses—which was understood as the Golden Age of racing even by the 1930s—faded, people started reminiscing. Exterminator's name often came up alongside Man o' War's, leading to a new round of comparisons. Quite a few racing people came out as Exterminator defenders, including Hall of Fame trainers Sunny Jim Fitzsimmons and Ben Jones. Grantland Rice saw Exterminator and Seabiscuit as "the two great horses, year by year, of the American turf." McDaniel weighed in, too. "Exterminator won $252,596 and in those days there were no one-sided 'specials' or more handed him on a silver platter," he wrote. "He had to battle with all a thoroughbred's natural courage and a warrior's gameness for all he earned." One turf writer claimed that "Uncle Henry McDaniels [*sic*] always swore Exterminator would have figured out some way to beat him [Man o' War]."

No matter how writers or trainers phrased it—he was more durable, more sympathetic, more sturdy or fast or strong—it came down to what it always had. "Exterminator was a fair trencherman, not a gourmand like Man o' War," wrote one reporter. "Turf fans worship many horses, greats of today and yesteryear. But they loved Old Bones."

Later, Exterminator was compared to newer stars, like the Australian Phar Lap, who really did look quite a bit like Exterminator. Both were very tall, high headed, and long in the barrel, although Phar Lap was more conventionally handsome. When Seabiscuit came along in the 1930s, he and Exterminator shared the title of racing's Cinderella. And many horsemen noticed that Native Dancer—the "Gray Ghost" of the 1950s—looked quite a bit like Exterminator when he ran, with a familiar ground-consuming stride.

McDaniel was asked, over and over, whether Exterminator was better than Sun Briar. He gave the same answer as always, that up to a mile and a furlong, Sun Briar would win. Beyond that, Exterminator would.

In the summer of 1936, McDaniel was sixty-nine. Some young trainers welcomed him to Saratoga. He told them he'd been coming to Saratoga since 1872, when his father was racing Harry Bassett against Longfellow. "I'm a greenhorn in this town," he joked. "You fellows should be a little lenient with a kid just starting out in his turf career. I don't know my way around a race track yet, but some day I'll catch up to you old fogies and show you I'm a horseman."

Exterminator and Peanuts appeared in an advertisement for Winchester cigarettes. "They didn't know what Exterminator could do for them until they put him in a race," it said. "You can't tell what Winchester Cigarettes can do for you till you put one between your lips and light it. Then you'll know you've picked a winner."

One day, went turf writer Nelson Dunstan's story, he was in the film mogul Louis B. Mayer's office. "Of all the horses you have seen, which one would you say would make a good story for a movie?" Mayer asked him.

"Exterminator," Dunstan said, without hesitating.

"Why don't you write the story?" Mayer asked.

"Because his story is such an unusual one that movie fans, who were not acquainted with the facts, would howl it down in the same manner they would howl down the story of the girl who rode a Kentucky Derby winner to pay the mortgage on the family homestead," Dunstan told him.

Early in 1940, a fire burned the main house at Remlik Hall, one of Kilmer's Virginia farms, while Kilmer was home. For some reason, the extensive sprinkler system wasn't turned on that night, a mystery that was never solved. Kilmer never really recovered, and his health suffered. That July, he died of pneumonia at Sky Lake, his upstate New York hunting lodge. He was seventy-one. Jane was at his side when he died. His body lay in state in a Binghamton Presbyterian church and was then taken to the Kilmer family mausoleum, in Floral Park Cemetery.

"Never a sycophant," wrote turf writer Neil Newman in an obituary. "He was a man who did much for the turf of this country and his contribution to the bloodlines will be a perpetual monument to his memory," wrote the president of the New York Turf Writers Association. "Exactitude of detail, standards of worth in things animate and inanimate played a tremendous part in the man's life," read his *Binghamton Press* obituary.

After Kilmer's death, Jane Kilmer held a dispersal sale at Court Manor, the Virginia farm near Newmarket. She would hold on to Exterminator, Peanuts, Sun Briar, and a few other horses to race, but the rest would be sold. It was the end of an era; Virginia had been an important site for Kilmer's racing establishment for many years. The auction was also a huge party, with many famous people from the racing and breeding worlds. Alfred G. Vanderbilt sat up front, and so did Seabiscuit's owner, Charles Howard. Auction guests were served lunch, and their dessert was individual ice cream cakes, decorated with the name "Sun Briar." The grooms ate Brunswick stew.

"There were sad hearts yesterday at the dispersal," wrote a Richmond reporter, "from executives down to stable hands, those men loved the stallions, weanlings and broodmares, and seeing them led into the ring to be sold must have caused a sharp pain."

As horses piled into vans, bound for their new homes, Exterminator watched them go. "His head got lower and lower," said Mrs. Kilmer. "He broke my heart the way he acted."

During a reporter's visit in 1940, a groom called to Exterminator, and he emerged, slowly, from a darkened stall into the light outdoors. Exterminator's height was still prepossessing, and his chest still muscled. He was winter furred and elderly, but the reporter still noticed the "way about him" that he had. The barn manager noticed that the writer didn't find Exterminator beautiful, and admitted it was true, but pointed out that "he was a mighty pretty horse coming in under the wire."

The Maryland Jockey Club honored Exterminator by naming a race after him. The first Exterminator Handicap was run at Baltimore's Pimlico Race Course in 1940, but Exterminator could not lead the post parade; it was too soon after Kilmer died, and Mrs. Kilmer thought it was unseemly for him to appear in public so soon. So in 1941, he was vanned up to Pimlico to appear at the second running. He was twenty-six years old.

Exterminator and Peanuts at Pimlico. *(Courtesy of Pimlico)*

Peanuts, of course, rode along, and Exterminator's groom, Mike Terry, came, too. Jockey Club president Alfred Vanderbilt offered a stall and knocked down a partition between two stalls so they would have plenty of room. The first thing Exterminator did was lie down and roll. Jim Milton, the Maryland starter, went to see Exterminator right away. "I just want to touch him again," he said. McDaniel came by, too, and told stories. "He actually seemed to be proud of his position as a champion, and, like all champions, he was always ready to give his best in any race," he said.

At first, there was an idea floating around that Willie Knapp would ride him, but that didn't happen, either because people were afraid Exterminator would get overexcited if he had a rider, or because Knapp had grown heavy. It was the opening day of the fall meeting, and the race was two miles and seventy yards. Fifteen thousand people came. Many pressed around Exterminator's stall as Terry prepared him for the parade. "If they want ribbons on this horse's bridle," Terry said, "they'll have to pin 'em on themselves. I'm no ribbon man. I'm a horseman." Exterminator looked at him, one reporter wrote, with "the gaze of a gentleman who won his fame without adornment and wishes to continue that way."

When Exterminator got out onto the track to lead the parade, he pranced and looked at the crowds and the grandstand. Peanuts came, too. Someone had managed to get Sun Briar Court–colored orange, green, and brown ribbons in Exterminator's tail, and they fluttered behind him. His ears were up. Some of the fans in the crowd had cheered for him twenty-five years before. A record of Guy Lombardo's orchestra playing "Auld Lang Syne" played, and Exterminator came through the paddock gate, seeming to turn and bow toward the stands. People began to cry. Over the PA system, an announcer listed Exterminator's accomplishments as racehorses paced behind him.

There hadn't been a well-thought-out plan for exactly where Exterminator should be during the race—he and Terry were supposed to get back to the paddock, although it was unclear how—and they were stranded in the infield, watching the horses run. "We thought for sure Old Bones would get all heated up watching those other horses race," said Terry, "but he just put his ears back and turned around in that field so he could see the leaders race by. He watched the whole race, two miles it was, too, as calmly as can be. Much calmer than the stands."

After the race, a woman flung her arms around Exterminator's neck. "I'm gonna follow him today," she said. "He won me my house in Maryland once." Track police waved and signaled at her, but she did not let go. Exterminator walked all the way back into the paddock with her hanging on, then "gave a backward look over his shoulder that, to a wishful thinker, easily seemed nostalgic," as Terry took him back to his stall.

"It was one of those things which start off as a bit of frill and then sweep the main program aside," said one onlooker.

McDaniel looked at Exterminator, quiet, stately, and tall, and cried.

Jane Kilmer brought Sun Briar, Exterminator, and Peanuts home to Binghamton from Virginia in 1942. "I think that is what my husband would have
wanted," she said. John Brady, the horse shipper, said there were two ways
he could take them from Court Manor. "One is to van them over the mountains," he said, "about 20 miles to—"

"No," Mrs. Kilmer said. "I don't want them to have to make a trip like
that. Why can't you get them out of Court Manor by rail?" Brady said that
he could, but it would mean hiring a separate locomotive. "All right," said
Mrs. Kilmer. "Get the locomotive."

"I suppose Exterminator will think he is off to the races again," said
Brady.

The horses, along with four grooms and a guard dog, got to Binghamton
at 6:30 A.M. Sun Briar went ahead in a van, and Exterminator, along with
Peanuts, retraced the walk he had taken so many times from the Lackawanna
station to Sun Briar Court. Mrs. Kilmer met them, patting their necks and
talking to them. Crowds gathered, just as they had when Sun Briar came
home as the juvenile champion and when Exterminator returned after the
Brooklyn. Virginia groom Mike Terry was there, too. He had cared for Sun
Briar and Exterminator for years, and moved to New York to stay with them.

Sun Briar died at Sun Briar Court in October 1943. He was twenty-eight
years old. When he died, his record for running a mile and a furlong in 1:50
still stood, and it wasn't beaten until 1956. Sun Briar's bloodlines have left
an indelible legacy on racing. His son Sun Beau was the leading money winner until Seabiscuit's earnings trumped his in 1940. His son Pompey was
the two-year-old champion of 1925, and his daughter, Suntica, won many
races for fillies.

Secretariat, Native Dancer, Seattle Slew, Funny Cide, California Chrome,
and 2015 Triple Crown winner American Pharoah (on both sides) all trace
their lineage back to Sun Briar.

Above: Mike Terry feeds Exterminator out of a trophy at his last birthday party as Peanuts looks on. Below: Jane Kilmer gives Exterminator birthday cake.

Binghamtonians adored Exterminator. Terry and Mrs. Kilmer gave him birthday parties on May 30, his actual foaling date. Mostly children came, and Terry patiently hoisted some up onto Exterminator and let them climb all over Peanuts. Mrs. Kilmer made an enormous cake out of an oat mash and put carrots in to represent candles. Peanuts had his own cake. The staff would line up Exterminator's trophies for the adults to admire, and Terry put bits of cake in some of the sterling cups, so Exterminator could eat from them.

Aubrey Clark was four years old when she celebrated Exterminator's birthday with him. (She got to feed Peanuts his cake.) "I think that a small community like this makes much of a person who is successful out in the big world," she said many years later. "Exterminator was successful, so there was respect and pride."

Epilogue

Many things about 1943 would put Americans in mind of Exterminator's Kentucky Derby year of 1918, with another world war, victory gardens, rationing, and meatless Mondays returned to the home front. As a reward for buying war bonds, a group of Binghamtonians got to name a Flying Fortress bomber. They decided on "Exterminator." But there was no mounted cavalry, no easy identification of racehorses with soldiers. For the most part, racing continued, although California's Santa Anita track was closed to house Japanese Americans.

But just as they had during the previous world war, stewards of thoroughbred racing pledged to help the war effort. A committee at Belmont decided to stage a "Back the Attack Day" to raise money for the third War Loan Drive, and asked for Exterminator as the feature. He would lead a parade and entertain visitors. Mrs. Kilmer hesitated; Belmont was about 200 miles from Binghamton, and Exterminator was twenty-eight years old. It would be a long, exhausting trip, his arthritic knees jolting in the van. But the idea that her warhorse could help his country again compelled her, and she told the organizers Exterminator would be there.

Exterminator and Peanuts loaded into the horse van and stood looking out. A photo of them that day bears the caption, "It's great to be going back to the races," and both look alert and comfortable, side by side, fresh straw at their feet. They arrived at Belmont a few days early, and William DuPont Jr. offered guest stalls in his barn.

Exterminator and Peanuts were hardly settled when old friends began to arrive. Walking toward the barn, Willie Knapp yelled "Shang!" and Exterminator stuck his head out. "He recognized me the minute he heard my voice," Knapp said. "I hadn't been near him in 15 years." When McDaniel came by, he went right into Exterminator's stall. McDaniel told a reporter that Exterminator was at home any place he landed. He added that Exterminator was never known to fret about anything and always tried to please his trainer whether it was in a race, trial, or stable. Exterminator nudged him, looking for sugar. Exterminator couldn't find any sugar in McDaniel's pockets and pinned his ears, which made him appear crotchety.

"You can't fool me, you old bluffer," said McDaniel. Exterminator whinnied.

On Back the Attack Day, people poured in to Belmont. Mars Cassidy rode a stable pony at the head of a parade of retired jockeys, who mounted up for an old-timers' exhibition race. Jane Kilmer watched from a box with a friend from Binghamton, two women with smoothed hair and light coats, binoculars at the ready. Their program listed the day's war-themed races: "The Guadalcanal Hurdles," "The Tunisia Handicap," and the "Coral Sea Purse."

Terry led Exterminator along the track. A young boy led Peanuts. Trainer Simon Healy teared up, along with many in the crowd, who remembered when Exterminator had raced there so many years before. The crowd of 31,336 clapped and shouted, and Exterminator and Peanuts stopped in front of the grandstand. "My horse sort of bowed to them and nodded his head," is how Terry described it, and a photo shows Exterminator, left front leg out straight, his head dipped, almost like a circus horse. Quietly facing the stands, Exterminator gave every impression of appreciating the applause. Over the loudspeaker, an announcer read out his record: 99 races, 50 wins, 17 seconds, 17 thirds. He was the oldest living Derby winner.

When the day's real racing began, the big winner was Princequillo, who would go on to be Secretariat's grandsire. Exterminator went back to his stall and rolled in the straw, which William DuPont decided would bring his horses luck.

The crowd bought a record $25 million in war bonds.

In the fall of 1944, the second Peanuts, now somewhere around thirty years old, got sick. He had choking spells, and although he still liked to romp around with Exterminator, he was failing. When he died, the *New York Times* ran his obituary. "Exterminator Loses Pal," the headline ran. Terry put a new pony named Teddy into the paddock with Exterminator, who chased him around, ears back. Terry had to cool Exterminator out, racehorse style, because he had worked himself into such a swivet. Eventually, though, Exterminator accepted Teddy. Soon everyone called Teddy Peanuts. "Exterminator, they say, acts as if he thoroughly understands the situation and is making the best of it," reported the *Binghamton Press*.

Exterminator stayed on American minds. The publisher Charles Scribner offered Ernest Hemingway 10 percent in royalties on some new editions. "I am an old horse like Exterminator that won for you every time but once," Hemingway wrote. "And I won't run for ten percent and you have that straight from [the] horse's mouth . . . The only thing that makes horses like Exterminator and me sore is when . . . the people that start you haven't got the guts to bet."

By the spring of 1945, Exterminator was thirty, nearing the upper limit of a horse's life expectancy. Jane Kilmer had remarried and was now Jane Kilmer Ellison. She remained dedicated to Exterminator, and she and veterinarian M. C. Markham checked on him often. During the years that Kilmer maintained the Virginia farms, Markham had traveled from Binghamton to tend the Kilmer horses. He knew Exterminator well.

The old horse was dropping weight. Terry dosed him daily with a flaxseed and cream of tartar health tonic, and chopped and soaked his hay, so he could chew it more easily. One day that summer, Exterminator lay down in his field and couldn't get up. Terry helped him to his feet. He didn't lie down again; Terry thought the old horse knew he wouldn't be able to stand if he did.

On September 25, the night watchman looked in on Exterminator around 3:30 in the morning. He was down, and Peanuts was nudging him, trying to rouse him. The watchman called Terry, who rushed over. Exterminator died with his head in Terry's lap.

Markham said Exterminator had died of a heart attack. Because of city ordinances, Exterminator couldn't be buried at Sun Briar Court. His body was wrapped and placed in a Virginia-made wooden coffin, to be buried at a pet cemetery outside of town, alongside Sun Briar. Terry stayed inside; he couldn't bear to watch Exterminator's body being taken away.

Jane Ellison cried while locals and children gathered to mourn. Terry cleaned the orange, brown, and green halter Exterminator was wearing when he died. He would take it home. A reporter asked what he would do now that the horse was gone.

"Well, I'll miss Slim, all right," he said, "but there's things for me to do around here." Then he laid straw in the stall he had just cleaned, so that Peanuts would have a fresh bed for the night.

Exterminator's obituaries ran everywhere. "Death sounded the 'call to post' for Exterminator today," one began. Here is part of a poem that ran in the *New York Sun*:

> *Old Bones they called him through the years*
> *Because he wasn't much*
> *To look at 'til you heard those cheers*
> *And saw that certain touch;*
> *Ungainly, not a "color horse,"*
> *He'd never hold your eye—*

Until you saw him on a course
Turn on the "do or die"
Now thirty, in his regal stall
The lights grow very dim
At last he hears a challenge fall
Which is too much for him!
For once there is in those great eyes
A little trace of fear
And dauntless to the last, he tries
The old straight course to steer
His body sways, he reels a bit
He hears a bugle call
And now he strives to answer it
Again this golden fall
He slumps . . . goes slowly to the floor . . .
While deadly darkness grows . . .
And "Old Bones" is forevermore
Where every gamester goes!

Henry McDaniel never left the turf. He died at eighty-two, in Coral Gables, Florida, three years after Exterminator. He had been in racing for sixty-six years; for his past two, he served as a steward at Tropical Park, in Miami. McDaniel had been the "oldest living active trainer," according to the *Saratogian*.

McDaniel's obituaries mentioned his father and centered around Exterminator. "His most famous charge was Exterminator, which McDaniel guided to a movie career in the world of racing," read one.

There was a funeral in Miami, and then McDaniel was buried beside Leonora, in Chicago's Forest Home Cemetery. He was inducted into the Hall of Fame in 1956, Exterminator in 1957.

Mildred Mastin Pace remembered her father coming home in 1918, when she was eleven, aglow with his win on a long shot to win the Kentucky Derby. She grew up to write a children's book called *Old Bones: The Wonder Horse,* a fictionalized story of Exterminator. It features a character named Mike Terry as a boy groom who grows up alongside him. "I knew the minute I laid eyes on him, he was the horse I'd been looking for all my life," the boy Mike tells Henry McDaniel in the book.

Wesley Dennis, who did all the pictures for Marguerite Henry's *Misty of Chincoteague* series, drew the illustrations. His trademark style rendered Exterminator's angles less harsh than they had been, and emphasized his wide, knowing eyes. The book was so popular, Pace said, that she was too busy writing letters to adoring children to start another.

Sun Briar Court was sold, and the property is now Lourdes Hospital. Long after Exterminator's death, Jane Kilmer Ellison tended his legacy, helping Pace with her book, and telling Exterminator's story to visitors. Ellison's great-nephew, Jonathan Davis, has spent much of his life involved with racing, as a pinhooker and an owner. "It really made me a racing fan," he says. As far as Exterminator, says Davis, "in terms of his greatness as a racehorse there is no question, to me anyway. Today that would be unheard of. They don't run races that long and it would never happen. And to have made as many starts as he did, and win or hit the board under arguably not the easiest of circumstances, and from trainer to trainer to trainer and keep that kind of form and race those distances. To me that is the remarkable part about the horse."

Sue McPeek, who has also spent a lifetime in the racing world, was one of the children who knew Ellison. "I remember my grandmother arranging to take me to her friend Jane Ellison's house," she told me. "She had one room just filled with all those beautiful silver trophies and I remember being awestruck by it all. It was a beautiful room. And she gave us charms for our charm bracelets, and a crystal statue of a horse, and a copy of *Old Bones: The Wonder Horse,* which she signed, and another book on horses and pictures of Peanuts and Exterminator grazing out in the field. It was like Christmas."

Ellison herself once said that she saw Exterminator this way: "He was superhuman, he was perfect."

In the late 1990s, an activist wanted to rebury Exterminator in Saratoga Springs. "Here we have a horse that had become a legend in his own time . . . and he's buried in some godforsaken little plot of land that no one knows about," she said. "That horse just does not deserve this. He ought to be in a place where he'll be remembered, where people who love horses will see him."

"That's our bit of history there," retorted a county official. "If they want to visit, that's fine. But we ought to keep our history right here. If the owners had wanted that horse buried at Saratoga Springs, he would have been buried there."

Sometimes it does seem that Exterminator isn't in a place "where he'll be remembered," and not just in geographic terms. His name is no longer a household word. Every once in a while, there will be a retrospective article. These usually either reiterate the rags-to-riches story—30–1, the truck horse—or debunk it—he wasn't *that* roughly bred, he did lose forty-nine races. But that we have the legend at all says so much about Exterminator, what people saw in him, what they needed from him, what they— we—still need.

"Perhaps it was the way Exterminator crashed into the big time that caught the public fancy so

Exterminator's grave. (*Author photo*)

completely," wrote Arthur Daley in the *New York Times* when Exterminator died. "Even in repetition it loses nothing because it follows unerr-
ingly the old [Horatio] Alger formula of poor-boy-gets-rich. As a success
story it has no counterpart in racing history." His deserving, unforeseen
ascent and incredible career make a great story. But it was Exterminator
himself—and what he meant to people—that made—and makes—him deserve our attention. He was born and he won the Derby and then he stayed
to race, year after year. The desire to watch him run, or bow to the stands,
never wavered, from world war to world war.

Exterminator's story is an American one, a story that we wrote and tell
ourselves.

I got lost a couple of times in the green, hilly countryside around Binghamton before I found Whispering Pines pet cemetery, where Exterminator is
buried. Finally, I turned onto the right road. I pulled in to the little parking
area and walked over to the cemetery.

It's quiet by Exterminator's headstone, which he shares with Sun Briar
and Suntica. The pet cemetery is small, with stone memorials to dogs
named Buffy and Max. Pine trees surround it on three sides and they
really do whisper in the slow breeze. The day I was there, there were hand-
fuls of pennies on top of the stone. I wondered who had left them, but
then I thought of all the people who used to send him apples and visit him
in his stall.

It makes sense to want Exterminator's grave moved to splendid Saratoga, where he was bought and sold, where he won four cups, where people
stamped their feet and shouted his name. His four Saratoga Cup trophies
stand polished, handsome, and gleaming in their own case at the National
Museum of Racing and Hall of Fame there.

But the shared headstone, the quiet field, and the little grassy plot make
more sense for Old Slim, the Abe Lincoln of racehorses. He is still with
Sun Briar.

He is at home.

Acknowledgments

Many, many people have helped me write this book.

I could not have written *Here Comes Exterminator!* without the help of Muriel and Garrett McDaniel, who were above-and-beyond generous with their time and with their McDaniel family materials. They believed in this project from before the beginning, and have helped me from proposal to final draft stages. I truly appreciate their contributions and support. In Binghamton, Bill Gorman, who performs in a play as Willis Sharpe Kilmer, spent an afternoon with me looking through the amazing amount of Kilmer material at the Broome County Historical Society. Bill has been on call for many Kilmer-related questions since. And in Saratoga, historian Allan Carter, who has long helped me with racing research, gave me a tour of the National Museum of Racing and Hall of Fame as well as offering research material, guidance, and advice.

I won't forget the morning that Jeff Ramsey spent showing me around his family's beautiful Ramsey Farm in Nicholasville, Kentucky, where Exterminator was born. Meeting Kitten's Joy was thrilling. Terri Busch, whose grandfather was Exterminator's veterinarian, shared her incredible collection of Exterminatoriana—including Exterminator's own stable trunk—and stories about Dr. Markham. Jonathan Davis, Sue McPeek, and Aubrey Clark all shared important memories, keeping Exterminator's legacy alive. Thanks, too, to Diana Bean and Stephen Spero for Binghamton assistance.

I am sorry that Jules Levitt, with whom I spoke about Exterminator on the phone and who may have been his number-one fan, died before I completed this book. The same is true of Dan Gill, who took an afternoon off in the summer of 2014 to give me a tour of his farm, which was Kilmer's Remlik Hall. At his family's excellent Something Different Restaurant in Urbanna, Virginia, you will see tables made from stall doors in the orange-green-and-brown Kilmer colors.

Grateful acknowledgment is made to the many librarians and researchers who helped me along the way, including Gracie Hale, equine librarian at the University of Kentucky, Jacob Nadal, director of Library and Archives at the Brooklyn Historical Society, Ivy Marvel at the Brooklyn Public Library, and Lisa Campbell at the National Sporting Library. Gerry Smith, at the Broome County Historical Society in Binghamton, dug deep to make sure I had everything I could want about Exterminator, Kilmer, and Swamp-Root. He maintains an incredible collection. Wade Clough gave me a wonderful tour of Temple Concord in Binghamton, which used to be a Kilmer mansion.

I spent one of the pleasantest days I can remember at the extraordinary Keeneland Library, with Cathy Schenck helping me access all the Exterminator, Kilmer, and McDaniel material held there. Chris Goodlett, curator of collections—including the Jim Bolus collection—at the Kentucky Derby Museum at Churchill Downs shared excellent material and his time.

I owe a great deal—including the title—to my agent, Rafe Sagalyn. He bet the long shot, which I appreciate enormously. Thanks to Elizabeth Shreve for introducing us. Many thanks, too, to the dedicated staff at ICM/Sagalyn, particularly Brandon Coward, Jake DeBacher, and Abby Keeble.

Peter Joseph, my editor at Thomas Dunne Books, has shared my enthusiasm for Exterminator from the beginning, and offered guidance on large and small decisions. He is also very, very patient. Associate editor Melanie Fried has been consistently available for my many requests, offering a huge amount of support. Many thanks also to production editor

Rafal Gibek, and copyeditor Cynthia Merman, who worked so hard on the book's final versions.

Laurie Prinz, the editor of *EQUUS*, has guided much of my work for the past fourteen years. She helped me learn how to write about horses, and has been very supportive of this latest project. The editorial and other assistance I received from Joel Achenbach, Anne Dickerson, Jill Drupa, J. D. Heyman, Kitson Jazynka, Anne Kornblut, MaryBeth Maeder, Tracey Madigan, Margaret McEvoy, Matt Mendelsohn, Lauri Menditto, Paula O'Rourke, Alison Piepmeier, Gary Richards, Christy Halvorson Ross, George Sengstack, and Florence Williams has seen me through.

And I am in great debt to my whole family. They take books and animals as seriously as I do. In particular, my parents, Rosemarie Howe and Beal Lowen, and Adam, Simon, and Macie: thank you.

Notes

Prologue

2 *"not given to sanguine prophecy"* "Horses Plentiful for Longer Stakes."

2 *"rubbed his nose against"* Quoted in "Return of 'Old Slim' to Racing Hailed by All Lovers of Horses."

Chapter 1

3 *McDaniel used to tell reporters* Vreeland, "Henry McDaniel Fills the Cloak of Skill Left by His Dad"; "McDaniel Training Horses Longer than Any Active Contemporary."

3 *McDaniel was one of the most famous horse trainers* Vreeland, "Henry Mc-Daniel Fills the Cloak of Skill"; "Col. McDaniel Critically Ill."

3 *Belmont stakes three times in a row* www.belmontstakes.com/UserFiles/file /Trainers.pdf.

3 *"From the time I could first toddle"* Henry McDaniel, "Fifty Years on the Turf."

3 *he moved to Hoboken* Daniels, "The Death of Colonel David McDaniel."

4 *by 1869 some horses had been seized* Ibid.

4 *"destined to shake the turf"* Ibid.

4 *Confederacy origin* "The McDaniel Confederacy."

4 *blue and red silks* "Jimmy Rowe's Colors Are the Same as Those Used by Colonel David McDaniel."

4 *earliest memories* King, "Modern Horses Less Rugged." Plus "Turf Bureau."

4 *biggest sporting events* "Saratoga Races."

4 *"My father thought there was no horse"* Vreeland, "Henry McDaniel and Gifford Cochran Flirt with Fortune and Win."

4 *"It really seemed as if Col. McDaniel"* "The Race Meeting at Jerome Park."

4 *He did celebrity endorsements* "To Owners of Horses."

4 *Harry Bassett declined* "The Death of Col. David McDaniel."

4 *three of his final twelve starts* Bouyea, "Harry Bassett, M. E. 'Buster' Millerick and Don Pierce Elected to Hall of Fame."

4 *because he had been raced too hard* Vosburgh, "The Belmont Stakes."

4 *may have taught Henry* Vosburgh, "The Passing of Jerome Park."

5 *too many horses in training* "Racing at Saratoga."

5 *learned about her death from a telegram* "Personal."

5 *"These visitors were clearly of the kind"* "A Sale of Thoroughbreds."

5 *series of setbacks* "Did Not Intend To Kill"; "Justice William McMahon's Side of the McDaniel Difficulty"; "A Veteran Turfman Retires."

5 *died in 1885* "The Death of Col. David McDaniel."

5 *"Col. McDaniel may have had enemies"* Ibid.

5 *More than a million horses . . . twenty-five million by 1900* Greene, *Horses at Work,* 166.

5 *Training for either work or racing* O'Dell, "Denton Offutt of Kentucky."

6 *"If the animal sulks"* Hayes, *Illustrated Horse-Breaking,* 147.

6 *"Any horse may be taught to do anything"* Rarey, *The Complete Horse Trainer.*

6 *Some claimed* Jennings, *Horse-Training Made Easy,* 6.

6 *"Old theories have been exploded"* Jennings, *The Horse and His Diseases,* 6.

6 *"Positing both as essentially innocent and good"* Pearson, *The Rights of the Defenseless,* 45.

7 *He was seventeen* Vreeland, "Marse McDaniel Inherited Training Skill from His Dad."

7 *Several other trainers had failed* Graham, "Setting the Pace."

7 *Afterward, Forest won* "His First Winner, No. 9. Henry McDaniel"; "Henry McDaniel," *Blood-Horse,* February 7, 1931.

7 *McDaniel kept a scrapbook* McDaniel collection.

7 *"Henry McDaniel, youngest son"* Broad Church, "Notes."

7 *"had his sterling character molded"* "Harry McDaniel," McDaniel collection.

7 *"the craving I've always had for race-horses"* Hildreth, *The Spell of the Turf,* 9.

8 *Animals* Acme Newspictures photograph with white German shepherd captioned, "with his dog Kleiner which never leaves his side," April 8, 1932; "Petted the Hen," 1931; terrier in pocket, photograph ca. 1930, McDaniel collection.

8 *"You are the most competent, capable"* Letter from M. H. Tichenor, McDaniel collection.

8 *Reporters called him "unassuming," "modest"* "Has Won Many Races," McDaniel collection.

8 *"thorough gentleman"* "Henry McDaniel, a Natural Born Horseman," McDaniel collection.

8 *"The better the horse, the better the master"* Gleason, *Oscar R. Gleason's Practical Treatise on the Breaking and Taming of Wild and Vicious Horses*, self-published, 1890, 7.

8 *"If he is tired and worn out"* Martin, *The Family Horse*.

8 *whipping tied-up horses, lighting fires, "bishoping"* Gleason, *Gleason's Horse Book*, 45.

8 *horse food, items, streetcar operators* Greene, *Horses at Work*, 174–75.

9 *"Intelligence is so clear as to almost startle"* Gleason, *Gleason's Horse Book*, 14.

9 *"If any year could be said"* Greene, *Horses at Work*, 174.

9 *the president of the Humane Association* Kean, *Animal Rights and Social Change*, 79.

9 *"Sweetheart of mine, remember this"* McDaniel collection.

9 *portrait shows Leonora*, McDaniel collection.

9 *lost a baby* 1900 census, courtesy Muriel McDaniel.

9 *she stayed in the private, small sanitariums* Ellen Holtzman, "Time Capsule."

9 *earned millions through mining* Mooney, *Race Horse Men*, 183.

9–10 *"the kind you never forget"* Hildreth, *Spell of the Turf*, 98.

10 *Baldwin's Rey el Santa Anita* "Domino Is Very Lame."

10 *"possibly the richest and the poorest man"* "Trainer M'Daniel's Career," McDaniel collection.

10 *Baldwin wired McDaniel* Ibid.

10 *"he came out of the race perfectly sound"* N.t., *Chicago Tribune*, June 26, 1894, McDaniel collection.

10 *"was the first really big race"* McDaniel, "Half a Century on the Turf," *The Washington Star*, June 1, 1930, p. 1 of section 7.

10 *"I had watched his work and made up my mind"* N.t., *Chicago Tribune*, June 6, 1894.

10 *McDaniel seemed to approve of hard work* "The Next Great 3-Year-Old Event in the Season."

10 *"From the way he won yesterday it would seem"* Ibid.

10 *He looks the consummate horseman* Photograph, McDaniel collection.

11 *"I have often been asked why"* "I Have Often Been Asked Why with My Success."

11 *trained his two hundredth winner for Bennett* "Local Turf Gossip," July 16, 1902.

11 *kept his numbers up* "Local Turf Gossip," August 23, 1902.

11 *a later season went less well* "Henry McDaniels, the expert trainer for G. C. Bennett"; "Ramiro Raced to Death in Front."

11 *A horse named Henry McDaniel* "Gossip of the Turf"; "Racing at New Orleans."

11 *McDaniel acted unruffled* "Trainer M'Daniel Loses Cheerfully," n.d. [during Bennett years], n.p., McDaniel collection.

11 *By January 1903*, Gossip of the Turf.

11 *he decided to send the horses back* "Gossip of the Turf."

12 *Coburn overweight* "Local Turf Gossip," May 21, 1903.

12 *"That boy"* "M'Daniel Gets After Coburn."

12 *Bennett took this so far* "In Quarters at Memphis."

12 *"That was the reason why Henry McDaniel"* "George C. Bennett Proud of His Horses."

12 *"a series of lucky strikes on the turf "* "Blue Grass Turf Gossip."

12 *but now they look a little cooler* Photograph, McDaniel collection.

13 *McDaniel accepted a standing offer* "Aladdin, Sheridan Stake Winner"; "Blue Grass Turf Gossip."

13 *Chicago millionaire* "Blue Grass Turf Gossip."

13 *overwhelmed by constant rumors of doping* "Chicago Owner to Campaign"; "Buys Jake Sanders."

13 *"There is something rotten in Denmark"* "Alarm Is Sounded at Ascot."

13 *A cranky debate wore on* "Hits Hard at Ascot Crooks"; "Supervisors Refuse to Close Ascot Park."

13 *"From the time he could toddle"* "Horses Trained by M'Daniel Capture Notable Stakes."

13 *"His own judgment is all he relies on"* Ibid.

13 *The accompanying photograph* "Henry McDaniel," McDaniel collection; "Horses Trained by M'Daniel Capture Notable Stakes."

14 *Spongers . . . ginger* Martin, "Dr. Ring and the Origins of Horse Doping."

14 *night watchmen* Drape, "Despite the Evidence, Trainers Deny a Doping Problem."

14 *saliva testing for drugs* Martin, "Dr. Ring and the Origins of Horse Doping."

14 *In February 1906* "Who Drugged the Horse?"

14 *one horse was so hopped up* Mulholland, "Stable May Get into Trouble if 'Dope' Was Used."

14 *"aroused the indignation"* "Will Decide the Huguenot Case Today."

14 *McDaniel and his friends* "They Accuse J. W. Brooks."

14 *Eventually, the dopers* "Notes of the Turf," March 7, 1906.

14 *"The turf scandal at Ascot"* "Ascot Needs Better Management."

15 *"The verdict in the Brooks case"* "Race Storm Blows Over."

15 *another sign of restlessness* "Tichenor Is to Have a New String"; Bergin, "McDaniel Has Good Chance to Annex Kentucky Derby This Year with Sun Briar."

15 *"While I feel very much disappointed"* M. H. Tichenor letter.

15 *"Horsemen get up early"* Kieran, "Uncle Henry Tells Some Stories."

15 *"Good horses have a lot of poor relations"* New Yorker, Volume 25, 2, 1949, 44.

15 *"I feel that I must go where I can win"* "Gossip from Juarez Track."

16 *Sheepshead Bay details* Vreeland, "McDaniel, Who Discovered Exterminator, Doing Well with Sun Briar Colts."

16 *The gambler Diamond Jim Brady jumping* Hildreth, *Spell of the Turf*, 87.

16 *Famous trainers* Goldberg, "The Golden Age of Brooklyn Racing."

17 *Uncle Henry's decency* "Prefers Job to $1000."

17 *He handed over his diamond pin* "Boy Jockey Accused of Stabbing R. L. Thomas."

17 *"Be quiet, not a move"* "Bold Resident Exchanged Shots with Burglar."

17 *through his bedroom door* "McDaniel Fought Duel With Burglar."

17 *the other in one of his boots* "Bold Resident Exchanged Shots with Burglar."

17 *"You can't settle down"* Hildreth, *Spell of the Turf*, 10.

18 *She had shot herself* "Trainer's Wife a Suicide."

18 *Just as his father had* "Notes of the Turf," February 17, 1914.

18 *"The Angel in Our House"* McDaniel collection. [in bibliography, poem's title is "The Angel of Our Home"]

18 *He would never marry again* Interview with Muriel McDaniel, June 11, 2012.

Chapter 2

20 *even other nouveau riche millionaires* West, "Willis Sharpe Kilmer and His Horses."

20 *"He was a millionaire"* Shay, *Bygone Binghamton*.

20 *"the number of horses employed"* U.S. Census, 1880.

20 *no electric railways . . . Brooklyn and New York* Tarr, "Urban Pollution."

20 *first international urban planning conference* Morris, "Horse Power to Horsepower," 2.

21 *about nine million in America today* "National Economic Impact of the U.S. Horse Industry."

21 *Horses transported almost all* Morris, "Horse Power to Horsepower," 3.

21 *As Ryan Goldberg writes . . . the one in England* Ryan Goldberg, "The Golden Era of Brooklyn Racing."

21 *Thomas Edison tested a camera* "Racing at Sheepshead Bay."

21 *Prospect Park and Coney Island, Brooklyn tracks information* Goldberg, "The Golden Era of Brooklyn Racing."

21 *Binghamton information* Interviews with Gerry Smith and Bill Gorman, Broome County Historical Society, Shay, *Bygone Binghampton*.

22 *S. Andral Kilmer and Swamp-Root* West, "Willis Sharpe Kilmer and Swamp-Root Tonic: Opportunist or Benefactor?"

22 *Medicine was not standardized yet* Stage, *Female Complaints*, 59.

22 *Doctors used* Ibid., 59, 63.

22 *In 1859, patent medicines generated* Young, *Toadstool Millionaires*.

22 *"A couple million a year"* West, "Willis Sharpe Kilmer and His Horses."

22 *Kilmer's innovations and attire* Hadsell, "Life and Times of Willis Sharpe Kilmer Told for First Time."

23 *Kilmer lashed a cyclist with a driving whip* "Willis Sharpe Kilmer Paid $605.99."

23 *"When we were doing a small business"* West, "Willis Sharpe Kilmer and Swamp-Root Tonic."

23 *became head of Swamp-Root's advertising* Ibid.

23 *"Miss Richardson, the bride"* "Kilmer-Richardson," clipping, BCHS, Kilmer file.

23 *Kilmer built a large home* "Mrs. Willis Sharpe Kilmer Has Begun an Action for Divorce at Binghamton."

23 *Sales were steady but slow* Hadsell, "Life and Times of Willis Sharpe Kilmer."

23 *Swamp-Root advertisements Swamp-Root Almanac 1916.*

23 *Swamp-Root jingle* "Musica-Medicus," sheet music with lyrics, BCHS.

24 *business owners needed to spend* Young, *Toadstool Millionaires*, 105.

24 *"an 1880s version of the infomercial"* Ibid.

24 *details of the Swamp-Root Almanac Swamp-Root Almanac 1916.*

24 *"If I am worth $25,000 to you"* Newman, "Willis Sharpe Kilmer."

24 *"Quick work necessary"* Adams, *Great American Fraud*, 129.

24 *The complaint she filed* "Mrs. Willis Sharpe Kilmer Has Begun an Action for Divorce"; "The Kilmer Divorce Case."

24 *Beatrice remarried in 1903* "Wedding Known to Few."

25 *"I'll get even with you"* National Reporter System, *Beardsley v. Kilmer*.

25 *The Herald's owners sued* Ibid.

25 *it went out of business* "How the Kilmers Ruled Binghamton."

25 *Christmas dinner details* "Mr. Kilmer Is Given Ovation by Newsboys."

25 *Adams spent plenty of his time* Young, *Toadstool Millionaires*.

25 *"The way to end Swamp-Root's career"* Adams, *Great American Fraud*, 135.

26 *Adams's book not sold in Binghamton* West, "Willis Sharpe Kilmer and Swamp-Root Tonic."

26 *An appellate court found* "Sweeping Decision by Appellate Court Is Filed Today."

26 *Kilmer married again* "Mrs. E. W. Kilmer Weds Maj. Sutton."

26 *His speedboat* Shepard, "The Frontenac Motor Boat Races."

26 *pacing the piazza* "Town and Country Life."

26 *foxhunting at Pinehurst* "Pinehurst."

27 *the Remlik Hounds* "Polo and Hunting."

27 *passengers snubbed Kilmer* West, "Willis Sharpe Kilmer and His Horses."

27 *"Membership in the American Jockey Club"* Mooney, *Race Horse Men,* 148.

27 *"would bring blushes to the foredeck"* Smith, *Strawberries in the Wintertime,* 145.

27 *Alice Roosevelt story* "Miss Roosevelt Eager to See Horses Start."

27 *"the new Eldorado of American racing men"* Rochecourt, "Americans Prosper on French Tracks."

27 *"It hardly seems credible"* Quoted in "English View of New York Legislation."

28 *"Perhaps you may not think so"* "Belmont Testifies in Graft Inquiry."

28 *Congress approved the creation of the Remount Service* Steve R. Waddell, *United States Army Logistics: From the American Revolution to 9/11* (Santa Barbara, CA: Praeger, 2010), 105.

28 *"It is upon you polo players"* . . . *"Where would they come from?"* "Belmont Horses as a Gift to Army."

29 *"I have not attempted to fix any definite standard"* Sanders D. Bruce, quoted in Boardman, *The Handbook of the Turf,* 18.

29 *no one in England liked* Robertson, *The History of Thoroughbred Racing in America,* 188–89.

29 *England started limiting how many American trainers* Ibid.

29 *Jersey Act* Elliott, *The History of Race Riding and the Jockeys' Guild,* 20.

29 *story of Durbar II* "Wraps American Flag Around Two Race Horses."

30 *Boer War remount* Koenig, *The Fourth Horseman,* 41–44.

30 *"vividly recall the short necked"* Charles L. Scott, quoted in Livingston and Roberts, *War Horse,* 48.

30 *stand 15-2 to 16-2 hands . . . between 1914 and 1918* Ibid., 32, 135.

30 *The color preference* "Painting White Horses for Camouflage During WWI."

30 *Front Royal* Livingston and Roberts, *War Horse,* 125.

30 *Sportsmen elected Major General Leonard Wood* " 'Save the Horse!' Slogan of Diners."

31 *Roosevelt was campaigning* Ibid.

31 *"In a nutshell"* "The Battle of Big Nations for Thoroughbred Horses."

31 *"Once he started buying racehorses"* "Recent New Recruit to Racing."

32 *"Billy Sunday didn't know a whole lot"* "How Willis Sharpe Kilmer Is Bringing Thoroughbreds."

32 *private Pullman car* "Gossip from Blue Grass Region."

32 *Frank Taylor* "Willis Sharpe Kilmer," *New York Morning Telegraph.*

32 *liner Mongolian* "Horses Arrive on S.S. Mongolian."

32 *entering racing on a "grand scale"* Railbird, "English 2-Year-Olds Here to Race in the Kilmer Silks."

32 *Atlantic Transport* Atlantic Transport Line advertisement; "Fire in Hold of Liner Minnehaha Admitted Due to Explosion."

32 *Horses ate well* "Rock Sand Cautious in Making a Landing."

32 *Stalls were padded* "Racers Off for Europe."

32 *famous driving team of grays, details of grooms* "Corrigan's Horses Arrive from London"; "Horses Traveling in Padded Stalls."

33 *Rock Sand* "Rock Sand Cautious in Making a Landing."

33 *onboard horse show* "Hold a Horse Show on an Ocean Liner."

33 *Muenter sabotages Minnehaha* "Muenter, Once German Teacher Here, Killed Wife, Shot Morgan, Sabotaged in World War 1"; "Minnehaha Sunk by a Submarine."

34 *"good-looking man"* Ross, *Boots and Saddles,* 102–03.

Chapter 3

35 *superstition that white socks* Alfred Stoddart, "Colors and Markings of Horses."

35 *eleven foals already,* "Dam of Exterminator."

35 *The Knight farm* "History."

35 *horse-birthing customs* Carlson, *Studies in Horse Breeding,* 195.

36 *Roosevelt's horses* Edmund Morris, *The Rise of Theodore Roosevelt* (New York: Coward, McCann, 1979).

36 *"the rhetoric of blood" . . . "was the same"* Kreyling, *A Late Encounter with the Civil War,* 8.

36 *"Cowboys . . . are certainly extremely good riders"* Roosevelt, *Ranch Life and the Hunting Trail,* 54.

36 *Roosevelt's riding rules* White House Historical Association, "The Theodore Roosevelt Family."

36 *Roosevelt considered* Morris, *Edith Kermit Roosevelt,* 412.

37 *"You all know what we mean"* Camp, "A Roosevelt Creed," 29.

37 *"The thoroughbred horse and the thoroughbred man"* "Battle of Big Nations for Thoroughbred Horses."

37 *"bred in the wilderness of obscurity"* Exile, "Exile's Note Book."

37 *August Belmont's ancestry* Birmingham, *"Our Crowd,"* 129.

37 *James Ben Ali Haggin* Mitchell C. Harrison, ed. *Prominent and Progressive Americans* (New York: New York Tribune, 1902), 2:146; Brackney, *Lost Lexington, Kentucky,* 106.

37 *"Big Ed" Corrigan* Wall, *How Kentucky Became Southern,* 143.

37 *unfashionably bred McGee* "Here and There on the Turf," September 1, 1922.

37 *named him after his insurance agent* "Latest Gossip and News from Churchill Downs."

37 *Knight family details* Boyd, 7; "Dam of Exterminator"; Estes, "The Exterminator Saga Ends"; "History."

37 *Charles W. Moore details* "C. W. Moore, the Breeder."

38 *McGee tended to get tired* Considine, "Old Bones."

38 *White Knight* Salvator, "Exterminator and the Figure System."

38 *his get were mud runners* "Exterminator Wins Kentucky Derby."

38 *"daily winners"* "C. W. Moore, the Breeder."

38 *She was born in 1899 . . . "washerwoman"* Considine, "Old Bones."

38 *"American hussy"* Sevier, " 'Tainted Blood' in Successful Racers."

38 *no dam on record* Salvator, "Exterminator and the Figure System."

38 *hardy and useful; details of Fair Empress's sales* "Dam of Exterminator."

38 *shares basis* "Exterminator Wins Kentucky Derby"; Estes, "The Exterminator Saga Ends."

38 *"Kentucky Paint"* " 'Kentucky Paint' Appears."

39 *recipes she attributed to a "Mammy"* Sharpless, *Cooking in Other Women's Kitchens.*

39 *"wanted them as examples"* Maria McCulloch-Williams, "Blood Will Tell in Horse as Well as Man."

39 *As Maryjean Wall . . . white jockeys ascended* Wall, *How Kentucky Became Southern*; Hotaling, *Great Black Jockeys.*

40 *McDaniel and Kilmer met* "Frank Taylor Quits as Trainer for Big Training Stable."

40 *leaving his brother William in charge* "Close Windsor Finishes."

40 *Crowds joined him* "Kilmer Racing String Is Fine."

40 *"Mr. Kilmer has organized his stud"* "Mr. Kilmer Will Help Breed Better Horses."

41 *"Mr. Kilmer is securing"* Ibid.

41 *McDaniel passport application* Woodrow Wilson, Executive Order 2285.

41 *"for W. S. Kilmer"* Passport application, Henry McDaniel, November 6, 1916. McDaniel collection.

41 *waiting for their ship* "30 Americans Held Up."

42 *navigation was hopeless* "German Bomb Narrowly Misses Binghamton Man in Streets of London.

42 *McDaniel in England, travel home* Ibid.

42 *"Somewhere out in the Atlantic"* "Current Notes of the Turf," January 13, 1917.

43 *needed five extra days* "Minnehaha Delayed by Accident."

43 *finally arrived on January 15* "Steamship Minnehaha Finally Arrives"; "Another of Minnehaha Shipment Dead."

43 *Four of the mares* "German Bomb Narrowly Misses Binghamton Man."

43 *specter of submarines* West, "Willis Sharpe Kilmer and His Horses."

43 *"The two torpedoes"* "Minnehaha Not Convoyed."

43 *Survivors clung to them* Ibid.

43 *"Have you anything for me, Sir?"* "Says Chained Mines Sunk Minnehaha."

43 *Forty-three people died* "Lost Minnehaha Officers"; "Minnehaha Is Sunk."

43 *"Oh heavens, horses!"* Quoted in Koenig, *The Fourth Horseman.*

43 *sixty-six hundred cavalry horses went down* Quoted ibid.

44 *like the ones that were aboard* Ibid.

44 *still lies underwater* "Lost Minnehaha Officers."

44 *Kilmer waited for the U.S. government* "Minnehaha Is Sunk."

44 *Atlantic Transport said* "Minnehaha Sunk by a Submarine"; "Minnehaha Is Sunk."

44 *turned out with the other 1915 foals* Carlson, *Studies in Horse Breeding,* 195.

44 *In August 1916* "Yearlings Sent East for Sale."

44 *"Racing and Saratoga are synonymous"* King, "Modern Horses Less Rugged."

44 *"At Saratoga they don't have paddocks"* Sherwood Anderson, "I Want to Know Why," http://xroads.virginia.edu/~hyper/Anderson2/triumph.html.

45 *examined hundreds of toddler thoroughbreds* "Saratoga Sales of Yearlings."

45 *seven sales scheduled* Ibid.

45 *"It takes a lot to make up a good horse"* Newman, "The Career of Uncle Henry," 296.

45 *Marcel Boussac* "French-Bred Yearlings Prove Popular."

45 *ringbone* Kilby, "How to Identify Pastern Problems."

45 *He was a very nice horse* Prime, "Uncle Henry."

45 *"I was prepared to go much higher"* "MacKay Yearlings Bring High Prices."

46 *story of Merrick* Livingston, *Old Friends.*

46 *Milam liked the sturdy* "Current Notes of the Turf," August 8, 1916.

46 *Bidding was lively* "Kentucky Yearlings Sell Well."

46 *Kilmer bought nothing* "Kentucky Yearlings Sell Well."

47 *Along with the other yearlings* Estes, "The Exterminator Saga Ends."

47 *he liked the McGee colt* "100 Years Old in March, He Says Horses Did It."

47 *"Why not Exterminator?"* Boyd, *Exterminator,* 24.

47 *Pancho Villa story* Livingston and Roberts, *War Horse,* 32.

47 *Sam Harris story* "8–1, Odds Faced at Carrizal by Pershing's Men."

48 *castration could help him bulk up* Estes, "The Exterminator Saga Ends."

48 *just wasn't well-bred enough* Boyd, *Exterminator,* 24.

48 *"Exterminator, from the beginning was doomed"* Salvator, "Exterminator and the Figure System."

49 *"carry a glass of water on his back"* "Roamer Iron Horse of American Turf."

49 *"Not one has missed a work-out"* "Kilmer Two-Year-Olds Are Now Ready."

49 *"Wizard of the Turf"* "Good Prices for Ogden Yearlings."

49 *"seemingly bottomless purses"* "Many Foreign-Bred Juveniles."

50 *"Racing Forecast"* Cole, "Looking Ahead for 1917."

50 *"had come to the front for war services"* "Baseball May Stop if New Order Stands."

50 *paid the rent on four homes* "Kilmer Again to Aid of Boys in Khaki"; "War Board Is Named Here to Aid Government."

50 *two hundred-foot* Remlik "Kilmer Gives Two Yachts."

50 Remlik *sailors won the Navy Yacht League* "Ship's Baseball Team"; Gill, "The U.S.S. *Remilk.*"

51 *Earl "Handy" Sande was punished* Barrett, "Alone at the Start."

51 *Starter Mars Cassidy* "Jockeys Must Keep Their Positions."

51 *"Cassidy's patience"* Ross, *Boots and Saddles,* 99.

51 *George Cassidy's stories* Barrett, "Alone at the Start."

51 *Others claimed that Exterminator watched* Considine, "Old Bones."

52 *the bettors' second choice* Estes, "The Exterminator Saga Ends."

52 *a short, cheap race* Boyd, *Exterminator,* 26.

52 *"Cal Milam's slab-sided gelding"* Alwes, "Backstretch Soliloquy."

52 *He came in fourth Gazette-Times,* May 19, 1918.

52 *he won a race there* Estes, "The Exterminator Saga Ends."

52 *he came from seventh place* "Exterminator Wins Kentucky Derby."

52 *Exterminator was to rest* Cromwell, "Trainer Milam's Horses in Charge."

52 *John Madden* Boyd, *Exterminator,* 60.

53 *Sun Briar won the Great American Handicap* "Local Horse Wins Greatest Two-Year-Old Race of Year."

53 *hung out giant placards* Ibid.

53 *women knitted socks* "Women at Racetrack Knitted Sox for Soldiers and Enjoyed It."

53 *Whitneys sailed* "Sun Briar in Van Before Big Crowd."

53 *Ral Parr passed around a box of chocolates* "Handsomely Gowned Women Show Interest in Races."

53 *"master hands"* "Jockey Willie Knapp."

54 *won the Albany Handicap* "Sun Briar Takes Albany."

54 *scratched Lucullite* "Sun Briar in Van Before Big Crowd," S2

54 *Grand Union Hotel Stakes* Dempsey, "Superb Saratoga Racing."

54 *Kilmer kept the whip* "Sun Briar in Van Before Big Crowd"; "Brilliant Gathering at Sun Briar Court."

54 *rode most of the race with just one stirrup* "Sun Briar King of 2-Year-Olds."

54 *Sun Briar won* "Sun Briar Now at the Top of His Form"; "Sun Briar Crowned Two-Year-Old King."

54 *kissed Esther* "Society's Adieu to Spa Season."

54 *salve of mercury and lard* Oscar Gleason, *Gleason's Veterinary Hand Book and System of Horse Taming*, 187.

54 *"They don't seem to hurt him"* "Midsummer Racing Attracts Crowds to the Spa."

54 *McDaniel made light* Jeffery, "Midway Shows Great Improvement."

54 *he just removed them* Smith, "Henry McDaniel."

54 *the most money of any horse* "Current Notes of the Turf," August 23, 1917, 1.

55 *Enormous banners* "Great Crowd Is in Frenzy of Joy as Colt Arrives."

55 *popular gramophone tunes* "Columbia Records That Should Be in Your Home This 'Fourth.'"

55 *out into the crowd, description of arrival and parade* "10,000 Binghamton Citizens Parade in Honor of Winning Race Horse."

55 *"This reception is not for me"* "Great Crowd Is in Frenzy of Joy."

56 *celebrate Sun Briar's turning three* "New Year Party for Sun Briar."

56 *Photographs* "Brilliant Gathering at Sun Briar Court."

56 *owner of other descendants of Lexington* "New Year Party for Sun Briar."

56 *Hundreds of people . . . McDaniel looked over Sun Briar* "Brilliant Gathering at Sun Briar Court."

57 *Negotiations with Churchill Downs* "Sun Briar to Go to Kentucky"; "New Year Party for Sun Briar."

57 *"Incidentally Mr. Kilmer took occasion"* "Big Price for Sun Briar."

Chapter 4

58 *"If I had my way"* "Baseball May Stop if New Order Stands."

58 *Matt Winn . . . glasses to soldiers* Winn, *Down the Stretch*, 160.

59 *ice-skated on frozen puddles* "Belmont Park Is Big Skating Rink."

59 *shortage of train cars* "Derby Again Has Value of $15,000."

59 *February 1* "Improvement in Sun Briar."

59 *frankly powerful body* "Sun Briar's First Work"; "Sun Briar Badly Beaten."

59 *ringbones were slowing him down* "Improvement in Sun Briar."

59 *the best of everything* "Sun Briar Is Carefully Guarded"; "Sun Briar the Derby Favorite."

59 *remained the Derby favorite* "Sun Briar the Derby Favorite."

60 *"The one crown"* "Henry McDaniel's Claim to Fame."

60 *racetrack: Exterminator* "Latonia Entries."

60 *"going wide"; "The ringbones seem to be bothering"* "Derby Candidates Doing Well."

60 *he would change things up* "Sun Briar Works Well in Blinkers."

60 *telegram* "Sun Briar Training Quite Soundly."

61 *would show reporters* "Latest Work of Derby Candidates"; "Sun Briar to Lexington"; "Lend Interest to Derby Trial."

61 *"One swallow don't make a summer"* "Ship Kilmer Horses to Louisville."

61 *"Something had to be done"* "Down the Stretch in the Derby."

62 *a lot of hazel in them* Dunstan, "Reflections."

62 *"He wouldn't have captured"* "Down the Stretch in the Derby."

62 *"born in a muddy stall"* "100 Years Old in March."

62 *buy the colt together* Fraley, "Today's Sports Parade."

62 *"I thought it over"* Wade, "One Tough Bag of Bones."

62 *"Kilmer got him"* "Three Old Timers Discuss Derby."

62 *Kilmer doubled immediately* "Trial Horse for Sun Briar."

62 *Exterminator was nowhere near as good* "War Cloud Reigns Favorite in Derby."

62 *Exterminator climbed aboard* "Ship Kilmer Horses to Louisville."

63 *a mile workout* "Sport Gossip"; "Manager Waite Wins the Camden"; "War Cloud Arrives at Louisville"; "Exterminator Brought $1,500 as Yearling at Saratoga."

63 *"I believe Mr. Kilmer made a wise move"* "War Cloud Arrives at Louisville."

63 *"It's all over but the shouting"* "Sun Briar Looks Good in Fast Workout."

63 *"In spite of the fact that Sun Briar"* McDaniel, "Down the Stretch in the Derby."

64 *So far, Exterminator had done his job* "Sun Briar Runs at Fair Speed in Derby Trial."

64 *"If I could guarantee the horse would win"* Boyd, *Exterminator*, 40.

64 *Al Jolson and Kilmer* "Kilmer Boosts Liberty Bond Sale."

64 *Camp Zachary Taylor description* Caroline Daniels, "'The Feminine Touch Has Not Been Wanting'"; "Unique Entertainment for Red Cross Society."

65 *Spanish flu epidemic* "Surgeon Blue Inspects Camp"; University of Michigan Center for the History of Medicine, www.influenzaarchive.org/cities/city -louisville.html.

65 *helped choose Sun Briar* "Mrs. Willis Sharpe Kilmer Gets Divorce and Remarries."

65 *Irving Wiles* "Mrs. Redondo Sutton," picture with "Mrs. Willis Sharpe Kilmer Divorced and Married Again, Sacrificing $25,000 a Year."

65 *large crowd from Binghamton, etc.* "The Churchill Downs Meeting."

66 *like a dress rehearsal for the* race "Sun Briar's Final Trial Today."

66 *owner and trainer conferred* "Liberator Delivers Goods."

66 *Kilmer telegram* "Sun Briar Will Be Sent East."

66 *"there are many who run fast"* McDaniel, "Down the Stretch in the Derby," 3.

66 *"nothing but a cussed billy goat!"* Wade, *One Tough Bag of Bones*, 60.

67 *livery stable* Brown, "Exterminator Resembled Hatrack."

67 *conversation between Winn and Kilmer* Winn, *Down the Stretch*, 158–59.

67 *"the pride of the Bluegrass"* "Bob Dundon Picks Escoba to Win Big Derby Race."

67 *had vowed to give his Derby winnings* "Escoba's Tussle with Sun Briar Derby Feature"; "Derby to Exterminator."

68 *details about the time* Kennedy, *Over Here*; "Meatless Mondays, Wheatless Wednesdays," Cornell University Library, http://exhibits.mannlib.cornell.edu /meatlesswheatless/meatless-wheatless.php?content=five; Eighmey, "Food Will Win the War"; United States Food Administration, "Potato Possibilities."

68 *Wilson and Mother's Day* " 'Mother's Day' for Army Abroad."

68 *Derby Day details* "War Coloring Given Derby."

68 *short plaits* Derby photos.

69 *"Earnest that our fighting forces"* Connor, *History of the Kentucky Derby*, 133.

69 *a foreign-born colt* Omar Khayyam.

69 *details of party the night before and the next morning* "Three Old-Timers Discuss Derby."

70 *Joe Notter sighed* Ibid.

70 *"hatful" of money* "Derby Day—Nuf Sed."

70 *"For you, $3,000 to 1"* Sporting edition of *Louisville Times,* quoted in "Exterminator's Victory Still Talk of Horse World."

70 *friends teased him so much* "Bourbon County Sports Not 'On' the Derby Winner."

70 *people kept coming* "Exterminator Is Winner of Derby, Was Trial Horse."

70 *Winn's team had encouraged* "To Avoid Delay Have Exact Change Ready."

70 *"Give me three conductors"* "War Coloring Given Derby."

71 *Spectators packed* "Kentucky Derby."

71 *capacity crowd of about forty thousand* "Derby to Exterminator, 30–1."

71 *carved out space* "East and West in Kentucky Derby."

71 *would take a very dark horse* "Around the Turf."

71 *"winner picked before it rained"* "Scenes in Betting Ring Are Graphically Described by Expert."

71 *"Two fives is lucky!"* "War Coloring Given Derby."

71 *More than $500,000* "Scenes in Betting Ring Are Graphically Described by Expert," 6.

71 *forbade women from betting* Derby program, Churchill Downs museum.

71 *inspired by the independence* "Scenes in Betting Ring."

71 *"It was with very mixed feelings"* McDaniel, "Down the Stretch in the Derby."

72 *"Hurry home"* "Exterminator Brought $1,500 as Yearling at Saratoga."

72 *a stretch battle* McDaniel, "Down the Stretch in the Derby."

72 *to improve the footing* "EXTERMINATOR a Worthy Substitute for Sun Briar."

72 *Each horse paraded past* "Derby to Exterminator, 30–1."

73 *And they were off* Ibid.

73 *spectators in the free section* "Great Crowd Sees Exterminator Win."

74 *"This is nothing to what I'll do"* McDaniel, "Down the Stretch in the Derby."

74 *the race* "Great Crowd Sees Exterminator Win"; "Derby to Exterminator, 30–1"; Boyd, *Exterminator.*

74 *"something up my sleeve"* "Derby Riders Make Statements About Mounts."

74 *"I never dreamed"* "Exterminator Brought $1,500."

74 *"After Exterminator beat Sun Briar so handily"* "Listen to What the Trainers Have to Say About It."

74 *"Gee, but it is great"* Ibid.

76 *Some of his friends* John I. Day, *New York Morning Telegraph,* quoted in "Exterminator's Victory Still Talk of Horse World."

76 *"It was the old story"* "Exterminator Brought $1,500."

76 *Mutual newsreel* "Derby Pictures Shown Day After Races."

76 *"The splendid victory"* "Triumph for American Breeding."

76 *The* Cincinnati Enquirer "The Overlooked Derby Winner."

77 *"the glorious uncertainty"* Ibid.

77 *"no one would take away Exterminator's glory"* The world of thoroughbred breeding also took Exterminator's victory to heart as a representative of "the Maria West family," tying Exterminator's breeding to such previous luminaries of the sport as Regret and Ben Brush, as Exile [M. M. Leach] wrote in the *Thoroughbred Record.* Also, many noted that Exterminator's half brother Donerail, also a son of McGee, had been the last long shot to win the Derby, in 1913.

77 *"That was the Derby"* "Three Old Timers Discuss Derby."

77 *hustled backward* "Exterminator Wins! 1918."

Chapter 5

78 *"Exterminator, the horse I bought"* "Mr. Kilmer's Entry Wins Classic Kentucky Derby."

78 *"If such a contingency ever occurs"* "Aftermath of the Kentucky Derby."

79 *August Belmont Sr. had Fenian declared* Vosburgh, "Analysis of Rules of Racing."

79 *"Racing in the United States"* "Geldings to Be Barred."

79 *winner would go to the government* "H. G. Bedwell's Success as a Trainer."

80 *"In well informed quarters"* "Major Belmont's Significant Words."

80 *"no excuse"* Macbeth, "Motor Cop Captures $5000 Withers Stakes at Belmont Park."

80 *"There was a jinx"* "Luck an Important Item in Racing."

80 *turf photographer C. C. "Red" Cook* "Jinx Haunting a Jockey's Cap."

80 *Sam Hildreth avoided $2 bills* Hildreth, *Spell of the Turf,* 258.

80 *He did not allow photographers* "Millions for a Horse."

80 *A mare named Kathleen* Dempsey, "Smashing Track Records."

80 *Even his head* "Exterminator Meets Defeat in East."

80 *People wondered if he was jinxed* "Likely Latonia Derby Starters."

80 *"Exterminator is mostly legs"* "Exterminator an Honest Horse."

81 *"not unbeatable"; details of race with Johren* "Uncle White a Good One"; "Johren's Latonia Derby."

81 *"Each cavalry man, as a rule"* "How Our Cavalry Horses Fare."

82 *"the Hun"* "Current Notes of the Turf," October 8, 1918, 2.

82 *"Get acquainted with your horse"* Articles from *Stars and Stripes,* November 29, 1918, quoted in "169,000 Horses in A.E.F."

82 *"An imaginary line is drawn"* United States War Department, *Manual for Stable Sergeants,* 161.

82 *only one, trusted man should be allowed to nurse him* Ibid., 69

82 *McDaniel had laid both colts off* "Three-Year-Old Supremacy."

82 *"Trainer Henry McDaniel has given Sun Briar"* Ibid.

83 *"would probably have to be satisfied"* "Great Outpouring of Society to Welcome Racing at the Spa."

83 *smell of liniment* Ross, *Boots and Saddles,* 98.

83 *fewer young men around* Morris, *Edith Kermit Roosevelt,* 414; "Automotive Gossip"; "Racing Notes," *Saratogian.*

83 *Julius Sighulz* "King Horse Again Draws Big Society Crowd to Saratoga."

83 *Others were supporting families* "Jockeys 'Doing Their Bit.'"

83 *"patriotic duty of every owner"* "Automotive Gossip."

83 *It sold for $5,300* "Society and Turf Patrons at Spa Contribute Largely to War Fund."

84 *"Football undoubtedly would make better"* "War Department Curbs Football"; "All Sports Are Off at Johns Hopkins."

84 *August 6 Delaware Handicap* Macbeth, "Sun Briar Smashes World's Mile Record."

84 *Racegoers crowded to congratulate* "Mile Time Is Lowered"; "Sun Briar Court May Aid Nation to Get Cavalry Horses."

84 *"If I had waved him on"* "Warm Spell No Bar to Society's Filling Club House at the Spa."

84 *"You see how much a woman respects"* Ibid.

84 *"The move would be made"* Ross, *Boots and Saddles,* 103.

85 *The Riddles were famous* Ibid., 166.

85 *Guests included Enrico Caruso* Ibid., 107.

85 *the Travers was only the second time* Carter and Kane, *150 Years of Racing in Saratoga,* 71–72.

86 *Even the jockeys rode for free* "Sun Briar Victor in Travers Stakes."

86 *To ride a horse knowing his stablemate* "An Elaborate Review of the Precedents of Racing."

86 *no matter what the rulebook said* More, "Great Sport in Sight."

86 *any challenger would find him* "Kilmer's Crack Racer Beats Johren by Nose."

86 *forced Johren into a pocket* "Sun Briar First in Turf Classic."

86 *giving Knapp a clear road* Dempsey, "Stars in Game Clashing."

86 *Exterminator came in fourth* "Jockey Knapp Tells How Sun Briar Won."

86 *sped off to find McDaniel and Knapp* "Sun Briar First in Turf Classic."

87 *whose warm laugh* Ross, *Boots and Saddles*, 106.

87 *"Sun Briar was the greatest"* Ibid., 101.

87 *"bully race"* "Sun Briar Creates Turf History"; "Sun Briar Victor in Travers Stakes"; "Sun Briar First in Turf Classic."

87 *"I am convinced that the farther he had to go"* Cole, "Latest Turf Gossip from Saratoga."

87 *While leafing through your copy* "Jockey Pays Supreme Sacrifice."

87 *leaving a widow and two children* "Donald Pons Is Killed in Action."

87 *wounded in action and confined to a hospital* "Current Notes of the Turf," October 8, 1918.

87 *he died the next day* "Turfman's Son Killed in France."

87 *twenty-three and just married* "James Butler's Son Dies in France."

87 *Martin Kearns* "Racing at Empire City."

88 *"blood counts with horses"* Wilfred Southwood, "Rockspring's Glorious Sacrifice."

88 *Democrat's picture on the cover* Thoroughbred Record, November 20, 1918.

88 *escaped from a German camp* "Good News for Thomas Hitchcock"; "How Thomas Hitchcock, Jr., Escaped."

88 *"It was an exciting thing, that race"* "Pudd'n McDaniel Wins Army Race."

88 *"The work is interesting"* "Jockeys Must Keep Their Positions."

88 *"I will send my colt against the record of Roamer's"* Cole, "Sun Briar After Roamer's Record."

89 *Exterminator joined him for the last mile* "Exterminator Horse That Shines on Any Sort of Racetrack."

89 *he did run it in 1:34 flat* "Sun Briar Runs Trial Mile in 1:34."

89 *"The mile was run in 1:34"* "Question Sun Briar's Mile in 1:34."

89 *"I timed it and know"* "Rice Suspended for Foul Riding at Belmont Park."

89 *"work or fight" rule; details of grooms' schedule* "Stable Work Is Hard Work Indeed."

90 *he also just lost* "Exterminator Is Third, Ticket Wins."

90 *had won the Derby by luck* "Derby Winner Left Far Behind in Race."

90 *Besides landscaping* "Laurel Park a Place of Beauty."

90 *the Spanish flu was taking hold* Barry, *The Great Influenza*, 239.

90 *one out of every sixty-seven soldiers* Ibid.

90 *including Earl "Handy" Sande* "Heard at Laurel."

90 *health authorities shut it down* "Laurel Racing Suspended."

91 *made everyone wear gauze masks* "Current Notes of the Turf," October 19, 1918.

91 *pine needle oil sprayed inside* "Influenza Precautions."

91 *Only sixteen of the Laurel meet's* "Closing Day at Laurel."

91 *donating $10,000 worth of bonds* "Exterminator Lands Feature."

91 *explanation of handicaps* Greene, *Kentucky Handicap Horse Racing*, 38–39.

92 *shouted until their voices rasped* "Enthusiasm Runs Wild."

92 *lift its ban on public gatherings* "No Change in Latonia Situation."

92 *By November 19, horses were running* "Drastic's Easy Triumph."

92 *Red Cross fund-raising* "Latonia Racing Extended."

92 *"crack three-year-old"* "Drastic's Easy Triumph."

92 *confident that Exterminator would win* "Latonia Cup to Be Decided Today."

92 *six ice spoons* Ibid.

92 *most successful foal* "Exterminator Wins Latonia Cup."

92 *bowl, cups, and spoons* "Exterminator's Cup Race."

92 *"shoulder top weight dependedly"* "Local Notes."

93 *Roosevelt tried to intervene for Leonard Wood; Kidron had been all over France* "'Kidron,' Pershing's War Horse, Must Remain in Quarantine While His Master Is Riding in Parades."

93 *saboteur named Anton Dilger* Koenig, *The Fourth Horseman*.

93 *before-parade details; Jeff* "Army of Children Cheer Pershing at Ceremony in Park."

94 *Kidron's later life* Koenig, *The Fourth Horseman*, 298.

94 *Esther was apparently finished* "Mrs. E. W. Kilmer Weds Maj. Sutton."

94 *process server and Esther* Conversations with Bill Gorman, July 2014 and 2015.

94 *divorced in the first place* "Mrs. E. W. Kilmer Weds Maj. Sutton."

94 *diamond-and-ruby bracelet* "Mrs. Willis Sharpe Kilmer Divorced and Married Again."

94 *"Sometime after the Kentucky Derby"* Shay, *Bygone Binghamton*, 376.

96 *"Up to a mile and a furlong"* "Henry M'Daniel."

96 *Sherwood Anderson details; "Middlestride . . . isn't such a much"* Rideout, *Sherwood Anderson*.

96 *he would not race any longer* "Last Year for Sun Briar."

97 *to race in French steeplechases* "Exterminator for Steeplechasing."

97 *to show the Europeans* "May Send Racers to France."

97 *Kilmer seemed to have two* Ours, *Man o' War*, 32

97 *"We have weeded the stable"* "Feature Race Captured by Hampton Dame."

97 *once Healy got to Saratoga* "Current Notes of the Turf," July 30, 1918.

97 *"W. S. Kilmer is going to turn one or two"* "Saratoga Track a Marvel."

97 *Mormon* "Breaks American Record," *Daily Racing Form*, September 13, 1918.

97 *"dark days, but no so dark"* Sevier, "Sun Briar and Johren to Remain Rivals This Year."

98 *With what Sun Briar and Exterminator* "Sun Briar Wintering Well."

Chapter 6

99 *"These swift and exquisite creatures"* "Sir Barton Wins."

100 *description of Sun Briar Court* "Improvements at Sun Briar Court"; Vreeland, "Sun Briar Court, a Million Dollar 'Horse Heaven.'"

100 *Binghamton's Riverside Drive* "Improvements at Sun Briar Court."

100 *shadow of a low mountain* Hadsell, "Life and Times of Willis Sharpe Kilmer."

100 *"hickory-boned" Kentucky foals* Wall, *How Kentucky Became Southern*, 55.

100 *"Kentucky luxuriance"* "Improvements at Sun Briar Court."

100 *"horse for horse"* Sevier, "Sun Briar Court Stud."

100 *"Economy in production"* Ibid.

100 *became a destination* Vreeland, "Sally's Alley and Exterminator Ready for 'Derby' and 'Cups.'"

100 *fireproof tile . . . underground steam plant* "Improvements at Sun Briar Court."

101 *three training tracks . . . quarter-mile riding ring* Ibid.

101 *sun through the glass warmed the track* Fitzgerald, "Racing Fixtures Should Be Annexed by Horses from Sun Briar Court."

101 *One led to the indoor track* Vreeland, "Sally's Alley and Exterminator Ready."

101 *Enough hay and grain* "Improvements at Sun Briar Court."

101 VISITORS ARE WELCOME Copland, "Sun Briar Court Stands Out."

101 *turf writers did gather* "Racing Experts Come to Sun Briar Court."

101 *Instead of a motor* Copland, "Sun Briar Court Stands Out."

101 *"This machine-like arrangement"* Vreeland, "Sally's Alley and Exterminator Ready."

102 *pouring oats into separate buckets* Copland, "Sun Briar Court Stands Out."

102 *"With the war, too"* Audax, in *Horse and Hound*, quoted in "Sun Briar Court."

102 *"I wanted to go right back to the hotel"* Rogers, "The Day's Worst Story."

102 *suited to his ground-covering speed* "Which Will Be the Greater Four-Year-Old?"

102 *Some of the jockeys* "Opening Day at Hot Springs."

102 *For McDaniel, this kind of competition* "Exterminator Sprints Fast."

102 *"well satisfied"* "Exterminator Beats Drastic and Lucky B."

103 *"the most widely known American"* "Champion Jess Willard Is Star in Big Production."

103 *Exterminator almost ran it down* "Exterminator Shares Honors with Willard in 'Challenge of Chance.'"

103 *"One end bites and the other end kicks"* Hillenbrand, *Seabiscuit,* 42.

104 *had been an amateur jockey* Burke, "It's a Helluva Long Time Since."

104 *Vreeland had worked as an assistant trainer* Inabinett, *Grantland Rice and His Heroes,* ix; Hughes, "Ed Hughes' column."

104 *"American obsession"* Allen, *Only Yesterday,* 65.

104 *writers of the postwar years* Inabinett, *Grantland Rice and His Heroes.*

104 *"This bird has been"* Collyer, "Collyer's Comment," November 7, 1922, 13.

104 *"What, then, made the Golden Age Golden?"* Inabinett, *Grantland Rice and His Heroes,* ix.

104 *"Would I were I a Homer"* Vreeland, "Exterminator Being Prepared to Capture Cups for Fourth Time."

105 *was a traditionalist* Hughes, "Ed Hughes' column"

105 *Henry V. King's description of the trains* Henry King, "Kilmer Horses Show the Way in Champlain"; "Sun Briar Breaks Record in Champlain Handicap."

105 *"whore's breakfast"* Cook, *Titanic Thompson.*

106 *"HAY IN THE BARN"* "W. E. Wilson."

106 *Mormon was supposed to be* "W. S. Kilmer Horses at Louisville."

106 *kept losing races* "Mormon Badly Beaten."

106 *didn't work with Mormon, either* "Derby the Principal Topic."

106 *had raced more and finished stronger* "W. S. Kilmer Horses at Louisville."

106 *"had taken great pains"* Leonard, "Exterminator Wins Ben Ali Handicap."

107 *tugged on McDaniel's coat* C. J. Savage, "Exterminator Proves Best in the Lexington Feature."

107 *"best mannered horse in the word"* Exile, "May 1."

107 *came to the front to win easily* "Exterminator in Triumph"; "Feature Is Easy for Exterminator."

107 *"he springs like a rubber ball"* Leonard, "Exterminator Wins Ben Ali Handicap."

107 *"I had my eyes open"* "Kilmer's 'Sun-Briar' Is Fine."

107 *"splendid fettle"* Exile, "May 8."

107 *sorry that Kilmer couldn't be there* "Lexington Meeting at End."

107 *"pleasure to see such a horse"* Savage, "Exterminator Is Winner over Midway in Lexington."

107 *told a reporter that he was happy* "Kilmer's 'Sun-Briar' Is Fine."

108 *Healy as just as underling* "Current Notes of the Turf," May 6, 1919; "Hopeless Cripple Made a Winner."

108 *the purchase was hopeful* "Here's Strong 'Hunch' for Derby."

108 *"flew off the handle"* McDaniel, "Fifty Years on the Turf."

108 *"Frogtown won handily enough"* Ibid.

108 *Kilmer even told people* Boyd, *Exterminator,* 101.

109 *if that was the plan, it didn't work* "All Favorites Overcome."

109 *an enormous 134 pounds* "Exterminator's Fine Trial."

109 *Exterminator could not pull ahead* "Midway Wins Rich Handicap"; "Midway Captures Kentucky Feature."

109 *not enough jockey* Sevier, "Sun Briar Likely to Face the Barrier at Aqueduct."

109 *Kilmer blamed McDaniel, too* Sevier, "Fastest 1919 4-Year-Old to Get Distance Tests."

109 *fairly heavy 128 pounds* "Weights for Suburban Handicap"; "Great Enthusiasm Shown."

109 *ready for the race* "Current Notes of the Turf," June 7, 1919.

109 *"He is a fine race horse"* "Suburban Handicap at Belmont Park."

110 *McDaniel gave him a rest* "Naturalist Is Easy Victor in Excelsior."

110 *since August 1918* "Fair Colleen Beats Ireland."

110 *bewildering jumble* "The Screen."

110 *movie prices* "Binghamton Will See."

110 *rewarded, instead, with his own ranch* "Exterminator Shares Honors with Willard."

110 *the good guys win* Ibid.; "Two Champions Star in Big Motion Picture."

110 *"best horse race that the screen has known"* "Exterminator Shares Honors With Willard."

110 *"A real horse race"* *Challenge of Chance* advertising poster.

111 *nicknamed him Dempsey* Ours, *Man o' War,* 74.

111 *Kilmer said that he didn't think* Sevier, "Sun Briar Likely to Face the Barrier at Aqueduct."

111 *The stallion looked strong* Ibid.; "Current Notes of the Turf," July 3, 1919.

111 *"Sun Briar's race"* "Sun Briar's First Race Impressive."

111 *no rationale was offered* "Loftus Is Called on Carpet"; "Double for S. C. Hildreth."

111 *"Kilmer has displayed admirable sportsmanship"* "Sun Briar Breaks Saratoga Record."

111 *A new entrance for racehorses* "Many Improvements at Saratoga."

112 *"You have proved it"* "Purchase Romps Off with Huron Under 134 Lbs."

112 *"a better balanced horse"* Exile, "Saratoga Special."

112 *"a living model"* "Sun Briar Superb Type of Horse."

112 *"He is 16.2 hands high"* "Exterminator an Honest Horse."

112 *McDaniel nicknamed Exterminator "Chang"* "Exterminator Adds to Fame by Winning Harford."

112 *Shang* "Willie Knapp: He'll Join Hall of Fame."

113 *"as if urging on his stable mate"* Day, "Fairy Wand Beats Gallant Sun Briar in the Delaware."

113 *"his gallantry"* Macbeth, "Cochran Mare Does 1:36 Mile in Winning the Delaware."

113 *came in second* Day, "Fairy Wand Beats Gallant Sun Briar in the Delaware."

113 *Exterminator came in third* Copland, "Sun Briar Is Beaten by a Head by Fairy Wand"; "Delaware Handicap."

113 *"If horses talked"* Day, "Fairy Wand Beats Gallant Sun Briar in the Delaware."

113 *"Sun Briar will win"* King, "Kilmer Horses Show the Way in Champlain."

113 *"Exterminator is the best horse"* "J. C. Milam."

113 *declared Champlain day a holiday* King, "Kilmer Horses Show the Way in Champlain."

113 *The crowd shouted* "Sun Briar Breaks Record in Champlain Handicap."

114 *trying to keep him behind Sun Briar* "Sun Briar's Flying Heels"; King, "Kilmer Horses Show the Way in Champlain"; "Keen Contest for Racing Laurels."

114 *finishing just behind Sun Briar* "Golden Broom a New Star."

114 *new mile-and-a-furlong track record* "Kilmer Rewards Trainer and Riders."

114 *"A majority of the thousands"* "Keen Contest for Racing Laurels."

114 *$500 each* "Kilmer Rewards Trainer and Riders."

114 *the one McDaniel remembered watching* "Sun Briar Breaks Record in Champlain Handicap."

115 *standing on Sam Hildreth's shoulders* "Turf Bureau."

115 *James Rowe* "Sun Briar Wins Champlain Handicap in Drive at Saratoga."

115 *Kilmer choosing Schuttinger* "Man o' War and Exterminator Win Feature Stakes."

115 *Rain had fallen* Ibid.

115 *pounding and splashing* Macbeth, "Great Purchase Defeated in Saratoga Cup Classic"; "Man o' War and Exterminator Win Feature Stakes."

115 *"hooked up at hurricane speed"; other race details* "Hopeful to Man o' War."

115 *"but he couldn't do it"* Harry Williams, "Exterminator and Man o' War Score in Stakes at Spa."

115 *"one of those things I like to forget"* Hildreth, *Spell of the Turf,* 237.

115 *Exterminator met the track record* "Man o' War and Exterminator Win Feature Stakes," 21; Sevier, "Another Cup Race Likely Next Month."

115 *drenched but alert* Macbeth, "Great Purchase Defeated in Saratoga Cup Classic."

115 *Kilmer ran from the stands* Ibid.

116 *Given the history* "Sun Briar Wins Champlain Handicap in Drive at Saratoga."

116 *any Exterminator victory seemed good* Copland, "$5000 Weight for Age Event Is Attractive."

116 *"Mr. Kilmer is setting a good example"* "Muddy Going at Belmont."

116 *"He will always be remembered"* "Sun Briar Fails over Distance."

116 *Sun Briar was finished* Ibid.

116 *"not nearly as great"* "Keen Contest for Racing Laurels."

116 *a venerable dowager* King, "Sun Briar's Dam Here from France."

116 *Man o' War* Harry Williams, "Exterminator and Man o' War Score," 1.

117 *"but somehow the conversation drifts"; Exterminator nudging McDaniel* "Exterminator an Honest Horse."

117 *"He didn't look it"* King, "Modern Horses Less Rugged."

117 *Horse and trainer went to Maryland* Cole, "Kilmer Horses Going to Maryland"; "Sunbriar in Cup Race."

117 *Exterminator lost the Harford* Price, "The Porter and Billy Kelly Take Big Events at Opening of Havre de Grace."

117 *he won the Republic Handicap* "Cudgel Is Beaten by Exterminator"; Price, "Exterminator Is Republic Victor"; "Exterminator's Gameness."

117 *Merchants' and Citizens'* "Keen Contest for Racing Laurels."

117 *Those two went back and forth* "Cudgel Runs Fine Race."

118 *Knapp and Exterminator* "Exterminator Easy Victor at Laurel"; "Exterminator Is Again a Winner."

118 *passed around the rumor* "Small Fields at Aqueduct."

118 *Guests received favors* "Mrs. R. L. Gerry Gives Dinner Dance."

118 *story ran that the Gerrys* Ours, *Man o' War,* 29

118 *the Gerrys' trainer* "Funeral Services of C. T. Patterson."

118 *On October 7* "H. McDaniel to Train for R. L. Gerry."

118 *went to Latonia next* "Be Frank Wins Latonia Cup."

119 *spectators could hardly move* "Royce Rools Wins Bowie Handicap."

119 *1919 Bowie* "Royce Rools Beats Stars at Pimlico."

119 *"thought he had been lost"* Vreeland, "In-and-Out Racing Marred Fall Meeting at Pimlico."

119 *Both McDaniel and Exterminator* Sparrow, "Easy for Exterminator."

119 *"He had all the pep"* Vreeland, "In-and-Out Racing Marred Fall Meeting at Pimlico."

119 *McDaniel and Exterminator headed back* "Exterminator Wins the Pimlico Cup."

119 *would sever his connection* "Pimlico Cup Goes to Exterminator"; "Exterminator the Winner."

119 *McDaniel told reporters* Fitzgerald, "The Round-Up."

119 *"I never had a horse in my charge"* "Great Exterminator, with $171,381, Leads World's Geldings."

120 *"Exterminator is no oil painting"* Exile, "Saratoga Cup."

Chapter 7

121 *Roamer's accident* "Roamer Breaks Leg at Red Bank."

121 *"Now that Roamer is sleeping the long sleep"* Vreeland, "Exterminator May Replace Roamer as 'Idol' of the Turf."

121 *"What we like most about Exterminator"* Daniel, "Exterminator Seems to Have Found Himself at Last."

122 *"Old Reliable" nickname* Vreeland, "Touch Me Not Wins Great American in Driving Finish."

122 *"Here comes Exterminator!"* Winn, *Down the Stretch*, 156.

122 *came in second* "Exterminator in First 1920 Race."

122 *Racegoers hoped Exterminator* Daniel, "High Lights and Shadows in All Spheres of Sport."

122 *Teddy Rice's jockey cap* Macbeth, "Paul Jones Adds Name to List"; "Paul Jones Is Home First in the Suburban."

122 *"bedraggled, wet and peevish throng"* Macbeth, "Paul Jones Adds Name to List."

123 *"No excuse"* Vreeland, "Paul Jones Suburban Winner."

123 *Some wondered* Ibid.

123 *won the Long Beach Handicap* King, "Exterminator Makes New Record at Jamaica Track."

123 *record of 1:51 1/5* Daniel, "Exterminator Seems to Have Found Himself at Last."

123 *a day so crowded* Vreeland, "Schuttinger a Real Jockey."

123 *Exterminator was the favorite* King, "Exterminator Is Choice for Brooklyn Handicap."

123 *came in fourth* King, "Cirrus Winner of Brooklyn Handicap."

123 *won the Luke Blackburn . . .* Vincent Treanor, "Dimmesdale Classy Colt," *Evening World*, June 20, 1920, 22.

123 *"one of the very best horse races"* Macbeth, "Exterminator Sets up New Track Record."

123 *won the Brookdale* "Great American to Maiden."

123 *lost the Frontier Handicap* "Frontier to Slippery Elm."

123 *and then the Saratoga Handicap* King, "Sir Barton Fast with Weight Up"; Dempsey, "Sir Barton at His Best."

123 *"suitcase horse"* Graham, "Setting the Pace.

123 *"He spent as much time on the road"* "To Keep Him Happy."

124 *McDaniel remembered once leaving* Graham, "Setting the Pace."

124 *Man o' War soared* Sevier, "Kilmer Racer Should Have Most Successful Campaign."

124 *which was the best horse?* Boyd, *Exterminator*, 107.

124 *came in second in the Champlain* Dempsey, "Tryster Still Unbeaten."

124 *Healy hustled him to Ontario* "Star Racers on the Way."

124 *Bedwell scratched him* "Exterminator the Winner."

124 *still in Canada, Exterminator won the Hendrie* "Gallant Exterminator."

124 *the following Tuesday* "These Victories Reflect the Training Ability of Healy."

125 *Healy obeyed* Treanor, "Healy To Train for Diaz, Isn't Sorry Quitting Kilmer."

125 *"easily be the greatest racing attraction"* Vreeland, "Today's Victory at 50 to 1."

125 *"There is nothing to be gained"* "Current Events in Sports."

125 *Other owners made a gentleman's agreement* Sevier, "Saratoga Cup Race May Be Three-Cornered Affair."

125 *If the two younger horses* Vreeland, "Man o' War Sure to Race for Historic Saratoga Cup."

125 *"The public which has made it possible"* "Real Championship Test."

125 *Schenectady Lodge of Elks* "Floral Piece for a Horse Is a Saratoga Novelty."

125 *Someone asked Healy* Treanor, "V. Treanor's Column."

126 *"being 'ridden and 'goaded' almost to distraction"* Ibid.

126 *Ross scratched Sir Barton* "Heard and Seen in Saratoga Paddock."

126 *"dodged the issue with Exterminator"* Vreeland, "Sir Barton, Travel Weary, 'Dodges' Man o' War."

126 *get those flowers* "Leonardo II Wins the Rich Hopeful."

126 *"Hello, Bill!"* "Schenectady Elks Present Mr. Kilmer with Magnificent Floral Horseshoe."

126 *Kilmer walked underneath* Ibid.

127 *"You can no longer hear"* "Auto Has Killed the Family Dobbin."

127 *Gerry had to pay a fine of $500* "Verdict Against R. L. Gerry."

127 *On just one summer day* "Motorcar Accidents."

127 *Once, a reporter asked McDaniel* Graham, "Setting the Pace."

128 *What was it like to see Exterminator now?* Hollingsworth, "Exterminator."

128 *" 'Tis an axiom of the track"* Curley, "Exterminator Smashes Record in Winning Aqueduct Feature."

128 *"On some of his forays Exterminator has been beaten"* "Wonderful Horse Keeps On Running Year After Year."

128 *description of the Autumn Gold Cup* Vreeland, "Exterminator Wins Gold Cup."

129 *Exterminator broke the record* "American Record Falls Before Exterminator."

000 *fourth race in four weeks* Ibid.

129 *"profound and sweeping bows"* Lyons, "Grandstand to Paddock."

129 *August Belmont shook his hand* Vreeland, "Exterminator Wins Gold Cup."

129 *"I'm all flustered"* Henry King, quoted in "Exterminator Sets American Running Record."

129 *spirited the cup away* Lyons, "Grandstand to Paddock."

129 *filled with champagne* Vreeland, "Exterminator Wins Gold Cup."

129 *Healy was in a more sober mood* King, "Exterminator Wins Cup and Makes New Record."

129 *"Exterminator is a great horse"* Lyons, "Grandstand to Paddock."

129 *"Healy isn't sorry"* Treanor, "Healy to Train for Diaz."

129 *put Exterminator up for sale* "Exterminator Will Be Sold."

130 *One buyer offered $50,000* Ibid.

130 *Exterminator wasn't for sale* Kenefick, "On the Sport Firing Line."

130 *Will was the more talented horseman* Interview with Muriel McDaniel, summer 2013.

130 *Other high earners* "Near the $100,000 Mark."

130 *"old time 'cup' horse"* Henry King, quoted in "Exterminator Sets American Running Record."

130 *"With the possible exception of Man o' War"* Ibid.

130 *could Man o' War beat Exterminator* Al Copland, quoted in "Racing Expert Asks for Real Test."

130 *Kenilworth Jockey Club* "Offers $50,000 for Race."

130 *Matt Winn tried to lure* "Plan Race for Man o' War and Two Rivals Today."

130 *offering $75,000* Dempsey, "$75,000 and $5,000 Gold Cup."

130 *Match race negotiations* Ours, *Man o' War*, 134.

131 *Kilmer hoped Vosburgh would allow* "Man o' War and Sir Barton to Race for $75,000 Purse."

131 *Kilmer felt slighted . . . cruising on his yacht* "How Kilmer Star Was Counted Out."

131 *"There can be no genuine championship"* Sevier, "Exterminator Should Go in Big Canadian Race."

131 *"lacks only the presence"* "In the Wake of the News."

131 *"Mr. Kilmer and not Mr. Riddle"* Salvator, "Man o' War—or Exterminator?"

132 *Kilmer and Exterminator were out* "$75,000 Horse Race for Two Champions"; "Shilling Says Race Is Sure."

132 *Exterminator won two races in the ten days* "Exterminator a Winner"; "Exterminator and Our Flags."

132 *Winn offered Riddle and Kilmer $50,000* "Man o' War May Race in England Next Year; Offer $50,000 for Race with Exterminator"; Vreeland, "Man o' War, the Miracle Horse."

132 *make Man o' War the highest money earner* "Man o' War–Exterminator."

132 *"I am considering the offer from Kentucky"* "Refuses $400,000 for Man o' War."

132 *Will McDaniel told reporters* "Plans Are Completed for Pimlico Meet"; "Cheaper Grade of Horses."

132 *Man o' War would not race again* "Man o' War Will Be Placed in Strictest Seclusion."

132 *"When racing officials offered"* Hillenbrand, *Seabiscuit*, 151.

132 *"the fact that Man o' War did not meet and beat"* Sevier, "Presses Man o' War for Winning Honors."

132 *Man o' War and Exterminator* Dempsey, "Sam's Boy Is Uncle Sam's"; "Man o' War Will Not Race Again, Says Samuel Riddle."

133 *"perhaps no greater nonsense"* Salvator, "Man o' War—or Exterminator?"

133 *"The color of the 1920s"* Alexander, *A Sound of Horses,* 130.

133 *Gerry's stable was unprepossessing* "Three Prominent Trainers."

133 *McDaniel hurried* Vreeland, "Burlew No Longer Trains Macomber Racing Stable."

133 *McDaniel briefly considered* "J. K. L. Ross' New Trainer."

134 *Exterminator, trapped in a pocket* "Exterminator Wins Big Moneyed Event."

134 *Ensor avenged* Vreeland, "Exterminator Wins the Pimlico Cup in Record Time."

134 *clipped twenty seconds* Sparrow, "Exterminator Breaks Record at Old Hilltop."

134 *two trophies* "Two Beautiful Trophies."

134 *attendance records were broken* "Saratoga's Greatest Meeting."

134 *"one-horse stable"* "Lucky Owner of Exterminator."

134 *"With the mighty Man o' War"* Vosburgh, "Great American Race Horses Are Contemporaneous."

134 *"My luck has always come in cycles"* Ibid.

135 *August Belmont spent $600,000* "New Belmont Park Today."

135 *Latonia was renovated* "All Set at Fair Latonia."

135 *"When great beauty of form"* "Foresee Wonderful Sport."

135 *Will with eight Kilmer horses* Omar Khayyam, "Out of the Feed Box."

136 *McDaniel nursed Thomas* "Shilling Receives His License."

136 *Shilling claimed* "Racing Notes," *Brooklyn Daily Standard Union.*

136 *The case was eventually dismissed* "Sporting Comment."

136 *He had been Bedwell's assistant trainer* Vreeland, "Burlew No Longer Trains Macomber Racing Stable."

136 *Belmont was acting in his capacity* "Noted Canadian Turfman Lets Head Trainer Go."

136 *Even the governor of Maryland* "To Fight New York Tracks to Finish."

136 *A mob attacked* "J. Kennedy Attacked by Pimlico Fans."

136 *Mired in dissent* "Pimlico Racing May Stop Today."

136 *"tired and sick of the trouble"* Vreeland, "Exterminator Wins the Pimlico Cup in Record Time."

136 *Ross let Bedwell go* Burnaugh, "Turfman Yields to Jockey Club"; "Turf War Starts over Bedwell Case."

136 *Ross hired Henry McDaniel* "J. K. L. Ross' New Trainer."

136 *the largest retainer ever* Ibid.

136 *made all Ross's troubles evaporate* "Ross Releases H. G. Bedwell."

136 *"The news that McDaniel would take charge"* "Commander Ross Averts Turf War."

137 *"Although his heart must have been heavy"* Sparrow, "Bedwell Has Field Day."

137 *"Bedwell has nobody but himself"* Vila, "Jockey Club Still Supreme on Track."

137 *He started drinking* Robertson, *The History of Thoroughbred Racing in America,* 206; Ross, *Boots and Saddles,* 224.

137 *Will McDaniel had Exterminator sharp* "Exterminator in Maryland."

137 *He was strong* Malone, "Belmont Park Almost Ready."

137 *Kilmer set a high goal* Sevier, "Exterminator May Reach $200,000 Mark in Purses."

138 *Hildreth didn't allow* "Mad Hatter Temperamental Horse."

138 *Kings County Handicap* "Hildreth's Day of Glory."

138 *Excelsior* "Great Racing at Jamaica."

138 *clocked the most people* "Long Beach Goes to Exterminator."

138 *biggest crowd for the New York tracks* Macbeth, "Exterminator and Thunderclap Clip Records at Jamaica."

138 *"were packed to choking suffocation"* Ibid.

138 *Earl Sande urged Mad Hatter on* "Exterminator Sets Track Record."

138 *"It will be many a day"* "Exterminator's Fast Race."

138 *"I believe that most students"* Sevier, "Exterminator May Reach $200,000 Mark in Purses."

139 *Kilmer's ambition still seemed ludicrous* Ibid.

139 *flying hoof slammed* W. J. Macbeth, "Audacious Takes Suburban."

139 *moved Mad Hatter to the far outside* Vreeland, "Audacious Wins Suburban."

139 *fell farther behind as they yelled* Burnaugh, "Exterminator Gains Thrilling Victory over Mad Hatter."

139 *"Just what would have been the result"* Vreeland, "Audacious Wins Suburban."

139 *"whalebone and steel Exterminator"* "Brooklyn to Grey Lag."

139 *Will McDaniel shipped* "In the Kentucky Racing Field."

139 *"Weight don't bother him"* Collyer, "Collyer's Comment," July 4, 1921.

139 *"Exterminator, of Course"* "Exterminator, of Course."

140 *Will McDaniel left Kilmer* "Exterminator May Win the Fourth Race."

140 *Willie Knapp* "Runstar Behaves and Wins."

140 *white cotton bandages* "Saratoga Battle Ground."

140 *turned Old Shang over to Knapp* "Much Activity at Saratoga."

140 *"Willie Knapp has all the qualifications"* Lowe, "Racing Folk Rejoice at Knapp's Success."

140 *Exterminator won* "Exterminator Is Handicap Winner."

140 *three Saratoga Cups?* "Exterminator Again Victor."

140 *"walkover" was still staged* "Modo Wins in Fast Time."

141 *"The old fellow took the track alone"* "Hunts Meet Is on Tomorrow."

141 *Autumn Gold Cup again* "Exterminator to Race at Woodbine."

141 *Only one other horse entered* Macbeth, "Final Belmont Feature Draws Only 2 Horses."

141 *"more or less of a joke and a travesty"* "Exterminator Takes Autumn Gold Cup and Edwina Wins Dunton."

141 *"That fellow ain't a horse"* Ibid.

142 *Kilmer said he would put his newest trophy* Vreeland, "Exterminator, King of Long Distance Horses, Wins the Autumn Gold Cup."

142 *At Aqueduct on the Fourth of July* Hotaling, *They're Off!*, 218; Pietrusza, *Rothstein*, 121.

142 *Rothstein and "The Brook"* Pietrusza, *Rothstein*.

142 *Rothstein and sports editor* Ibid., 113.

142 *Belmont and Rothstein* Ibid., 110.

143 *Exterminator won the Toronto Autumn Cup* "Exterminator Once Again."

143 *"No horse can do the impossible"* Helgesen, "The Porter Wins Annapolis Handicap."

143 *"all was over but the shouting"* Omar Khayyam, "Careful and Exterminator Win."

143 *went to Lexington, lost* "Laurel's Largest Crowd."

143 *now a public figure* Helgesen, "Audacious Wins Pimlico Feature."

143 *most formidable opponent to Boniface* Burnaugh, "Exterminator on Man o' War's Trail."

143 *the crowd roared* "Pimlico Cup Won by Exterminator."

143 *"the ancient warrior's head"* Ibid.

143 *"Exterminator pulled a knife"* Anderson, *Horses Are Folks*.

143 *"It seems that seasons"* "Comment on Current Events in Sports."

Chapter 8

144 *some turf writers took advantage* "Visit to Sun Briar Court."

144 *Susquehanna river* Hadsell, "Life and Times of Willis Sharpe Kilmer."

144 *"Exterminator, seen in his box"* " 'Slim' Is as Good as Ever."

144 *"on all sides"* Jackson, *Constellation of Genius, 1922.*

145 *"double triple"* " 'Slim' Is as Good as Ever."

145 *greatest distance runner in the country* Salvator, "Repeats and Comebacks."

145 *"A horse as sound and kind"* Sevier, *Thoroughbred Record*, March 24, 1922.

145 *a "real she-flapper"* "Flapper Jockey Is Awaited by Turf Followers."

145 *Babe Ruth's 1921 season* Ham, *Larceny and Old Leather.*

145 *first million-dollar boxing gate* Inabinett, *Grantland Rice and His Heroes*, 28.

145 *He wanted Exterminator's winnings* Burnaugh, "Bright Array of Turf Talent at Havre de Grace."

146 *The answer, of course* Vreeland, "Sprinters Not the 'Whole Show' in Racing Year 1922."

146 *Gene Wayland* Sevier, "Kilmer's Foreign Stakes Entries."

146 *"Exterminator is a wonderful horse"* Vreeland, "Exterminator Being Prepared To Capture Cups for Fourth Time."

146 *Wayland particularly appreciated* "Bob Dornan in Extollation of Exterminator."

146 *"in love" with Exterminator* Sevier, "Tribute to a Great Horse."

146 *"Exterminator is the kind of stout"* "Kilmer Stable in Maryland."

147 *Fourteen Kilmer employees would make the trip* "Sun Briar Court Juveniles Leave to Take up Racing."

147 *"Binghamton is just right"; train details* Ibid.

147 *Susquehanna* "Westerners Interested in New Track."

147 *"the Graw"* Bates, "Havre de Grace"; Boyd, *Exterminator,* 95.

147 *"would be the jockey if women"* "Havre de Grace Track Fit for Fast Racing."

147 *"one hundred pint-bottles"* "Supposed Airplane Liquor Confiscated."

148 *"An incident on the way up"* "Dry Agents Allege Tip-Off Before Raid."

148 *"in his cups"* Williams, "Off to a Banquet."

148 *They streamed in* Burnaugh, "Class of Eastern Turf Awaits Havre de Grace Meeting, Starting Saturday."

148 *put on about a hundred pounds* Vreeland, "Upsets Precedent in Winning Sprint"; "Veteran Gelding Exterminator Ready for Western Campaign"; Sevier, "Presses Man o' War for Winning Honors."

148 *Cassius* Vreeland, "Upsets Precedent in Winning Sprint."

148 *Johnson, meanwhile* "Kilmer Stable in Maryland."

148 *"like hickory saplings"* Sevier, "Presses Man o' War."

149 *He said he worried* John I. Day, *New York Telegraph*, April 16, 1922, quoted in "Exterminator Adds to Fame by Winning Harford Handicap."

149 *special opening-day trains* Omar Khayyam, "Exterminator Defeats Billy Kelly in Harford"; "Opening Day at Havre de Grace"; John I. Day, quoted in "Exterminator Adds to Fame by Winning Harford Handicap."

149 *Ross arrived in a private Pullman* John I. Day, quoted in "Exterminator Adds to Fame"; Omar Khayyam, "Exterminator Defeats Billy Kelly."

149 *Pullman details* "Mulligan, "The Delights of Pullman Dining"; Omar Khayyam, "Exterminator Defeats Billy Kelly."

149 *not without plenty of shoving* Quoted in "Exterminator Adds to Fame."

149 *Kilmer was there* Omar Khayyam, "Exterminator Defeats Billy Kelly."

149 *"good workout for the horse"* Collins, "Stars of the Paddocks and Tracks."

149 *Fans cheered for both* Omar Khayyam, "Exterminator Defeats Billy Kelly."

149 *The race started clumsily* Quoted in "Exterminator Adds to Fame."

150 *Exterminator had won* "Exterminator Wins Harford Handicap"; "Season's First Stake Goes to Exterminator."

150 *"chestnut avalanche"* Quoted in "Exterminator Adds to Fame."

150 *"Passing the eighth pole"* Collins, "Stars of the Paddocks and Tracks."

151 *thrilled to see him do it* "Season's First Stake Goes to Exterminator"; George Daley, quoted in "Exterminator Adds to Fame."

151 *unleash their power right away* Burnaugh, "Bright Array of Turf Talent at Havre de Grace."

151 *gave Boniface the win* "Wonderful Turf Battle."

151 *Pimlico Spring Handicap* "Champlain in Limelight."

151 *had been a fluke* "Battle of Turf Giants."

151 *long head safely in front* Ibid.

151 *"homage that is the right of kings"* Ibid.

152 *Clark Handicap victory* "Magnificent Exterminator"; "Boniface Beats Exterminator."

152 *eight other horses* Salvator, "American Champion Weight Carriers."

152 *won the Kentucky Handicap* Boyd, *Exterminator,* race chart.

152 *passed the $200,000 mark* "Exterminator Now a $200,000 Winner"; "Exterminator's Record for Six Years on Track Breaks All Records."

153 *Bayside purse* Burnaugh, "Exterminator Wins Bayside"; Vreeland, "Exterminator, the Richest Gelding in the World, Wins His Fifth Handicap."

153 *"as John D. Rockefeller earns that amount"* Vreeland, "Exterminator, the Richest Gelding in the World, Wins His Fifth Handicap."

153 *"He's the best yearling"* "Exterminator an Easy Winner in Belmont Feature."

153 *"Exterminator won the Kentucky Derby"* "Kilmer Gelding Wins Bayside Handicap Under Heavy Wraps."

153 *Douglas Fairbanks "The Three Musketeers* Coming to Hippodrome Last Week in January."

153 *Charlie Chaplin pillow fight; other Fairbanks details* "Marilynn and Jack Are Made One at Fairbanks' Home in Los Angeles"; "Home to Be Made Perfect"; "Doug Fairbanks Calls on Man Hit by Arrow."

154 *glorified "workout"* Vreeland, "Morvich Had Better Watch Out or Big Exterminator Will Chase Him Leg Weary"; "Exterminator! That's All."

154 *"My operative thinks"* "Viewing Exterminator at Belmont Park."

154 *Jack Sharkey* Ibid.

154 *happy, satisfied trainer* "Exterminator! That's All."

154 *"He's an iron horse"* "Bob Dornan in Extollation of Exterminator."

154 *"There's no telling how great"* Vreeland, "Morvich Had Better Watch Out."

154 *"Talk about your Man o' War!"* Ibid.

155 *gray goose* Vreeland, "Exterminator Shows He Has Lost Most of His Speed of the Early Spring."

155 *Harry Sinclair* Sann, *The Lawless Decade,* 84.

155 *the Brooklyn Handicap* Brossman, Editorial.

155 *the Brooklyn gained even more import* "Exterminator! That's All"; Vreeland, "No Champion Among the Young Race Horses"; "Year of 1922 Ranks High in Sport World."

156 *"a sort of left-handed compliment"* Vreeland, "Mr. Racegoer, Do You Believe Exterminator Is 7 Pounds Better than Morvich?"; "Weights in the Brooklyn"; Brossman, Editorial.

156 *scratched their horses* "Grey Lag Beaten by Exterminator."

156 *"Certainly the prospects are excellent"* "Stars in Brooklyn Handicap" 1.

156 *Philadelphia and New Orleans* "Exterminator Day at Old Aqueduct."

156 *continue doing the impossible* "Exterminator in Stirring Victory."

156 *On Brooklyn Day* "Exterminator Wins Brooklyn Handicap," *New York Times,* 16

156 *As the horses went to the post* Photograph, "Exterminator, on the Inside."

156 *could not raise his arm* Boyd, *Exterminator.*

156 *out-of-control yelps* Burnaugh, "Exterminator Wins Brooklyn."

157 *flung his tail* "More Laurels for Great Exterminator."

157 *Was he giving up?* "More Laurels for Great Exterminator."

157 *swept under the finish line* Vreeland, "Exterminator Earns a Great Ovation by Beating Grey Lag a Head for the Brooklyn."

157 *their applause increased* "More Laurels for Great Exterminator."

157 *could not remember any horse* "Crowd Wild as Exterminator Wins Great Race."

157 *"like a perfect equine god"* Ibid.

157 *"seemed to know he had done something"* Treanor, "Morvich Races in First Real Defense of Championship."

157 *seeming to pose* Vreeland, "Exterminator Earns a Great Ovation."

158 *said they saw Exterminator bow* Ibid.

158 *pushed to the finish line* "Crowd Wild as Exterminator Wins Great Race."

158 *straining to pat him* Vreeland, "Exterminator Earns a Great Ovation"; "Exterminator Wins."

158 *"dance of ecstasy"* Vreeland, "Exterminator Earns a Great Ovation."

158 *"Seldom if ever before"* Ibid.

158 *"They all look alike"* "Exterminator Day at Old Aqueduct."

158 *"Old Bones" poem* McGee, "Old Bones."

158 *"beats a heart whose gameness"* "Bob Dornan in Extollation of Exterminator."

159 *"Talk about bulldog courage!"* Vreeland, "Exterminator Earns a Great Ovation."

159 *ship Exterminator abroad* Pond, "The Horses of 1921."

159 *"the old fashioned American"* Brossman, Editorial.

160 *"I have watched many races"* Vreeland, " 'Sunny Jim' Fitzsimmons Says Exterminator Greatest of His Time."

Chapter 9

161 *"good doer"* Belknap, *Horsewords,* 190.

161 *every scrap of bran* Alexander, *A Sound of Horses.*

161 *"He turned his tail to the feed box"* Neil Newman, quoted in Boyd, *Exterminator,* 134.

161 *"He was all in"* Vreeland, "Sally's Alley and Exterminator Ready."

161 *did not even seem ridiculous anymore* "Exterminator and Morvich May Meet."

162 *"American racing epic"* Sevier, "Exterminator: A Wonder Horse."

162 *"Behold Exterminator"* Burnaugh, "Burden of a Base Name."

162 *"A bet on Exterminator has come to be reckoned"* Walsh, "Exterminator Greatest Race Horse of All Time."

162 *cartoon* "Exterminator, the Wonder Horse."

163 *assigned 138 pounds* "Crushing Impost on Exterminator."

163 *Wayland didn't send him* "Weight Concession Causes Exterminator to 'Decline Issue.' "

163 *highest weight ever carried* Dempsey, "Heavy Going and Upsets."

163 *Joe Estes's poem* "Exterminator," *Blood-Horse.*

163 *Firebrand got very few cheers* "Firebrand Wins Independence Handicap"; "Exterminator Runs Sixth in Handicap."

163 *"would be benefited by a rest"* Dempsey, "Metric's Amazing Victory."

163 *Wayland gave him a rest . . . back in training* "Rest for Exterminator"; "Tuning Up at Saratoga."

163 *There were flowers* "Spa Has Come Back as Big Stakes and Great Horses Prove"; "Saratoga Prepares for Race Meeting."

164 *Exterminator Avenue* "Halt Saratoga Training."

164 *"did not impress as possessing"* Welton, "Biggest Money Maker on the Course."

164 *"If Exterminator can carry 137 pounds"* Vreeland, "Can Exterminator Concede 7 Pounds to Grey Lag in the Saratoga Handicap?"

164 *Saratoga details; "enthusiasts balanced themselves"* "Grey Lag Captures Saratoga Handicap," *New York Times,* August 2, 1922, 23.

165 *"Old Poison was a complete"* Vreeland, "Exterminator Shows He Has Lost Most of His Speed."

165 *Grey Lag got only a "ripple"* "Grey Lag Wins Saratoga Handicap."

165 *"He's done all and more"* "Exterminator," *Ogden Standard-Examiner.*

165 *He felt obligated* "Exterminator in New Hands."

165 *"the ambition of his life"* "Exterminator, Horse of Iron, Has Run His Last Track Race."

165 *"We had better not start him"; details of conversation* Vreeland, "Sally's Alley and Exterminator Ready."

165 *Kilmer agreed* "Turf," August 7, 1922.

165 *"Horses like Man o' War"* "A Great Campaigner."

166 *they had a chance to win* "Here and There on the Turf," August 27, 1922, 1.

166 *No one would take it easy* Ibid.

166 *"If Exterminator is beaten"* Burnaugh, "Year's Great Two-Year-Olds Compete for Hopeful Prize."

166 *jeopardized their chances* "Exterminator in New Hands."

166 *details about the night before the cup* Vreeland, "Sally's Alley and Exterminator Ready."

166 *Exterminator stepped along briskly* "Here and There on the Turf," September 2, 1922.

166 *scratched Grey Lag* "Saratoga."

167 *"he's throwing up his tail!"* Vreeland, "Exterminator Wins Cup for Fourth Time."

167 *"Go on, Exterminator!"* "Veteran Shows Real Speed in Feature at Spa."

167 *cried as Exterminator* "Exterminator in Great Triumph."

167 *wore Mad Hatter down* "Exterminator and Dunlin Victors."

167 *"The greatest cup horse of history"* Macbeth, "J. S. Cosden's Dunlin Wins $38,950 Hopeful Stakes."

167 *Mrs. Wayland's story* Vreeland, "Sally's Alley and Exterminator Ready."

167 *twenty-five-thousand-person crowd* "Old Exterminator Sets New Record by Taking Cup Again."

167 *"Hail to the Chief"* Vreeland, "Exterminator Wins Cup for Fourth Time."

167 *fourth Saratoga Cup* "President Wilson Presents Cup."

168 *poem* "Exterminator," *Thoroughbred Record.*

168 *"He has earned his retirement"* Fitzgerald, "Exterminator in 4th Straight Victory for the Saratoga Cup."

168 *"He well deserves repose"* "Exterminator and Dunlin Victors."

168 *"If he doesn't show a desire"* Vreeland, "Exterminator Should Be Retired."

168 *"It will still be remembered"* "Here and There on the Turf," October 26, 1922.

169 *"Earnings Second Only"* "Exterminator in Stirring Victory."

169 *sent a telegram* "Exterminator Again"; "Here and There on the Turf," September 22, 1922.

169 *he did not need the money* "Great Exterminator."

169 *Kilmer's message fired up the locals* "Good News for Chicago."

169 *The stable manager reserved* Ibid.; "Big Feature for Chicago."

169 *Kilmer sent a telegram* "Exterminator on the Way."

169 *last-minute arrangements* Lane, "Exterminator Here Tomorrow for Races."

169 *gallop him slowly around the track* "3,000 at Hawthorne Track; Exterminator Parades, Then Rests"; "Chicagoans See Exterminator."

169 *"the homage in a regal way"* "Chicagoans See Exterminator."

170 *"so much for the turf"* "Here and There on the Turf," September 27, 1922.

170 *more people could come see Exterminator* "Everyone Welcome."

170 *Carpenters worked on the racetrack* "Hawthorne."

170 *Kilmer took his private car* "Exterminator Arrives for Hawthorne Races."

170 *cup for Kilmer* "Everyone Welcome."

170 *"Track builders of the future"* "Here and There on the Turf," October 4, 1922.

170 *flags and banners* "Racing's Glorious Return."

170 *A crowd gathered around* "Hawthorne."

170 *She ran out* Ibid.

170 *"I've been here an hour"* Rodenbach, "New Hawthorne Conjures Ghosts for Riders of '04."

171 *looked like "Ku Kluxers"* Ibid.

171 *stayed standing and clapping* Woodruff, "20,000 Cheer Race Revival at Hawthorne."

171 *Kilmer accepted the big silver cup* Ibid.

171 *"a household word"* "Chivalric Generosity of W. S. Kilmer."

171 *"Chicagoans will not forget"* "Here and There on the Turf," September 30, 1922.

171 *"Now, the great running horse"* "Exterminator the Great," *Cherry Creek* (NY) *News.*

172 *"When one considers"* Vreeland, "Stewards Make Exterminator, Best Horse in U.S.A., an 'Outcast' by Their Rules."

172 *"like asking patrons of a theater"* Vreeland, "Will Grey Lag Have a Chance to Regain His Prestige?"

173 *"usual cyclonic rush"* "Great Exterminator," *Daily Racing Form.*

173 *"that unconcerned manner"* "Exterminator Wins Laurel Stakes."

173 *"There are many who would take exception"* Ibid.

173 *"not so much of a turf aristocrat"* "Exterminator vs. Man o' War."

173 *"If Exterminator were able"* Walsh, "Exterminator Greatest Race Horse of All Time."

173 *"Exterminator never had a chance"* "Splendid Chance for Exterminator."

173 *he had enough races* "Exterminator Hailed as Country's Greatest Horse."

174 WHERE EVERYTHING GOES Vanderwood, *Satan's Playground,* 86.

174 *a bordello called the Molino Rojo* Alexander, *A Sound of Horses,* 136.

174 *Clubs lining Tijuana's main street* Vanderwood, *Satan's Playground,* 107.

174 *They would eat at San Diego* "Angelenos to Go South."

174 *The track drew Hollywood stars* Vanderwood, *Satan's Playground,* 109.

174 *climbed into the plane* Ibid., 136.

174 *ordered extra train cars* "Off-Day at Laurel Park."

174 *Even after the opening bugle* "Exterminator Fails," October 29, 1922.

175 *"May the best horse win"* "Exterminator's Great Opportunity."

175 *"Man o' War's Mark"* "Man o' War's Mark in Danger Today."

175 *Nothing went Exterminator's way* Omar Khayyam, "World's Greatest Gelding Will Go to Post Favorite in $25,000 Handicap."

175 *"On he came with the courage"* "Exterminator Fails," October 29, 1922.

175 *Oceanic wasn't impressive overall* "Here and There on the Turf," October 31, 1922.

175 *"There is not the slightest doubt"* Vreeland, "Oceanic, Stable Mate of the Great Man o' War."

175 *"The Association of Ex-Trainers of Exterminator"* Burnaugh, "Exterminator in New Hands."

175 *"Jolly Willie" Shields* Ibid.

176 *"One would never think to look"* Fitzgerald, "Shields to Train Kilmer Racers."

176 *Wayland kept working Exterminator* "Captain Alcock Wins."

176 *"Mr. Riggs, I am sending"* Collins, "Stars of the Paddocks and Tracks."

176 *huge crowd crossed their fingers* "Exterminator's Great Chance."

176 *"Old Slim—the whole wide world"* Collyer, "Collyer's and Other Handicaps."

176 *Albert Johnson was sick* "Pimlico Smashes Record."

177 *Johnson had told* Burnaugh, "Marinelli Blamed for Defeat in Cup."

177 *Marinelli had never "let him know"* Ibid.

177 *As the horses swept* Collins, "Stars of the Paddocks and Tracks."

177 *they almost seemed to wait* Ibid.; "Captain Alcock Wins."

177 *"Men turned away with lumps in their throats"* Collins, "Stars of the Paddocks and Tracks."

177 *"bungling ride"* Boyd, *Exterminator,* 140.

177 *"was about the maddest man"* Burnaugh, "Marinelli Blamed for Defeat in Cup."

177 *Everyone clapped louder* "Defeat of Exterminator Stuns Racegoers."

178 *"trying struggles"* Ibid.

178 *"Summing it all up"* "Here and There on the Turf," November 14, 1922.

178 *"[Captain Alcock] beat Exterminator"* "Captain Alcock Wins."

178 *"still be found trying"* "Captain Alcock Wins Pimlico Cup."

179 *"That could readily be picked up"* "Here and There on the Turf," November 17, 1922.

179 *"It would have been better for his reputation."* Sevier, "Exterminator After Thanksgiving Stakes," 64.

179 *"I need only mention one"* Colin Campbell, letter, "Man o' War and Exterminator."

179 *"Insofar as the personal equation"* Newman, "Man o' War Versus Exterminator."

180 *"Horse of the Century"* Colin Campbell, letter, "The Noblest Roman of
Them All."

180 *Coffroth was a long race* Sevier, "Exterminator After Thanksgiving Stakes";
"First Far Western Venture."

180 *agonizing less than $5,000* "W. S. Kilmer's 1923 Stable."

180 *"I felt again the tightening"* Herring, "A Visit to Sun Briar Court."

Chapter 10

181 *osselets* Briggs, "Osselets."

181 *"The scene must have bordered"* Burnaugh, "Trainer Confident of Kilmer's
Filly."

181 *For Exterminator, pin firing* "Exterminator Ready."

181 *before midsummer* Burnaugh, "Trainer Confident of Kilmer's Filly."

181 *neither did Wayland* Ibid.

182 *It made him feel at home* Vreeland, "Exterminator in Fine Fettle for New
Record."

182 *"Race Men"* "Always Welcome."

182 *a little heavier* Vreeland, "Exterminator in Fine Fettle."

182 *"bracelets" around his fetlocks* Ibid.

182 *"letting him know"* "Here and There on the Turf," February 22, 1923.

182 *Airedale terrier* Vreeland, "Sally's Alley and Exterminator Ready."

182 *"Exterminator is the greatest horse"* Ibid.

183 *"acute dilation of the heart"* "Eugene Wayland, Veteran Trainer for Willis
Sharpe Kilmer, Dies"; "Exterminator Won for Him."

183 *interviewing prospective trainers* "W. S. Kilmer at Baltimore."

183 *"What trainer would not strive?"* "Here and There on the Turf," March 26,
1923.

183 *His goal in life* "Ponce at Idle Hour Farm."

183 *Their names included Sunfey* "W. S. Kilmer Horses."

183 *McDaniel was thrilled* "Rebuke's Splendid Victory."

183 *comfortable situation for McDaniel* "Ross' Horses for Havre."

184 *"No less an authority"* "Tia Juana Boasting Many Speedy Horses."

184 *looked better with each passing week* "Exterminator Ready"; "Here and
There on the Turf," March 28, 1923; Ogle, "Opening of Race Season in East at
Bowie Today."

184 *"The old fellow was on the bit"* "Exterminator and Sally's Alley Rapidly Nearing Racing Form."

184 *He was so close* Vreeland, "Exterminator in Fine Fettle."

184 *"Those who have never been to the races"* "Here and There on the Turf,"
April 24, 1923.

184 *"magic name has appeared"* "Fine Opening Card at Havre de Grace."

184 *Gamblers came from New York* "Blazes Beats Exterminator."

184 *couldn't rally* "Havre de Grace Tomorrow."

184 *Lately, crowds clapped more* "Blazes Beats Exterminator."

185 *Onlookers agreed* "Blazes Outruns Exterminator"; "Havre Opens in Blaze of
Glory."

185 *"Listen Baltimore"* Collyer, "Collyer's Comment," April 21, 1923.

185 *As soon as Exterminator emerged* "Exterminator in Old Time Form; Wins
Handicap."

185 *Hoping they would see him get closer* "Exterminator Wins Maryland Feature."

185 *"But darn if that Exterminator"* Considine, "Old Bones."

185 *McAtee kept him under control* "Great Exterminator Wins Big Handicap."

185 *McAtee asked Exterminator* Vreeland, " 'Snapper' Garrison Says Exterminator
Is the Best Gelding Bred in U.S.A."

185 *"big hearted piece of racing machinery"* "More Glory for Exterminator."

186 *"No event in thoroughbred racing"* "Turf," April 23, 1922.

186 *"He is now in an unfinished race"* "Here and There on the Turf," April 22, 1923.

186 *management of Havre de Grace* "Purse Increased to Help Exterminator Set
Record."

186 *performance in the Philadelphia* "Latest Turf News from Havre."

186 *"He came through"* "Here and There on the Turf," April 26, 1923.

186 *a bare second* " 'Old Slim' Loses by Nose Decision."

186 *"To say that the defeat of Exterminator"* "Exterminator Fails," April 29, 1923.

186 *"Many sportsmen regretted"* "Pal Purchased for Famous Exterminator."

187 *home from work on horseback* "Lamanda Park Calm Again."

187 *nostalgic renewal of the Pony Express* "Pony Express Sees Colorado Ten
Hours Ahead of Schedule."

187 *"High tide for the horse"* Chapman, "What's Become of the Horse?"

187 *"Should the old son of McGee"* "Here and There on the Turf," May 5, 1923.

187 *Kilmer did take some sweeping actions* "Exterminator to Retire when Racing
Season Ends."

187 *a New York record* Ibid.

188 *Exterminator perked up* "Pal Purchased for Famous Exterminator."

188 *"iron horse in action"* "Exterminator: A Wonder Horse."

188 *Tijuana scene* "Exterminator May Be Entered in Rich Stakes at Tiajuana
Track."

189 *"If he is brought back"* "Here and There on the Turf," November 9, 1923.

189 *Zev's record* Stringer, "Along the Rail."

189 *Exterminator was supposed to beat Man o' War* "Eastern Nags Invade Tijuana."

189 *"I would be satisfied"* "Exterminator Scheduled to Arrive Friday."

190 *They were nothing serious* "'Old Slim' Ready for Coast Trip"; "Exterminator Going West," *Morning Telegraph*, November 5, 1923, 1.

190 *"The man who found Exterminator"* "'Old Slim' Ready for Coast Trip"; "Exterminator Going West," *Morning Telegraph*, November 5, 1923, 1.

190 *"This theory was based on his knowledge"* "Exterminator After Rich Tia Juana Purses."

191 *A crowd of horsemen* "Exterminator Given Ovation."

191 *The trip took* Ibid.; Exterminator Entrains."

191 *when he got to Tijuana* "'Old Slim' Ready for Coast Trip."

191 *A crowd applauded* "Judge Nelson Welcomed at Tijuana Track."

191 *Exterminator had come west* "Exterminator Given Ovation."

191 *McDaniel watched Exterminator's legs* "Exterminator in Triumphant Return"; "Here and There on the Turf," February 1, 1924.

191 *"There is an old saying"* McDaniel, "Fifty Years on the Turf."

191 *"triumphant comeback"* "Exterminator Today."

191 *On Christmas Day, Exterminator paraded* "Horses Plentiful for Longer Stakes."

191 *"Henry McDaniel will have him fit"* "Osprey, in Great Form."

191 *"fit and ready after careful"* "Exterminator in Triumphant Return."

191 *"training wonderfully"* "Horses Plentiful for Longer Stakes."

191 *ready for his first race* "Racing Attracting Turf Enthusiasts at Tijuana."

192 *"If McDaniel is successful"* "Here and There on the Turf," January 10, 1924.

192 *"14 times"* Boyd, *Exterminator*, race chart.

192 *McDaniel booked Johnson* "Osprey, in Great Form."

192 *"Two hopheads were kicking the stem"* "Speaking of Exterminator."

192 *owners of the other horses* "Billy Evans Says."

192 *They would try again later* "Exterminator Can't Get Any Competition."

193 *his signal that it was time to go New York Times,* quoted in "Return of 'Old Slim' to Racing Hailed by All Lovers of Horses."

193 *all eyes fixed on Exterminator* "High Lights Mark Week's Racing at Tia Juana Track."

193 *trademark stretch drives* Ibid.

193 *No one could remember* "Exterminator Wins in Comeback Race," *Chicago Daily Tribune*.

193 *"The crowd simply went wild"* "Exterminator in Triumphant Return."

193 *"The old fellow"* "Exterminator Wins in Come-Back Race," *New York Times*.

193 *"It was a little race"* "Here and There on the Turf," February 19, 1924.

193 *"as if he knew just why"* "Exterminator Wins in Comeback Race," *Chicago Daily Tribune.*

193 *McDaniel had passed the test* "Old Exterminator Comes Back to Races with Win."

193 *brought the old hero back* "High Lights Mark Week's Racing at Tia Juana Track"; "Here and There on the Turf," February 19, 1924.

193 *"It is small wonder"* "Here and There on the Turf," February 19, 1924.

193 *"Horses may come and go"* *New York Times,* quoted in "Return of 'Old Slim' to Racing Hailed by All Lovers of Horses."

194 *a local horse named Osprey* "Exterminator Withdrawn."

194 *track vet said* "Exterminator Withdrawn"; "Exterminator Out Owing to Lameness."

194 *was not impervious* "Round-up," *New-York Tribune,* quoted in "Return of 'Old Slim' to Racing Hailed by All Lovers of Horses."

194 *"couldn't say whether the lameness"* "Exterminator Lame; Match Is Called Off."

194 *not during his workouts* "Exterminator to Carry Top Weight in Coffroth."

194 *stunning onlookers* "Here and There on the Turf," March 23, 1924.

194 *"Of course Henry McDaniel is bringing"* Ibid.

195 *pulling on his exercise rider* Ibid.

195 *would carry the top weight* "Rain at Tijuana Track."

195 *"sobriquet of the turf's miracle man"* Ibid.

195 *watching Winn's preparations* "Runstar Winner of the Coffroth Handicap."

195 *course would be dry and fast* "Exterminator Favorite."

195 *come to watch him break that record* Ibid.

195 *"I will have no excuses"* Ibid.

196 *no more room at Tijuana* "Runstar Winner of the Coffroth Handicap."

196 *All across the country* "'Old Bones' to Run Today Against Sinclair Horse."

196 *Hollywood came* "Pick Exterminator to Win at Tijuana"; "$51,400 Feature at Tiajuana Is Won by Runstar."

196 *had the infield opened* "Runstar Winner of the Coffroth Handicap."

196 *the biggest crowd in the track's history* Ibid.

196 *ten thousand from Los Angeles* "Runstar Wins Coffroth Handicap."

196 *"Here comes Exterminator!"* "Pacific Coast Horse Critics Pay Tribute to Old Exterminator."

196 *"The old fellow's heart"* "8 Placed Horses in Blanket Finish."

197 *Everyone cheered and whistled* "Runstar Captures $40,000 Coffroth"; "Here and There on the Turf," April 1, 1924.

197 *"Exterminator's goal has been achieved"* Menke, "Exterminator Has Eclipsed the Record of Man o' War."

Chapter 11

198 *"The son of McGee"* "Turf Gossip from Havre de Grace."

198 *It was chilly* "Exterminator the Attraction."

198 *Exterminator was set up to succeed* "Old Exterminator Wins at Havre de Grace."

198 *"his amiable face beamed"* "Buck Pond Wins at Havre de Grace."

198 *Applause started* Omar Khayyam, "Exterminator, Hero of Many Turf Battles, Is Victorious."

198 *"brought the old fellow back"* "Exterminator the Attraction."

199 *"Here I have been doing everything"* Stringer, "Old Bones Shows Return to Form in Winning Edgewood."

199 *"The statement frequently is made"* "Buck Pond Wins at Havre de Grace."

199 *"His action in defeat"* Ibid.

200 *McDaniel wanted to see Exterminator retired* Boyd, *Exterminator,* 149.

200 *devoted himself to Ross's string* Ibid.

200 *telling onlookers about all the races* "Exterminator Had Numerous Visitors."

200 *He won one race* French, "Seven Rancocas Stars Named in Chicago Derby."

200 *tried to pull him up* "Exterminator Loses."

200 *"Exterminator moved up"* Considine, "Old Bones."

200 *Kilmer interview with King* "Exterminator Remains in Training Because He Likes Turf Life."

202 *a sort of assistant trainer* "Exterminator Fathers Bunch of Youngsters."; "Exterminator Back in New Turf Role."

202 *usher the two-year-olds* "Exterminator Has Chance to Come Back."

202 *would balk if the whole string* "Exterminator Is Hard to Handle."

202 *"Come on if you think"* Corum, "How Exterminator Came Back to the Races."

202 *New York State Fair* "Exterminator To Run."

202 *Franklin Roosevelt* "Exterminator and Franklin D. Roosevelt at State Fair," photograph, 17.

202 *"Sunny Man was poisoned"* "Two Inquiries Are Expected in Colt's Death"; "Sunny Man Poisoned with Intent to Kill."

202 *Insurance officials ran to recover* "Seek Poison in Sunny Man's Stomach Today."

202 *into an acid bath* "Colt's Carcass Destroyed Quickly."

202 *Kilmer offered a reward* "Kilmer to Sell Nags, but Won't Quit Game."

203 *"Racing authorities have become"* Baxter, "Turf Can't Survive if Officials Refuse to Do Their Duty."

203 *bought another breeding farm* "Kilmer Buys Harris Farm."

203 *Exterminator settled right down* Durden, "The Sportview."

204 *interview with Lew Williams* "Exterminator Arrives at Aqueduct."

205 *"The old fellow was raced too long"* "Here and There on the Turf," May 8, 1925.

206 *"It would be great to spend a day here"* "Will Rogers Visits Sun Briar Court."

206 *posed for pictures* "Binghamton Depicture at Work and Place."

207 *"Pitchfork" Peanuts story* Boyd, *Exterminator,* 153–4.

207 *Exterminator would shove him over* Considine, "On the Line with Considine."

207 *pony always in front* Bob Considine, "Old Bones."

207 *"slow burn"* Daley, "Farewell to Old Bones."

207 *He chased Luckner* Dunstan, "Exterminator Thrives on Easy Life at Farm"; Considine, "Old Bones."

207 *cycled through trainers* "Well, Willis Sharpe Kilmer Has Another Trainer."

207 *"Whimsical Willis"* Vreeland, "Racing Fans Ask, 'How Long Will M'Daniel Train for Kilmer?'"

207 *missing a few* "So Schuttinger Has Joined the Kilmer Club."

208 *"I wonder if you know all that you have missed"* "Dinner Is Held for Willis Sharpe Kilmer."

208 *gave Kilmer a floral horseshoe* Ibid.

208 *Ross decamped* Ross, *Boots and Saddles,* 221.

208 *McDaniel contract* Contract between Willis Sharpe Kilmer and Henry McDaniel.

208 *including Reigh Count and Sun Beau* "Willis Sharpe Kilmer to Seek Juvenile Racing Honors at Saratoga."

208 *"Racing is an uncertain proposition"* Lamb, "McDaniel Is Back at Sun Briar Court."

209 *"Just as he had defended Sun Briar"* Bowen, "How the Great Kidney Specific Influenced History at Hawthorne." *Blood-Horse.*

209 *Reigh Count went on to win* Henry McDaniel obituary, *Blood-Horse.*

209 *Widener telegram* McDaniel collection.

210 *"All visitors are anxious"* Linthicum, "Spotlight on Sports."

210 *"Hello, Slim!"* Dunstan, "Exterminator Thrives on Easy Life at Farm."

210 *"When the gallant deeds"* "Exterminator. A Gallant Steed."

211 *"How long will Henry McDaniel train?"* Vreeland, "Racing Fans Seeking the Path to Wealth May Find It in Golden Way."

211 *"No one had ever taught Exterminator"* Newman, "I Remember."

211 *"I think of all his achievements"* Vreeland, "Racing Fans Seeking the Path to Wealth."

211 *manicurist on board a cruise ship* Shay, *Bygone Binghamton,* 379–80.

212 *"Mark Twain of the turf"* "Henry McDaniel," *Blood-Horse.*

212 *"A good listener"* Graham, "Graham's corner."

212 *smashed a radio* "Mr. Kilmer."

212 *Tom Mix's "wonder horse"* Mitchum, *Hollywood Hoofbeats,* 23.

212 *"A hero who is questioned"* Orlean, *Rin Tin Tin.*

212 *"the two great horses"* Rice, "Seabiscuit Tops Admiral"; Rice, "The Sportlight."

212 *McDaniel weighed in, too* King, "Modern Horses Less Rugged"; Vreeland, "Henry McDaniel Fills the Cloak"; King, "Old Bones Big and Fat at 25."

213 *"He had to battle"* "Exterminator Is Most Popular Horse Ever Known, Says Trainer."

213 *"Uncle Henry McDaniels"* Considine, "On the Line with Considine," 3.

213 *"Exterminator was a fair trencherman"* Brown, "Exterminator Resembled Hatrack."

213 *Phar Lap* Vreeland, "Exterminator Did Greater Deeds than 'Down Under' King."

213 *"Gray Ghost" of the 1950s* Smith, "The People's Horse."

213 *McDaniel was asked* Newman, "I Remember."

213 *up to a mile and a furlong* "Henry M'Daniel."

213 *"I'm a greenhorn in this town"* King, "Modern Horses Less Rugged."

213 *cigarette advertisement* "The Test of a Horse—or Cigarette."

214 *Louis B. Mayer* Dunstan, "Reflections."

214 *Kilmer died at Sky Lake* "Willis Sharpe Kilmer, Noted Turfman, Dies."

214 *"Never a sycophant"* Newman, "Wills Sharpe Kilmer."

214 *"man who did much for the turf"* "Mr. Kilmer."

214 *"Exactitude of detail"* "Willis Sharpe Kilmer," *Binghamton Press.*

215 *grooms ate Brunswick stew* Durden, "The Sportview."

215 *"There were sad hearts"* Craigie, "Dispersal Sale at Kilmer Farm."

215 *"His head got lower and lower"* Considine, "On the Line with Considine."

215 *"he was a mighty pretty horse"* "Exterminator, 'Old Bones' to His Many Turf Followers."

215 *thought it was unseemly* "Exterminator Won't Appear at Pimlico."

216 *lie down and roll* "Exterminator, 26, at Pimlico Track."

216 *"I just want to touch him again"* Linthicum, "Spotlight on Sports."

216 *"He actually seemed to be proud"* Williams, "Exterminator Returns to Track."

216 *there was an idea floating around* Considine, "On the Line with Considine."

216 *the opening day of the fall meeting . . . prepared him for the parade* Hagner, "Exterminator Lion of Hour."

217 *"the gaze of a gentleman"* *Morning Telegraph,* quoted in "15,000 Give 'Old Bones' Big Ovation."

217 *orange, green, and brown ribbons* Brunson, "Market Wise Beats Haltal in Pimlico Special."

217 *some of the fans* Philadelphia Enquirer, quoted in "15,000 Give 'Old Bones' Big Ovation."

217 *as racehorses paced behind him* Morning Telegraph, quoted ibid.

217 *"We thought for sure"* Shay, "The Story of Exterminator."

217 *"He won me my house in Maryland"* Priore, "Mike Terry and West Side Kids Chief Mourners."

217 *"gave a backward look"* Hagner, "Exterminator Lion of Hour."

217 *"It was one of those things"* Philadelphia Enquirer, quoted in "15,000 Give 'Old Bones' Big Ovation."

217 *McDaniel looked at Exterminator* Murray Tynan, *New York Herald,* quoted ibid.; Shay, "The Story of Exterminator."

218 *Exterminator and Sun Briar shipped home* "Sun Briar and Exterminator Brought Here to Spend Rest of Their Days"; "Exterminator, Sun Briar Back at Old Home."

218 *death of Sun Briar* "Sun Briar, Thoroughbred Champion, Dies in Stall Here."

218 *Secretariat, Native Dancer* www.pedigreequery.com.

219 *birthday parties* Kelly, "Before and After."

219 *carrots in to represent candles* Dunstan, "Reflections."

219 *Aubrey Clark* Interview with Aubrey Clark, April 2015.

Epilogue

221 *name a Flying Fortress bomber* "Missing."

221 *closed to house Japanese Americans* Bell, "Santa Anita Racetrack Played a Role in WWII."

221 *"Back the Attack Day"; Mrs. Kilmer hesitated* "Mrs. Kilmer Will Send Great Gelding to Belmont"; Richardson, "Sports of the Times."

221 *"It's great to be going back"* "Off to War."

222 *"He recognized me"* "Former Jockey Knapp to Enter Saratoga's Racing Hall of Fame."

222 *Exterminator was never known to fret* King, "Old Bones Here for Bond Sales, Spry as a Colt."

222 *"You can't fool me"* Shay, "The Story of Exterminator."

222 *old-timers' exhibition race* Millar, "Paddock Parade."

222 *binoculars at the ready* "Mrs. Willis Sharpe Kilmer," photograph.

222 *war-themed races* Glueckstein, *Of Men, Women, and Horses,* 29.

222 *A young boy led Peanuts* Lamb, "Spinning the Sports Top."

222 *Simon Healy teared up* Millar, "Paddock Parade."

222 *remembered when Exterminator had raced there* Field, "31,336 at Belmont: 25 Million Bond Sale."

222 *stopped in front of the grandstand* "Gallant Exterminator Takes a Bow."

222 *"My horse sort of bowed to them"* Priore, "Mike Terry and West Side Kids Chief Mourners."

222 *almost like a circus horse* "Gallant Exterminator Takes a Bow."

222 *Exterminator gave every impression* "Exterminator, King of the Turf, Dies, Aged 30."

222 *Over the loudspeaker* Lamb, "Spinning the Sports Top."

223 *Exterminator rolled in the straw* Ibid.

223 *bought a record $25 million in war bonds* Richardson, "Sports of the Times."

223 *Peanuts got sick* "Exterminator Loses Pal."

223 *the* New York Times *ran his obituary* Ibid.

223 *worked himself into such a swivet* Kelly, "Before and After"; "Exterminator Gives 'Derby Week' Exhibition."

223 *"Exterminator, they say"* Lamb, "Spinning the Sports Top."

223 *Ernest Hemingway* Ernest Hemingway letter to Charles Scribner, quoted in Voss, *Picturing Hemingway,* 76.

224 *a flaxseed and cream of tartar health tonic* King, "Old Bones, 30, Grows Weary."

224 *He didn't lie down again* Priore, "Mike Terry and West Side Kids Chief Mourners."

224 *trying to rouse him* Ibid.

224 *died with his head in Terry's lap* Ibid.

224 *Exterminator buried alongside Sun Briar* Shay, "The Story of Exterminator."

224 *Terry stayed inside* Priore, "Mike Terry and West Side Kids Chief Mourners."

224 *gathered to mourn* Ibid.

224 *A reporter asked what he would do* "Exterminator Dies at Sun Briar Court."

224 *laid straw in the stall* Priore, "Mike Terry and West Side Kids Chief Mourners."

224 *"Death sounded the 'call to post'"* Stewart, "We Just Have to Laugh."

224 New York Sun *poem* Phillips, "Death of a Champion."

225 *"His most famous charge was Exterminator"* "H. E. McDaniel, Famed Trainer of Racehorses, Dead at 82."

225 *buried beside Leonora* "Henry McDaniel" Obituary.

226 *Mildred Mastin Pace* Basler, "Exterminator."

226 *Wesley Dennis* Carley, "Matter of Fact."

226 *"I knew the minute I laid eyes"* Pace, *Old Bones,* 76.

226 *The book was so popular* Basler, "Exterminator."

226 *"It really made me a racing fan"* Interview with Jonathan Davis, April 2015.

226 *"I remember my grandmother"* Interview with Sue McPeek, August 2014.

227 *"He was superhuman"* Shay, "Story of Exterminator."

227 *"If the owners had wanted that horse buried"* Sbarra, "Enthusiast Wants Horse Reburied."

227 *"Perhaps it was the way Exterminator crashed into the big time"* Daley, "Sports of the Times."

Works Consulted

Abbreviations

BCHS Broome County Historical Society, Binghamton, NY

BDE *Brooklyn Daily Eagle*

BP *Binghamton Press*

DRF *Daily Racing Form,* www.drf.com

NYT *New York Times*

TR *Thoroughbred Record*

WP *Washington Post*

"McDaniel collection" refers to material kindly shared by Garrett and Muriel Mc-Daniel. Other sources for my research include the National Sporting Library, the Bolus collection at the Kentucky Derby Museum, the Keeneland Library, the Library of Congress, the Louisville Public Library, the National Museum of Racing and Hall of Fame, SUNY–Binghamton's library, Tom Tryinski's Web site fultonhistory.com, the *Daily Racing Form*'s archives, and the private collections of Terri Busch, Bill Gorman, and the late Dan Gill.

"8 Placed Horses in Blanket Finish." *WP,* March 31, 1924, S2.

"8–1, Odds Faced at Carrizal by Pershing's Men." *Chicago Daily Tribune,* June 26, 1916, 2.

"30 Americans Held Up." *NYT,* January 8, 1916, 2.

"100 Years Old in March, He Says Horses Did It." *Baltimore Afro-American,* November 10, 1973, 9.

"3,000 at Hawthorne Track; Exterminator Parades, then Rests." *Chicago Daily Tribune,* September 25, 1922.

"10,000 Binghamton Citizens Parade in Honor of Winning Race Horse." *Buffalo Courier,* September 4, 1917, 13.

"$10,000 Dominion Handicap." *DRF,* August 10, 1920, 1.

"15,000 Give 'Old Bones' Big Ovation." *BP,* October 31, 1941.

"$51,400 Feature at Tiajuana Is Won by Runstar." *Saratogian,* March 31, 1924, 9.

"$75,000 Horse Race for Two Champions." *NYT,* September 25, 1920, 1.

"169,000 Horses in A.E.F." *DRF,* December 21, 1918, 2.

Adams, Samuel Hopkins. *The Great American Fraud.* New York: P. F. Collier, 1906.

"Aftermath of the Kentucky Derby." *DRF,* May 16, 1918, 2.

"Aladdin, Sheridan Stake Winner, and His Trainer." McDaniel collection.

"Alarm Is Sounded at Ascot." *Los Angeles Express,* December 29, 1905. www.ulwaf .com/LA-1900s/06.01.html.

Alexander, David. *A Sound of Horses.* Indianapolis: Bobbs-Merrill, 1966.

"All Favorites Overcome." *DRF,* May 16, 1919, 1.

"All Set at Fair Latonia." *DRF,* June 4, 1921, 1.

"All Sports Are Off at Johns Hopkins." *New York Herald,* September 13, 1918, 8.

Allen, Frederick Lewis. *Only Yesterday: An Informal History of the 1920s.* New York: Harper, 1931.

"Always Welcome." Advertisement, ca. 1923.

Alwes, Clinton B. "Backstretch Soliloquy." *Turf and Sport Digest,* November 1945.

"American Mile Record Tied." *DRF,* August 6, 1919, 1.

"American Record Falls Before Exterminator." *Baltimore Sun,* September 16, 1920, 14.

Anderson, C. W. *Horses Are Folks.* New York: Harper, 1950.

"Angelenos to Go South." *Los Angeles Times,* December 16, 1922, III4.

"Another of Minnehaha Shipment Dead." *DRF,* January 17, 1917, 1.

"Army of Children Cheer Pershing at Ceremony in Park." *NYT,* September 10, 1919, 1.

"Around the Turf." *New York Morning Telegraph,* May 3, 1918.

"Ascot Needs Better Management." *San Francisco Chronicle,* quoted in *DRF,* March 10, 1906, 1.

Atlantic Transport Line advertisement. 1897. National Horse Show program.

"Auto Has Killed the Family Dobbin." *BP,* September 4, 1920, 18.

"Automotive Gossip." *New York Herald,* August 7, 1918, 9.

Barrett, Janet. "Alone at the Start." *TR,* November 5, 1980, 2182.

Barry, John M. *The Great Influenza.* New York: Viking, 2004.

"Baseball May Stop if New Order Stands." *NYT,* May 24, 1918, 14.

Basler, George. "Exterminator." *BP,* May 4, 1985.

Bates, Bill. *Havre de Grace*. Charleston, SC: Arcadia, 2006.

"The Battle of Big Nations for Thoroughbred Horses." *NYT*, May 3, 1914, SM9.

"Battle of Turf Giants." *DRF*, May 7, 1922, 1.

Baxter, N.P.W. "Turf Can't Survive if Officials Refuse to Do Their Duty." *WP*, May 5, 1925, 13.

"Be Frank Wins Latonia Cup." *TR*, October 18, 1919, 200.

Belknap, Maria. *Horsewords: The Equine Dictionary*, North Pomfret, VT: Trafalgar Square, 1997.

Bell, Alison. "Santa Anita Racetrack Played a Role in WWII." *Los Angeles Times*, November 8, 2009. http://articles.latimes.com/2009/nov/08/local/me-then8.

"Belmont Horses as a Gift to Army." *NYT*, February 16, 1911, 1.

"Belmont Park Is Big Skating Rink." *DRF*, January 15, 1918, 2.

"Belmont Testifies in Graft Inquiry." *NYT*, November 30, 1910, 1.

Bergin, Charles E. "McDaniel Has Good Chance to Annex Kentucky Derby This Year with Sun Briar," February 8, 1918. McDaniel collection.

"Big Feature for Chicago." *DRF*, September 20, 1922, 1.

"Big Price for Sun Briar." *DRF*, January 20, 1918.

"Billy Evans Says." *Saratogian,* February 22, 1924, 9.

"Binghamton Depicture at Work and Place." *BP*, September 12, 1929, 17.

"Binghamton Will See." Advertisement, *BP*, June 27, 1919.

Birmingham, Stephen. *"Our Crowd."* New York: Harper, 1967, 129.

"Blazes Beats Exterminator." *New York Evening Telegram,* April 16, 1923, 1.

"Blazes Outruns Exterminator." *Buffalo Courier,* April 17, 1923, 11.

"Blue Grass Turf Gossip." *Cincinnati Enquirer,* July 9, ca. 1900, McDaniel collection.

Boardman, Samuel. *The Handbook of the Turf.* New York: Judd, 1910.

"Bob Dornan in Extollation of Exterminator." *BP*, June 22, 1922, 15.

"Bob Dundon Picks Escoba to Win Big Derby Race." *Louisville Times,* May 10 1918.

"Bold Resident Exchanged Shots with Burglar." *Vancouver World*, February 15, 1914, McDaniel collection.

"Boniface Beats Exterminator." *TR,* April 29, 1922, 366.

"Bourbon County Sports Not 'On' the Derby Winner." *Paris* (KY) *Bourbon News,* May 17, 1918, 2.

Bouyea, Brian. "Harry Bassett, M. E. 'Buster' Millerick and Don Pierce Elected to Hall of Fame." *Racing Through History* blog, racinghallblog.wordpress.com /2010/06/09/harry-bassett-buster-millerick-and-don-pierce-elected-to-hall-of -fame/.

Bowen, Edward. "How the Great Kidney Specific Influence History at Hawthorne." *Blood-Horse,* October 4, 1971, 3545.

"Boy Jockey Accused of Stabbing R. L. Thomas." *BDE,* November 1, 1909, 2.

Boyd, Eva Jolene. *Exterminator.* Lexington, KY: Eclipse, 2002.

Brackney, Peter. *Lost Lexington, Kentucky.* Charleston, SC: History Press, 2014, 106.

"Breaks American Record." *DRF,* September 13, 1918, 1.

Brereton, J. M. *The Horse in War.* New York: Arco, 1976.

Briggs, Karen. "Osselets." www.thehorse.com/articles/10119/osselets-traumatic -arthritis-of-the-fetlock.

"Brilliant Gathering at Sun Briar Court." From *BP,* quoted in *TR,* January 12, 1918, 16.

Broad Church. "Notes." *Spirit of the Times,* October 23, 1886, 402.

"Brooklyn to Grey Lag." *DRF,* June 18, 1921.

Brossman, Charles. Editorial. *TR,* June 24, 1922, 470.

Brown, Ned. "Exterminator Resembled Hatrack; You Could Hang Your Coin on Him." *Gloversville* (NY) *Morning Herald,* January 26, 1944.

Brunson, Mason. "Market Wise Beats Haltal in Pimlico Special." October 31, 1941, 2.

"Buck Pond Wins at Havre de Grace." *New York Evening Post,* April 21, 1924, 16.

Burke, Doc. "It's a Helluva Long Time Since." *Turf Digest,* September, 1930, 937.

Burnaugh. Peter. "Bright Array of Turf Talent at Havre de Grace." *New York Evening Telegram,* April 16, 1922, 10.

———. "Burden of a Base Name." *NYT,* October 22, 1922, 70.

———. "Class of Eastern Turf Awaits Havre de Grace Meeting, Starting Satur-day." *New York Evening Telegram,* April 9, 1922, 10.

———. "Exterminator Gains Thrilling Victory over Mad Hatter." *New York Eve-ning Telegram,* June 4, 1921, 1, sporting final.

———. "Exterminator in New Hands." *New York Evening Telegram,* November 2, 1922, 13.

———. "Exterminator on Man o' War's Trail." *New York Evening Telegram,* May 22, 1922, 2.

———. "Exterminator Wins Bayside." *New York Evening Telegram,* June 5, 1922, 1.

———. "Exterminator Wins Brooklyn." *New York Evening Telegram,* June 16, 1922, 1.

———. "Marinelli Blamed for Defeat in Cup." *New York Evening Telegram,* Sep-tember 12, 1922, 12.

———. "Trainer Confident of Kilmer's Filly." *New York Evening Telegram,* Janu-ary 7, 1923, 9.

———. "Turfman Yields to Jockey Club." *New York Evening Telegram,* April 16, 1921, 9.

———. "Year's Great Two-Year-Olds Compete for Hopeful Prize." *New York Evening Telegram,* August 31, 1922.

"Buys Jake Sanders." *Los Angeles Herald,* October 26, 1905, 3.

"C. W. Moore, the Breeder." *DRF,* June 8, 1922, 1.

Camp, Walter. "A Roosevelt Creed." *Labor Digest* 12 (March 1920): 28–29.

Campbell, Colin. "Man o' War and Exterminator." *TR,* September 30, 1922.

———. "The Noblest Roman of Them All." *TR,* November 25, 1922.

"Captain Alcock Wins." *New-York Tribune,* November 12, 1922, 23.

"Captain Alcock Wins Pimlico Cup." *TR,* November 18, 1922, 247.

Carley, Tom. "Matter of Fact." *BP,* May 17, 1955.

Carlson, George Lloyd. *Studies in Horse Breeding: An Illustrated Treatise on the Science and Practice of Horse Breeding.* Norfolk, NE: Published by the author, 1910.

Carter, Allan, and Mike Kane. *150 Years of Racing in Saratoga.* Charleston, SC: History Press, 2013.

"Cella's Horses at Memphis." *DRF,* November 16, 1906, 1.

Challenge of Chance advertising poster. *New York Morning Telegraph,* June 15, 1919, 12.

"Champion Jess Willard Is Star in Big Production." *Atlanta Constitution,* June 29, 1919, D10.

"Champlain in Limelight." *DRF,* May 6, 1922, 2.

Chapman, Arthur. "What's Become of the Horse?" *McClure's,* April 1928, 50.

"Cheaper Grade of Horses." *DRF,* October 16, 1920.

"Chicago Owner to Campaign." *Los Angeles Times,* July 4, 1904, 11.

"Chicagoans See Exterminator." *DRF,* September 26, 1922, 1.

"Chivalric Generosity of W. S. Kilmer." *DRF,* September 30, 1922, 2.

"The Churchill Downs Meeting." *TR,* May 4, 1918, 206.

"Close Windsor Finishes." *DRF,* August 18, 1916, 1.

"Closing Day at Laurel." *DRF,* November 1, 1918, 1.

Cole, Edward W. "Kilmer Horses Going to Maryland." *DRF,* August 27, 1919, 1.

———. "Latest Turf Gossip from Saratoga." *DRF,* August 17, 1918, 1

———. "Latest Turf Gossip from Saratoga." *DRF,* August 18, 1918, 2.

———. "Looking Ahead for 1917." *DRF,* January 1, 1917, 1.

———. "Sun Briar After Roamer's Record." *DRF,* August 23, 1918, 1.

Collins, Leonard. "Stars of the Paddocks and Tracks." *WP,* April 28, 1929, SM3.

"Colt's Carcass Destroyed Quickly." *WP,* May 6, 1925, 15.

Collyer, Bert. "Collyer's and Other Handicaps." *Buffalo Courier,* November 11, 1922, 11.

———. "Collyer's and Other Handicaps." *Buffalo Courier,* March 29, 1924, 9.

———. "Collyer's Comment." *WP,* July 4, 1921, 6.

———. "Collyer's Comment." *WP,* November 7, 1922, 13.

———. "Collyer's Comment." *WP,* April 21, 1923.

"Col. McDaniel Critically Ill." *Weekly Saratogian,* November 30, 1884.

"Columbia Records That Should Be in Your Home This 'Fourth.'" Advertisement, *BP,* July 2, 1917, 5.

"Commander Ross Averts Turf War." *NYT,* April 16, 1921, 17.

"Comment on Current Events in Sports." *NYT,* November 28, 1921, 18.

Considine, Bob. "Old Bones." *Collier's,* May 10, 1941, 44–46.

———. "On the Line with Considine." *WP,* October 30, 1941, 23.

Contract between Willis Sharpe Kilmer and Henry McDaniel. McDaniel collection.

Cook, Kevin. *Titanic Thompson.* New York: Norton, 2011.

Cooper, Jilly. *Animals in War.* New York: Lyons Press, 2002.

Copland, Al. "$5000 Weight for Age Event Is Attractive." *New York Evening Telegram,* September 7, 1919, 14.

———. "Sun Briar Court Stands Out." *New York Evening Telegram,* 1920.

———. "Sun Briar Is Beaten by a Head by Fairy Wand." *New York Evening Telegram,* August 6, 1919, 14.

———. "Turf Kings Bow to Paul Jones." *New York Evening Telegram,* June 6, 1920, 5.

"Corrigan's Horses Arrive from London." *NYT,* February 12, 1902, 10.

Corum, W. M. "How Exterminator Came Back to the Races." *New York Evening Journal,* quoted in *BP,* November 25, 1925.

Craigie, Walter. "Dispersal Sale at Kilmer Farm." *Richmond Times Dispatch,* October 27, 1940, 5.

Cromwell, T. B. "Trainer Milam's Horses in Charge." *DRF,* September 6, 1917, 1.

"Crowd Wild as Exterminator Wins Great Race." *Chicago Daily Tribune,* June 17, 1922, 8.

"Crushing Impost on Exterminator." *BP,* June 22, 1922, 15.

"Cudgel Is Beaten by Exterminator." *NYT,* September 23, 1919, 25.

"Cudgel Runs Fine Race." [Washington, D.C.] *Sunday Star,* September 26, 1919, 29.

Curley, Ed. "Exterminator Smashes Record in Winning Aqueduct Feature." King Features.

"Current Notes of the Turf." *DRF,* August 8, 1916, 2.

"Current Notes of the Turf." *DRF,* January 13, 1917, 2.

"Current Notes of the Turf." *DRF,* August 23, 1917, 1.

"Current Notes of the Turf." *DRF,* July 30, 1918, 2.

"Current Notes of the Turf." *DRF,* October 8, 1918, 1, 2.

"Current Notes of the Turf." *DRF,* October 19, 1918, 2.

"Current Notes of the Turf." *DRF,* May 6, 1919, 4.

"Current Notes of the Turf." *DRF,* June 7, 1919, 2.

"Current Notes of the Turf." *DRF,* July 3, 1919, 2.

"Current Events in Sports." *NYT,* August 23, 1920, 16.

Daley, Arthur. "Farewell to Old Bones." *NYT,* September 28, 1945, 24.

———. "Sports of the Times." *NYT,* May 29, 1945, 11.

"Dam of Exterminator." *DRF,* September 23, 1922, 1.

Daniel. "Exterminator Seems to Have Found Himself at Last." *Sun and the New York Herald,* July 6, 1920, 13.

———. "High Lights and Shadows in All Spheres of Sport." *New York Herald,* June 5, 1920.

Daniels, Caroline. "Fairy Wand Beats Gallant Sun Briar in the Delaware." *New York Morning Telegraph,* August 6, 1919, 1.

———. " 'The Feminine Touch Has Not Been Wanting': Women Librarians at Camp Zachary Taylor, *1917–1919.*" *Libraries & the Cultural Record* 43, no. 3 (2008): 286–307.

Day, John I. "Fairy Wand Beats Gallant Sun Briar in the Delaware." *New York Morning Telegraph,* August 6, 1919, 1.

"The Death of Col. David McDaniel." *Spirit of the Times,* January 31, 1885, 16.

"Defeat of Exterminator Stuns Racegoers." *Washington Star,* November 12, 1922, 4.

"Delaware Handicap." *TR,* August 1919.

Dempsey, J. L. "$75,000 and $5,000 Gold Cup." *DRF,* September 25, 1920.

———. "Heavy Going and Upsets." *DRF,* June 29, 1922, 1.

———. "Metric's Amazing Victory." *DRF,* July 6, 1922, 1.

———. "Sam's Boy Is Uncle Sam's." *DRF,* October 15, 1920.

———. "Sir Barton at His Best." *DRF,* August 3, 1920, 1.

———. "Smashing Track Records." *DRF,* August 23, 1918, 2.

———. "Stars in Game Clashing." *DRF,* August 18, 1918, 1.

———. "Superb Saratoga Racing." *DRF,* August 26, 1917, 1.

———. "Tryster Still Unbeaten." *DRF,* August 15, 1920, 1.

"Derby Again Has Value of $15,000." *NYT,* February 10, 1918.

"Derby Candidates Doing Well." *Thoroughbred Record,* April 20, 1918, 220.

"Derby Day—Nuf Sed." *Louisville Courier-Journal,* May 11, 1918.

"Derby Pictures Shown Day After Races." *Moving Picture World,* June 1, 1918, 1306.

"Derby Riders Make Statements About Mounts." *Louisville Courier-Journal,* May 12, 1918.

"Derby the Principal Topic." *DRF,* March 28, 1919, 1.

"Derby to Exterminator, 30–1." *Chicago Tribune,* May 12, 1918, A1.

"Derby Winner Left Far Behind in Race." *NYT,* August 31, 1918, 5.

"Did Not Intend to Kill." *New York Herald,* November 2, 1879, 14.

"Dinner Is Held for Willis Sharpe Kilmer." *BP,* September 18, 1926, 1.

"Domino Is Very Lame." *Chicago Tribune,* June 26, 1894, McDaniel collection.

"Donald Pons Is Killed in Action." *DRF,* November 9, 1918, 1.

"Double for S. C. Hildreth." *DRF,* July 18, 1919, 2.

"Doug Fairbanks Calls on Man Hit by Arrow." *NYT,* October 5, 1922, 21.

"Down the Stretch in the Derby." *Washington Sunday Star,* May 11, 1930, 3.

Drape, Joe. "Despite the Evidence, Trainers Deny a Doping Problem." *NYT,* November 22, 2013, D5.

"Drastic's Easy Triumph." *DRF,* November 20, 1918, 1.

"Dry Agents Allege Tip-Off Before Raid." *Baltimore Sun,* September 29, 1922, 24.

Dunstan, Nelson. "Exterminator Thrives on Easy Life at Farm." *New York Morning Telegraph,* September 8, 1935.

———. "Reflections." 1945, McDaniel collection.

Durden, Chauncey. "The Sportview." *Richmond Times-Dispatch,* October 31, 1940.

Durell, Frank. "Will Sell Kilmer Horses." *New York Evening Telegram,* February 12, 1925.

"East and West in Kentucky Derby." *New York Morning Telegraph,* May 11, 1918.

"Eastern Nags Invade Tijuana." *Los Angeles Daily Times,* November 23, 1923, III, 2.

Eighmey, Rae Katherine. "Food Will Win the War." *Minnesota History* (Fall 2005): 272–86.

"An Elaborate Review of the Precedents of Racing." *DRF,* April 4, 1912, 2.

Elliott, Ron. *The History of Race Riding and the Jockeys' Guild.* Nashville: Turner Publishing, 1999.

"English View of New York Legislation." *DRF,* September 4, 1910, 1.

"Enthusiasm Runs Wild." *DRF,* October 17, 1918, 1.

"Escoba's Tussle with Sun Briar Derby Feature." *New-York Tribune,* April 17, 1918.

Estes, J. A. "The Exterminator Saga Ends." *Blood-Horse,* October 6, 1945, 581.

"Eugene Wayland, Veteran Trainer for Willis Sharpe Kilmer, Dies." *BP,* March 11, 1923.

"Everyone Welcome." *DRF,* September 28, 1922, 4.

Exile [M. M. Leach]. "Exile's Note Book." *TR,* April 19, 1919, 234.

———. "May 1." *TR,* 1919, 265.

————. "May 8." *TR*, May 10, 1919, 282.

————. "Saratoga Cup." *TR*, September 1919.

————. "Saratoga Special." *DRF*, August 1919, 1.

"Exterminator" poem. *TR*, September 23, 1922.

"Exterminator." *Blood-Horse*, October 6, 1945, 582.

"Exterminator." *Ogden Standard-Examiner*, August 11, 1922, 9.

"Exterminator, 26, at Pimlico Track." *NYT*, October 29, 1941, 30.

"Exterminator. A Gallant Steed." *New York Press*, October 10, 1934.

"Exterminator a Horse That Shines on Any Sort of Racetrack." *New-York Tribune*, December 1, 1918, 4.

"Exterminator a Winner." *DRF*, September 26, 1920, 1.

"EXTERMINATOR a Worthy Substitute for Sun Briar." *DRF*, May 12, 1918, 1.

"Exterminator Adds to Fame by Winning Harford Handicap." *BP*, April 17, 1922, 10.

"Exterminator After Rich Tia Juana Purses." *WP*, December 16, 1923, 60.

"Exterminator Again." *DRF*, September 21, 1922, 1.

"Exterminator Again Victor." *DRF*, August 28, 1921, 1.

"Exterminator an Easy Winner in Belmont Feature." *New York Morning Telegraph*, June 6, 1922, 8.

"Exterminator an Honest Horse." *New York Herald*, September 7, 1919, 6.

"Exterminator and Dunlin Victors." *NYT*, September 1, 1922, 18.

"Exterminator and Franklin D. Roosevelt at State Fair." Photograph, in Tom R. Underwood, ed., *Thoroughbred Racing and Breeding*. New York: Coward-McCann, 1945.

"Exterminator and Morvich May Meet," *WP*, June 24, 1922, 13.

"Exterminator and Our Flags," *DRF*, October 3, 1920, 1.

"Exterminator and Sally's Alley Rapidly Nearing Racing Form, *Binghamton Press*, April 6, 1923.

"Exterminator Arrives at Aqueduct," *New York Telegram*, May 7, 1925, n.p.

"Exterminator Arrives for Hawthorne Races," *Buffalo Evening News*, September 26, 1922, 2.

"Exterminator Back in New Turf Role," *New York Telegram*, April 8, 1925, n.p.

"Exterminator Beats Drastic and Lucky B," *BP*, March 24, 1919, 7.

"Exterminator Brought $1,500 as Yearling at Saratoga," *Louisville Courier-Journal*, May 12, 1918, n.p.

"Exterminator Can't Get Any Competition" *Los Angeles Times*, February 4, 1924, 8.

"Exterminator Day at Old Aqueduct." *New York Morning Telegraph*, June 17, 1922.

"Exterminator Dies at Sun Briar Court." *BP*, September 26, 1945, 21.

"Exterminator Easy Victor at Laurel." *Baltimore Sun*, October 4, 1919, 15.

"Exterminator Entrains." *Los Angeles Times*, November 13, 1923, III, 3.

"Exterminator Fails." *DRF,* October 29, 1922, 1.

"Exterminator Fails." *DRF,* April 29, 1923, 1.

"Exterminator Fathers Bunch of Youngsters." *Buffalo Evening News,* April 9, 1925, 35.

"Exterminator Favorite." *DRF,* March 30, 1924, 1.

"Exterminator for Steeplechasing." *DRF,* December 1, 1918, 1.

"Exterminator Given Ovation." *BP,* November 19, 1923, 13.

"Exterminator Gives 'Derby Week' Exhibition." *BP,* May 3, 1944, 19.

"Exterminator Going West." *DRF,* November 7, 1923, 1.

"Exterminator Had Numerous Visitors." *Montreal Gazette,* June 2, 1924, 16.

"Exterminator Hailed as Country's Greatest Horse." *Binghamton Press and Leader,* October 21, 1922, 13.

"Exterminator Has Chance to Come Back." *New York Evening Journal,* April 4, 1925.

"Exterminator, Horse of Iron, Has Run His Last Track Race." *Eau Claire Leader,* August 6, 1922, 2.

"Exterminator in First 1920 Race." *BP,* June 2, 1920.

"Exterminator in Great Triumph." *DRF,* September 1, 1922, 1.

"Exterminator in Maryland." *DRF,* March 29, 1921, 1.

"Exterminator in New Hands." *New York Evening Telegram,* November 2, 1922, 13.

"Exterminator in Old Time Form; Wins Handicap." *Chicago Daily Tribune,* April 22, 1923, A4.

"Exterminator in Stirring Victory." *Buffalo Courier,* June 17, 1922, 11.

"Exterminator in Triumph." *DRF,* May 2, 1919, 1.

"Exterminator in Triumphant Return." *DRF,* February 18, 1924, 1.

"Exterminator Is Again a Winner." *NYT,* October 4, 1919, 13.

"Exterminator Is Handicap Winner." *NYT,* August 28, 1921, 78.

"Exterminator Is Hard to Handle." *Washington Post,* August 26, 1925, BCHS.

"Exterminator Is Most Popular Horse Ever Known, Says Trainer." *BP,* January 7, 1929.

"Exterminator Is Third, Ticket Wins." *New York Sun,* August 31, 1918.

"Exterminator Is Winner of Derby, Was Trial Horse." *New York Morning Telegraph,* May 12, 1918.

"Exterminator, King of the Turf, Dies, Aged 30." *BP,* September 26, 1945, 22.

"Exterminator Lame; Match Is Called Off." *WP,* March 1, 1924, S2.

"Exterminator Lands Feature." *Washington Herald,* October 5, 1918, 10.

"Exterminator Looks Fine." *DRF,* January 31, 1924.

"Exterminator Loses." *DRF,* June 22, 1924, 1.

"Exterminator Loses Pal." *NYT,* November 25, 1944, 19.

"Exterminator May Be Entered in Rich Stakes at Tiajuana Track." *Milwaukee Sentinel,* October 15, 1922, 2.

"Exterminator May Win the Fourth Race." *New York Globe,* August 27, 1921. BCHS.

"Exterminator Meets Defeat in East." *DRF,* May 29, 1918, 1.

"Exterminator Now a $200,000 Winner." *DRF,* May 28, 1922, 1.

"Exterminator, of Course." *DRF,* July 5, 1921, 1.

"Exterminator, 'Old Bones' to His Many Turf Followers." *WP,* April 28, 1940, SP6.

"Exterminator Once Again." *DRF,* September 25, 1921, 1.

"Exterminator, on the Inside." *Guide to the Official National Thoroughbred Racing Hall of Fame,* 2011–2012, 7.

"Exterminator on the Way." *DRF,* September 23, 1922, 1.

"Exterminator Out Owing to Lameness." *NYT,* March 1, 1924, 11.

"Exterminator Ready." *DRF,* April 3, 1923, 1.

"Exterminator Remains in Training Because He Likes Turf Life." *BP,* June 30, 1924, 1.

"Exterminator Runs Sixth in Handicap." *Baltimore Sun,* July 5, 1922, 16.

"Exterminator Scheduled to Arrive Friday." 1924, McDaniel collection.

"Exterminator Sets American Running Record." *BP,* September 16, 1920, 8.

"Exterminator Sets Track Record." *New York Evening Telegram,* May 21, 1921, 9.

"Exterminator Shares Honors with Willard in 'Challenge of Chance.'" *BP,* June 21, 1919.

"Exterminator Sprints Fast." *DRF,* April 1, 1919, 2.

"Exterminator, Sun Briar Back at Old Home." *WP,* June 14, 1942, C4.

"Exterminator Takes Autumn Gold Cup and Edwina Wins Dunton." *BP,* September 17, 1921, 14.

"Exterminator! That's All." *DRF,* June 14, 1922, 1.

"Exterminator the Attraction." *DRF,* April 18, 1924, 1.

"Exterminator the Favorite." *DRF,* May 27, 1922, 1.

"Exterminator the Great." *Cherry Creek* (NY) *News.*

"Exterminator the Great." *DRF,* April 16, 1922, 1.

"Exterminator the Winner." *DRF,* November 14, 1919, 1.

"Exterminator, the Wonder Horse." *Duluth Herald,* November 14, 1922, 16.

"Exterminator to Carry Top Weight in Coffroth." *WP,* March 23, 1924, S2.

"Exterminator to Race at Woodbine." *DRF,* September 16, 1921, 1.

"Exterminator to Race in England." *DRF,* September 17, 1921, 1.

"Exterminator to Retire when Racing Season Ends." *WP,* June 16, 1923, 16.

"Exterminator to Run." *New York Evening Telegram,* August 11, 1925.

"Exterminator Today." *DRF,* February 17, 1924, 1.

"Exterminator, Victor in Derby Classic, Not Yet Three Years Old." Pittsburgh *Gazette-Times,* May 19, 1918, 20.

"Exterminator vs. Man o' War." *Putnam County* (NY) *Republican,* 1923.

"Exterminator Will Be Sold." *New York Evening Telegram,* August 22, 1920.

"Exterminator Wins! 1918." Film. www.kentuckyderby.com/history/year/1918.

"Exterminator Wins Big Moneyed Event." *NYT,* November 13, 1920, 16.

"Exterminator Wins Brooklyn Handicap." *NYT,* June 17, 1922, 16.

"Exterminator Wins Clark Handicap." *TR,* April 27, 1922, 420.

"Exterminator Wins Harford Handicap." *NYT,* April 16, 1922, 27.

"Exterminator Wins in Comeback Race." *Chicago Daily Tribune,* February 18, 1924, 24.

"Exterminator Wins in Come-Back Race." *NYT,* February 18, 1924, 18.

"Exterminator Wins Kentucky Derby." *TR,* May 18, 1918, 278.

"Exterminator Wins Latonia Cup." *TR,* November 20, 1918, 257.

"Exterminator Wins Laurel Stakes." *TR,* October 28, 1922, 206.

"Exterminator Wins Maryland Feature." *NYT,* April 22, 1923, S1.

"Exterminator Wins the Pimlico Cup." *BP,* November 15, 1919, 9.

"Exterminator Withdrawn." *DRF,* March 1, 1924, 1.

"Exterminator Won for Him." *Baltimore Sun,* March 10, 1923, 10.

"Exterminator Won't Appear at Pimlico." *WP,* October 29, 1940, 19.

"Exterminator's Cup Race." *DRF,* November 24, 1918.

"Exterminator's Fast Race." *DRF,* May 22, 1921, 1.

"Exterminator's Fine Trial." *DRF,* May 23, 1919, 1.

"Exterminator's Gameness." *DRF,* September 23, 1919, 1.

"Exterminator's Great Chance." *DRF,* November 11, 1922, 2.

"Exterminator's Great Opportunity." *DRF,* October 28, 1922, 1.

"Exterminator's Record for Six Years on Track Breaks All Records." *BP,* June 6, 1922.

"Exterminator's Victory Still Talk of Horse World." *BP,* May 18, 1918, 3.

"Fair Colleen Beats Ireland." *New York Sun,* June 15, 1919, 3.

"Feature Is Easy for Exterminator." *New York Morning Telegraph,* May 2, 1919, 1.

"Feature Race Captured by Hampton Dame" *TR,* July 17, 1915, 32.

Field, Bryan. "31,336 at Belmont: 25 Million Bond Sale." *NYT,* October 3, 1943, S1.

"Fine Opening Card at Havre de Grace." *NYT,* April 16, 1923, 15.

"Fire in Hold of Liner Minnehaha Admitted Due to Explosion." *Saratogian,* August 8, 1915, 1S.

"Firebrand Wins Independence Handicap." *TR,* July, 1922, 491.

"First Far Western Venture." *DRF,* December 6, 1921, 1.

Fitzgerald, C. J. "Racing Fixtures Should Be Annexed by Horses from Sun Briar Court." *BP,* February 4, 1922, 17.

Fitzgerald, J. V. "The Round-Up." *WP,* January 6, 1920, 9.

Fitzgerald, John I. "Exterminator in 4th Straight Victory for the Saratoga Cup." *New York Morning Telegraph,* September 1, 1922, 1.

———. "Shields to Train Kilmer Racers." *New York Morning Telegraph,* November 2, 1922, BCHS scrapbook.

"Flapper Jockey Is Awaited by Turf Followers." *New York Evening Telegram,* April 9, 1922, 10.

"Floral Piece for a Horse Is a Saratoga Novelty." *NYT,* August 26, 1920, 19.

"Foresee Wonderful Sport." *DRF,* July 27, 1921, 1.

"Former Jockey Knapp to Enter Saratoga's Racing Hall of Fame." *Gloversville* (NY) *Leader-Herald,* August 2, 1969, 13.

Fraley, Oscar. "Today's Sports Parade." *Auburn* (NY) *Citizen Advertiser,* February 16, 1952, B2.

"Frank Taylor Quits as Trainer for Big Training Stable." *New York Evening Sun,* August 17, 1916, BCHS.

French, Lane. "Seven Rancocas Stars Named in Chicago Derby." *Chicago Daily Tribune,* June 15, 1924, A6.

"French-Bred Yearlings Prove Popular." *DRF,* August 16, 1916, 1.

"Frontier to Slippery Elm." *DRF,* July 15, 1920, 1.

"Funeral Services of C. T. Patterson." *TR,* April 6, 1918, 182.

"Gallant Exterminator." *DRF,* August 29, 1920, 1.

"Gallant Exterminator Takes a Bow." *BP,* October 4, 1943, 15.

"Gallops away from His Rival." *Baltimore Sun,* June 14, 1922, 11.

Gatto, Kimberly. *Saratoga Race Course.* Charleston, SC: History Press, 2011.

"Geldings to Be Barred." *DRF,* August 7, 1918, 1.

"George C. Bennett Proud of His Horses." *New York Morning Telegraph,* quoted in *DRF,* August 8, 1906, 1.

"German Bomb Narrowly Misses Binghamton Man in Streets of London." *BP,* January 4, 1917, 2.

Gill, Dan. "The U.S.S. *Remilk*." www.pine3.info/USS%20Remlik.htm.

Gleason, Oscar R. *Gleason's Horse Book.* Philadelphia: Hubbard Publishing, 1892.

———. *Gleason's Veterinary Hand Book and System of Horse Taming.* Chicago: C. C. Thompson, 1900.

Glueckstein, Fred. *Of Men, Women, and Horses.* Xlibris, 2006.

Goldberg, Ryan. "The Golden Age of Brooklyn Racing." *DRF,* November 11, 2010.

"Golden Broom a New Star." *DRF,* August 10, 1919, 1.

"Good News for Chicago." *DRF,* September 21, 1922, 9.

"Good News for Thomas Hitchcock." *DRF,* September 1, 1918, 1.

"Good Prices for Ogden Yearlings." *DRF,* June 30, 1917, 1.

"Gossip from Blue Grass Region." *DRF,* April 28, 1915, 2.

"Gossip from Juarez Track." *DRF,* March 23, 1913, 2.

"Gossip of the Turf." *DRF,* December 4, 1902, 3.

Graham, Frank. "Setting the Pace." *New York Sun,* February 28, 1939.

Graham, Frank. "Graham's Corner," n.p., n.d., 1948.

"Great American to Maiden." *Daily Racing Form,* July 4, 1920, 1.

"A Great Campaigner." *Cincinnati Times-Star,* quoted in *Maysville* (KY) *Public Ledger,* August 10, 1922, 2.

"Great Crowd Is in Frenzy of Joy as Colt Arrives." *BP,* September 4, 1917, 3.

"Great Crowd Sees Exterminator Win." *Washington Evening Star,* May 12, 1918.

"Great Enthusiasm Shown." *DRF,* June 6, 1919, 1.

"Great Exterminator." *DRF,* September 7, 1922, 1.

"Great Exterminator Wins Big Handicap." *Buffalo Courier,* April 22, 1923, 100.

"Great Exterminator, with $171,381, Leads World's Geldings." *Saratogian,* November 17, 1921, 8.

"Great Outpouring of Society to Welcome Racing at the Spa." *New York Herald,* August 2, 1918, 9.

"Great Racing at Jamaica." *DRF,* May 15, 1921.

Greene, Ann Norton. *Horses at Work.* Cambridge, MA: Harvard University Press, 2008.

Greene, Melanie. *Kentucky Handicap Horse Racing.* Charleston, SC: History Press, 2014.

"Grey Lag Beaten by Exterminator." *Baltimore Sun,* June 17, 1922, 9.

"Grey Lag Wins Saratoga Handicap." *DRF,* August 2, 1922, 1.

"H. E. McDaniel, Famed Trainer of Racehorses, Dead at 82." *Saratogian,* January 26, 1948, 10.

"H. G. Bedwell's Success as a Trainer." *DRF,* September 29, 1918, 1.

"H. McDaniel to Train for R. L. Gerry." *DRF,* October 8, 1919.

Hadsell, Jerome. "Life and Times of Willis Sharpe Kilmer Told for First Time." *BP,* July 13, 1940, 4.

Hagner, Anne. "Exterminator Lion of Hour." *WP,* October 31, 1941, 25.

Haight, Walter. "Wanted: Exterminator of Tall Tales." *WP,* January 2, 1968, C4.

"Halt Saratoga Training." *DRF,* July 25, 1922, 1.

Ham, Eldon. *Larceny and Old Leather.* Chicago: Academy Publishers, 2005.

"Handsomely Gowned Women Show Interest in Races." *Saratogian,* August 26, 1917, 8.

"Harry McDaniel." N.p., n.d., McDaniel collection.

"Havre de Grace Tomorrow." *DRF,* April 15, 1923, 1.

"Havre de Grace Track Fit for Fast Racing." *New York Morning Telegraph,* April 17, 1922.

"Havre Opens in Blaze of Glory." *DRF,* April 17, 1923, 1.

"Hawthorne." *DRF,* October 1, 1922, 1.

Hayes, M. Horace. *Illustrated Horse Breaking.* London: Thacker & Co., 1889.

"Heard and Seen in Saratoga Paddock." *WP,* August 31, 1920, 9.

"Heard at Laurel." *WP,* October 12, 1918, 12.

Helgesen, Ray. "Audacious Wins Pimlico Feature." *Washington Star,* November 15, 1921.

———. "The Porter Wins Annapolis Handicap." *Washington Herald,* November 9, 1921, 14.

"Henry McDaniel." *Blood-Horse,* 1933, McDaniel collection.

"Henry McDaniel." *Blood-Horse,* week ending February 7, 1931, 226.

"Henry McDaniel." Obituary, *Blood-Horse,* 1948.

"Henry McDaniels, the expert trainer for G. C. Bennett," McDaniel collection.

"Henry McDaniel's Claim to Fame." *DRF,* February 11, 1918, 1.

"Henry M'Daniel." *New York Morning Telegraph,* December 14, 1930.

"Here and There on the Turf." *DRF,* August 27, 1922, 1.

"Here and There on the Turf." *DRF,* September 1, 1922, 2.

"Here and There on the Turf." *DRF,* September 2, 1922, 2.

"Here and There on the Turf." *DRF,* September 22, 1922, 2.

"Here and There on the Turf." *DRF,* September 27, 1922, 2.

"Here and There on the Turf." *DRF,* September 30, 1922, 1.

"Here and There on the Turf." *DRF,* October 4, 1922, 2.

"Here and There on the Turf." *DRF,* October 26, 1922, 2.

"Here and There on the Turf." *DRF,* October 31, 1922, 2.

"Here and There on the Turf." *DRF,* November 14, 1922, 2.

"Here and There on the Turf." *DRF,* November 17, 1922, 2.

"Here and There on the Turf." *DRF,* February 22, 1923, 2.

"Here and There on the Turf." *DRF,* March 26, 1923, 2.

"Here and There on the Turf." *DRF,* March 28, 1923, 2.

"Here and There on the Turf." *DRF,* April 22, 1923, 2.

"Here and There on the Turf." *DRF,* April 24, 1923, 2.

"Here and There on the Turf." *DRF,* April 26, 1923, 2.

"Here and There on the Turf." *DRF,* May 5, 1923, 1.

"Here and There on the Turf." *DRF,* November 9, 1923, 2.

"Here and There on the Turf." *DRF,* January 10, 1924, 2.

"Here and There on the Turf." *DRF,* February 1, 1924, 2.

"Here and There on the Turf." *DRF,* February 19, 1924, 2.

"Here and There on the Turf." *DRF,* March 23, 1924, 2.

"Here and There on the Turf." *DRF,* April 1, 1924, 2.

"Here and There on the Turf." *DRF,* May 8, 1925.

"Here's Strong 'Hunch' for Derby." *DRF,* May 8, 1919, 2.

Herring, Charles Griffin. "A Visit to Sun Briar Court." *TR*, December 12, 1922, 151.

"High Lights Mark Week's Racing at Tia Juana Track." *WP*, February 24, 1924, S4.

Hildreth, Samuel C. *The Spell of the Turf*. Philadelphia: Lippincott, 1926.

Hildreth's Day of Glory." *DRF*, May 8, 1921, 1.

Hillenbrand, Laura. *Seabiscuit*. New York: Random House, 2001.

"His First Winner, No. 9. Henry McDaniel." Ca. 1935, McDaniel collection.

"History." Ramsey Farm. www.ramseyfarm.com/history.shtml.

"Hits Hard at Ascot Crooks," *Los Angeles Times*, March 1, 1906, II7.

"Hold a Horse Show on an Ocean Liner." *NYT*, August 2, 1910, 7.

Hollingsworth, Kent. "Exterminator." *Blood-Horse*, 1969, 2020.

Holtzman, Ellen. "Time Capsule: A Home away from Home." *Monitor on Psychology* 3, no. 43 (March 2012): 24. www.apa.org/monitor/2012/03/asylums .aspx.

"Home to Be Made Perfect: Former Society Leader to Decorate Fairbanks Home at Beverly Hills." *Los Angeles Times*, October 27, 1922, 18.

"Hopeful to Man o' War." *Baltimore Sun*, August 31, 1919, 13.

"Hopeless Cripple Made a Winner." *DRF*, July 29, 1919, 4.

"Horses Arrive on S.S. Mongolian." *New York Morning Telegraph*, February 21, 1916, BCHS.

"Horses Plentiful for Longer Stakes." *WP*, February 10, 1924, S4.

"Horses Trained by M'Daniel Capture Notable Stakes." McDaniel collection.

"Horses Traveling in Padded Stalls." *NYT*, February 24, 1907, 13.

Hotaling, Edward. *Great Black Jockeys*. Rocklin, CA: Forum, 1999.

———. *They're Off!* Syracuse: Syracuse University Press, 1995.

"How Kilmer Star Was Counted Out." *New York Morning Telegraph*, October 6, 1920, BCHS scrapbook.

"How Our Cavalry Horses Fare." *DRF*, December 5, 1918, 2.

"How Thomas Hitchcock, Jr., Escaped." *DRF*, September 11, 1918, 1.

"How the Kilmers Ruled Binghamton, Stalled Post Office Fraud Order." *Binghamton Sun-Bulletin*, October 2, 1961, 9, BCHS.

"How Willis Sharpe Kilmer Is Bringing Thoroughbreds." *BP*, 1918, BCHS scrapbook.

Hughes, Ed. "Ed Hughes' Column," *BDE*, January 18, 1931, ac.

Hughes, Johnny. *Famous Gamblers, Poker History, and Texas Stories*. iUniverse, 2012, 120.

"Hunts Meet Is on Tomorrow." *New York Evening Telegram*, August 31, 1921.

"I Have Often Been Asked Why with My Success." McDaniel collection.

"Improvement in Sun Briar." *DRF*, February 7, 1918, 1.

"Improvements at Sun Briar Court." *DRF*, September 5, 1918, 1.

"In Quarters at Memphis." *Louisville Courier-Journal,* quoted in *DRF,* November 19, 1903, 1.

"In the Kentucky Racing Field." *DRF,* July 23, 1921, 1.

"In the Wake of the News." *Chicago Daily Tribune,* October 10, 1920, A1.

Inabinett, Mark. *Grantland Rice and His Heroes: The Sportswriter as Mythmaker in the 1920s.* Knoxville: University of Tennessee Press, 1994.

"Influenza Precautions." *DRF,* October 27, 1918, 2.

"It would have been better for his reputation." *Berkeley Daily Gazette,* December 22, 1922, 6.

"J. C. Milam." *Thoroughbred Record,* October 1921.

"J. K. L. Ross' New Trainer." *DRF,* April 16, 1921, 1.

Jackson, Kevin. *Constellation of Genius: 1922, Modernism Year One.* New York: Farrar, Straus and Giroux, 2013.

"James Butler's Son Dies in France." *DRF,* November 27, 1918, 1.

Jennings, Robert. *The Horse and His Diseases.* Philadelphia: J. E. Potter, 1860.

———. *Horse-Training Made Easy.* Philadelphia: J. E. Potter, 1866.

Jeffery, J. R. "Midway Shows Great Improvement." *DRF,* August 18, 1917.

"Jimmy Rowe's Colors Are the Same as Those Used by Colonel David McDaniel." *DRF,* October 1, 1908, 2.

"Jinx Haunting a Jockey's Cap." *DRF,* January 25, 1917, 1.

"J. Kennedy Attacked by Pimlico Fans." *Baltimore Sun,* November 12, 1920, 20.

"Jockey Knapp Tells How Sun Briar Won." *BP,* August 19, 1918, 5.

"Jockey Pays Supreme Sacrifice." *DRF,* November 3, 1918, 1.

"Jockey Willie Knapp." *TR,* February 23, 1918.

"Jockeys 'Doing Their Bit.'" *DRF,* July 24, 1918, 1.

"Jockeys Must Keep Their Positions." *DRF,* July 17, 1918, 1.

"Johren's Latonia Derby." *DRF,* June 23, 1918, 1.

"Judge Nelson Welcomed at Tijuana Track." *Los Angeles Times,* November 6, 1923, III3.

"Justice William McMahon's Side of the McDaniel Difficulty." *BDE,* December 3, 1881, 1.

Kean, Hilda. *Animal Rights: Political and Social Change in Britain Since 1800.* London: Reaktion Books, 1998, 79.

"Keen Contest for Racing Laurels." *New York Sun,* August 24, 1919, 5.

Kelly, Billy. "Before and After." *Buffalo Courier-Express,* June 11, 1944, 4B.

Kenefick, Bob. "On the Sport Firing Line." *Syracuse Journal,* September 1, 1920.

Kennedy, David M. *Over Here: The First World War and American Society.* New York: Oxford University Press, 1980.

"Kentucky Derby." *TR,* May 17, 1918.

"Kentucky Paint Appears." *DRF,* April 12, 1938, 20.

"Kentucky Yearlings Sell Well." *DRF,* August 19, 1916, 1.

" 'Kidron,' Pershing's War Horse, Must Remain in Quarantine While His Master Is Riding in Parades." *WP,* September 10, 1919, 8.

Kieran, John. "Uncle Henry Tells Some Stories." *NYT,* August 10, 1932, 22.

Kilby, Emily. "How to Identify Pastern Problems." *Equus,* March 1997. http://equusmagazine.com/article/pasternproblems_012706.

"Kilmer Again to Aid of Boys in Khaki." *Binghamton Herald,* July 1, 1916, BCHS.

"Kilmer Boosts Liberty Bond Sale." April 25, 1918, BCHS.

"Kilmer Buys Harris Farm." *Atlanta Constitution,* May 16, 1925, 10.

"The Kilmer Divorce Case." *Binghamton Herald,* April 4, 1899, 5.

"Kilmer Gelding Wins Bayside Handicap Under Heavy Wraps." *BP,* June 6, 1922.

"Kilmer Gives Two Yachts." *NYT,* May 31, 1917, 5.

"The Kilmer Racing String Is Fine." *New York Evening Telegram,* September 17, 1916.

"Kilmer Rewards Trainer and Riders." *DRF,* August 12, 1919.

"Kilmer Stable in Maryland." *DRF,* March 29, 1922, 1.

"Kilmer–Richardson." Clipping, BCHS, Kilmer file.

"Kilmer to Sell Nags, but Won't Quit Game." *Chicago Daily Tribune,* May 8, 1925, 21.

"Kilmer Two-Year-Olds Are Now Ready." *DRF,* March 20, 1917, 1.

"Kilmer's Crack Racer Beats Johren by Nose." *New-York Tribune,* August 18, 1918, II, 1.

"Kilmer's 'Sun-Briar' Is Fine." *Elmira* (NY) *Telegram,* May 4, 1919, 1.

King, Henry V. "Cirrus Winner of Brooklyn Handicap." *Sun and New York Herald,* June 25, 1920, 10.

———. "Exterminator Is Choice for Brooklyn Handicap." *Sun and New York Herald,* June 24, 1920, 11.

———. "Exterminator Makes New Record at Jamaica Track." *Sun and New York*

———. "Exterminator Wins Cup and Makes New Record." *New York Sun and Herald,* September 16, 1920, 13.

Herald, June 20, 1920, 9.

———. "Kilmer Horses Show the Way in Champlain." *Baltimore Sun,* August 10, 1919, 1, Sec. 2.

———. "Modern Horses Less Rugged." *New York Sun,* July 25, 1936, 33.

———. "Old Bones, 30, Grows Weary." *New York Sun,* May 4, 1945, 30.

———. "Old Bones Big and Fat at 25." 1938.

———. "Old Bones Here for Bond Sales, Spry as a Colt." *New York Sun,* September 29, 1943, 31.

———. "Sir Barton Fast with Weight Up." *Sun and New York Herald,* August 3, 1920.

———. "Sun Briar's Dam Here from France." *New York Sun,* December 12, 1919, 18.

"King Horse Again Draws Big Society Crowd to Saratoga." *New York Herald,* August 3, 1918, 8.

Koenig, Robert. *The Fourth Horseman.* New York: PublicAffairs, 2006, 41–44.

Kreyling, Michael. *A Late Encounter with the Civil War.* Athens: University of Georgia Press, 2013.

Kruse, Holly. "Media, Marketing, and Memory: Sport Promotion and *Seabiscuit.*" In *Visual Economies of/in Motion,* ed. C. Richard King and David J. Leonard, New York: Peter Lang, 2006.

"Lamanda Park Calm Again." *Los Angeles Times,* August 25, 1923, III3.

Lamb, Al. "McDaniel Is Back at Sun Briar Court," *BP,* January 4, 1927, 15.

———. "Spinning the Sports Top." *BP,* December 1, 1944, 27.

———. "Sun Briar, Thoroughbred Champion, Dies in Stall Here." *BP,* October 18, 1943.

Lane, French. "Exterminator Here Tomorrow for Races." *Chicago Daily Tribune,* September 23, 1922, 9.

"Last Year for Sun Briar." *Saratogian,* July 27, 1918, 8.

"Latest Gossip and News from Churchill Downs." *DRF,* May 6, 1939.

"Latest Turf News from Havre." *DRF,* April 25, 1923.

"Latest Work of Derby Candidates." *DRF,* April 18, 1918, 1.

"Latonia Cup to Be Decided Today." *DRF,* November 23, 1918, 1.

"Latonia Entries." *TR,* April 6, 1918, 187.

"Latonia Meeting Finished." *DRF,* July 10, 1921, 1.

"Latonia Racing Extended." *DRF,* November 21, 1918, 1.

"Laurel Park a Place of Beauty," *DRF,* September 26, 1918, 2.

"Laurel Racing Suspended." *DRF,* October 13, 1918, 1.

"Laurel's Largest Crowd." *DRF,* October 23, 1921, 1.

"Lend Interest to Derby Trial." *DRF,* April 12, 1918, 1.

Leonard, Andrew G. "Exterminator Wins Ben Ali Handicap." *Lexington Leader,* May 2, 1919.

"Leonardo II Wins the Rich Hopeful." *Saratogian,* September 1, 1920.

Letter from M. H. Tichenor. N.d. but post-1901, McDaniel collection.

"Lexington Meeting at End." *DRF,* May 9, 1919, 1.

"Liberator Delivers Goods." *Louisville Courier-Journal,* May 9, 1918, 1.

"Likely Latonia Derby Starters." *DRF,* June 20, 1918, 1.

Linthicum, Jesse A. "Spotlight on Sports." *Baltimore Sun,* May 19, 1935, S2.

"Listen to What the Trainers Have to Say About It." *Louisville Courier-Journal,* May 12, 1918.

Livingston, Barbara D. *Old Friends: Visits with My Favorite Thoroughbreds.* Lexington, KY: Eclipse Press, 2002.

Livingston, Phil, and Ed Roberts. *War Horse.* Albany, TX: Bright Sky, 2003, 125.

"Local Horse Wins Greatest Two-Year-Old Race of Year." *BP,* July 2, 1917, 5.

"Local Notes." *TR,* November 20, 1918, 256.

"Local Turf Gossip." *DRF,* July 16, 1902, 1.

"Local Turf Gossip." *DRF,* August 23, 1902, 1.

"Local Turf Gossip." *DRF,* May 21, 1903, 3.

"Loftus Is Called on Carpet." *NYT,* July 18, 1919, 13.

"Long Beach Goes to Exterminator." *NYT,* May 22, 1921, 94.

"Lost Minnehaha Officers." *NYT,* September 16, 1917, 2.

Lowe, Dan. "Racing Folk Rejoice at Knapp's Success." *New York Evening Telegraph,* August 30, 1929, BCHS.

"Luck an Important Item in Racing." *DRF,* July 25, 1918, 2.

"Lucky Owner of Exterminator." *DRF,* December 8, 1920, 1.

Lyons, Dan. "Grandstand to Paddock." *New York Globe,* September 16, 1920.

M. H. Tichenor letter. October 3, 1906. McDaniel collection.

Macbeth, W. J. "Audacious Takes Suburban." *New-York Tribune,* June 5, 1921, 18.

———. "Cochran Mare Does 1:36 Mile in Winning the Delaware." *New-York Tribune,* August 6, 1919, 11.

———. "Exterminator and Thunderclap Clip Records at Jamaica." *New-York Tribune,* May 22, 1921, 20.

———. "Exterminator Sets Up New Track Record." *New-York Tribune,* June 30, 1920.

———. "Final Belmont Feature Draws Only 2 Horses." *New-York Tribune,* September 16, 1921, 15.

———. "Great Purchase Defeated in Saratoga Cup Classic." *New-York Tribune,* August 31, 1919, 19.

———. "J. S. Cosden's Dunlin Wins $38,950 Hopeful Stakes." *New-York Tribune,* September 1, 1922, 15.

———. "Motor Cop Captures $5000 Withers Stakes at Belmont Park." *New-York Tribune,* June 2, 1918, 2.

———. "Paul Jones Adds Name to List." *New-York Tribune,* June 6, 1920, 18.

———. "Sun Briar Smashes World's Mile Record." *New-York Tribune,* August 7, 1918, 12.

"MacKay Yearlings Bring High Prices." *DRF,* August 13, 1916, 1.

"Mad Hatter Temperamental Horse." *DRF,* August 31, 1921, 2.

"Magnificent Exterminator." *DRF,* May 21, 1922, 1.

"Major Belmont's Significant Words." *DRF,* June 26, 1918, 1.

Malone, Tom. "Belmont Park Almost Ready." *New York Evening Telegram*, March 29, 1921, 7.

"Manager Waite Wins the Camden." *New York Morning Telegraph*, May 5, 1918.

"Man o' War and Exterminator Win Feature Stakes." *NYT*, August 31, 1919, 21.

"Man o' War and Sir Barton to Race for $75,000 Purse." *Sun and New York Herald*, September 25, 1920, 12.

"Man o' War–Exterminator." *DRF*, October 14, 1920, 1.

"Man o' War May Race in England Next Year; Offer $50,000 for Race with Exterminator." *NYT*, October 14, 1920, 1.

"Man o' War Will Be Placed in Strictest Seclusion." *Buffalo Evening News*, October 16, 1920.

"Man o' War Will Not Race Again, Says Samuel Riddle." *WP*, October 16, 1920, 12.

"Man o' War's Mark in Danger Today." *NYT*, October 28, 1922, 19.

"Many Foreign-Bred Juveniles." *DRF*, April 13, 1917, 1.

"Many Improvements at Saratoga." *TR*, 1919, 56.

"Marilynn and Jack Are Made One at Fairbanks' Home in Los Angeles." *WP*, July 31, 1922, 5.

Martin, George A. *The Family Horse*. New York: Orange Judd, 1889.

Martin, Kevin. "Dr. Ring and the Origins of Horse Doping." April 13, 2009. http://colinsghost.org/2009/04/dr-ring-and-origins-of-horse-doping.html.

"May Send Racers to France." *Chicago Eagle*, March 22, 1919.

McCulloch-Williams, Maria. "Blood Will Tell in Horse as Well as Man," *DRF*, October 5, 1918, 2.

McCullough, Edo. *Good Old Coney Island*. New York: Scribner, 1957, 128.

McDaniel, Henry. "Down the Stretch in the Derby." *Washington Sunday Star*, May 11, 1930.

———. "Half a Century on the Turf." *Washington Sunday Star*, June 1, 1930, 2.

"The McDaniel Confederacy." Simpson, Joseph. Quoted in *DRF*, December 18, 1897.

"McDaniel Fought Duel with Burglar." *Enquirer*, n.d., McDaniel collection.

"McDaniel Training Horses Longer than Any Active Contemporary," *DRF*, McDaniel collection.

McGee, Guy. "Old Bones." *DRF*, June 20, 1922, 1.

McShane, Clay, and Joel A. Tarr. *The Horse in the City*. Baltimore: Johns Hopkins University Press, 2007.

"M'Daniel Gets After Coburn." *Chicago Daily Tribune*, May 17, 1903, 11.

Menke, Frank O. "Exterminator Has Eclipsed the Record of Man o' War." *Wheeling News*, April 14, 1924.

"Midsummer Racing Attracts Crowds to the Spa." *New York Herald*, August 12, 1917, 8.

"Midway Captures Kentucky Feature." *Washington Sunday Star,* May 25, 1919, 22.

"Midway Wins Rich Handicap." *New York Sun,* May 25, 1919, 2:1.

"Mile Time Is Lowered." *DRF,* August 7, 1918, 1.

Millar, Harry. "Paddock Parade." *Long Island Daily Press,* October 6, 1943, 3.

"Millions for a Horse." *Santa Ana Register,* April 13, 1930, 22.

"Minnehaha Delayed by Accident." *DRF,* January 18, 1917, 1.

"Minnehaha Is Sunk." *BP,* September 13, 1917.

"Minnehaha Not Convoyed." *NYT,* October 30, 1917, 15.

"Minnehaha Sunk by a Submarine." *NYT,* September 13, 1917, 1.

"Missing." *BP,* August 18, 1943, 3.

"Miss Roosevelt Eager to See Horses Start." *NYT,* April 1, 1905, 9.

Mitchum, Petrine Day. *Hollywood Hoofbeats.* Irvine, CA: I-5 Press, 2014.

"Modo Wins in Fast Time." *DRF,* August 31, 1921, 1.

Mooney, Katherine C. *Race Horse Men.* Cambridge, MA: Harvard University Press, 2014.

"More Glory for Exterminator." *DRF,* April 22, 1923, 1.

"More Laurels for Great Exterminator." *DRF,* June 17, 1922, 1.

More, T. R. "Great Sport in Sight." *Los Angeles Times,* November 12, 1891, 3.

"Mormon Badly Beaten." *DRF,* April 4, 1919, 2.

Morris, Eric A. "Horse Power to Horsepower." *Access* 30 (Spring 2007): 2.

Morris, Sylvia Jukes. *Edith Kermit Roosevelt: Portrait of a First Lady.* New York: Modern Library, 2001.

"'Mother's Day' for Army Abroad." *Morning Telegraph,* May 12, 1918, 1.

"Motorcar Accidents." *BDE,* June 25, 1920, 3.

"Mr. Kilmer." *BP,* July 15, 1940, 21.

"Mr. Kilmer's Entry Wins Classic Kentucky Derby." *BP,* May 13, 1918.

"Mr. Kilmer Is Given Ovation by Newsboys." *BP,* December 26, 1916.

"Mr. Kilmer Will Help Breed Better Horses." *BP,* September 15, 1916, 2.

"Mrs. E. W. Kilmer Weds Maj. Sutton." *Washington Times,* July 15, 1919, 11.

"Mrs. Kilmer Will Send Great Gelding to Belmont." *Binghamton Press,* n.d.

"Mrs. R. L. Gerry Gives Dinner Dance." *NYT,* February 4, 1911, 13.

"Mrs. Willis Sharpe Kilmer." Photograph, *BP,* October 4, 1943, 15.

"Mrs. Willis Sharpe Kilmer Divorced and Married Again, Sacrificing $25,000 a Year." *New York Herald,* July 15, 1919, 10.

"Mrs. Willis Sharpe Kilmer Gets Divorce and Remarries." *Elmira Star-Gazette,* July 16, 1919, 2.

"Mrs. Willis Sharpe Kilmer Has Begun an Action for Divorce at Binghamton." *Elmira Daily Gazette,* April 6, 1899.

"Much Activity at Saratoga." *DRF,* July 26, 1921, 1.

"Muddy Going at Belmont." *DRF,* September 3, 1919, 1.

"Muenter, Once German Teacher Here, Killed Wife, Shot Morgan, Sabotaged in World War 1." *Harvard Crimson,* February 14, 1942. www.thecrimson.com /article/1942/2/14/muenter-once-german-teacher-here-killed/.

Mulholland, Fred E. "Stable May Get into Trouble if 'Dope' Was Used." *San Francisco Call,* February 20, 1906, 10.

Mulligan, Terence. "The Delights of Pullman Dining USA 1866–1968." Pullman Car Services Supplement Edition, April 2007, 20.

"Musica-Medicus." Sheet music with lyrics, BCHS, Kilmer folder.

"National Economic Impact of the U.S. Horse Industry." www.horsecouncil.org /national-economic-impact-us-horse-industry.

National Reporter System, *The New York Supplement,* Containing the Decisions of the Supreme and Lower Courts of Record of New York State," January 1, 1922, *Beardsley v. Kilmer.*

"Naturalist Is Easy Victor in Excelsior." *New York Sun,* June 15, 1919, 3.

"Near the $100,000 Mark." *DRF,* September 3, 1920, 1.

"New Belmont Park Today." *DRF,* May 27, 1921, 1.

Newman, Neil. "The Career of Uncle Henry McDaniel." *National Turf Digest,* April 1929.

———. "I Remember." *New York Morning Telegraph,* n.d.

———. "Man o' War Versus Exterminator." *TR,* November 4, 1922, 222.

———. "Willis Sharpe Kilmer." *TR,* July 6, 1940, 39.

"New Year Party for Sun Briar." *DRF,* January 5, 1918, 1.

"The Next Great 3-Year-Old Event in the Season." McDaniel collection.

Nicholson, James C. *The Kentucky Derby.* Lexington: University Press of Kentucky, 2012.

"No Change in Latonia Situation." *DRF,* October 26, 1918, 1.

"Noted Canadian Turfman Lets Head Trainer Go." *Auburn* (NY) *Citizen,* April 1, 1921, 2.

"Notes of the Turf." *DRF,* March 7, 1906, 2.

"Notes of the Turf." *DRF,* February 17, 1914, 1.

N.t. *Chicago Tribune,* June 26, 1894, McDaniel collection.

O'Connor, John. *History of the Kentucky Derby, 1875–1921,* 1923. https://archive .org/details/historyofkentuck00ocon.

O'Dell, Gary A. "Denton Offutt of Kentucky: America's First 'Horse Whisperer'?" *Register of the Kentucky Historical Society* 108, no. 3 (Summer 2010): 173–211.

"Off-Day at Laurel Park." *DRF,* October 27, 1922, 1.

"Off to War." *BP,* September 28, 1943, 17.

"Offers $50,000 for Race." *NYT,* September 17, 1920, 23.

Ogle, Tasker. "Opening of Race Season in East at Bowie Today." *Buffalo Courier,* April 2, 1923, 11.

"'Old Bones' to Run Today Against Sinclair Horse." *Atlanta Constitution,* March 30, 1924, A2.

"Old Exterminator Comes Back to Races with Win." *Buffalo Courier,* February 18, 1924, 11.

"Old Exterminator Sets New Record by Taking Cup Again." *Saratogian,* September 1, 1922, 98.

"Old Exterminator Wins at Havre de Grace." *Buffalo Courier,* April 18, 1924, 11.

"'Old Slim' Loses by Nose Decision." *WP,* April 29, 1923, 59.

"'Old Slim' Ready for Coast Trip." *New York Morning Telegraph,* November 5, 1923.

Omar Khayyam. "Careful and Exterminator Win." *Baltimore Sun,* October 23, 1921, SP4.

———. "Exterminator Defeats Billy Kelly in Harford." *Baltimore Sun,* April 16, 1922, 19.

———. "Exterminator, Hero of Many Turf Battles, Is Victorious." *Baltimore Sun,* April 18, 1924, 12.

———. "Out of the Feed Box." *Baltimore Sun,* March 6, 1921, ED25.

———. "World's Greatest Gelding Will Go to Post Favorite in $25,000 Handicap." *Baltimore Sun,* October 28, 1922, 11.

"Opening Day at Havre de Grace." *TR,* April 15, 1922, 346.

"Opening Day at Hot Springs." *TR,* March 29, 1919.

Orlean, Susan. *Rin Tin Tin.* New York: Simon & Schuster, 2011.

"Osprey, in Great Form." *WP,* January 13, 1924, S2.

Ours, Dorothy. *Man o' War.* New York: St. Martin's Press, 2007.

"The Overlooked Derby Winner." *TR,* May 25, 1918.

Pace, Mildred Mastin. *Old Bones: The Wonder Horse.* New York: Scholastic, 1955.

"Pacific Coast Horse Critics Pay Tribute to Old Exterminator." *BP,* April 11, 1924.

"Painting White Horses for Camouflage During WWI." http://camoupedia .blogspot.com/2015/04/painting-white-horses-for-camouflage.html.

"Pal Purchased for Famous Exterminator." *New York Morning Telegraph,* 1923.

"Paul Jones Is Home First in the Suburban." *New York Herald,* June 6, 1920, 2.

Pearson, Susan J. *The Rights of the Defenseless.* Chicago: University of Chicago Press, 2011.

"Personal." *Saratoga Sentinel,* August 23, 1877.

Phillips, I. "Death of a Champion." Poem, *New York Sun,* October 1, 1945, 15.

"Pick Exterminator to Win at Tijuana." *Chicago Daily Tribune,* March 30, 1924, A2.

Pietrusza, David. *Rothstein.* New York: Basic Books, 2003.

"Pimlico Cup Goes to Exterminator." *New York Sun,* November 14, 1919, 18.

"Pimlico Cup Won by Exterminator." *NYT,* November 13, 1921, S4.

"Pimlico Racing May Stop Today." *NYT,* November 11, 1920, 21.

"Pimlico Smashes Record." *DRF,* November 14, 1922, 8.

"Pinehurst." *Town and Country,* March 16, 1907, 14.

"Plan Race for Man o' War and Two Rivals Today." *Chicago Daily Tribune,* September 24, 1920, 15.

"Plans Are Completed for Pimlico Meet." *Baltimore Sun,* October 17, 1920, 20.

"Polo and Hunting." *Town and Country,* May 27, 1911, 36.

"Ponce at Idle Hour Farm." *DRF,* April 2, 1923, 1.

Pond, Wilf. "The Horses of 1921." *New York Spur,* reprinted in *TR,* January 28, 1922, 67.

"Pony Express Sees Colorado Ten Hours Ahead of Schedule." *Chicago Daily Tribune,* September 3, 1923, 5.

Pratt, Charles Edward. "The Angel of Our Home." Poem, McDaniel collection.

"Prefers Job to $1000." *WP,* October 19, 1907, 9.

"President Wilson Presents Cup." *New York Morning Telegraph,* September 21, 1922.

Price, Harry N. P. "Exterminator Is Republic Victor." *WP,* September 23, 1919, 12.

———. "The Porter and Billy Kelly Take Big Events at Opening of Havre de Grace." *WP,* September 12, 1919, 14.

Prime, Cornelia. "Uncle Henry." *TR,* December 3, 1938, 871.

Priore, Louise M. "Mike Terry and West Side Kids Chief Mourners." *New York Sun,* September 26, 1945.

"Pudd'n McDaniel Wins Army Race." *DRF,* December 11, 1918, 1.

"Purchase Romps Off with Huron Under 134 Lbs." *New York Herald,* August 27, 1919, 7.

"Purse Increased to Help Exterminator Set Record." *NYT,* April 25, 1923, 19.

"The Question Came Up." *New York Press,* April 7, 1927.

"Question Sun Briar's Mile in 1:34." *DRF,* September 12, 1918, 1.

"The Race Meeting at Jerome Park." *Spirit of the Times,* 1872, 265.

"Race Storm Blows Over." *Los Angeles Times,* March 2, 1906, 113.

"Racers Off for Europe." *NYT,* January 13, 1895, 6.

"Racing at Empire City." *DRF,* October 15, 1918, 1.

"Racing at New Orleans." *NYT,* February 26, 1904, 6.

"Racing at Saratoga." *New York Daily Graphic,* July 26, 1876, 168.

"Racing at Sheepshead Bay." Film, July 23, 1897, Library of Congress. www.loc.gov /item/00694285.

"Racing Attracting Turf Enthusiasts at Tijuana." *WP,* January 20, 1924, S2.

"Racing Expert Asks for Real Test." *BP,* September 18, 1920.

"Racing Experts Come to Sun Briar Court." *BP,* March 3, 1920.

"Racing Folk Rejoice at Knapp's Success." *New York Telegraph,* August 30, 1929, BCHS.

"Racing Notes." *Brooklyn Daily Standard Union,* May 3, 1910, 10.

"Racing Notes." *Saratogian,* July 27, 1918, 8.

"Racing's Glorious Return." *DRF,* October 1, 1922, 1.

Railbird. "English 2-Year-Olds Here to Race in the Kilmer Silks." *New York Evening Sun,* February 23, 1916, BCHS.

"Rain at Tijuana Track." *DRF,* March 28, 1924, 1.

"Ramiro Raced to Death in Front." *Chicago Daily Tribune,* March 29, 1900, 4.

Rarey, John Solomon. *The Complete Horse Tamer.* rarey.com/sites/jsrarey/jsrbook .html.

"Real Championship Test." *DRF,* August 23, 1920, 1.

"Rebuke's Splendid Victory." *DRF,* March 27, 1923, 1.

"Recent New Recruit to Racing." *TR,* n.d.

"Refuses $400,000 for Man o' War." *NYT,* October 15, 1920, 22.

"Rest for Exterminator." *DRF,* July 8, 1922, 2.

"Return of 'Old Slim' to Racing Hailed by All Lovers of Horses." *BP,* March 5, 1924, 17.

Rice, Grantland. "Seabiscuit Tops Admiral." *Baltimore Sun,* November 2, 1938, 1.

———. "The Sportlight." *Washington Evening Star,* March 2, 1940, A13.

———. *The Tumult and the Shouting.* New York: A. S. Barnes, 1954.

"Rice Suspended for Foul Riding at Belmont Park." *New York Herald,* September 13, 1918, 8.

Richardson, William D. "Sports of the Times." *NYT,* August 2, 1945, 24.

Rideout, Walter B. *Sherwood Anderson: A Writer in America.* Madison: University of Wisconsin Press, 2005.

"Roamer Breaks Leg at Red Bank." *New-York Tribune,* January 1, 1920, 17.

"Roamer Iron Horse of American Turf." *NYT,* September 15, 1918, E4.

Robertson, William H. P. *The History of Thoroughbred Racing in America.* New York: Bonanza, 1964.

Rochecourt, Pierre. "Americans Prosper on French Tracks." *NYT,* January 14, 1912, C5.

"Rock Sand Cautious in Making a Landing." *NYT,* July 17, 1906, 3.

Rodenbach, C. C. "New Hawthorne Conjures Ghosts for Riders of '04." *Chicago Daily Tribune,* September 30, 1922, 11.

Rogers, Will. "The Day's Worst Story." *Baltimore Sun,* October 27, 1925, 12.

Roosevelt, Theodore. *Ranch Life and the Hunting Trail.* New York: Century Company, 1888, 54.

Ross, J.K.M. *Boots and Saddles.* New York: Dutton, 1956.

"Ross Releases H. G. Bedwell." *New York Sun,* April 15, 1921, 9.

"Ross' Horses for Havre." *DRF,* April 6, 1923, 1.

"Royce Rools Beats Stars at Pimlico." *New York Sun,* November 9, 1919, 5.

"Royce Rools Wins Bowie Handicap." *TR*, November 8, 1919, 233.

"Runstar Behaves and Wins." *DRF*, July 29, 1921, 1.

"Runstar Captures $40,000 Coffroth." *NYT*, March 31, 1924, 13.

"Runstar Winner of the Coffroth Handicap." *DRF*, March 31, 1924, 1.

"Runstar Wins Coffroth Handicap." *Los Angeles Times*, March 31, 1924, B1.

"A Sale of Thoroughbreds." *NYT*, February 27, 1878, 8.

Salvator [John Hervey]. "American Champion Weight Carriers." *DRF*, July 9, 1922, 1.

———. "Exterminator and the Figure System." *DRF*, September 9, 1922, 1.

———. "Man o' War—or Exterminator?" *TR*, September 14, 1940, 178.

———. "Repeats and Comebacks." *DRF*, May 30, 1922, 11.

Sann, Paul. *The Lawless Decade: Bullets, Broads & Bathtub Gin*. Mineola, NY: Dover Courier, 2010.

"Saratoga." *DRF*, August 31, 1922, 16.

"Saratoga Battle Ground." *DRF*, July 19, 1921, 1.

"Saratoga Prepares for Race Meeting." *NYT*, July 2, 1922, 17.

"Saratoga Races." *New York Herald*, July 17, 1872, 10.

"Saratoga Sales of Yearlings." *DRF*, August 2, 1916, 1.

"Saratoga Track a Marvel." *DRF*, July 31, 1918, 1.

"Saratoga's Greatest Meeting." *DRF*, September 2, 1920, 1.

Savage, C. J. "Exterminator Is Winner over Midway in Lexington." *Louisville Courier-Journal*, May 9, 1919, 9.

———. "Exterminator Proves Best in the Lexington Feature." *Louisville Courier-Journal*, May 2, 1919, 1.

" 'Save the Horse!' Slogan of Diners." *NYT*, February 20, 1912, 20.

"Says Chained Mines Sunk Minnehaha: Captain of Vessel Does Not Believe." *NYT*, December 19, 1917, 6.

Sbarra, Don. "Enthusiast Wants Horse Reburied." *BP*, February 25, 1998, 6B.

"Scenes in Betting Ring Are Graphically Described by Expert." *Louisville Courier-Journal*, May 12, 1918.

"Schenectady Elks Present Mr. Kilmer with Magnificent Floral Horseshoe." *BP*, August 26, 1920.

"The Screen." *NYT*, June 19, 1919, 9.

"Season's First Stake Goes to Exterminator." *New York Evening Telegram*, April 15, 1922, 1.

"Seek Poison in Sunny Man's Stomach Today." *Chicago Daily News*, May 5, 1925, 21.

Sevier, O'Neil. "Another Cup Race Likely Next Month." *WP*, September 21, 1919, 23.

———. "Exterminator: A Wonder Horse." *Vanity Fair*, December 1922.

———. "Exterminator After Thanksgiving Stakes." *WP,* November 19, 1922, 64.

———. "Exterminator May Reach $200,000 Mark in Purses." *WP,* May 30, 1921, 6.

———. "Exterminator Proves Best Distance Racer." *WP,* December 25, 1921, 15.

———. "Exterminator Should Go in Big Canadian Race." *New York Globe,* September 29, 1920, BCHS scrapbook.

———. "Fastest 1919 4-Year-Old to Get Distance Tests." *WP,* February 1, 1920, 19.

———. "Kilmer Racer Should Have Most Successful Campaign." *WP,* June 27, 1920, 19.

———. "Kilmer's Foreign Stakes Entries." *TR,* January 28, 1922, 43.

———. "Presses Man o' War for Winning Honors." *DRF,* June 4, 1922, 11.

———. "Saratoga Cup Race May Be Three-Cornered Affair." *WP,* August 15, 1920, 19.

———. "Sun Briar and Johren to Remain Rivals This Year." *WP,* February 23, 1919, 19.

———. "Sun Briar Court Stud." January 11, 1919.

———. "Sun Briar Likely to Face the Barrier at Aqueduct." *WP,* June 8, 1919, 19.

———. " 'Tainted Blood' in Successful Racers." *WP,* December 31, 1922, 31.

———. *TR,* March 24, 1922, 297.

———. "Tribute to a Great Horse." *DRF,* April 10, 1922, 1.

Sharpless, Rebecca. *Cooking in Other Women's Kitchens.* Chapel Hill: University of North Carolina Press, 2011.

Shay, Jack Edward. *Bygone Binghamton.* Bloomington, IN: Author House, 2012.

———. "The Story of Exterminator," *Susquehanna Magazine,* May 7, 1978, 10.

Shepard, Edwin H. "The Frontenac Motor Boat Races." *Town and Country,* September 10, 1904, 22.

"Shilling Receives His License." *New York Herald,* May 3, 1910.

"Shilling Says Race Is Sure." *DRF,* September 23, 1920, 1.

"Ship Kilmer Horses to Louisville." *DRF,* April 30, 1918, 1.

"Ship's Baseball Team." Photograph. www.history.navy.mil/photos/sh-usn/usnsh-r/sp157.htm.

"Sir Barton Wins." *DRF,* May 11, 1919, 1.

" 'Slim' Is as Good as Ever." *DRF,* February 7, 1922, 2.

"Small Fields at Aqueduct." *DRF,* September 24, 1919.

Smith, E. C. "Henry McDaniel." *Blood-Horse,* n.d., McDaniel collection.

Smith, Marshall. "The People's Horse." *Life,* September 21, 1953, 190.

Smith, Red. *Strawberries in the Wintertime.* New York: Crown, 1974.

"So Schuttinger Has Joined the Kilmer Club." *New York Evening Graphic,* July 17, 1931.

"Society and Turf Patrons at Spa Contribute Largely to War Fund." *New York Herald,* August 28, 1918, 7.

"Society's Adieu to Spa Season." *New York Herald,* August 31, 1917, 6.

Southwood, Wilfred. "Rockspring's Glorious Sacrifice," *DRF,* October 25, 1918, 2.

"Spa Has Come Back as Big Stakes and Great Horses Prove." *Philadelphia Evening Public Ledger,* August 4, 1922, 15.

Sparrow, C. Edward. "Bedwell Has Field Day." *Baltimore Sun,* April 17, 1921, SS1.

———. "Easy for Exterminator." *Baltimore Sun,* November 14, 1919, 13.

———. "Exterminator Breaks Record at Old Hilltop." *Baltimore Sun,* November 13, 1920, 9.

"Speaking of Exterminator." *New York Morning Telegraph,* n.d.

"Splendid Chance for Exterminator." *Baltimore Sun,* October 24, 1922, 13.

"Sport Gossip." *Louisville Courier-Journal,* May 4, 1918.

"Sporting Comment." *Auburn* (NY) *Citizen,* January 14, 1911, 3.

"Stable Work Is Hard Work Indeed." *DRF,* October 5, 1918, 2.

Stage, Sarah. *Female Complaints.* New York: Norton, 1979.

"Star Racers on the Way." *DRF,* August 20, 1920, 1–2.

"Stars in Brooklyn Handicap." *DRF,* June 16, 1922, 1.

"Stayer Exterminator's Deeds." *DRF,* December 16, 1920, 1.

"Steamship Minnehaha Finally Arrives." *DRF,* January 16, 1917, 1.

Stewart, Walter. "We Just Have to Laugh." McDaniel collection.

Stoddart, Alfred. "Colors and Markings of Horses." *Journal of the United States Cavalry Association* 26 (July 1915): 83–86.

Stringer, Harry. "Along the Rail." *Washington Post,* April 23, 1924, S2.

———. "Old Bones Shows Return to Form in Winning Edgewood." *WP,* April 18, 1924, S2.

"Suburban Handicap at Belmont Park." *DRF,* June 7, 1919, 2.

"Sun Briar and Exterminator Brought Here to Spend Rest of Their Days." *BP,* June 13, 1942.

"Sun Briar Badly Beaten." *DRF,* April 26, 1918, 1.

"Sun Briar Breaks Record in Champlain Handicap." *BP,* August 11, 1919, 8.

"Sun Briar Breaks Saratoga Record." *New York Morning Telegraph,* August 10, 1919, 1.

"Sun Briar Court." *TR,* n.d., ca. 1919.

"Sun Briar Court Juveniles Leave to Take up Racing." *BP,* March 15, 1922, 20.

"Sun Briar Court May Aid Nation to Get Cavalry Horses." *BP,* August 13, 1918, 3.

"Sun Briar Creates Turf History." *BP,* August 19, 1918, 5.

"Sun Briar Crowned Two-Year-Old King." *NYT,* August 26, 1917, 25.

"Sun Briar Fails over Distance." *Morning Telegraph,* August 24, 1919.

"Sun Briar First in Turf Classic." *NYT,* August 18, 1918, 25.

"Sun Briar in Van Before Big Crowd." *NYT,* August 12, 1917, S2.

"Sun Briar Is Carefully Guarded." *DRF*, March 3, 1918, 1.

"Sun Briar King of 2-Year-Olds." *New York Evening Telegram*, September 2, 1917.

"Sun Briar Looks Good in Fast Workout." *BP*, May 2, 1918, 1.

"Sun Briar Now at the Top of His Form." *DRF*, August 29, 1917.

"Sun Briar Runs at Fair Speed in Derby Trial." *Chicago Tribune*, May 8, 1918.

"Sun Briar Runs Trial Mile in 1:34." *DRF*, September 12, 1918, 1.

"Sun Briar Superb Type of Horse." *DRF*, August 14, 1919.

"Sun Briar Takes Albany." *NYT*, August 9, 1917, 10.

"Sun Briar the Derby Favorite." *TR*, March 20, 1918, 167.

"Sun Briar, Thoroughbred Champion, Dies in Stall Here." *BP*, October 18, 1943.

"Sun Briar to Go to Kentucky." *Saratogian*, December 20, 1917, 6.

"Sun Briar to Lexington." *DRF*, April 11, 1918, 1.

"Sun Briar Training Quite Soundly." *DRF*, April 15, 1918, 1.

"Sun Briar Victor in Travers Stakes." *New York Sun*, August 18, 1918, 5.

"Sun Briar Will Be Sent East." *BP*, May 10, 1918.

"Sun Briar Wins Champlain Handicap in Drive at Saratoga." *New York Herald*, August 10, 1919, 3.

"Sun Briar Wintering Well." *DRF*, December 20, 1918, 1.

"Sun Briar Works Well in Blinkers." *TR*, April 13, 1918, 200.

"Sun Briar's Final Trial Today." *DRF*, May 9, 1918, 1.

"Sun Briar's First Race Impressive." *DRF*, July 15, 1919, 2.

"Sun Briar's First Work." *DRF*, February 15, 1918, 1.

"Sun Briar's Flying Heels." *NYT*, August 10, 1919, 1.

"Sunbriar in Cup Race." *NYT*, October 5, 1919, 12.

"Sunny Man Poisoned with Intent to Kill, Veterinarian Reiterates." *WP*, May 5, 1925, 13.

"Supervisors Refuse to Close Ascot Park." *Los Angeles Examiner*, January 23, 1906. www.ulwaf.com/LA-1900s/06.01.html.

"Supposed Airplane Liquor Confiscated." *Baltimore Sun*, September 18, 1922, 26.

"Surgeon Blue Inspects Camp." *Louisville Courier-Journal*, May 11, 1918, 1.

Swamp-Root Almanac 1916. https://ia600801.us.archive.org/20/items/swamprootalmanac1916kilm/swamprootalmanac1916kilm.pdf.

"Sweeping Decision by Appellate Court Is Filed Today." *BP*, January 4, 1917.

"Sweetheart of Mine, Remember This." McDaniel collection.

Tarr, Joel A. "Urban Pollution: Many Long Years Ago." *American Heritage*, 1971. www.banhdc.org/archives/ch-hist-19711000.html.

"The Test of a Horse—or Cigarette." Advertisement, Winchester cigarettes, 1944.

"*The Three Musketeers* Coming to Hippodrome Last Week in January." *Gloversville* (NY) *Morning Herald*, January 21, 1922.

"These Victories Reflect the Training Ability of Healy." Ca. 1920, BCHS scrapbook.

"They Accuse J. W. Brooks." *Los Angeles Times,* February 19, 1906, 112.

"Three Old Timers Discuss Derby." *DRF,* May 5, 1949, 1.

"Three Prominent Trainers." *DRF,* February 21, 1921, 2.

"Three-Year-Old Supremacy." *DRF,* July 24, 1918, 1.

"Tia Juana Boasting Many Speedy Horses." *WP,* December 9, 1923, 61.

"Tichenor Is to Have a New String." *DRF,* March 6, 1906, 1.

"To Avoid Delay Have Exact Change Ready." Advertisement, *Louisville Times,* May 4, 1918.

"To Fight New York Tracks to Finish." *NYT,* April 15, 1921, 23.

"To Keep Him Happy." *Milwaukee Journal,* February 15, 1934, 18.

"To Owners of Horses." *Puck,* September 27, 1892, McDaniel collection.

"Top o' th' Morning Wins in Fleetwing." *NYT,* July 15, 1917, 27.

"Town and Country Life." *Town and Country,* July 14, 1906, 22.

"Trainer M'Daniel's Career." N.d., McDaniel collection.

"Trainer's Wife a Suicide." *NYT,* February 15, 1914, 3.

Treanor, Vincent. "Dimmesdale Classy Colt." *New York Evening World,* June 20, 1920, 22.

———. "Healy to Train for Diaz, Isn't Sorry Quitting Kilmer." *New York Evening World,* September 16, 1920, 18.

———. "Morvich Races in First Real Defense of Championship." *New York Evening World,* June 17, 1922, 6.

———. "$75,000 Match Will Bring Man o' War, Exterminator, and Sir Barton Together." *New York Evening World,* September 23, 1920.

———. "V. Treanor's Column." *New York Evening World,* August 30, 1920, 15.

"Trial Horse for Sun Briar." *DRF,* April 30, 1918, 1.

"Triumph for American Breeding." *DRF,* May 14, 1918.

Tuchman, Barbara. *The Guns of August.* New York: Macmillan, 1962.

"Tuning Up at Saratoga." *DRF,* July 21, 1922, 1.

"Turf." *NYT,* April 23, 1922, 13.

"Turf." *NYT,* August 7, 1922, 17.

"Turf Bureau." *Morning Telegraph,* August 12, [1933?], McDaniel collection.

"Turf Gossip from Havre de Grace." *DRF,* April 16, 1924, 2.

"Turf Notes." *TR,* ca. 1919.

"Turf War Starts over Bedwell Case." *NYT,* April 12, 1921, 26.

"Turfman's Son Killed in France." *DRF,* November 26, 1918, 1.

"Two Beautiful Trophies." *BP,* September 4, 1920.

"Two Champions Star in Big Motion Picture." *BP,* July 1, 1919, 7.

"Two Inquiries Are Expected in Colt's Death." *Baltimore Sun,* May 4, 1925, 20.

"Uncle White a Good One." *DRF,* June 22, 1918, 1.

Underwood, Tom R., ed. *Thoroughbred Racing and Breeding.* New York: Coward-McCann, 1945.

"Unique Entertainment for Red Cross Society." *Kentucky Kernel,* April 26, 1918. http://camptaylorhistorical.org.

United States War Department. *Manual for Stable Sergeants.* Washington, D.C.: Government Printing Office, 1917.

U.S. Census, 1880. www.agcensus.usda.gov/Publications/Historical_Publications /1880/1880a_v3-01.pdf.

Vanderwood, Paul. *Satan's Playground: Mobsters and Movie Stars at America's Greatest Gaming Resort.* Durham, NC: Duke University Press, 2010.

"Verdict Against R. L. Gerry." *NYT,* May 22, 1911, 1.

"Veteran Gelding Exterminator Ready for Western Campaign." *New-York Tribune,* April 9, 1922, 17.

"Veteran Shows Real Speed in Feature at Spa." *WP,* September 1, 1922, 17.

"A Veteran Turfman Retires." *Spirit of the Times,* 1877, 501.

"Viewing Exterminator at Belmont Park." *New York Morning Telegraph,* June 14, 1922, 8.

Vila, Joe. "Jockey Club Still Supreme on Track." *Philadelphia Inquirer,* April 28, 1921.

"Visit to Sun Briar Court." *DRF,* January 24, 1922, 1.

Von Borries, Philip. *RaceLens.* Gretna, LA: Pelican, 2014.

Vosburgh, W. S. "Analysis of Rules of Racing." *DRF,* January 18, 1920, 2.

———. "The Belmont Stakes." *DRF,* April 23, 1922, 1.

———. "Great American Race Horses Are Contemporaneous." *DRF,* February 23, 1921, 3.

———. "The Passing of Jerome Park." *Outing Magazine,* March 23, 1901, 519.

Voss, Frederick. *Picturing Hemingway.* New Haven, CT: Yale University Press, 1999.

Vreeland, W. C. "Audacious Wins Suburban." *BDE,* June 5, 1921, 1, sporting section.

———. "Burlew No Longer Trains Macomber Racing Stable." *BDE,* March 23, 1921, 2.

———. "Can Exterminator Concede 7 Pounds to Grey Lag in the Saratoga Handicap?" *BDE,* July 24, 1922, 2A.

———. "Exterminator Being Prepared to Capture Cups for Fourth Time." *BDE,* February 17, 1922, 2A.

———. "Exterminator Did Greater Deeds than 'Down Under' King." *BDE,* March 23, 1932, 25.

———. "Exterminator Earns a Great Ovation by Beating Grey Lag a Head for the Brooklyn." *BDE,* June 17, 1922, 11.

———. "Exterminator in Fine Fettle for New Record." *BDE,* February 6, 1923, 2A.

———. "Exterminator, King of Long Distance Horses, Wins the Autumn Gold Cup." *BDE,* September 17, 1921, 12.

———. "Exterminator May Replace Roamer as 'Idol' of the Turf." *BDE,* February 22, 1920, 2.

———. "Exterminator Should Be Retired." *BDE,* September 13, 122, 4A.

———. "Exterminator Shows He Has Lost Most of His Speed of the Early Spring." *BDE,* August 2, 1922.

———. "Exterminator, the Richest Gelding in the World, Wins His Fifth Handicap." *BDE,* June 6, 1922, 2A.

———. "Exterminator Wins Cup for Fourth Time." *BDE,* September 1, 1922, 6.

———. "Exterminator Wins Gold Cup." *BDE,* September 16, 1920, 2.

———. "Exterminator Wins the Pimlico Cup in Record Time." *BDE,* November 13, 1920.

———. "Henry McDaniel and Gifford Cochran Flirt with Fortune and Win." *BDE,* December 7, 1930, 4C.

———. "Henry McDaniel Fills the Cloak of Skill Left by His Dad." *BDE,* October 19, 1930, C5.

———. "Henry McDaniel Is Great Trainer." *BDE,* August 18, 1935, 4D.

———. "In-and-Out Racing Marred Fall Meeting at Pimlico." *BDE,* November 14, 1919, 3.

———. "Man o' War Sure to Race for Historic Saratoga Cup." *BDE,* August 19, 1920, 2.

———. "Man o' War, the Miracle Horse." *BDE,* October 17, 1920, 5.

———. "Marse McDaniel Inherited Training Skill from His Dad." *BDE,* July 23, 1939, 4D.

———. "McDaniel, Who Discovered Exterminator, Doing Well with Sun Briar Colts." *BDE,* July 24, 1927.

———. "Morvich Had Better Watch Out or Big Exterminator Will Chase Him Leg Weary." *BDE,* June 14, 1922, 2A.

———. "Mr. Racegoer, Do You Believe Exterminator Is 7 Pounds Better than Morvich?" *BDE,* June 12, 1922, 2A.

———. "No Champion Among the Young Race Horses During 1922, but Exterminator the Hero." *BDE,* December 24, 1922, 2A.

———. "Oceanic, Stable Mate of the Great Man o' War, Saves the Record of the Super-Horse." *Brooklyn Daily Eagle,* December 2, 1922, 12.

———. "Paul Jones Suburban Winner." *BDE,* June 6, 1920, 2.

———. "Racing Fans Ask, 'How Long Will M'Daniel Train for Kilmer?'" *BDE,* November 15, 1933, 23.

———. "Racing Fans Seeking the Path to Wealth May Find It in Golden Way." *BDE,* April 9, 1933, 66.

————. "Sally's Alley and Exterminator Ready for 'Derby' and 'Cups.'" *BDE,* February 25, 1923, D5.

————. "Schuttinger a Real Jockey." *BDE,* June 20, 1920, 2.

————. "Sir Barton, Travel Weary, 'Dodges' Man o' War." *BDE,* September 7, 1920, 3.

————. "'Snapper' Garrison Says Exterminator Is the Best Gelding Bred in U.S.A." *BDE,* April 23, 1923, A3.

————. "Sprinters Not the 'Whole Show' in Racing Year 1922." *BDE,* January 22, 1922.

————. "Stewards Make Exterminator, Best Horse in U.S.A., an 'Outcast' by Their Rules." *BDE,* October 9, 1922, 2A.

————. "Sun Briar Court, a Million Dollar 'Horse Heaven.'" *BDE,* March 9, 1919, 3.

————. "'Sunny Jim' Fitzsimmons Says Exterminator Greatest of His Time." *BDE,* December 3, 1929, 30.

————. "Today's Victory at 50 to 1." *BDE,* August 10, 1920.

————. "Touch Me Not Wins Great American in Driving Finish." *BDE,* June 4, 1920, 2S.

————. "Upsets Precedent in Winning Sprint." *WP,* April 20. 1922, 19.

————. "Will Grey Lag Have a Chance to Regain His Prestige?" *BDE,* September 5, 1921, 8.

"W. E. Wilson." Advertisement, *New York Morning Telegraph,* May 1, 1922.

"W. S. Kilmer at Baltimore." *DRF,* March 20, 1923, 1.

"W. S. Kilmer Bids for Racing Fame." *New York Morning Telegraph,* May 18, 1916, BCHS scrapbook.

"W. S. Kilmer Horses." *DRF,* April 17, 1923, 1.

"W. S. Kilmer Horses at Louisville." *DRF,* April 16, 1919, 2.

"W. S. Kilmer's 1923 Stable." *TR,* December 28, 1922, 329.

Wade, Horace. "One Tough Bag of Bones." *Spur,* November/December 1983, 60–61.

Wall, Maryjean. *How Kentucky Became Southern.* Lexington: University Press of Kentucky, 2010.

Walsh, Davis J. "Exterminator Greatest Race Horse of All Time." *Farrell* (PA) *News,* June 17, 1922.

"War Board Is Named Here to Aid Government." *BP,* January 4, 1917, BCHS scrapbook.

"War Cloud Arrives at Louisville." *DRF,* May 3, 1918, 1.

"War Cloud Reigns Favorite in Derby." *NYT,* May 5, 1918, 32.

"War Coloring Given Derby." *Louisville Courier-Journal,* May 12, 1918.

"War Department Curbs Football." *New York Herald,* September 13, 1918, 8.

"Warm Spell No Bar to Society's Filling Club House at the Spa." *New York Herald,* August 7, 1918, 9.

Wedding Known to Few." *NYT*, January 31, 1903, 5.

"Weight Concession Causes Exterminator to 'Decline Issue.'" *BP*, June 24, 1922, 17.

"Weights for Suburban Handicap." *DRF*, June 5, 1919, 1.

"Weights in the Brooklyn." *DRF*, June 13, 1922, 1; Editorial, *TR*, June 24, 1922, 470.

"Well, Willis Sharpe Kilmer Has Another Trainer." *Bridgeport Herald*, July 19, 1931.

Welton, Charles. "Biggest Money Maker on the Course." *Buffalo Sunday Express*, 1922, 5.

West, Floyd. "Willis Sharpe Kilmer and His Horses." Talk presented to the Broome County Historical Society, June 17, 1989, 1.

———. "Willis Sharpe Kilmer and Swamp-Root Tonic: Opportunist or Benefactor?" Talk presented to the Broome County Historical Society, ca. 1995.

"Westerners Interested in New Track." *DRF*, May 9, 1912, 2.

"What the Owners Had to Say About the Big Race." *Louisville Courier-Journal*, May 12, 1918.

"What Will Win the Derby?" *TR*, April 27, 1918.

"Which Will Be the Greater Four-Year-Old?" *TR*, March 1, 1919, 125.

White House Historical Association. "The Theodore Roosevelt Family." www .whitehousehistory.org/presentations/white-house-horses/white-house-horses -02.html.

"Who Drugged the Horse?" *DRF*, February 21, 1906, 1.

"Will Decide the Huguenot Case Today." *DRF*, February 22, 1906, 1.

"Will Rogers Visits Sun Briar Court." *BP*, October 3, 1925, 11.

Williams, Harry. "Exterminator and Man o' War Score in Stakes at Spa." *New York Morning Telegraph*, August 31, 1919, 1.

Williams, Joe. "Exterminator Returns to Track." *New York World-Telegram*, reprinted in *BP*, October 30, 1941.

———. "Off to a Banquet." *Rome* (NY) *Daily Sentinel*, April 27, 1944, 14.

Williamson, S. T. "When Pershing Came." *NYT*, June 12, 1927, SM6.

"Willie Knapp: He'll Join Hall of Fame." *New York Morning Telegraph*, 1969.

"Willis Sharpe Kilmer." *BP*, July 7, 1940, 6.

"Willis Sharpe Kilmer." *New York Morning Telegraph*, December 23, 1915, BCHS scrapbook.

"Willis Sharpe Kilmer, Noted Turfman, Dies." *WP*, July 13, 1940, 13.

"Willis Sharpe Kilmer Paid $605.99." *Oswego Times*, 1896.

"Willis Sharpe Kilmer to Seek Juvenile Racing Honors at Saratoga." *New York Telegram*, July 16, 1927, 10.

Winn, Matt J. *Down the Stretch*. New York: Smith & Durrell, 1944.

"Women at Racetrack Knitted Sox for Soldiers and Enjoyed It." *Elmira Morning Telegram,* September 9, 1917.

"Wonderful Horse Keeps On Running Year After Year." *Saratogian,* November 17, 1921, 8.

"Wonderful Turf Battle." *DRF,* April 23, 1922, 2.

Wood, Michael. *America in the Movies.* New York: Columbia University Press, 1975.

Woodrow Wilson, Executive Order 2285—Requiring American Citizens Traveling Abroad to Procure Passports, December 15, 1915.

Woodruff, Harvey T. "20,000 Cheer Race Revival at Hawthorne." *Chicago Daily Tribune,* October 1, 1922, 1.

"Wraps American Flag Around Two Race Horses." *Reading Eagle,* September 12, 1914, 5.

"Year of 1922 Ranks High in Sport World." *NYT,* December 31, 1922, 25.

"Yearlings Sent East for Sale." *DRF,* August 13, 1916, 1.

Young, James Harvey. *Toadstool Millionaires.* Princeton, NJ: Princeton University Press, 1961.

Index